Modern Germany

Modern Germany

A Social, Cultural, and Political History

Henry M. Pachter

Westview Press / Boulder, Colorado

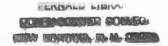

Copyright © 1978 by Westview Press, Inc.

Published in 1978 in the United States of America by
  Westview Press, Inc.
  5500 Central Avenue
  Boulder, Colorado 80301
  Frederick A. Praeger, Publisher

Library of Congress Cataloging in Publication Data
Pachter, Henry Maximilian, 1907-
  Modern Germany.
  Bibliography: p.
  Includes index.
  1. Germany—History—William II, 1888-1918. 2. Germany—History—
20th century. I. Title.
DD228.P33   943.08   78-2030
ISBN 0-89158-166-9

Printed and bound in the United States of America

For Hedwig and Renée,
who have given this book much help

Contents

Tables, Figures, and Charts

Abbreviations

ADGB	General German Trade Union Association (pre-1933)
APO	Extraparliamentary Opposition (West)
BRD	Federal Republic of Germany (West)
CDU	Christian-Democratic Union (West)
COMECON	Council for Mutual Economic Assistance (East)
CSU	Christian-Social Union (Bavaria)
DDP	German Democratic Party (Weimar period)
DDR	German Democratic Republic (East)
DGB	German Trade Union Association (West)
DKP	German Communist Party (Moscow-oriented; West)
DNVP	German Nationalist People's Party (Weimar period)
DP	German Party (right-wing farmers' party; West)
DRP	German Neo-Nazi Party (underground; West)
DVP	German People's Party (Weimar period)
ECSC	European Coal and Steel Community (in German: EGKS)
EEC	European Economic Community (Common Market; in German: EG)
FDGB	Free German Trade Union Association (East)
FDJ	Free German Youth (East)
FDP	Free-Democratic Party (West)
HO	State-run department stores (East)
KPD (1)	Communist Party of Germany, member of the Comintern (1919-1945)
KPD (2)	Communist Party of Germany (Peking-oriented; West)
LDP	Liberal-Democratic Party (liberal, legal; East)
NPD	National-Democratic Party of Germany (neo-Nazi, legal; West)
NSDAP	National Socialist German Workers' Party (Nazi)
SA	Storm Squads; Nazi militia (brown shirts)
SALT	Strategic Arms Limitation Talks
SED	Socialist Unity Party of Germany (East)
SPD	Social-Democratic Party of Germany (West)
SS	Security Squads; Nazi elite guards (black uniforms)
WEU	West European Union

The German Self-Image

Why is it that with us the tradition of princely states, of centralism, militarism, and finance, has been stronger than the tradition of the Reich, whose idea was Unity, Justice, and Freedom?

—Ricarda Huch

A NATION LIVES BY ITS LEGENDS, its popular novels, its histories. These form the idea it has of itself, the models it strives for. Obviously, this self-image changes from time to time, and it also reflects conflicting forces. But at any moment the prevalent values may appear most clearly in the texts that are read in schools and in the juvenile literature that parents see fit to give their children. Thus, German schoolboys at the turn of the century were shown a glorious and colorful pageant of their venerable past. Here are some of its important panels:

In the beginning of German history, treacherous Roman invaders found virtuous tribes of woodsmen. Tacitus, the traveler and historian, admired their community spirit, their upright simplicity, and their love of freedom. Eighteen hundred years later, the German playwright Heinrich von Kleist wrote a passionate patriotic drama on Hermann the Cheruscian, the leader of a German uprising against the Roman Empire. Both Tacitus and Kleist were read in school, and school libraries carried Felix Dahn's popular novels narrating how the Teutonic tribes overran the decadent Roman Empire and founded German kingdoms in the west, leaving their names to countries which today are still called England, France, Normandy, Burgundy, Lom(Lango)bardy, (V)Andalucia, after the Anglo-Saxons, Franks, Normans, Burgundians of *Nibelungen* fame, etc. It was Germany's Homeric Age, whose fame is preserved in the *Nibelungen* saga, a great poem which was revived in the Romantic period and retold on all levels, from the juvenile reader to Richard Wagner's *Ring* cycle to Fritz Lang's two-part movie pageant.

This was the pagan past. Charlemagne, king of the Franks, founded the first Christian *Reich* (realm) in the west. For a thousand years— from 800 to 1805, with a few interruptions—German princes wore the crown of the Holy Roman Empire, and the height of medieval splendor was reached around 1200 under the reigns of Frederic I and Frederic II. The legends of these two Hohenstaufen emperors were blended in the tale of Barbarossa, who sleeps in Mount Kyffhäuser, waiting to revive the old grandeur of imperial Germany. That wonderful age lives on in many monuments all over the country: cloisters, palaces, city halls, marketplaces. The cathedrals of Strasbourg and Bamberg especially are symbols of national culture. Novelists have celebrated the glamour of the Crusades, of jousting, of courtly love and chivalrous adventure.

Another panel of past glory shows the Teutonic knights and the Guelph party, rivals of the Hohenstaufen and champions of Germany's *Drang nach Osten*—the eastward thrust, subjugating or expelling the Slavic population from places and areas that still bear Slavic names: Prussia, Brandenburg, Berlin, Poznan. It is roughly along the Elbe River that the line runs separating this colonized country from the areas of original German settlements in the west; interestingly, this same line divided Germany into zones of French and Russian influence at the time of Napoleon, and today it is once again the border between the two Germanies. At all times the two parts had different systems of land tenure: large estates were the rule in the east, peasant holdings in the west. East of the Elbe the nobles (Junkers, or country squires) ruled the land from the manor and reduced the tenants to serfdom. They were the prince's judges, army officers, and administrators, the pride and the curse of a system that lasted until the beginning of this century.

Another panel: all along the coasts and trade routes flourished the great merchant cities—the *Hanse,* whose League was the greatest power factor in northern Europe at the end of the Middle Ages. Today only Hamburg and Bremen have retained a measure of independence; the League's sway once reached from Bruges to Novgorod and included Danzig, Lübeck, Rostock, Wismar, places like Visby that have disappeared from the map, and others whose majestic plazas still tell of former greatness. This patrician culture was still much alive at the time of the classical writers, but is often forgotten in analyses of the German tradition.

Turning our gaze from the east to the south, we see the lands of the Hapsburg crown: Austria with the Tyrol, Carinthia, Styria, and Salzburg; Bohemia and Moravia, which today are Czechoslovakia; Hungary with her eastern dependencies; southern Slavic areas along the Dalmatian coast; and at times large parts of northern Italy.

The Hapsburgs had also been emperors of Germany from 1273 to 1806. They lost their Italian possessions in 1859 and 1866, but the remaining Austro-Hungarian monarchy was still, at the beginning of the twentieth century, one of the five great European powers.

Confronting the Slavic nations of the east, it was the natural ally of the northern Germans: two Reichs conjoined in *Nibelungen* loyalty.

Those were memories of German unity. Another series of panels represents moments of world-historical confrontations. Dr. Martin Luther led a German revolt against the universalist claims of the emperor and the Pope. The temperamental son of a sturdy Thuringian miner, an inspiring and vociferous leader of the Reformation, he translated the Bible into the Saxonian vernacular and thereby gave the Germans—Protestants and Catholics alike—a standard language.

Simultaneously with the Reformation, all over southwest Germany the peasants and radical townsmen arose under the flag of messianic religion. They were allied with impoverished knights and with some of the foremost artists and humanists of the Renaissance in Germany. The movement was crushed; but its leaders have been immortalized in German poetry and drama (Goethe's *Götz von Berlichingen,* Ferdinand Lassalle's *Sickingen,* Conrad Ferdinand Meyer's *Huttens letzte Tage* and *Jürg Jenatsch,* Gerhart Hauptmann's *Florian Geyer*), and in some folk songs.

The religious wars of the seventeenth century split the nation but gave rise to a new idea of the state: that sovereign territorial organism which, under inspiring leadership, could become the embodiment of a national will. Prussia, in particular, emerged as such a dynamic state, forged by the iron hands of a few gifted rulers (of the Hohenzollern house) and loyally supported by their subjects' industry and discipline. In the eighteenth century Frederick II of Prussia challenged the power of the Hapsburg Empire and won the admiration of Germany's classical writers. He is called "the Great" although he was saved from utter ruin only by the succession to the Russian throne of a feeble-minded czar. But the Germans drew two lessons from the Seven Years War and, to their ruin, heeded them in two world wars: (1) if one holds the inner line, one can hold out against superior forces; and (2) by thus "holding out" (see page 72) long enough, one has a chance of being saved by a miracle. Frederick's legend reverberates in novels, plays, movies, poems, and children's books; his residence in Potsdam is a national shrine—even under the communist regime of East Germany.

Time of troubles—both the vaunted Prussian army and the pompous Empire collapsed before the fiery onslaught of the great French Revolution. To liberate itself from French domination, Germany had to adopt the liberal principles that had defeated it. To foment a "people's war," Prussia first had to become a modern nation. The cities were granted a measure of self-administration; a citizens' army was created through universal military training; the peasants were freed from servitude and allowed to buy their farms (it is true that half of them became farm laborers, and neither the property nor the power of the Junkers in eastern Germany was diminished). Thus, the War of Liberation (1812-14) against Napoleon became Germany's substitute for the national revolution; notably in Prussia, it hammered the king, the upper classes, and the people into one fatherland. Volunteers fought in Free Corps under the black, red, and gold flag which a girl's fancy had designed for them.

Alas! the War of Liberation did not bring the much-desired German unity. The Congress of Vienna reinstated the three dozen petty princes, along with their courtiers and concubines, and gave the Reich the constitution of a loose confederation *(Deutscher Bund)* whose notorious futility made it the butt of cartoonists and lampoons. The causes of freedom and unity were taken up by the student movement *(Burschenschaften)*; persecuted by the police of all the states and unanimously denounced by philosophers as divergent as Hegel and Schopenhauer, the fraternities nevertheless distributed pamphlets, organized festivals, and displayed the black, red, and gold flag, which now became the symbol of revolutionary patriotism: "from the black present through blood to the golden future." Karl Sand assassinated a hated flunky of the old regime, and at his execution people fought for scraps of his clothes, locks of his hair, and chips from his scaffold. Enthusiastic youths flocked to Greece to help liberate the Hellenes from the Turkish yoke. Seven professors at the University of Göttingen rebuked the King of Hanover (uncle of Queen Victoria) for violating the constitution; they were fired and became famous. A new literature, provocatively called "Young Germany," attacked old customs, old morality, and old beliefs with spirited satire. Even the beneficiaries of the old regime knew that its days were numbered.

In 1841 Hoffmann von Fallersleben composed the anthem that was to become the German "Marseillaise." "Unity and justice and freedom," says its third stanza, which is now the anthem of the Federal Republic of Germany. But its first stanza calls on the various German tribes to put "Germany above all," and it spells out the borders: "From the Meuse to the Niemen, from the Adige to the Belt." That is to say, the republican movement was "Great-German," *Grossdeutsch,* embracing all German-speaking people but no non-Germans; Austria's and Prussia's Slavic minorities would have to shape their own destinies. For German patriotism still seemed compatible—nay, allied—with the patriotic aspirations of other nations: Young Poland, Young Italy, Young Germany, all the disenfranchised nations forming "Young Europe."

But humanist and liberal patriotism had to contend with a more chauvinistic type. At the same time two other songs were more popular than Hoffmann's anthem: "The Watch on the Rhine" with its trumpetlike chorus, and "They Shall Not Have the Free German Rhine." The athletic clubs *(Turnerschaften)* also propagated marching songs and a chauvinistic ideology.

In March 1848, the long-expected revolution (sparked in France a month earlier) seized the German lands. Barricades rose in Berlin, Vienna, Budapest, Munich, Dresden, Brunswick; and at first the people seemed to have won. The king of Prussia stood bareheaded before the coffins of two hundred victims; hastily, state assemblies were convened to write constitutions, and an all-German National Assembly met in St. Paul's Church in Frankfurt (which ever since has been revered as a symbol of German democracy).

But then the aims of unity and justice and freedom fell apart. Those who wanted unity above all refused to fight for freedoms which the princes were loath to grant; those whose aim was freedom above all could not accept realistic compromises to achieve unity. Austria, anxious to retain its multinational empire, rejected all plans for a Great-German solution. When, however, the National Assembly voted to offer the emperor's crown to the Prussian king, he turned it down on the ground that he could not wear headgear soiled by democratic hands. The insurrection in Vienna was smashed with the help of Croatian regiments; Kossuth's insurrection in Budapest was subdued with the help of Russian cossacks; the assembly in Berlin was dissolved; uprisings in Baden and elsewhere were beaten down by Prussian troops. In Dresden, court music director Richard Wagner, charged with having attempted to set fire to the royal palace, had to flee in a hurry (in Paris he was to set his pyromaniacal dreams to music); Dr. Karl Marx, editor of the *Rheinische Zeitung*, was first muzzled, then expelled from Cologne; Ferdinand Freiligrath, a popular poet, somberly explained the colors of the republic: "Black is the powder, Red is the blood, Golden blazes the flame."

Like the Peasant Insurrection of 1525, the "March Revolution" of 1848-49 was beaten, but it lived on in the memory of the German left as its greatest moment, while the right referred to it as "the mad year."

If German unity could not be won under democratic insignia, the historic opportunity fell to the one state that had both the motive and the power: Prussia. Heinrich Heine, the poet, warned that "that eagle has talons." Yet gradually men who had once been Great-Germans were converted to the idea of a "smaller Germany" under the leadership of Prussia. Although her government was reactionary, it seemed to offer the strutting young bourgeoisie unification, industrialization, trade, and perhaps a share of that power in the world which so far had not fallen to

Germany's lot. In an age of rising nationalism everywhere, the German *Bürger* (citizens) were tired of being known as "the people of poets, thinkers, and dreamers"; Prussia stood for efficiency. The Rhenish provinces which Prussia had acquired in the War of Liberation were as much advanced industrially as England, then the foremost economic power. Prussia had forced a customs union on the other German states, some of which its territories held clamped as in a vise anyway; it was building a formidable army; and it now proposed to bring to the Germans, by statecraft, that unity which had eluded their democratic enthusiasm. If in 1848 the slogan had been that "Prussia will be absorbed into Germany," the question now was just when Germany would be absorbed into Prussia.

By and large, the intellectuals began to rally to the cause: Gustav Freytag and Felix Dahn, who were both novelists and historians; Johann Gustav Droysen and his impassioned disciple Heinrich Treitschke, who created a legend of the Prussian state and its historic mission; even some old-time liberals who had despised the spiked helmet and the corporal's baton or had feared to lose their Bavarian, Hanoverian, etc., identities. Among this group were the great historian Theodor Mommsen and three of the Göttingen Seven. Liberals under Rudolf von Bennigsen, a Hanoverian, formed a *Nationalverein* to support Prussia's cause. The young socialist leader Ferdinand Lassalle, too, imbued with Hegel's philosophy and Fichte's ethics, dreamed of an alliance between the workers and the Prussian crown toward a "social empire."

*   *   *

BEFORE WE CONTINUE THE PANORAMA of a German citizen's historical horizon, we must ask what caused this remarkable turnabout of the middle class and particularly of the intelligentsia. Prussia had never been popular with the educated classes; it had been poor and boorish, an upstart state with a Slavic name and a collection of haphazardly annexed provinces. Nor had these *Bürger* been brought up to admire power and military prowess; their culture was *Biedermeier* (probity, naiveté, and *Gemülichkeit*), humanist studies, and Schubert *Lieder*. Classical German literature had set forth the ideal of the all-around human personality, and the Romantic poets had developed still more sensitively the image of the beautiful soul, or gone in search of the "blue flower" and sung of fair mermaids. (Rosa Luxemburg, that great revolutionary of Polish-Jewish origin, knew half of Eduard Mörike's most lyrical poems by heart.)

There could have been no sharper contrast than that between Potsdam and Weimar—the symbols, respectively, of Prussian militarism and classical German literature. The *Bürger* who cherished his classical *Bildung* (cultural education) had no use for nationalism, militarism, fanaticism. He was urbane, cosmopolitan, and, above all, a private person minding his own business. He felt that "a political song is a nasty song"; he heeded Kant's practical imperative: one must obey one's sovereign—whether a legitimate one, a usurper, or even a revolutionary. An almanac written by Goethe and Schiller had dedicated this distich to the German patriots:

> Germans, a nation to build I fear you vainly endeavor.
> Aim to become instead, can't you, freer as men!

Not the citizen but the man is here the locus of authenticity; *unpolitisch* (nonpolitical) was long a word of honor. Thomas Mann used it during World War I to argue his antidemocratic, antiwestern cause. Freedom, in the conception of the German classics, is man's internal immunity to coercion; it is not, as it is in western political theory, a system of public rights; therefore it can be realized (once more according to a well-known Schiller poem) only "in the realm of dreams." It is, above all, the freedom to think. During the Nazi regime, Schiller's *Don Carlos* had to be taken out of the repertory because the audiences waited to cheer when the Marquis Posa asks of King Philip: "Sire, grant us freedom of thought!"

Yet here precisely lay the weakness of the German middle classes. Their quietism allowed the state to develop its power unchecked. They knew no link between freedom to think and freedom to act; society was apart from politics. As a result, the middle class had no experience with power; it had left all state business to the nobles, who in turn had no desire to share the privileges and perquisites that went with public office. Without any practice of power, the liberal middle class had no theory of revolution. There were German speakers whose ideas might have been compared to those of the Girondins and Jacobins; but there was no Gironde and no Jacobin Club.

A western-type patriotism that was at the same time liberal and populist might still have emerged in Germany had not the War of Liberation, back in 1812, aligned patriots and princes against revolutionary France: the national enemy had been the protagonist of democratic and egalitarian ideas. To fight against Napoleon one had to reject liberalism and the great Enlightenment of the eighteenth century; whoever preached its message in Germany was denounced as a "Frenchling." For a century German writers had been struggling against French dominance in taste and thought. Even the cosmopolitan thinkers of Goethe's generation had pitted German *Geist* (spirit) against French formalism. The Romantic movement of the nineteenth century turned this resentment into a new philosophy with a nationalist slant: it condemned the antihistorical, rationalistic, mechanistic, and super- ficial *esprit* of the French and exalted the history-minded, worshipful, sensitive, and profound *Geist* of the Germans.

Although these romantic ideologies had come from Joseph de Maistre and René de Chateaubriand (not to mention Edmund Burke), their German partisans gave them a distinctively national and even racial flavor. They claimed that only Germans had a sense of com- munity, understood the sacred old myths, and respected the traditional institutions. In fighting France they defended not just the fatherland but these old values. Hence, Germans would not be tempted by the spurious lure of "equality" or "citizen's rights"; on the contrary, they were proud of their organic order of estates where king, noblemen, middle class, and peasants each had an assigned place. Full humanity could be developed only in the community, and that community was best organized in the inherited structure of the state. The philosopher Johann Gottlieb Fichte designed a sort of German socialism; Georg Friedrich Hegel declared the state "the realization of the ethical idea"; the great historian Leopold von Ranke proclaimed that "states are like individuals and must follow their life instinct toward the fulfillment of their power potential." Power was the new word that was on everyone's lips. To quote Lassalle once again:

> History is the struggle with nature, with misery, with ignorance, poverty, and powerlessness—that is, unfreedom. The progressive con- quest of this powerlessness is freedom. In this struggle we could not advance one step were we to wage it as individuals. It is the state that must achieve this march toward freedom.

Even humanism was harnessed to the chariot of the new politics. Plato's *Politeia* was translated under the title *Der Staat*, and Socrates' *Apologia* was read to show that even the greatest individual's life belonged to his country. Theodor Mommsen's Roman studies culminated in a passionate vindication of Julius Caesar: "I have heard Ciceros in 1848," he exclaimed, "who talked eloquently but acted feebly."

Germany was ready for a Bismarck. When he became prime minister of Prussia in 1862, he told the Diet with brutal frankness: "Germany does not look to Prussia's liberalism but to its power. Speeches and majority resolutions will not decide the great questions of our time; blood and iron will." He promised unity without liberty.

The Diet to which Bismarck spoke had been elected under "three-class suffrage"—an outrageous electoral law that provoked many bitter demonstrations but remained in force until 1918. Balloting was unequal, open, and indirect. In each district voters were divided into three unequal groups according to the amount of taxes they paid. Those voters in the highest bracket who among themselves paid one-third of the total tax formed one group; those whose total in the middle brackets constituted another third formed a second group; and all the rest formed the third. Each group elected the same number of delegates to the electoral college, so that 100 rich men had as many votes as 1,000 moderately well-to-do, and those 1,000 had as many votes as 10,000 poor. Even so, the representatives so elected had little power: they could neither nominate nor dismiss a minister, and their law-making ability was severely curtailed by a House of Lords where the nobility and the king's appointees held sway.

But the Diet had the power of the purse, and the liberal majority refused to vote a budget. A constitutional crisis ensued, but Bismarck governed against the Diet, against public opinion, and against the sentiments of the other German states. An unscrupulous adventurer and a reckless gambler, he recognized no principles; no sentimental codes stood in the way of his one idea: to make Prussia great. He allied himself with revolutionary movements, started a fratricidal war between the German states, ruthlessly deposed princes, and annexed their territories.

Yet Bismarck's success created the strongest legend in German history. Thanks to their meticulous military preparation, superior weapons, and brilliant staff work, the Prussians won swift victories in 1864 against Denmark, in 1866 against Austria, and in 1870-71 against France. In these wars Prussia acquired the northern provinces of Schleswig-Holstein, the kingdom of Hanover, the electorate of Hesse, the grand duchy of Nassau, the old imperial city of Frankfurt, and, under the title of "Reichsland," Alsace-Lorraine. Austria was expelled from the German *Bund*, and rump Germany was reorganized under Prussian leadership.

When Napoleon III was taken prisoner at Sedan, the preponderance of France on the continent was ended. In the Hall of Mirrors of the Versailles palace—as if on enemy ruins—King Wilhelm I of Prussia was proclaimed German emperor. Richard Wagner composed an ode for the ceremony, and King Ludwig of Bavaria read the proclamation. A large painting immortalizing the scene was reproduced in every schoolbook. It showed all the princes, Bismarck, and the bemedaled generals, but not a single civilian. This was the new German fatherland.

Once united by military prowess, the nation was held together by the memory of its victories. Sedan Day and the emperor's birthday became the national holidays; the national anthem was *"Heil dir im Siegerkranz"* ("Hail to thee in the conqueror's laurel," to the tune of "God Save the King"). But "The Watch on the Rhine" remained the most popular song for another generation, and black, white, and red (an extension of the Prussian black and white) became the national flag.

Having become "the man of the century," Bismarck now dominated European politics. The domestic opposition mellowed—or rather rushed to the succor of victory. The Great-Germans and the minor-state patriots overcame their shock and accepted Bismarck's "Small-German" solution. The liberals forgave his violations of the constitution.

Among the few who refused to accept success as proof of right was Wilhelm Liebknecht, a cofounder of the Social-Democratic Party. He jeered at the sudden change of values: "Yesterday's oppressors are hailed as today's liberators; what had been right is now wrong and what was wrong has become right; the mystical power of bloodshed has transformed Satan's disciple into an angel of light." More significantly, some spokesmen of the middle class who had originally prepared Germany for the spirit of 1870 now turned away from Bismarck. Thus Leopold Sonnemann, editor of the *Frankfurter Zeitung*, tried in vain to introduce a bill of rights into the constitution; Theodor Mommsen called the new constitution a sham.

Some conservatives, former Great-Germans, and southern Catholics also compared the Second Reich unfavorably with the First: "Can it really be the German people's mission to form a great, centralized state when its entire history points in the opposite direction?" asked Konstantin Frantz (whose vindication came only after the fall of the Third Reich). In annexed Hanover and Alsace and in idiosyncratic Bavaria there lingered hatred and contempt for the overweening Prussians. The extravagant, romantic Ludwig of Bavaria, sponsor of Richard Wagner and builder of dream castles, was popular with the peasants, and they kept faith with his dynasty even through the republic.

Eventually, some of Germany's finest minds became disgusted with the opportunism, the power worship, the greed and vulgarity, of the new Reich. Theodor Fontane lets the main character in *Der Stechlin* muse: "We Germans are on top again—I fear a little too much so."

And Nietzsche warned that "the German *Geist* might be defeated by the German Empire."

However, these were isolated voices. The vast majority of the German middle class followed Bismarck gratefully and enthusiastically into a future that promised them greatness. "Put Germany in the saddle—it will know how to ride," Bismarck had said. Indeed, with Bismarck as the jockey, the dynamism of the new state overrode all opposition.

According to its constitution, the Second Reich was a confederation of princes. It consisted of four kingdoms (Prussia, Bavaria, Württemberg, Saxony), six grand duchies, five tiny duchies, seven minuscule principalities, three free cities (Hamburg, Bremen, Lübeck), and the Reichsland, Alsace-Lorraine. Sovereignty was vested in the *Bundesrat* (Federal Council), an upper house to which the princes sent their deputies. As a concession to southern pride, the Bavarians were permitted to have their own army, railway, and postal service. The kaiser (emperor) was supreme commander only in time of war. But the pull of the unitarian state was strong. Bismarck created a national railway office (Reichsbahn), a national post office (Reichspost), and a national bank (Reichsbank). Moreover, Prussia, with more than half of the total territory and two-thirds of the Reich's population, made its weight felt in all affairs of more than local interest. With the help of just one small state, it could block any constitutional amendment in the *Bundesrat*, and in routine affairs this body was too unwieldy to function as a check on the administration.

The centralist principle was represented by the kaiser (who also was king of Prussia). The Prussian prime minister was also chancellor of the Reich. He, and the departmental secretaries, served at the kaiser's pleasure.

However inadequately, the Reichstag (parliament) represented the democratic principle. It was elected by near-universal, direct, equal, and secret male suffrage. The voting age was twenty-five; residential and literacy requirements, and underrepresentation of the heavily populated cities, weighted the election returns in favor of the right. Despite one-man districts, six major parties—(from left) Social-Democratic, Progressive, Center, National-Liberal, Free-Conservative, and Conservative—contended for most seats, in addition to Poles, Alsatians, Guelphs, and Danes. The Reichstag could ask questions of the administration (as in England), debate and vote on laws, and approve the budget (although part of the Reich's income derived from state contributions). It had no say in foreign and military affairs, and it could neither appoint nor dismiss a chancellor or secretary. Even

Bismarck, however, tried to obtain majority support at all times, and he skillfully manipulated the Reichstag by raising issues—worthy or unworthy—on which he could rally the nation.

In Prussia, however, three-class suffrage was retained, and the civil service was an obedient tool of the chancellor. Its proverbial reliability, honesty, and discipline made it the backbone of the administration and the main instrument of power. Promotion was given preferentially to members of the Junker caste. Their life-style, code of honor, customs, and beliefs became the butt of cartoons, skits, and even full-length comedies (such as Gerhart Hauptmann's *The Beaver Coat*), but they furnished the role model for the rising middle class, which adopted their values.

The ambitious young man's aim now was to be a lieutenant of the reserve, to earn a medal or a title, to be received at court, and if possible to be knighted. Social status was measured not by the money he made but by his rank in the hierarchy of command. Each person was categorized by his title and wives were addressed by their husbands' titles: *Herr Doktor* was any Ph.D. or LL.D., *Herr Ministerialrat* an assistant secretary, *Herr Justizrat* an elderly lawyer, *Herr Assessor* a lawyer or teacher in training; *Frau Apotheker* was the pharmacist's wife, *Exzellenz* a general's widow. In business, a new hierarchy of *Herr Direktor* and *Herr Generaldirektor* began to establish itself. Those who had no other distinction could buy the title *Kommerzienrat*. Thus, everyone knew his place, and society was thoroughly stratified.

The school system, too, reflected the class division. Lower-class children went to the eight-grade "people's school," where they learned the four Rs (including religion) and discipline; they had to serve three (later two) years in the army. Although tuition fees were nominal, only the upper 10 percent sent their children at the age of nine to "high school" (*Gymnasium* or *Realschule* for boys), which started them on a foreign language and led, after five years, to a commercial career and the privilege of serving in the army for only one year. Those who took another three years of high school and earned the "Matura Certificate" could go into higher management or enroll in a university or technical academy. Only 5 percent of the population thus acquired the *Bildung* that was the prerequisite of privileged positions in society—provided they also were admitted to the right fraternities (*Korporationen*). These were the insensitive judges, the ignorant county presidents, the conceited government officials whom the cartoonists drew with bulldog faces, monocles, and dueling scars. The industrialist Walther Rathenau and Max Weber feared that unless the schools were opened to talent, the country would train fewer competent leaders than it actually needed.

Middle-class daughters attended a *Lyzeum,* which taught two languages but did not, of course, prepare its students for a career.

Access to the hierarchy was severely limited by birth. Nobility always had precedence; connections and good breeding usually mattered more than ability. The status system allowed advancement for each category of people only within well-circumscribed boundaries. The bourgeoisie could not hope to replace the aristocracy, but the individual man of property, education, and merit could hope to prepare the way for his sons to enter the hierarchy. This view from the middle rungs of the ladder fragmented the middle class and distorted the goals it could set for itself. Bismarck had opened a wide field of activities for businessmen, but he would never allow them to share the satisfactions of government. The lowliest government official exercised more authority than the wealthiest banker.

Those who did rise in the professions, in the civil service, and in business, therefore, did not feel like pioneers or vanguards of their class. They were co-opted into the ruling class only because they could be integrated into the system and become its supporters. An American observer was struck by this paradox of an alert and effective business class which was still politically immature as late as 1915:

> Germany carried over from the recent past . . . institutions and a frame of mind suitable to coercive and irresponsible control and dynastic domination. The Prussian spirit has permeated the rest of the federated people. . . . This united Germany took over from the more advanced neighbors the latest and highly developed technology, wholly inconsistent with her institutional backwardness but highly productive. . . . Taken over in so short a time this technology has not suffered from waste, obsolescent usage, or class animosities . . . [but] has not yet induced new habits of thought as among the English-speaking peoples. (Thorsten Veblen, *Imperial Germany and the Industrial Revolution*)

In its political immaturity the patriotic bourgeoisie followed Bismarck's slogans fanatically. There was to be one nation, one state, one school system; why not one church, one race? Poles and Danes were to be Germanized. The king of Prussia was *ex officio* head of the Lutheran Church; why not of the Catholic Church too? Bismarck tried to complete the Reformation: no "ultramontane power" (power residing "beyond the mountains," i.e., in Rome) was to be able to influence German politics. He encouraged a movement "away from Rome" among the Catholics, and when the faithful remained loyal to their clergy, the furies of the Prussian police were unleashed against cloisters, orders (especially the Jesuits), and Catholic schools. Catholics constituted three-eighths of the population and voted primarily for the Center Party, which also offered a haven to the recalcitrant minorities—disgruntled Poles, annexed Hanoverians and Alsatians, and southern particularists. Patriots dubbed the Center Party a Reichsfeind (enemy of the state); Bismarck considered it "an anachronistic challenge to the state" and proposed to crush it.

Liberals saw the church as a reactionary power—the main enemy of the secular state, public education, and civil marriage. Forgetful of other people's civil rights, they eagerly joined the good fight against obscurantism (the Pope had just declared himself infallible). The radical leader Dr. Rudolf Virchow—one of the great pathologists of his time—coined the term *Kulturkampf* (cultural crusade). An ugly coalition of Prussian police, liberal freethinkers, arrogant Junkers, Protestant bigots, and secularists pounced on the Catholic minority.

For once, however, Bismarck failed, and he had to call off the crusade. Compromise agreements ruled that the government must be advised of clerical appointments and that civil marriage must precede church marriage; schools were required to provide religious instruction for each faith; the state was to collect the tithe and pay the clergy's salaries; the Jesuits remained banned, but other orders were allowed.

Turning against the next Reichsfeind, Bismarck then proposed to outlaw internationalist, democratic socialism. Again the National-Liberals put their principles aside. After an anarchist had shot at the kaiser, the Reichstag majority approved the Anti-Socialist Law (*Sozialistengesetz*). All socialist organizations and propaganda were banned. The police suspended 150 socialist papers, arrested 1,500 agitators, and seized numerous books, but the increase of socialist votes was stopped for only a moment. By 1890 the Social-Democrats had become the strongest party (by popular votes, not by seats).

Trying to alternate the stick and the carrot, Bismarck offered the German workers a system of social insurance which was indeed pioneering, unique, and effective. All wage earners had to be insured against sickness, accident, disability, and old age, with the premiums to be paid by employers, employees, and the state. Unemployment insurance was still missing, but even so the German legislation was far ahead of that in any other country. It was carried with the help of Conservative and Center Party votes, against bitter resistance from the employers and the liberal parties.

Having long considered the state neutral on social issues, Bismarck now returned to the conservative notion of paternalistic government; he even spoke of state socialism. As we have seen, he had political reasons, too, for bringing the railways, the Reichsbank, the telegraph and telephone, and the post office under federal control. Individual states took over some prestigious businesses such as porcelain manufacturing. At the same time Bismarck switched from a long-standing practice of free trade to protectionism, and from territorial nationalism to "world politics."

The new tariffs benefited the big grain-producing estates and the large steel mills. This policy was intended to forge a new conservative coalition and to make Germany self-sufficient in case of a continental war. It made consumers pay for stepped-up capital accumulation, and forced them to help finance the new arms race. "We Germans fear God, but no one else in the world," said Bismarck in defense of his new military budget.

He had once said that the Middle East was not worth the bones of a single Prussian musketeer. Now he began to acquire colonies in Africa and in the South Pacific. He taught the Germans to place "foreign policy first." After having conducted a cautious foreign policy, he launched out into colonialism and imperialism. A literary magazine in 1882 expressed the new self-image of the German nation: "Germany wants nothing but her place in the sun."

* * *

WITH THIS TWIST, Bismarck had completed his "revolution from the top." He transformed the democratic drive for German unity into an instrument of a Great-Prussian power drive; he deflected a movement *for* Germany into a challenge *to* the world; and he perverted the Reich idea into the concept of an all-powerful state.

The middle classes had followed Bismarck step by step on this perilous road. They were now his ideological prisoners. Having accepted Bismarck's rule by coups, they continued to expect their salvation from the state, even though they did not dominate this state or control it. They idolized it and identified with the nation, much as they identified the ruler's decision with the national will.

A great German historian, Friedrich Meinecke, who also considered himself a liberal, wrote in his powerful book *The Idea of Reason of State*:

> In Bismarck we see the most sublime and successful synthesis between the old Reason of State and the new popular forces. He made use of these for the power needs of the state. With Machiavellian ruthlessness he created the German state. An intimate connection exists between his suppression of democratic tendencies and his cautious foreign policy after 1871.

Max Weber, the father of German sociology, arrived at this verdict:

> Bismarck bequeathed to Germany a nation without any political education, even below the level it had attained twenty years earlier; a nation accustomed to allow the great statesmen at its head to look after it; a nation acquiescing, under the cover of constitutional monarchy, to anything that was decided for it.

Of the two forces that struggled in the German mind—the humanist-democratic and the nationalist-authoritarian—the one that prevailed for the moment was younger and better organized. The older one, for the moment reduced to a few private voices and an ineffective, disaffected opposition, was condemned to play the role of "the other Germany." But it was not silent and it had its own traditions. To the Prussian legend of Potsdam (see p. 6) it opposed that of classical Weimar, to the memory of Sedan that of St. Paul's Church, to the splendor of the new empire those of German scholarship and industry. However, this other Germany was necessarily meshed with and dependent upon the ideas and institutions of official Germany. Its idea, formulated by Richarda Huch (see the epigraph beginning this Prelude) with such imprecision, was either not clear or expressed with many doubts and uncertainties.

Above all, the democratic forces in Germany lacked a clear understanding of power. It was always assumed that power was the business, or even the prerogative, of those who traditionally exercised it. Neither German democracy nor those who prided themselves on representing German *Geist* were prepared to wield power themselves. Impotent, they fell into line with those who did. Therein lies the tragedy of German history.

PART ONE

The Empire

1

State and Society at the Turn of the Century

*He who never held a gold coin in his hand does not know
the golden era of bourgeois certainty.*

—Thomas Mann

THE SECOND REICH, which had emerged from the cauldron of war, extended from the fortress of Metz in Lorraine to the fortress of Tilsit in East Prussia, and from the Alps to the Baltic shore. Its longest diagonal, from Metz to Memel, measured 1,305 kilometers (815 miles), but its waist along the Neisse and Oder Rivers, from the tip of Bohemia to the Baltic resort of Swinemünde (today Swinoujscie), was only 315 kilometers (200 miles). Its total area was four-fifths that of the state of Texas. The population in 1871 numbered forty-one million.

It was bounded in the west by France, the archenemy whose revenge it had to fear, Belgium, and Holland; in the north it looked across the sea to England, whose trade it was challenging, and to the Scandanavian countries; its southern flank was secured by the neutrality of Switzerland and the alliance with the Hapsburg monarchy; but in the east loomed the ever-expanding Russian empire (still in possession of Poland and the Baltic states and fomenting trouble in the Balkan Peninsula).

Industry was concentrated in the western provinces of Prussia, especially in the Rhine-Ruhr valleys, in Saxony, and of course in the big cities. Cattle were raised in the northern and western areas; the large estates of the northeastern plains produced grains (though not wheat) and potatoes.

Two-thirds of the population still lived in rural areas, and half were occupied in farming, fishing, and forestry. Of all cities, only Berlin was approaching the million mark (if communities that were absorbed later are included; but at that time Charlottenburg and Wilmersdorf were separated from Berlin by a vast expanse of unbuilt area which today is covered by the "New West" and the *Kurfürstendamm*). Munich, the art capital, and Hamburg, the commercial capital, had less than half a million people each.

But by 1900 Berlin counted 1,880,000, Hamburg 722,000, and Munich 659,000 heads. By 1914 Berlin had passed two million, Hamburg one million. New centers of urbanization developed in the Rhine-Ruhr valley, Saxony, and Silesia. With prosperity, early marriages, and improved sanitation, the total population rose to fifty-six million in 1900 and to sixty-five million in 1914; thanks to the decline in infant mortality, one-third of the population was under fifteen years of age. Significantly, at the outbreak of World War I, only 40 percent of the German people lived in places with less than 2,000 inhabitants, and less than one-third of the total were employed in agriculture.

The rise of German industry had been well on its way before unification. In the war of 1871, Germany acquired the Alsatian iron and potash mines. Then, thanks to the ingenuity, efficiency, and organizing ability of German industrialists and bankers, pig-iron output increased from 1.5 million tons in 1871 to 8.5 million tons in 1900 and to 16 million tons by 1914. Coal output tripled. Exports of mostly manufactured goods rose from 2.5 billion marks in 1871 to 5 billion in 1900 and 10 billion in 1914.

The early 1870s were known as "founders' years" because many new firms began their astounding careers at that time—among them the world-famous Zeiss works, which also pioneered in social policy. This people, which had long thought of itself as a nation of poets and dreamers, or perhaps of thinkers, had suddenly poured its energies into the vigorous pursuit of industrial business. By 1880 Germany had outstripped her archrival on the continent, France, which was stagnating in population and remained strongly rural. During the 1890s German industrial output had overtaken that of England, the premier industrial nation and Germany's economic rival. National income had doubled in twenty years; it was 40 billion marks in 1912, or 600 marks per capita, while England enjoyed the equivalent of 900 marks (one gold dollar = 4.25 marks gold).

Germany shared with the United States the advantages of the latecomer. Unhampered by dated technology and business methods, it was able fully to exploit the new inventions of the second industrial revolution: the dynamo, the internal combustion engine, the chemistry of dye and carbon derivatives. In this century, the American Leo H. Baekeland invented synthetic resin, which gave rise to the new industry of plastics; Fritz Haber produced nitrogen from the air, liberating German farming from the import of Chilean saltpeter and enabling the kaiser's armies to defy the blockade in World War I.

A. W. von Hoffmann made synthetic rubber; Wolfgang Ostwald published the pioneering work on colloid chemistry. The Badische Anilin- und Sodafabrik produced "artificial silk" (rayon), and Krupp produced stainless steel. (Cynically, he offered the British navy an armored plate that would resist any existing shell, and the kaiser a shell that would pierce that armor.) Emil Rathenau founded the electrical trust Allgemeine Elektrizitäts-Gesellschaft; his son Walther expounded the economics of the new industries:

> Older industries produced articles that consumers needed, but left their use to the customers' discretion. While using new techniques, the old manufacturers continued, or improved upon, that which the old handicrafts had done. With electromechanics [and today, we would add, with chemical engineering] a new *field* of industry is opening. It will transform a large part of human life. Production no longer caters to the consumers' needs; rather, these needs are *created* by the producer, or even imposed. Electricity is not an industry but a complex; it creates new demands, controls new industries, penetrates all spheres of life from lighting to transportation to power to the use of new, centralized machinery.

The new industries also differed from the old ones in their attempt to control their suppliers and their outlets. Huge concerns teamed up with the leading banks to organize an industry or a market; cartels such as the Rhenish-Westphalian Coal Syndicate or the Potash Syndicate introduced the era of "organized capitalism." Interlocking directorships and financial manipulations assured the domination of the economy by "finance capital" (the Marxist Rudolf Hilferding, who was to be finance minister under the republic, coined the term in 1912). There were 385 cartels in Germany, and 100 of them were international. Rathenau, who himself held no fewer than sixty-eight directorships, said that the planet's fate was in the hands of 400 persons who all knew each other. He also drew the political conclusion that the era of liberalism (in the European sense of laissez-faire for business and ideas) was over. Small-scale middle-class enterprise, thrift, and free trade were no longer adequate. Anyway, the petit-bourgeois intellectuals and their Progressive Party had not been able to create a political structure such as Bismarck had given to the new German enterprise. Monopoly capital tended to associate itself with the state, imperialism, and political reaction.

Those developments had not failed to produce some shifts in the structure of the leading elites. The expansion of overseas grain production had ruined many estates, and their owners had been forced to gild their escutcheons by marrying bankers' daughters—in some cases even Jewish bankers' daughters. Conversely, merchants, professors, and civil servants had been ennobled and commoners promoted to high offices. Thus, General Erich Ludendorff became the strategist of World War I (though it is true that for want of a nobility "von" he could not be created a field marshal); neither the chancellor, Theobald von Bethmann-Hollweg, nor the naval secretary, Admiral Alfred von Tirpitz, had noble ancestors. At court, too, the old aristocracy now mingled with people whose credentials lay in their financial, legal, or technical ability, and whose business interests made them useful for the kaiser's ambitious designs in global politics.

Thus, Albert Ballin, president of the Hamburg-America Line, and the banker Max Warburg, although Jewish, were received at court. Among the older barons of industry were the established masters of the mining and steel companies: Krupp, Röchling, Vögler, and Baron von Stumm (the latter known for his patriarchal views on labor); but besides them there were shrewd and rapacious newcomers like Thyssen and Stinnes. There were the grandsons of the old machine builder, von Siemens: Georg, founder of the Deutsche Bank, and Werner, pioneer in the field of electrical engineering. The owners of the new inventions quickly rose to prominence: Bosch and Daimler for the automotive industry, Duisberg for the chemical industry, Rathenau for the electrical industry. Another new breed were the bankers who promoted industrial ventures, financed German investments abroad, and then went into politics to support and protect these plans. Among them were Bernhard Dernburg and Karl Helfferich, men of power in or out of office, although they were not owners themselves of the enterprises they directed.

Similarly, the corporation lawyers who represented cartels and other trade associations—a new profession, called *Syndikus* in German—wielded immense influence and often found their way into politics. Among these men were Gustav Stresemann, the future chancellor, whose father had been an innkeeper; Emil Kirdorf, founder of the Rhenish-Westphalian Coal Syndicate; and Alfred Hugenberg, who used his position in the Land Credit Bank to build a newspaper and movie empire which became the basis for his nefarious role in politics.

Friedrich Meinecke, the liberal historian, wrote in 1912:

> A new aristocracy is forming. Without any plan it arises out of the need to meet the most modern conditions. The new masses cannot govern themselves; everywhere decisions are made by a few leading heads. The associations which present the problems to the government are mere

sounding boards for a few purposeful leaders. Nor can the many goods we produce find their way to the customer through the accidental encounter in a free market. Everywhere the few organize the many to regulate syndicates, cartels, tariffs. They stay in power as long as they justify the confidence which the many have to give them. No other way is possible. The specifically modern reform of administration and government results in a temporary *dictatorship of trust* [*Diktatur des Vertrauens*—italics by Meinecke].

This new elite at the top of the social pyramid was supported by a growing infrastructure: the "salaried employees" and officials. Being paid monthly rather than on an hourly or weekly basis, they constituted the "salariat" or "new middle class." A business bureaucracy grew at the side of the state bureaucracy and adopted its service mentality. By 1912, 12 percent of the working population were in this class. Teachers and professors, although ranking high in esteem, also found their place in this hierarchy and, in addition to being civil servants economically, shared the mental attitude of civil servants (*Beamte*), eager for promotion and for the honors that the system provided: medals, titles, perhaps even nobility.

The majority of intellectuals, too, had adopted a civil service mentality. They were sensitive to the viewpoint of state and nation and often looked down on the bourgeoisie and up to the symbols of the state. The government was seen as standing above the interests of the various classes and representing the national will.

A sudden change of the guard had given the new tendencies a premature access to the levers of power. In 1888, the "old emperor" and his son Frederick died within a hundred days of each other. The "crown prince"—as he had continued to be called even as emperor from long usage and affection—had passed for a liberal, and his British wife had been a critic of Bismarck. Their liberal-minded generation—those who had been young in 1848—had been kept from power during the long reign of Wilhelm I and Bismarck. Now the untimely death of the crown prince deprived it of its turn to influence the course of government. The successor was twenty-nine-year-old Wilhelm II—inexperienced but enthusiastic, imbued with his generation's progressive ideas but arrogant and brash. Born with a short left arm and disliked by his mother, he had a deep need to be admired—a desire catered to by courtiers, subordinates, and the rich bourgeois whom he favored with his company. His unstable mind and restlessness exposed Germany to perpetual shifts of policy. He wanted to be a "people's kaiser," or even a *Socialkaiser*, promoting the well-being of the laboring classes; but he also wanted to lead his nation to world power and prestige. He lifted the ban on socialist organizations, but his police went on harassing them. He let himself be celebrated as the "peace kaiser," but at the same time he missed no opportunity to challenge the power of other nations and remind them of his military might. He had his picture taken clasping the hilt of his saber.

As all Germany was jealous of England, Wilhelm II was envious of his cousin Edward VII, and he challenged British sea power. He congratulated the Boers on a victory over the Jameson Raiders. When a German ambassador was murdered in Peking, he sent a punitive corps to China with the instruction, "Behave so that you will be remembered as Huns!" At the disarmament conference at the Hague, the powers found it embarrassing to think up excuses for adjourning without result, but Wilhelm brazenly picked up the "old maid" and took the blame for the conference's failure. The Foreign Office often had to burn the midnight oil to mitigate, repair, or prevent some faux pas of the indefatigable monarch. The pacifist writer Ludwig Quidde published a historical pamphlet, *Caligula, a Study of Megalomania in a Roman Caesar*; it was full of allusions but could not be banned because the censors could not admit that they understood the unflattering parallels between the mad Roman and the ruler of Germany.

While the emperor's panache gave Germans the reputation of being boisterous, boorish meddlers, it is not suggested that a more polished monarch could have avoided the world war. The sad truth is that in provoking other nations Wilhelm acted out the dreams of all German patriots. He was in tune with his generation: it wanted a kaiser who led with the sword. Nothing could be more symbolic than the upturned, waxed, and twisted mustache which the kaiser modeled and every patriotic, strutting young man copied. The cartoonists had fun with it, and his "court barber" advertised it as the "we-have-ascended mustache." It illustrated the German mind at the turn of the century. The kaiser did not mislead the people; they wanted to be led to where he pointed.

The structure of the imperial government excluded the checks and balances of informed opinion. While secret diplomacy was the practice of all countries, Wilhelm's most momentous decisions were made on the advice of courtiers and secret councilors whose influence was hardly suspected by the public and by foreign chancelleries. The kaiser's volatile temperament attracted flatterers who exploited his insecurity and encouraged his worst inclinations, his muscle flexing, his bragging, his display of power. They belonged to his own generation, which still felt that, as a newcomer to the world theater, Germany had to show more than mere self-confidence. They were parvenus and exhibited the swagger of nouveaux riches—which some of them indeed were. They introduced a new style of life at the court and in politics. It was natural that they felt ill at ease with the old chancellor who thought himself indispensable.

The inevitable clash came in 1890. The young kaiser and Bismarck disagreed about social legislation, which Wilhelm wished to expand, and the Anti-Socialist Law, which he did not want to renew, and about Bismarck's reckless scheme to abrogate the powers of the Reichstag. In foreign affairs, too, the kaiser's advisers felt that Bismarck's house of cards—of contradictory treaty obligations— could not be maintained for long, and that decisions had to be made that might require a new defense posture.

When Bismarck was dismissed, with very little dignity, many feared that "the pilot had left the boat." But the younger generation was eager to show that they had grown up, and many were glad to be relieved of the oppressive presence that had anguished Europe for three decades. On his eightieth birthday, the Reichstag rejected a motion to send the founder of the Reich a congratulatory telegram.

The young kaiser proclaimed that a "new course" was taking Germany into a "new era." The ban on Social-Democratic organizations was dropped; new measures were adopted to protect workers, especially women and children, from exploitation and health hazards; tariffs were lowered; a progressive income tax was introduced for the first time; the period of military service was cut from three years to two years; minorities were given better treatment.

But industrialists remonstrated against these intrusions of the state into their God-given right to be masters in their own houses, and the Junkers protested that they would be ruined unless the state's hand were held over them. This was true: they were bankrupt economically; in addition, they no longer supplied political leaders but merely *Beamte* (as Max Weber said in 1895). Yet they still claimed that they were the backbone of the state and entitled to its special protection. Socially they were still influential enough to force the resignation of Caprivi, the new chancellor, who had offended their interests. Nor did they hesitate to blackmail the kaiser with unsavory disclosures about persons in his entourage.

This was the system: court intrigues took the place of politics; a commoner could gain influence only if he adapted his own thinking to that of the Junker class and became a courtier himself. Industrialists acquired the habit of involving government officials in their ventures. This symbiosis of Junker and financier also suggested an easy way out of conflicts over policies and conflicts within the establishment: they were resolved by exporting the problem. Internal antagonisms were deflected by naming targets of envy and greed abroad. Nationalism thus was converted into imperialism, and high-minded patriotism was used as a cover for narrow interests. (Foreign policy will be discussed in Chapter 5; here we are interested only in its relation to the domestic structure.)

But there was no national interest; there were only fitful sallies in all directions, responding to this or that pressure. The new course soon turned into a zigzag course. Pressure groups sought mass support on economic and patriotic grounds. The Agriculturists' League, the trade unions and employers' associations, the Pan-German (*Alldeutsche*) League, the Naval League, marched their throngs into the free-for-all fight that caused many intellectuals to turn away from the materialism of the age, from its egoism, its cant, its vulgarity.

The main problem of domestic policy at the time was known as "the social question," and that meant, specifically, the rising vote of the Social-Democratic Party. Many people inside and outside the government pleaded that something be done for the workers. But the Social-Democrats, in their "program" of 1891, had declared that the workers had to liberate themselves. In a class society where workers never could rise above their station, revolution was the only remedy. All the other parties were, at one time or another, in league with the administration. The leaders of the Social-Democratic Party had never talked to a chancellor, even in private. It was as if the workers did not belong to the nation. Therefore they voted for the overthrow of the "system."

It is true that Karl Marx's dire prophecy about the poor getting poorer had been proven incorrect. Wages were rising, working conditions were improving. Strikes were successful, and trade unions were able to bargain. But all this only made the workers more confident that they had to receive full recognition. Meeting that desire, listening to just grievances, was the purpose of the Association for Social Policies—mostly professors of sociology and economics—which organized a vast research program into the causes of poverty and maladjustment. Their proposals earned them the epithet "socialists of the lectern."

Some optimistic reformers pointed to the increasing opportunities for lower-class children to rise into white-collar occupations. But actually, advancement stopped at the middle rungs, where the "glass walls of education" became impenetrable. Speech habits, dress, and table manners marked the ineligible candidate; family connections and membership in the right student fraternities were more important than exams.

As this was a class society, the income pyramid was not gradated but jagged. One percent of all families earned over 10,000 marks a year, and 6 percent earned over 3,000 marks; these two categories accounted for one-third of all incomes. Twenty million families had less than 1,200 marks a year. A Krupp worker earned 30 to 36 marks a week when a kilo of rye bread cost twenty-eight pfennigs and a pound of beef eighty-seven pfennigs. Food usually took one-half of a worker's income. In the textile town of Barmen, the average consumer ate 39 kilos of meat per year; in the resort spa of Wiesbaden, 102 kilos. For factory workers the working week was still sixty hours, with never a Saturday off, and there were neither fringe benefits nor union rights—though small employers usually recognized moral obligations toward their workers and would keep workers even when work was slow.

But new processes, new products, and increased productivity had given higher incomes to more people. Skilled workers could afford a bicycle, a daily shave, and chicken every Sunday. What was missing can clearly be seen from the demands of the Social-Democratic Party in its 1891 program: free education all the way; free dispensation of justice; free health care; free burial; a progressive income tax; the right to organize; the eight-hour day and the thirty-six-hour weekend; total prohibition of child labor and of the cottage industry.

One category of workers saw no improvement of its condition. The "Regulation for Servants" (*Gesindeordnung*) held the laborers on the eastern states in a semifeudal dependence. Otto Braun, later prime minister of Prussia, recalled how the Junkers sicced their dogs on him when he tried to organize laborers. Despite their protestations of patriotism, the Junkers also employed thousands of Polish migrants for seasonal work; Max Weber charged that this policy depopulated the area and prevented its economic development.

*   *   *

EAST OF THE ELBE WERE THE HEARTLANDS OF traditional conservatism—agrarian, Protestant, authoritarian, militaristic, opposed to "modernism." A small faction, the Free-Conservatives (also called Reichspartei), had supported the chancellor at all times. Together the two conservative parties had once commanded one-fourth of the vote; under Wilhelm II they had dropped to 14 percent and less. But, through the powerful Agriculturists' League, the Junkers kept a tight hold on medium and small peasants in other areas, too, although truck farms and vineyards had interests of their own. Desperate, the conservatives denounced the "Jewish Empire," for indeed money had conquered Berlin. Court chaplain Adolf Stoecker deployed a viciously anti-Semitic campaign in the vain hope of winning the masses of the poor over to a reactionary policy. This attempt proved disastrous. The party disowned Stoecker, but it continued to emphasize its Christian and traditionalist character. It was narrowly chauvinistic rather than imperialistic; its intellectuals followed the Romantic and racist teachings of Langbehn, Lagarde, and Houston Stewart Chamberlain (see page 31).

After Bismarck abandoned the *Kulturkampf* and Leo XIII became Pope, the Center Party turned into an establishment party. It represented the Catholic peasants and middle class of the smaller states, but it had a more liberal wing in the Rhineland, where Catholic trade unions were competing with the Socialist unions. The Center adopted the social teachings of the encyclical *Rerum novarum* (1891) and supported social legislation. Its problem was to democratize its base and to "get out of the Catholic tower." When it criticized the kaiser's colonial policies it was once again denounced, in the "Hottentot Campaign" of 1905, as the "enemy of the Reich." In 1918 it helped to assure a smooth transition from monarchy to republic, and it took part in every government from 1919 to 1932.

The main support of the government, throughout the Bismarckian and Wilhelmian eras, was the National-Liberal Party. It was the party of the bourgeoisie, which enthusiastically followed the kaiser's military, naval, and colonial policies; many of its representatives were promoters of the Pan-German League, a frankly imperialistic pressure group. Having abandoned civil rights, it jettisoned free trade and formed a "cartel" with the conservatives to raise protective tariffs on grains and manufactured goods. The National-Liberals usually received 14 percent of the vote (down from twice that much in the honeymoon of the Bismarck era).

The liberal tradition, however, was continued by smaller groups, which frequently split and changed names, such as the Progressives, the Freethinkers, and the People's Party; among them they polled from 9 to 12 percent of the vote. They remained in opposition and upheld the banner of civil rights, free trade, and small enterprise. They boasted the support of distinguished scholars like Max Weber, the economist Lujo Brentano, Theodor Heuss, a future president of the second republic, and Friedrich Meinecke, whose *Cosmopolitanism and National State* almost pathetically exhibits the illusions of liberal idealism. Liberalism was the creed of the *Frankfurter Zeitung* and

Berliner Tageblatt as well as the venerable *Vossische Zeitung* in Berlin.

Progressivism gained a fresh face when in 1903 Pastor Friedrich Naumann joined the left. He had been a follower of Adolf Stoecker and wanted to bring genuine help to the lower classes. His influential weekly, *Die Hilfe* (*Social Aid*), and his National-Social Association may be compared to the "social liberalism" of David Lloyd George in England or to William Jennings Bryan's populism in the United States. Like Lassalle before him, Naumann dreamed of a "social monarchy"; he strove for a national community, scorned selfish interests, and fought bitterly against the agrarian-aristocratic caste and the big capitalists. He scorned the submissiveness of the German middle class and deplored their lack of political will; he called on the citizens to assert their rights and he tried to develop a constitutional regime that would deliver Germany from the shackles of its antiquated state.

The outlines of his social-liberal "people's state," however, remained dim, and he blurred them further with his vision of a central European union (*Mitteleuropa*), forecasting an empire in which the Germans would be the first among the associated nations. As a result, he was attacked by the Right as a radical and by the socialists as a "social-imperialist." Nevertheless, among German politicians before the war, he stood out. After the war he converted the Progressives into the Democratic Party, which at first raised many hopes for a radical republic; but Naumann's death in 1919 and Max Weber's in 1920 plunged the party back into its tradition of bourgeois liberalism.

The only party radically opposed to the monarchy, the caste state, and all its institutions was the SPD (Social-Democratic Party of Germany), a branch of the International Workingmen's Association. Its program of 1891 called for the emancipation of the workers through their own efforts, i.e., through class war—democratically where the workers had the rights of association and representation, and in revolutionary ways where the state withheld these rights. Although its ultimate goals transcended the system, it participated in elections and vigorously supported trade union activity. As the strongest party in the Reichstag, it did its share in shaping social legislation. But on budget day it voted "not a dime for this system"; outside Parliament, it led mass demonstrations on May Day and fought against unequal suffrage, against colonialism, against the arms race. Many went to jail for picketing, trespassing, or *lèse majesté*; on one occasion a police saber cut a worker's hand off. The kaiser referred to them as "bums without a fatherland"; the government persecuted them as "enemies of the state" or "nigger-lovers."

Yet if the socialists did not belong to the nation, they had their one million members, their hundred newspapers and magazines, their unions and meeting halls, their own theater and sports clubs—all in all, a vigorous organization life. In fact, they had created their own counter-nation, with a counter-establishment and a counter-kaiser, their beloved leader August Bebel, a turner by trade. The Marxist theory as presented by Karl Kautsky promised a "necessary," almost automatic, breakdown of capitalism; it claimed to possess scientific proof that socialism was inevitable. And since the age believed in science, this apocalyptic vision fired the workers with infinite confidence that their suffering and fighting were not in vain.

In the southern states Parliament had more power than in Prussia, and young activists felt that socialists might achieve more practical reforms if they were to talk less of revolution. "What you call the final goal is nothing, the movement is everything," said Eduard Bernstein in proposing to revise doctrinaire Marxism. He stated that Marxian dialectics no longer explained what Social-Democrats now were doing: instead of rallying to the revolution, they were pursuing day-to-day reform. This, he declared, was not only possible but necessary; for capitalism was obviously not going to break down all at once, but was changing gradually, and the most recent developments in industry might open new possibilities.

This view was called revisionism or reformism. It was rejected, after an ardent debate, by the party's Dresden Convention of 1903. But their revolutionary ideology did not prevent Social-Democrats from pursuing practical goals of the day. They proposed social legislation, approved municipal projects, designed a formula for a "people's army," etc. Above all, they had to support the trade unions in collective bargaining. Although formally the two organizations were separate, the Free Trade Unions (ADGB) with their 2.5 million members were under socialist leadership. Moreover, there were 110 socialist members of the Reichstag from 1912, and as many representatives in state and municipal assemblies; the party gave employment to thousands of editors, printers, organizers, and "labor-union secretaries"—a new profession—who would not wantonly expose their offices and homes to the risk of police raids.

Hence, when revolutionary events in Russia raised the issue of political mass strikes, or when the left (Rosa Luxemburg) proposed to the Socialist International that it should answer war with a general strike, the parties balked: in most countries socialists made a distinction between "the system," which they hated, and the country, in which they had a stake. Many socialist intellectuals felt that their party should also appeal to those "intermediate classes" that were its potential allies in its fight against big capitalism and the class state: small peasants, salaried employees, and especially that newly important stratum, the technical intelligentsia.

Although Marxists were still strong on economic theory, they had nothing to say to the most recent trends in philosophy, criticism, and the arts. Social democracy attracted very few intellectuals. It proposed to take over the state—the Bohemians would have preferred to abolish it. Marxism is based on rationality and the work ethic; the prevailing philosophies of the young intelligentsia were antirationalist and libertine. Many artists, students, and freethinkers reacted emotionally against the harsh realities of the work ethic; but their protest was moral or romantic (see Chapter 2). They tended toward an individual anarchism or a backward-looking nativism. Socialism in its Marxist form was no answer to their nostalgia. The world, Max Weber complained, had been "deprived of its mystery"; business and the state alike pursued a bureaucratic state rationality that tended to destroy the human substance.

Weber's colleague, Emil Lask, analyzed the problem of alienation as early as 1902, decades before the word became fashionable on the left. Playwrights like Frank Wedekind and poets like Richard Dehmel castigated the uptight (a favorite German word was *verkrampft*) morality of middle-class society and confronted it with brutal, naked sexuality. Nietzsche's radical individualism and his teaching of the "wisdom of the body" stirred other writers to search for values beyond the confines of state and society. The youth movement sought a community of man and nature in the German people's ancient customs. Richard Wagner's *Ring of the Nibelungen* was generally understood as portraying the revolt of the naive, natural German Siegfried against the alien dragon of capitalism. "Mammon" and calculating vulgarity were often identified as western, especially English or "Welsh" (meaning French), or as Jewish.

Julius Langbehn flattered would-be elites by telling them that the Germans had a deep, metaphysical soul which was in danger of succumbing to the plebian assault of state and business organizations. His *Rembrandt as Educator* (1870), confused and unoriginal but brilliantly written, had tremendous success and in turn influenced Wagner's son-in-law Houston Stewart Chamberlain, who chose Germany as his fatherland and wrote *Foundations of the Nineteenth Century* (1900). Both substituted anti-Semitism for any political solution. But Bebel's quip, "Anti-Semitism is the morons' socialism," overlooked the fact that anti-Semitism expressed the intellectuals' malaise rather than the needs and hopes of the masses. It was an upper-class complaint that pushy Jews were crowding around the kaiser, that they dominated newspapers and the theater, were successful lawyers and doctors, and sponsored the avant-garde through their predominant publishing houses (Cassirer, S. Fischer, Hegner, Wolff). Small shopkeepers also resented the Jewish-owned department stores. In every election anti-Semites received 1 to 3 percent of the vote; the Conservatives, too, appealed to "Christian" voters.

But resentment could not be a political platform as long as the system produced no problems that did not seem capable of rational solutions, and as long as all people and classes saw opportunities ahead. There was room at the top for newcomers, and there were new outlets abroad.

Above all, the system itself seemed to be as stable as the currency; every criticism seemed to point to potential improvements rather than to rupture. And it was tolerated gladly. The regime was able to laugh at its foibles. The leading satirical weekly, *Simplicissimus*, castigated the abuses and vanities of the ruling caste, and even of the court, without fearing censorship. Its cartoonists, Olaf Gulbransson and Thomas Theodor Heine, were honored members of the artists' profession. Wilhelm Busch was even more popular. His gently irreverent jeers and taunts made the philistines laugh at themselves, in the sure knowledge that his naughty urchins would grow up and be solid citizens. Neither of them attacked the foundations of society.

And nowhere do we find the uncertainty and insecurity that was to turn the ensuing period into a spectacle of crises, despair, and revolution. Without falling prey to the fallacy that sees the past in the golden hues of nostalgia, we may envy the decade before World War I for its confidence in the continued progress of mankind, its assurance that most problems could be solved, its certainty that God rewards the good and that evil is a deviation from the natural.

2

Wilhelminian Culture

The son hates nothing so much as the rules and conventions that confine his father. Punching piety's face frees a young man from his mother's apron strings. The young generation rejoices at the decline of the middle-class world under whose whip it grew up for decades.
—Hermann Hesse

AT THE TURN OF THE CENTURY, most of Germany was still rural or small-town. "Residential cities" in each state had been built around the sovereign's palace; they had gardens and theaters. Even in the big cities most streets were still paved in stone, and most country roads would today be called dirt roads. Few automobiles circulated on them; horse feed accounted for one-fifth of the grain that was harvested. Railway trains, drawn by steam engines, still had a romanticism of their own, and in popular novels people spent much time in stations. Because of the smoke, railway stations had to have large halls and so became the first examples of modern architecture—iron structures boldly showing their tectonic elements.

Elsewhere such honesty was still uncommon. Factories had battlements like barracks buildings, but little effort was spent to make them safe and sanitary, much less airy and pleasant to work in. The same must be said of worker's tenements, or the "backhouses" in the big cities. They had gas lighting and WCs that had to be used by several families each. Middle-class houses tried to look like castles, with balconies and turrets, just as the bourgeois *intérieur* pretended to imitate the nonchalant elegance of the aristocratic salon. While the stock exchange was always fitted with the columns of a Greek temple, city halls borrowed Gothic or Romanesque motives for spires that had no function. The architecture exposed the falseness of Wilhelminian culture: its churches without inspiration, its monuments with empty postures, its public buildings designed to display pompousness.

But remedies were at hand. The new generation was trying to liberate itself from the taffeta and tassels, from the pseudo-Gothic windows and the pseudo-Baroque furniture of its fathers. The un-

79455

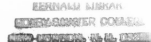
BERNALD LIBRARY
CONBY-SAWYER COLLEGE
NEW LONDON, N. H. 032

inhibited Munich magazine *Jugend* (*Youth*) sported illustrations inspired by flowing ribbons and imaginary vegetation. Similar ornaments on furniture were in the style called *Jugendstil* (in France, *art nouveau*). Its flowing lines continued to deny the function of the objects they decorated. But after a while, designers took up impulses from the crafts movement and the life-style reformers who pleaded for "truth in building" and "loyalty to the material." When the exuberant vegetation disappeared, the twentieth century had acquired a distinctive style which made good use of structural elements and was capable of producing noble lines.

Adolf Loos, who belonged to the "truth in living" movement, designed the "house without eyebrows" in Vienna. Alfred Messel erected the breathtaking "glass structure" of Wertheim's department store in Berlin. Munich, too, had its "glass palace," and Hamburg was building the proud Mönckebergstrasse. Peter Behrens, the most fertile mind among the functional architects, found an intelligent sponsor in Rathenau's electric trust (AEG); his student, Walter Gropius, later directed the Bauhaus (originally, the Weimar School of Design), which emphasized conformity with the natural characteristics of the material. The *Werkbund* (Craft's League) movement, inspired by Langbehn's romantic philosophy, also aimed to renew the traditions of craftsmanship and helped the new middle classes to proclaim their independence from the sham-patrician tastes of their fathers.

Modern apartment houses were equipped with electricity, elevators, and central heating; new districts were being built up with all the modern conveniences. Horse-drawn buses were replaced by electric tramways and, in Berlin, by the elevated. People could clearly see progress happening and, more important, its possibilities were in their minds when they set goals for their own advancement.

Every year brought new inventions and new scientific insights. Huge crowds traveled to an open field to watch bold aviators perform acrobatics in the air. They hailed the mighty zeppelin as it circled above the cities. (The question of whether flying ships should be lighter or heavier than air had not been decided yet.) They heard of powerful telescopes that penetrated into the Milky Way and of instruments that unveiled the secrets of the atom. Recent discoveries like X rays and radioactivity were to change notions about the structure of the universe. Popular science and the magazine sections of the newspapers spread new attitudes toward science among the masses; we may speak of a democratization of knowledge. Newly invented machines and gadgets—linotype, phonograph, motion picture, wireless telegraph, the one-horsepower dynamo—were to affect everyone's style of living. Although home sewing was still the proper thing, the ready-to-wear industry democratized fashion; every girl could wear an imitation of a Paris creation. The phonograph, though still of abominable tone quality, brought Caruso to those who could not afford an opera ticket; the movie permitted everybody to see the great Eleanore Duse—although of course most people preferred the current hit song to *Aïda*, and Tom Mix or slapstick comedy to Feuillade's screen presentation of social strife.

Innovations in the press gave the masses a sense of belonging, of participating in their age's culture. The novel format of the *Generalanzeiger* (mass circulation daily) no longer spoke to the educated, the partisans, and the committed alone, but brought general information, both useful and trivial, as entertainment to a larger audience. Even the old and respected papers were forced to publish magazine supplements. A great publishing house like Ullstein or Scherl might own several dailies and weeklies and subsidize a highbrow paper out of general revenue.

These were ambiguous blessings. While the media spread the enjoyment of the arts, they also affected the art of enjoying and using them. The new media could not simply transpose highbrow culture into the language of the masses, but they carried their own message, forced upon them by their technical potential. The movie camera failed whenever it tried to photograph a stage performance; it succeeded when it used its own characteristic themes or exploited its mobility. It could photograph tumbling mountains and onrushing locomotives which put Wagner's *Magic Fire* to shame; it could photograph a manhunt, and it especially pleased its audiences with slapstick comedies, thrillers, and romantic love stories.

Above all, movies produced the worship of the star, or rather, as the female of the species was called, the diva, whose personality submerged her role—exactly the opposite of what a good actor does— and with whose character and suffering the audience tried to identify. The Danish actress Asta Nielsen became famous as gypsy, as fallen beauty, and as working girl. The German firm of Messter promoted the beautiful Henny Porten.

Accompanying the silent film, the piano banged out the "Ride of the Valkyries" while the villain was being hunted, or tinkled a schmaltzy melody while the diva submitted to a strictly measured footage of kisses. In comparison with the realistic French film, the German movie industry was artistically and technically under-developed. It offered escape and vicarious participation in the envied experiences of others. During the war the Army command became interested in providing patriotic entertainment; it helped organize the UFA company, which for thirty years was to dominate German filmmaking.

Paperback thrillers and movies may symbolize the new patterns of consumer culture. In contrast to the hardcover book, pulp publications are consumed instantly; the experience provided by the movie is fleeting, seen only once and therefore inviting repetition in a hundred varieties. We are entering the age of sensationalism, of reportage, of frequent changes in scenery and in fashion. On-the-spot enjoyment whets the appetite for more and lends itself to manipulation and direction; fashion is "made." Although larger masses participate, their taste is unsure and does not build up cultural values. The old handcrafted articles of daily use are replaced by cheap imitations or, worse, by trash of insipid inspiration, like the ashtray decorated with a galleon figure, the pipe bowl in the shape of Bismarck's head, or the beer mug that played the "Lorelei." The German word *Kitsch* has meanwhile won currency throughout the world.

Like the movie, the popular operetta proclaimed the prevailing view that women were to be conquered after token resistance and that marrying a millionaire was preferable to most other ways of being provided for. The genre declined from Johann Strauss's *Die Fledermaus* and *The Gypsy Baron* to Franz Lehár's *The Merry Widow* and Leo Fall's *The Dollar Princess,* and then dropped to the shallowness of Oskar Straus's *A Waltz Dream* and, immediately before World War I, to *Puppchen* (*Dolly*), whose hit song professed the same philosophy in four-quarter time.

Before the advent of soap operas, Germany produced a type of ladies' novel unrivaled for sentimentality in any other country or age. Johanna Schopenhauer, the philosopher's mother, had been a practitioner of the art; a hundred years later E. P. Marlitt, Nathalie von Eschtruth, and Hedwig Courths-Mahler were still at it, describing how noble-hearted and innocent young girls sigh after uniformed counts, or how poor girl and rich boy find one another. Miss Courths-Mahler wrote this novel a hundred times, but in her off hours she was a courageous pacifist and feminist. In their own sugary way, her plots sometimes reflect the class tensions between lovers.

Literature had to be edifying and was supposed to express noble feelings. Even the lower classes were not interested in seeing an honest picture of their condition. Readers of the Social-Democratic *Vorwärts* objected to a serialization of Zola's *Germinal.* Their ideas on taste and decency in literature did not differ from those of the empress, who personally intervened to prevent the staging of Richard Strauss's

Rosenkavalier in Berlin. (Fortunately the queen of Saxony was less squeamish, so the opera was premiered in Dresden.)

No survey of German culture would be complete without mentioning the uninterrupted presence of Grimm's *Fairy Tales*, Heinrich Hoffmann's *Struwwelpeter*, and Wilhelm Busch's cartoon stories. Psychologists and sociologists have pointed out their sadism and their revealing dream projections. Busch's pranksters, though, display a good-humored yet epigrammatically acute contempt of middle-class ways and of authority. Karl May's and Friedrich Gerstäcker's "wild west" stories were Germany's answer to James Fenimore Cooper; they depicted dreams of freedom and asserted the superiority of the white race. For adolescents, the patriotic novel in historical garb was offered by writers like Walter Bloem, Viktor von Scheffel, or Felix Dahn—all of whom may scarcely rate a footnote in a modern history of German literature, but would not have been missing in any pre-World War I library or bookstore. Regrettably, better historical novels, such as those by Ricarda Huch, were less widely read.

This was mass culture for the masses. The high school produced mass culture for the elite, or *Kultur*: the correct use of standard German, the shelf with the collected works of the classical authors, gilt edged and bound in linen or leather; the piano with the Wagner or Beethoven bust on top of it. This was the middle class's intellectual defense against attacks from both its betters and its inferiors. Their *Bildung* proved that they were the true defenders of the national heritage and had a right to their share of the spoils. *Kultur* did for the liberal middle class what faith had done for the Puritans: it justified worldly success by pointing to the higher purposes. A sterile class of academics exploited and perpetuated this affectation; a veritable priesthood, it did not cultivate independent minds but produced Ph.D.'s. Manifestations of this attitude can be found in neoclassical literature and even in the parodies which Thomas Mann, Christian Morgenstern, and others were beginning to write at that time.

It is anomalous that Marxists too held on to this classical German idea of *Bildung* and turned their backs on the modernist, naturalist writings of their contemporaries. They had to refute the suspicion that sordid material interest was the motive of their movement. Their aim was to inherit the world of the bourgeoisie with its classical education; their watchword was not reform of the entire educational system but "gangway for talent"—i.e., integration of smart sons of working people into the leading strata.

The attack on Wilhelminian *Kultur* did not come from the left but from modernizing patriots. They strove to replace Greek and

Latin with modern languages and science, and to change the humanist curriculum into nationalistic indoctrination. "We want to train German boys, not Greek boys," the kaiser told an educators' conference. Liberation from stuffy studies and formalism may have been the program of some bohemians and progressives; but it also was part of the reaction against the liberal philosophy of the preceding era. The contempt for mass culture united anticapitalist and antidemocratic critics of the modern age. Nietzsche was alarmed by the vulgarity of Wilhelminian culture, Max Weber by its brutality, Ferdinand Tönnies by its loss of the old values, Langbehn by its insensitivity. In his *German History*, Karl Lamprecht tried to show that an era of "sensualism" was following one of materialism. Karl Kraus denounced journalism as the typical expression of a culture that craved novelty for its own sake and dealt with the superficial aspect of events rather than their significance. Langbehn's diatribe against "barbarism with gaslight," his exaltation of handicrafts and of native German virtues, inspired the youth movement, down to the Weimar period.

Life reformers also deepened Tönnies' distinction between *Gemeinschaft* and *Gesellschaft*, the latter being the artificial, mechanical conglomerate of people who have nothing in common but the business at hand, whereas in the true *Gemeinschaft* (community) interaction between people is embedded in the web of values and traditions that modern society (*Gesellschaft*) is about to forget.

The romantic, antiliberal, and anti-intellectualist reaction found its strongest expression in the philosophy and poetry of Friedrich Nietzsche. Little read in his lifetime, and lost in mental darkness during his last twelve years, he gradually became the most influential ideologist of the new century. The modernists hailed him as the Attila ravaging middle-class morality and as the prophet of a new aristocracy. A critic of European nihilism and, at the same time, the man who ultimately consummated it, he gave pathetic expression to the nausea of western civilization.

Nietzsche charged that the educational system had squashed creativity and was hostile to "life." He hated the canonized, sterilized, and mind-killing way in which heroes were served up for students. He looked at Socrates and Christ as doers rather than thinkers, as living men whose ideas were one way of asserting their "will to power." By the same token he interpreted the great systems of morality as instruments of power, and he proposed to "smash the old tablets." For law, too, was nothing but the expression of a will. He proclaimed the individual's freedom from the mass and especially great men's right to unmake and remake the rules. Many an officer in World War I carried *Also sprach Zarathustra* in his knapsack. It denounced squares, academicians, the prisoners of middle-class morality. But at the same time all this raving about "power" and "superman," about "masters' morality" and "blond beast," fitted the temper of those lusty, greedy, arrogant bourgeois whom Nietzsche despised. They imagined that by donning a reserve lieutenant's uniform they were the barbarians whose dawn Nietzsche had predicted. His finely honed sentences and his well-measured, dithyrambic language shrouded his message in a prophet's and poet's mantle. But the message clearly was that European culture was on the wane and that it was better to join those who would destroy it.

Nietzsche was a deliberately obscure thinker, and many readers— those whom he liked to call "the all-too-many"—readily mistook his aesthetic rebellion for a political one, his experimental thinking for radicalism, his "superman" for the master race. But his language and his message inspired the next generation of creative thinkers. "He was the earthquake of our epoch," said Gottfried Benn. Stefan George imitated Nietzsche's style and mannerisms. Carl Spitteler's *Olympischer Frühling* followed Nietzsche's ideas on religion, and Hermann Hesse's philosophy is deeply indebted to both Spitteler and Nietzsche. More important in its immediate consequences, Nietzsche's aesthetics liberated the life-affirming lyricism and frank eroticism of Richard Dehmel, whose cycle of poems, *The Metamorphoses of Venus*, was a challenge to the censor and a symbol of the rebellion against middle-class values. The youth movement merrily "smashed the tablets" of bourgeois morality. Eroticism, or rather frankness about it, was Frank Wedekind's weapon against mediocrity. His cabaret verses exposed the establishment to ridicule. Following his crusade, the expressionist (originally called neopathetic) movement expanded its aims beyond aesthetics and supported life reform, the cult of nature as against reason, of feeling against law, of freedom against authority. Nor was this movement confined any longer to the small circles of artists and freethinkers. It meant to be the champion of all young people. In 1908 the first public beach "for families" (giving men and women access at the same time) was opened at the Wannsee near Berlin.

Freedom for women was still far away. They had no suffrage, poor schooling; often they were ignorant of their own bodies. Before modern appliances and contraception, household chores and children would wear them out physically and mentally. A small, not very militant movement under the leadership of Dr. Helene Stöcker fought for family planning and against the double standard of morality. After Ibsen had taught men to see their wives as persons in their own right, another Scandanavian made the same plea on behalf of children. Ellen Key's *The Century of the Child* (1900) was acclaimed as a breakthrough. It asked that parents no longer treat their children as small adults but as young people whose age had values in itself. We see relativism wherever we look. The family was far from breaking down, to be sure; nor were other institutions in danger of falling. But a free look at them revealed that maintaining authority might sometimes be costly. Much of the new century's stirring was seen as a generational fight.

From Wedekind's *Spring Awakening* (1891, performed in 1906) to Walter Hasenclever's *The Son* (1918), German playwrights created a long series of father-son tragedies. Disgusted with the mores and views of their parents, German schoolboys and university students formed groups to cultivate friendship, to worship nature, to read new books together, to shape their own lives under their own responsibility, to celebrate festivals of their own. A group in Berlin-Steglitz led by Karl Fischer called itself *Wandervögel* (migrant birds); later the name was used for the entire movement, setting it apart from the state-sponsored Pathfinders and similar Boy Scout–like outfits. In 1913 a few thousand young people, defying the official celebration of a patriotic centenary, assembled on Mount Meissner and swore an oath to be different. They revived the old folk songs and dances, celebrated the summer solstice around campfires, and wore distinctive clothes testifying to their contempt of bourgeois culture. Even though they had no answers to the problems of that society, they had better dreams and greater awareness. They looked for "something that was genuine and true," said Friedrich Meinecke, the historian, when he looked back on his youth. Similar testimony has come from people as different as Werner Heisenberg, the atomic physicist, and Karl August Wittfogel, the sinologist. Leonhard Frank's *Die Räuberbande* (1914) and Hesse's *Demian* were to be "*the* books" for the initiated in the 1920s.

The youth movement was idealistic, deliberately naive and unworldly, but nativist and patriotic. Many of its followers volunteered in World War I; many of the younger *Wandervögel* went over to the Nazis when the harsh realities of life in the republic clashed with their romantic dreams of a "Reich"—and then, characteristically, fell out with the Nazis when the Third Reich fell short of those dreams.

In its beginning, the German movement for school reform also breathed this spirit of flight from the world. Hermann Lietz founded his boarding school in Ilsenburg, Gustav Wyneken the famous "Free School Community" at Wickersdorf (where his unchallenged authority secured the success of a student self-government); others followed. These were all elite schools, and their alumni retained the sense of mission that united school reform, life reform, youth movement, and literary avant-garde.

It is hardly possible to describe German middle-class culture without mentioning the following of Richard Wagner, the non-conformist conformist, the conservative radical, the bourgeois artist, the enfant terrible who preached resignation but, at the same time, created a national cult that was to take the place of religion lost. The Wagner opera displayed all the pompousness and sensuousness in which the Wilhelminian age wallowed. But under Wagner's musical successors—Anton Bruckner, Gustav Mahler, above all Richard Strauss and the young Arnold Schönberg—the public myth gave way to the elaboration of private sensibilities, even to a hothouse lasciviousness which betrayed the first signs of morbidity in bourgeois culture. Inwardness (*Innerlichkeit*) would now be the watchword of advanced cultural experience. Bruckner and Mahler explored the phenomena of experiencing (*Erleben*).

Just as the impressionists did in painting, the composers tried to put together a world out of patches of perception; where they achieved their most grandiose effects, the listener lost the sense of structure. The banal and the flamboyant, the cute and the sublime dwell next to each other in Mahler's symphonies, which seem to be paroxysms of sensations. The classical rules of composition, which even the naturalists had observed, were now eased to accommodate the sensuous colors; the sheer enjoyment of textures and orchestration could break down the borders between different arts. The following quotation, from a program note to Richard Strauss's *Don Juan*, may illustrate the intimate meshing of musical and painterly values in impressionism:

> In the coloring by groups of instruments, individual tone values assume significance. By isolating individual color [*Farbe*, perhaps meaning "timbre"], the artist gains an ever-changing pattern of extremely differentiated compositions. As the quiet harmony dissolves into an abundance of melodious events, so the unity of the color plane is dissolved into several substances. The color becomes flexible, it breathes. . . .

When Schönberg's *Verklärte Nacht* was performed in 1900 for the first time, the audience demonstrated against the vehemence of the dissonances. But they soon learned that the composer's intention had been to confront them with a new kind of experience—the unresolved dissonance which the classical teaching of harmony had rejected. Whether in music, painting, or poetry, the artist's world must be accepted as his private sphere; his message is one man's utterance. This development was diametrically opposed to the notion of *Bildung* which the middle class had absorbed in school. The creations of classical culture claimed objective validity and represented an objective reality that could serve as a norm for future generations and guarantee the stability of the world. The new art by its very existence denied these principles; it guaranteed nothing and obligated its audience to nothing.

In the theater, the great days of naturalism and social realism were drawing to a close. Frank Wedekind's great puberty drama *Spring Awakening* and his challenge to bourgeois morality in *Earth Spirit* (1895) had no sequel. Gerhart Hauptmann's early plays of social protest yielded to sentimental, neoromantic, and Christian themes. The successors of Henrik Ibsen—Hermann Sudermann, Max Halbe, Otto Erich Hartleben, and Otto Ernst—did not create lasting works, although Ernst's irreverent comedy *Flachsmann as Educator* (1901) held the stage for some time. Hermann Bahr's Free Theater produced modern plays of social criticism in closed performances. Typical is Hartleben's *Last Day of Carnival* (1900), in which a young lieutenant shoots himself because he can abandon neither a poor girl with whom he is in love nor his class, which forbids him to marry her. (Even some thirty years later, Hitler could break a general who had married a woman with a dubious past.)

The successful new novelists showed tendencies of decadence; their characters suffered their fate instead of shaping it. The problem was often conceived in purely personal terms, and the solutions were sentimental or religious, as in Hermann Stehr's *Der Heiligenhof* (1918); in Gustav Frenssen's *Jörn Uhl* (1901) the hero loses his property but finds his soul. The writers spiritualize (*vergeistigen*) that which naturalism, in the previous generation, had perhaps tried to despiritualize.

More advanced works dealt more openly with decadent themes. They either commented tenderly and melancholically on the ambiguity of life (Arthur Schnitzler) or explored complexities of the soul (Robert Musil), and pushed self-destruction, despair, and helplessness to the limits of possible expression. The sensitive Hugo von Hofmannsthal—Richard Strauss's librettist, of mixed ancestry, and heir to all the secrets of European culture—defined the poet as one who suffers from all the experiences that give him pleasure (*Genuss*) and takes pleasure in suffering from his experiences.

Rainer Maria Rilke, sweetest of all poets, listened enraptured to the "inwardness of things." In his novel *The Notebook of Malte Laurids Brigge* (1910), he asked whether "it is possible that with all our inventions and advancements, in spite of culture, religion, and science, we have remained on the surface of the universe." Both Hofmannsthal and Rilke were increasingly plagued by the problem of death and by the impossibility, for modern man, of grasping the world as real. Both also wrote silly verses on the blessings of being poor and a subject of the Hapsburg monarchy. Like Schnitzler, Musil, and Kafka, they belonged to that charmingly decrepit empire.

But the northern writers, too, felt the sting of decadence. Thomas Mann approached life with a tinge of nostalgic irony. In *Buddenbrooks* (1901) he described the decline of a patrician family in the old Hanse town of Lübeck (his own). Two characters portray the problem that pursued Thomas Mann throughout his life. Toni, the robust business-man who enjoys living and acting, is intellectually insignificant, but survives; his cousin Hanno, the delicate, sensitive artist, perishes under the burden of merely watching the others perform. In *Tonio Kröger* (1903), Mann discussed the condition of art in society; in *Death in Venice* (1912) he faced the problem of destructive demonic power. He was recognized early in his long career as an outstanding writer of European stature.

Next to him, Hermann Hesse laid claim to significance as a witness of his epoch. His novels are intimate journals of solitude; his tone, too, is elegiac. Ricarda Huch, little known outside the orbit of the German language, was concerned with the changing morality of her contemporaries, and she painted great frescoes of turning points of world history. In *The Great War* (1912-14), which deals with the Thirty Years War, she seems to have anticipated the horrors of the war that was imminent.

Throughout the decade before World War I, the writers speak of personal problems in a daring new way, setting the individual's passion against society's demands; they try to free man from con-ventions and to assert the right of life against the dead letter of the law. Yet, in the tradition of classical German literature, they also bear witness to the price that must be paid for freedom. The young rebel may end in resignation as an innkeeper, as in Hesse's *Under the Wheel*, the ardent lover as a fat, selfish husband; happiness must be purchased by cruelty inflicted on friends and loved ones. Above all, freedom and contentment must never be sought in selfishness, but may be claimed only by the inspired, spiritualized genius in the name of highest principles. This bliss, obviously, is not attainable for the bourgeois and not even for the man of power: only for the artist. The cult of bohemia, which had begun in the middle of the previous century, the gap between "philistines" and the elect, which had been endemic in German literature since *Sturm und Drang* days, now ended in a complete break. Artists did not even condescend to *"épater le bourgeois"* anymore: "Those who have the money imagine that they are striving for ideals when they support art," said Ricarda Huch contemptuously. Stefan George formed his *Gemeinde* away from society and allowed his disciples to speak of him as The Poet. Musil was offended by Rathenau's attempt to justify business by spirituality. Johannes Schlaf ridiculed the dispensers of *Bildung*.

Nowhere was the break with society and tradition more clearly visible than in the new school of painters that emerged all over Europe at about the same time. Picasso's *Demoiselles d'Avignon* (exhibited in 1905) had proclaimed that the world was not what it seemed to be. In the same year Karl Schmidt-Rottluff, Ernst Ludwig Kirchner, and Erich Heckel founded *Die Brücke* (The Bridge) in Dresden; as their models they took primitive art and the French group known as *Les Fauves* (The Wild Beasts).

These artists were called expressionists not because they were expressing their emotions (that had been done before), but because they tried to heighten, to intensify, the expression of whatever their object might be; in the process they were forced to change the object, to rearrange its elements, to develop their own idea of what the object ought to be. In this way, an activist factor was injected into art, or developed out of it. The artist was no longer at the mercy of nature; he shaped it. What might have been true for all art was here shown radically for the first time: art does not reflect the world but constitutes it; one has not seen a tree until the artist has shown him how to look at it. The movement was joined by Max Pechstein and others. Its theory was spelled out by the artist Hans Arp and by the writer Wilhelm Worringer in *Abstraction and Empathy* (1908).

In Munich, meanwhile, another group had been working along similar, even bolder lines. It included Vassily Kandinsky, Franz Marc, Paul Klee, and others, and it formalized itself by adopting the name *Der blaue Reiter* (The Blue Rider). In 1912 Kandinsky exhibited the first canvas that was totally abstract; although "modern art" in all its features was fully developed before World War I, it was not yet a recognized movement. On the contrary, these were individualists who were very conscious of swimming against the mainstream. In the words of Gottfried Benn, the foremost expressionist poet, theirs was "a mating with ecstasies, eruptions, and hatreds." Witness the cadaverous bankers' faces on the canvases of Otto Dix and Oskar Kokoschka. The artists were seeking neither beauty nor resemblance, but meaning.

Not all expressionists, however, subscribed to the same philosophy. To Emil Nolde, the brooding genius of the north, who was plagued by the demons of racism, expressionism was the German revolt against "French" impressionism and its Jewish satrap, Max Liebermann. He thought he was renewing the Gothic tradition; in this effort he was supported by Wilhelm Lehmbruck and Ernst Barlach. They were all disappointed, thirty years later, when Hitler not only failed to embrace expressionism as a German art but declared them degenerates.

They were indeed destructive of bourgeois values, and most expressionists found their political home on the far left. Georg Kaiser and Carl Sternheim satirized the bourgeois in their plays. Ernst Bloch became a philosopher of unorthodox, utopian communism. His *Spirit of Utopia* and *Thomas Münzer as Theologian of Revolution* tried to relate the cause of revolution to the sources of religon and mysticism in German history. Expressionism also found a voice in Franz Pfempfert's anarchist magazine *Die Aktion* and in *Der Sturm*, edited by Herwarth Walden, the first husband of the ethereal Else Lasker-Schüler and creator of the term "expressionism." Berlin expressionists, led by Kurt Hiller and Alfred Kerr, met in the famous Café Megalomania.

Most expressionists—like their successors, Dadaists and surrealists—rejected modern technology, science, psychology, sociology; but also politics and any other form of action in the world, except that which would explode it. "If only there were a war, even an unjust one! This peace is so rotten and filthy," wrote the expressionist poet Georg Heym, who fittingly perished in a violent act. Ernst Stadler, who was killed in the first month of the war, anticipated that "liberation" in a desperate wish to be "flame, thirst, outcry, and firebrand." Even Rilke joined the danse macabre around the fire.

European nihilism, the disease of the avant-garde, prepared the nations for the catastrophe into which their rulers were driving them. On the lower level, Germany no longer enjoyed the cultural tradition that gives stability to a society. On the middle level, cultural orientations lagged behind the technical and social potentials and indeed the needs of the age. On the highest and most refined level, the creators of culture were in open rebellion against the latest trends of social development. It is not an exaggeration to speak of a crisis of the European spirit.

This was even clearer to the few who were able to follow the most recent development of the sciences.

3

Science and Philosophy
at the Crossroads

If Einstein is right, posterity may regard him as the Copernicus of the twentieth century.

—Max Planck, 1905

THE ADVANCE OF SCIENCE DURING THE NINETEENTH CENTURY had not shaken the power of the Christian churches in Germany, but it had reshaped the faith of many Germans. Religion had become more personal—*innerlich*—but could no longer interfere with business and science. The coexistence of the two was shown emphatically when Adolf von Harnack, the famous theologian, urged the kaiser to establish an institute for basic research—to keep Germany abreast of other nations. This was the beginning of the Kaiser Wilhelm Institut, now the Max Planck Institut. Planck, the famous physicist, reciprocated by proclaiming that he believed in God.

This symbiosis had as its academic underpinnings the vogue of neo-Kantian philosophy, which asserted just that: scientific truth is valid in its own realm, but the scientific method fails where values are at stake. What is good, beautiful, and sublime we know by intuition; reason alone cannot determine what we should do. The rationalism of the Enlightenment had always been suspect in Germany because it was "French," mechanical, and potentially republican. Likewise, determinism and materialism had enjoyed only a brief vogue around the time of the Revolution of 1848; thereafter, the Social-Democrats alone continued to adhere to these philosophies. In their program, however, they merely asked for freedom of belief and for a secular school.

Traditional religion was strongly entrenched in the rural areas. But critical reading of the Bible and archaeological research had revealed that the authors of the Old Testament had been influenced by Babylonian, the New Testament by gnostic and other sources. Geological evidence and Darwin had dethroned fundamentalism; the Bible could no longer be accepted as revelation; advanced theologians were content to interpret Christ as the symbol of exemplary life. Harnack (ennobled by the kaiser and president of the Evangelical Congress) was the perfect embodiment of liberal theology. His *History of Dogma* (1886-90), which is still in use, relieved Jesus of all mystery, doctrine, or theology. The dogma, he explained, became necessary to the church when it had to speak to the Greeks in terms of their philosophy and to the Romans in terms of a law. But dogma had never been compatible with the human soul; it had now become incompatible with the known facts of nature and of history. He wished to replace dogma with knowledge of the human heart, and revealed religion with the inner experience of the divine. To him, Christ was moral energy.

Most scientists could accept this theology, and despite the wide gap that existed between the catechism and the most elementary facts of natural science, few people felt that a crisis was imminent or that a new Reformation was necessary.

That God is an ethical idea was also the opinion of the neo-Kantian philosophers who were prominent at Marburg, Freiburg, Heidelberg, and Berlin. Somewhat complacently they admitted that man lives in a plurality of worlds: those of knowing, of feeling, and of willing—no need to reconcile the findings of science with the notion of freedom, with ethical commands, or with religion! Scientific and technological progress depended on the certainty that nature is subject to immutable laws and hence predictable and exploitable; but political action rests on the belief that a great mind is sovereign over inertial forces and can master the problems they may create. The neo-Kantian formula of coexistence therefore satisfied the political compromise of the regime.

It also solved a major ideological problem. As economic and sociological research expanded, many social scientists were looking for "laws" governing the development of human societies. Marx had considered himself the Darwin of history, and the Social-Democrats believed that inexorable laws govern the course of society, carrying its political and ideological superstructure along. Naturally, conservatives and liberals alike rejected this view with great passion. Heinrich Rickert and Wilhelm Windelband, both neo-Kantians, argued that historical events are unique, hence unpredictable. Wilhelm Dilthey went further: sociology may "explain" but history must "understand"; there will always be an irrational element in the creation of something new. The natural sciences, said Rickert, can make experiments, verify their predictions, and generalize their conclusions in the form of "laws": they are nomothetic; history records great individuals' free acts and therefore is ideographic.

More important, moral philosophy and the creative arts proclaimed the freedom of the individual: freedom to choose his happiness and freedom to escape into realms where necessity does not rule. To this day the mainstream of German philosophy and sociology recognizes this division between natural science and humanities. To the latter Dilthey assigned the function of giving meaning (hermeneutics), and he defined their method as *Verstehen* (empathy). Since these premises allow for a number of ethical and religious choices, relativism was the temper of the age. "Man has no nature, only history," said Dilthey in his most Nietzschean vein—all possibilities are open.

But materialism still had its adherents, especially among the working classes. In 1899 Ernst Haeckel, a noted biologist and spokesman for Darwin in Germany, published a book that within ten years sold 100,000 copies. Entitled *The Riddles of the Universe*, it enumerated seven enigmas that the metaphysicians with their antiquated methods had vainly tried to solve. Haeckel declared that four of these alleged enigmas existed only in the imagination of backward people (for instance: What is Time? What is the Soul?). The remaining three, he thought, would be solved in due time by scientific methods. He looked at the origin of life as an explorer might look at the North Pole: he knew where it was, how to get there, and approximately what to expect when he got there; all that was needed was someone to go and look—and Haeckel was on his way! He marveled at the properties of certain crystals which seemed to bridge the gap between inorganic and organic substances, between inanimate and animate matter. Of course he knew nothing of the double helix yet. But he was convinced that there was only one great chain of being, one principle, one material in nature. He denied the hiatus between body and soul, matter and mind, substance and spirit. Like Spinoza, he saw nothing but beauty and reason in nature, all flowing from one energy; he called this system "monism." Wilhelm Ostwald, a famous chemist, went even further in claiming wisdom for his principle of energy and revived the mystical ideas of *Naturphilosophie*. Thus materialism was happily wedded to an aesthetic-religious world view.

The blow against materialism as a system, however, came from the development of physics. In 1900 Max Planck read to the Physicists' Society in Berlin a paper which inaugurated the modern theory of the universe. Radiant energy, he showed, is not emitted in a continuous flow but in discrete "quanta" or parcels, not in fractions but always in integers; that is, it is discontinuous. This was like saying that water can leave a tub only in drops of a certain size, a view contrary to what physicists had held sacred since Newton. Above all, it seemed impossible to predict which "quantum" would be discharged at any moment; and where would that leave causality?

Five years later Einstein showed that the quantum had wider applications, and when atomic scientists investigated the behavior of the smallest particles, the Roman proverb "Nature makes no leaps" became untenable. In 1914 Niels Bohr published his theory on the structure of the atom, which is basically the one we hold today, and again the quantum h turned out to be irreducible and therefore indivisible in its constitution.

Even more disturbing was a second paper which Einstein published in 1905; it subsequently became known as "The Special Theory of Relativity." Up to then, whenever experiments produced conflicting results, scientists would wait for better experiments or would somehow explain the "exception." Einstein resolved such a conflict in a revolutionary way: by changing the basic assumptions that had dominated physics since at least Galileo, or even since Euclid. It had been found that light always seemed to travel at the same speed, whether we moved toward its source or away from it. This made no sense unless we discarded our accustomed view of space; and Einstein proposed that we comprehend space and time as a four-dimensional continuum. Similarly he proposed to comprehend gravity as a property not of things but of space, and it followed that mass could be transformed into energy—the famous formula $E = mc^2$ was to make history forty years later.

All of this seemed not only utterly strange to common sense but contrary to the majestic laws Newton had laid down for physics. The general public, of course, was unable to share either the excitement of these discoveries or the confusion they created. A true understanding of the problem requires mathematical tools that few laymen master; a non-Euclidian geometry had to be worked out by Hermann Minkowski. Thus, when the philosopher Ernst Cassirer wrote *Substance and Function* (1910), in which he tried to adapt logic to the modern developments in science, he mentioned neither Planck nor Einstein, although he was dealing with the same fundamental problem.

Scientists were now exploring new frontiers behind which entirely new continents were opening—worlds in which some basic axioms of experience had to be amended. Scientists needed to rethink their assumptions about reality. A new theory of investigation had been developed by Richard Avenarius and Ernst Mach: "empiriocriticism," which Moritz Schlick and his Vienna Circle were to develop into neopositivism. These thinkers had no use for "metaphysical assumptions" such as Kant's "thing-in-itself," causality, and substance. They told scientists that they should not ask "What is it?" but "How does it work?" But in these quests, philosophy, which had once been the queen of sciences, became their handmaiden. Once philosophy had asked the questions and unified the answers. Now Cassirer admitted that the various sciences had reached questions and formulated concepts for which philosophy had prepared no tools of logic.

It must be said that philosophical questions about the nature of reality and our knowledge of it have nothing to do with the physicist's ability or inability to define matter. Only in popular science are these questions confused. But it may not be a mere coincidence that physicists, philosophers, and popular science writers were worrying about "matter" just then. In Berlin, some clever tenant had conducted a wire around his electric meter; when the company haled him into court, his lawyer proved that theft can be charged only if a "thing" has been stolen. With "thingishness" missing in so many modern things, the public was left wondering about the solidity of its world.

Nor did the mechanical laws seem to hold up in the fields of biology and genetics. Hans Driesch showed that lower animals are capable of reproducing or replacing organs that have been artificially excised; he concluded that cells are possessed of a wisdom that cannot be explained by the workings of biochemistry. He assumed a "life force" that works in the genes; he even spoke of "entelechy," a word not heard since Goethe, meaning an innate drive, proper to organic matter, to reach a final goal. Driesch called his new view "vitalism," and it was widely accepted. It seemed to be in harmony with Dilthey's "philosophy of life"—once again by a popular misunderstanding. Dilthey meant to separate natural from human sciences; but now nature too was asking for "understanding" rather than explanation.

Genetics was another field where nineteenth-century science had to be amended. Darwin still thought that evolution takes place in small steps when organisms make useful adjustments to their environment and bequeath them to their progeny. Now, also in 1900, Hugo de Vries was able to vindicate Mendel's theory of mutation: he showed that sudden, fortuitous changes in the genetic substance produce chance variations that then may enter into the competition for survival. Here again nature permitted leaps, eluded man's attempt to predict or anticipate the results, and in fine behaved quite "irresponsibly" unless one assumed, with Driesch, an entelechy.

It never fails: obscurantists would see in these developments new proof for the possibilities of miracles or for "spiritualistic" interpretations. As in earlier periods of intellectual history, precisely when science and a general scientific orientation made great strides, there was also a backlash, as though people were shrinking from the consequences. Oriental cults and new spiritualistic cults sprang up in many western countries; and Germany, which had always prided itself on being a metaphysical country, received more than its share of *Ernste Bibelforscher* (Jehovah's Witnesses), Vitalists, Theosophists, Christian Scientists, etc. In 1912 Rudolf Steiner split from the Theosophical Movement, founded his own Anthroposophical Society, and built the deeply symbolic Goetheanum near Basel and a well-known free school.

At this stage it would be premature to speak of an intellectual crisis; or if there was one, the critique of the scientific world view had certainly gone much farther in France, and been better articulated by Bergson than by any German. Dilthey's "philosophy of life" and the contributors to Eugen Diederichs' monthly *Die Tat* reflect the exuberance of a new departure rather than the "cultural despair" which some of these same writers were to express after the war. Nevertheless, Arthur Moeller von den Bruck, the translator of Dostoevsky (from whose Pan-Slavic writings he probably picked up the title of his own pamphlet, *The Third Reich*) was already inveighing against "western" civilization and extolling "eastern culture"; and Oswald Spengler was working on his mammoth elegy, *The Decline of the West*. If we can trust the testimony that Thomas Mann gave later, in his *Magic Mountain*, the intellectual leaders had come to an impasse from which the hero knew no egress except going to war.

The nineteenth century had believed in progress, or the linear view of history. Spengler taught that civilizations have come and gone, and none was an advance over the other. Rather, each of them had its period of heroic advance and then declined into sterile contentment. This thesis, not entirely new, had nevertheless not been worked out in detail by anyone since Vico. It fitted the relativistic trend of twentieth-century philosophy and sociology. What made it sensational was its brutal acknowledgment of immoralism and antihumanism, its almost joyful prediction that the age of individualism, freedom, and humanism was over. If Spengler had predicted the future correctly, the cool technocrat was the new hero.

Spengler was not in the mainstream of German sociology, however. Max Weber, Georg Simmel, and Robert Michels had also studied the nature of bureaucracy; they had found in modern society, even in such revolutionary organizations as the SPD, tendencies to become ossified and to fall into the hands of routine organizers. But they had sorted the technocratic trend out from the moral and political potentials: Max Weber studied "Protestant ethics" precisely because of his search for spiritual motives in history. They had tried to define the room for moral choices in politics; and scholars like Franz Oppenheimer in particular had shown the voluntaristic element in the formation of states. There was no fear and no presentiment of a European *Götterdämmerung* (twilight of the gods).

4

World Politics

*The contempt of other nations for ours, because we
tolerate the regime of this man, has become a factor in
world politics. We are isolated because this is the way he
rules us and we justify him. . . . No person and no party
that pursues democratic and national ideals can assume
responsibility for this regime, whose continued existence
is more dangerous than all the colonial problems put
together.*

—Max Weber to Friedrich Naumann, 1906

IN MOST COUNTRIES, THE ERA OF LAISSEZ-FAIRE was drawing to a
close. Powerful economic interests allied themselves with militaristic
chauvinists, with colonialists and empire builders, to plunge the
nations into a contest for world domination. England had skirted war
with France over Africa, and with Russia over central Asia. Japan
and Russia were fighting over China; Austria and Russia were rivals
in the Balkans. Bismarck, reversing his earlier reticence, acquired Togo
and the Cameroons; his successors annexed more territory in east and
west Africa, led expeditions into China, and staked out claims at both
ends of the Mediterranean.

A fever of world politics had seized the nations, involving them
in an almost uninterrupted series of crises that led to World War I. In
this struggle Germany was a latecomer, trying to muscle in where
established powers already had squatters' rights. Faced with the
intruder, the older powers settled their colonial differences amicably.
France and England granted each other a free hand—for the one in
Morocco, the other in Egypt—to the exclusion of other claimants
(Entente Cordiale of 1904). A similar entente was formed between
England and Russia.

Could Germany have received its share by agreement, too? In
1906 a piece of the Congo was adjudicated to it as "compensation" for
France's protectorate over Morocco. When further difficulties arose,
British diplomats cynically suggested that Germany might help itself
to one of weak Portugal's colonies. They also looked the other way

when Germany's Italian and Hapsburg allies got chunks of the moribund Ottoman Empire.

But colonial possessions were not the real bones of contention between the rivaling powers; colonies were treated like pawns which only marked the power relationship between them, or the rank each had won in the great world political game of one-upmanship. An interesting instance was the German attempt to penetrate Turkey economically, politically, and militarily. After the Young Turk Revolution of 1908 a German general was appointed to reorganize Turkey's army and a British admiral its navy. A German bankers' consortium held the concession to build a railway through Anatolia, linking Berlin and Vienna (via Budapest and Sofia) with Constantinople, Baghdad, and ultimately with Basra on the Persian Gulf. It was too close to India, the British decided, and negotiated to stop the railway at Baghdad. Then Russia objected that the line had been planned too close to the Black Sea, and obtained its relocation near the Mediterranean. Finally it turned out that the Germans did not have the money to complete the ambitious project. British capitalists were happy to come in as partners—on equal terms—but the Germans were not willing to grant that. They would rather have let the rails rust and rot. It was clear that the German bankers were not simply looking for profit but were being directed by the German government. The name of the game was power, not money, and the Germans reaped their reward in 1914 when Turkey joined the Central Powers.

The same game was played in Morocco. In 1905, France was about to establish a protectorate over the sultan, a clear violation of international statutes. Here German diplomacy saw an opportunity to overthrow French Foreign Minister Théophile Delcassé, an ardent revanchist and promoter of the Franco-Russian alliance. The kaiser landed in Tangier for three hours to proclaim that he would support the sultan. The German papers claimed that he was protecting the mining interests of the Mannesmann concern in Morocco; but this was soon forgotten in the ensuing power play. Delcassé had to resign for lack of aggressive support in either Paris or London.

Now the Germans could have obtained a bilateral understanding with France on their mutual interests in Morocco. But that was not their aim. They demanded an international conference on the Morocco question, hoping that it would provide them with an opportunity to drive a wedge into the young entente between France and England. The opposite happened. When the conference convened at Algeciras (1906), the Germans found themselves facing a united front of ten nations that had been angered by the kaiser's high-handed, intransigent manner.

A memorandum circulated in the British Foreign Office at the time stated that reasonable, legitimate aspirations for colonies should not be opposed, but attempts to establish a German hegemony on the European continent must be frustrated. Foreign Minister Edward Grey therefore allowed British staff officers to deliberate with their French colleagues on common measures of defense. For what was at stake was "mastery in Europe," as A.J.P. Taylor described the hundred years' struggle of the powers.

A widely accepted theory holds that imperialism is essentially the fight for financially lucrative colonies. In the case of the German possessions, this is demonstrably incorrect. All the German overseas territories put together did not absorb as much as 1 percent of German exports; they offered practically no opportunity for capital investment; and in forty years they took in only 50,000 German immigrants—less than the United States did in one year.

Of Germany's 20-billion-mark investment abroad, only 505 million—2.5 percent—had gone to the colonies. The German opportunities pointed to Spain and Latin America, and it is well known that the great powers did more business with each other than with their empires. British Foreign Secretary Sir Edward Grey felt that economic interests ought to create ties among the nations but that their political and military interests interfered with peace; the German ambassador to London, Count Metternich, reported that "not our economic upsurge but the rise of our naval power is here considered a serious danger." To the treasury the colonies were a burden; the arms race was profitable only for the few industrialists directly concerned, while for the vast majority it meant higher taxes.

However, the entire German defense budget, in those blessed days, constituted only 3 percent of the national income, and the question is: why did the majority of those who were interested in the other 97 percent not carry as much weight as the shipbuilders and the steel industry? They had surrendered their birthright. When Bismarck made Germany great, he made the Germans small. German imperialism was the creature of the German regime and of the monopolistic structure supporting it. Foreign policy was made, after Bismarck's dismissal, largely by underlings and nonresponsible favorites of the kaiser. The daily details were in the hands of Friedrich von Holstein, a mere councilor, who did not report directly to the kaiser but manipulated him through Prince Philipp Eulenburg, Wilhelm's friend, and Chancellor Bernhard von Bülow, a charming phrasemonger. On basic policy they saw eye to eye with the court clique, which enjoyed the muscle-flexing, saber-rattling posture of the young Reich. But when that policy failed at Algeciras, they jettisoned Holstein and gave the press reports about the sinister role he had played behind their backs. He was described as a schemer, a recluse, and a sort of *éminence grise*. History books that claim that his maneuverings were discovered only after the revolution are in error; actually, Holstein often intrigued to hold the kaiser back from foolish, impulsive actions and indiscretions. In his memoirs (1909, published in 1955), he wrote:

> That the Kaiser, who was well beyond the age of youthful exuberance and had reigned more than ten years, lacked, and one must regretfully say still lacks, all sense of what is fitting, is a misfortune both for him and for the German Reich. Future historians will compile a long list of the Kaiser's sudden impulses in conversation, in writing, in telegrams, which collectively and singly have had the effect of gradually diminishing the prestige of the Kaiser and the Reich, of wrecking diplomatic negotiations, and even of provoking immediate danger of war.

The strategic plan on which kaiser, chancellor, and councilor agreed was based on the fear of war between the Austro-German and the Franco-Russian allies; in such a conflict England would have to be neutralized. To achieve this, Germany had to show her strength, her nuisance capability if hostile, her value as a friend if benevolent.

The axis of German foreign policy under this leadership was *Nibelungen* faith with Austria. In one of the many Balkan crises, Holstein wrote: "We must stand by Austria calmly and resolutely, imposing no restrictions or conditions, for in defending *her own* cause she [is] fighting *our* battle against the encircling powers, England, Russia, and France. This basic principle must take precedence over all other considerations."

He was insensitive to the danger that Germany might become isolated in pursuing her ambitious goals. Often he went to the brink of war (bluffing, and gambling that the others were bluffing) in order to make his point. At the Algeciras conference his bluff was called. When Bebel told the Reichstag that this policy was leading to war, the chancellor fainted. Word went out to the press that the king of England had conducted a deliberate campaign to "encircle" Germany. With equal justice critics of Bülow's policy said that Germany had "excircled" herself, and indeed some German nationalists boasted: "The more enemies, the more honor."

King Edward VII had a rather low opinion of his imperial nephew;

he thought of him as an ill-mannered upstart and an immature bore. Nor did Sir Edward Grey like Germany's rise in world politics; if he did not actively encircle Germany, he tried to contain her power drive and hence was not altogether unhappy to find the Germans uncooperative at all international conferences. In an interview with the *London Daily Telegraph* Wilhelm II complained about encirclement and then, obviously to show his benevolence to the British people, hinted that in the Boer War the winning strategy had been his idea. It was a blunder. The uproar on both sides of the channel sobered the kaiser; his interest in foreign affairs flagged, and henceforth he interfered less often.

Bülow was dismissed; the Foreign Office was given to Alfred von Kiderlen-Wächter, a man of perhaps greater integrity and intelligence but equally unable or unwilling to change policies. He thought he could do better than Bülow in Morocco—and in 1911 sent the gunboat *Panther* to Agadir. The German press was enthusiastic about the "leap of the *Panther*"; but it was almost a leap into war, and it caused a major shift in British public opinion. Even David Lloyd George, who was supposed to be pro-German, made a passionate speech for British intervention. In that crisis, Germany received a small compensation; but again her truculence had tightened the coalition against her. The more victories she won, the more she was encircled. But when Kiderlen-Wächter finally did seek an agreement with England on a limitation of armaments, he encountered stiff opposition at the highest level in Berlin. The British negotiator, Lord Haldane, complained that he never got to see the man who had the power to veto the rapprochement.

For in fact German policy was controlled by military considerations, and it had been laid down for good when two strategic plans were adopted. One was the continental war plan of General Alfred von Schlieffen, chief of the Army General Staff from 1891 to 1905, the other the naval building program promoted by Grand Admiral Alfred von Tirpitz, secretary of state at the admiralty.

The Schlieffen Plan was designed to meet the danger of a two-front war, posed by the Franco-Russian alliance, and it fulfilled the *Nibelungen* pact that united Germany and Austria. The Hapsburg monarchy lived in great fear of Pan-Slavism and was locked in century-old rivalry with Russia over domination of the Balkan Peninsula. The disintegration of the Ottoman Empire in Europe let this struggle come to a head.

Now the system of alliances required that if Austria were attacked by Russia, Germany had to come to her aid; and if Russia were under attack from those two countries, France had to march against Germany. Since both Austria and Russia were likely to be drawn into any Balkan conflict, a small incident could trigger the infernal machine. Instead of trying to defuse it, General Schlieffen topped it with another: he would counter the calamity of a two-front war by dealing a preventive blow to France! As soon as Russia mobilized her unwieldy armies and before she had time to strike in the east, the German armies were to thrust through unsuspecting, neutral Belgium, appear at the back of the French deployment, reach Paris with swift, forceful punches, and there dictate the peace before other powers could make up their minds.

The plan was risky because England was a guarantor of Belgian neutrality and rather touchy on the subject of North Sea ports. Therefore, all depended on speed and ruthlessness. Once mobilization was under way, there was no time to reflect or negotiate.

With such a contingency in mind, the kaiser ought to have courted the British king, appeased the English in every possible way, and tried to compose the colonial and naval differences with Britain as other nations had done. Instead, Holstein, Tirpitz, and Wilhelm decided that England had to be bullied to acquiesce in German hegemony on the continent. Grand Admiral Tirpitz proposed building so many battleships that soon a German force would be able to meet the British navy in the North Sea. The British themselves had made this plan look realistic when they put the new class of "dreadnoughts" into commission—superbattleships that could outrun and outgun all existing naval craft; their cruiser fleet thereby was made obsolete. The Germans had to match only the British dreadnought program. By 1914 Germany had thirteen of these ships, to England's twenty in the home waters. All England was seriously concerned about this wanton challenge. Ironically, during the war the German battleships were mostly at anchor.

While the British were ahead, however, the kaiser engaged in a war of nerves, which then was called "zigzag course"—letting the British know one day that he wished to be their ally, then having his chancellor brusquely declare: "We cannot be England's sword on the continent." When the British seriously asked what Germany's price would be for halting the naval race, the kaiser named a condition no British government could accept: that England promise neutrality in any conflict between Germany and her neighbors. Hegemony on the continent was the prize England would not concede to anyone.

Contrary to the Clausewitz doctrine that war must serve politics, the kaiser's diplomacy was completely dependent upon his military conceptions. He wanted Germany to be the dominant power in Europe and the second on the sea, simultaneously to expand into the Middle East and Africa, and to impose Austrian preponderance on the Balkans. In pursuing so many goals the kaiser had forgotten which were means and which were goals; he had no priorities, and all fights seemed good against all comers. In the end, he had everybody convinced that as long as he was around there certainly would be war sometime.

But the show he gave the Germans was popular. Both the aims and the style of his policy were actively supported by the Pan-German League with its one million members, the Naval League, the Colonial League, the state-sponsored Young Germany, the Association of German Industrialists; by many intellectuals, by the Liberals, and, with qualifications, by the "social imperialists"—the Rathenau-Naumann wing of the Progressive Party. Even those who were critical, like Meinecke, couched their warnings in cautious language: "The real battlefields still lie ahead of us. . . . [We must therefore] follow our Kaiser on the steep trail toward the clouded summit." Such misgivings or ambivalent feelings may have been shared by many voters. In 1907 the "Hottentot elections" provided a test. They came right after a tariff increase and under the shadow of rising prices; but the government chose colonialism as the battleground. At the time Germany was engaged in a cruel war against the Herero tribe; atrocities and corrupt practices were revealed, but only the Center Party and the SPD protested. A vast flood of bigoted, racist propaganda was released against "blacks" (priests), "nigger-lovers," and "*Sozis*" (socialists); the result was an unchanged distribution of the vote, although electoral alliances among all bourgeois parties deprived the SPD of half its seats. Interestingly, the victorious coalition of conservatives and liberals fell apart over the proposed inheritance tax: the conservatives wanted a big navy, but they did not want to pay for it; the liberals, though deemed to represent capitalistic interests, were prepared to tax wealth in order to be first on the seas.

During the tense years that ensued, international crises followed on each other's heels. War might have broken out in 1908, when Austria annexed Bosnia-Herzegovina, or in 1911, the "*Panther*-leap" year, or in 1912, when Austria opposed the Serbian drive to the Adriatic. In that year the British made a last desperate attempt to offer Germany colonies in return for a stabilization of the naval forces. But Tirpitz was confident that he who has ships will have colonies. The flag did not follow trade but preceded it. The German price for a naval pact was not this or that piece of geography but British neutrality in a future European war. The kaiser and his military paladins aspired to supremacy on the European continent, no less, and by that time they felt that Germany was ready to take on a European coalition.

The new chancellor was Theobald von Bethmann-Hollweg, a solid and stolid civil servant with a philosophical countenance who considered himself a mere technician. He saw the approaching catastrophe, but he had neither the power nor the will to prevent it. He might have opposed the arrogance of specific interests whose forwardness threatened to entangle him in conflict with foreign countries; but he was helpless against the intoxicating words that he heard from the mouths of his sovereign and his friends: *Weltgeltung* and *Seegeltung*—prestige in the world and prestige at sea. According to Joseph Schumpeter, the Vienna (later Harvard) economist, the source of imperialism is precisely that megalomania which forgets that other nations have interests and have power, too; that desire to expand and expand, to excel and to subdue others; that lust to conquer; and that atavistic idea that honor can be won with the sword. Even financial magazines spoke in those inebriated tones and quoted leading businessmen to the effect that Germany must fight for first place, that "a decision by the sword must not be shunned," and that "the stock exchange has a Special Duty Toward the Nation." It was as though people were deliberately engaging in profitless confrontations and heroic postures in order to deny that their real interests were in vulgar profit making. The flag was not following trade; trade was sought in order to create pretexts for the flag to follow. Colonies were sought only to justify the need for a navy. Professors at German universities spoke of the fight of giant powers for supremacy, of the need to grow in order to measure up to the best, of creating large economic spheres capable of sustaining a long war. Erich Marcks and Max Lenz, historians of the Ranke school, declared that Germany had a mission to increase its power and to display it, to gain its fitting "share of that world dominion which the spirit of humanity has assigned to the cultured nations."

Friedrich Naumann was more specific. First he tied social progress solidly to imperial policies: "Social reform is the strongest armor in any future war." He wanted monarchy plus democracy, imperialism plus equality. But he saw no value in sea power and colonies. Instead, he set up before the Germans the great vision of *Mitteleuropa*—a central European economic association that was to comprise Germany, Austria-Hungary, Belgium, Holland, Luxemburg, Italy, Switzerland, Rumania, and if possible Serbia and Bulgaria, which would have to be weaned away from Russian protection.

During the war, businessmen translated this lofty vision into concrete desiderata: the mining basin of Lorraine; the wide spaces of the Ukraine for the settlement of German peasants; "protectorates" over Poland, Lithuania, and Latvia; Belgium as a vassal state. But we must keep in mind that these ideas did not jell into a coherent system until the war made it necessary to have "war aims." Up to August 1914 one may, rather, indict German policymakers for pursuing conflicts without aims, for seizing every opportunity to throw their weight around. Superiority of arms dictated foreign policy. In the final analysis, responsibility for the war of 1914 rests with the military leaders in Germany and Austria, who felt that they had reached the peak of their preparations and therefore were ready to start the war; they fully expected the crisis of 1914 to take its fatal course. "The Chief of Staff is using all his influence to make sure that the favorable situation should not be allowed to pass by," reported the Bavarian military attaché in Berlin. Franz Conrad von Hötzendorf, Austria's chief of staff, felt that war with Russia was a risk to be taken if the emperor did not want to live in eternal fear of Greater Serbian aspirations and Pan-Slavic agitation.

This is not to exonerate the revenge-craving factions in Paris or the Pan-Slavic schemers in St. Petersburg and Belgrade, nor those statesmen who merely failed to stop the warmongers and—out of laziness, incompetence, stupidity, negligence, misjudgment, or fear of intransigent opposition at home—allowed their machines to run on a collision course. Thus the czar was pushed by the Pan-Slavists, the French president by the chauvinists. Worse, everybody talked about "the coming war" as a foregone conclusion and as if no one could do anything to prevent it.

* * *

HISTORIANS ARE OFTEN TEMPTED to look for the chain of antecedents that made an event inevitable. In the case of World War I, escalating rivalries between the powers seemed indeed to lead them inexorably into collision. They all seemed to be caught in a whirlpool of one-upmanship from which they were unable to withdraw.

The "war guilt" debate starts out from the opposite assumption: that war might have been avoided if A had refrained from doing X, and if B had done Y. Long after it was all over, Sir Edward Grey mused:

Did we have to interpret every German move as directed against us? It is true that the number of variants was not inexhaustible and, given the propensities of the system, the chances of a peaceful settlement were limited. But to accept the outcome as inevitable means to absolve those who could have made it avoidable. If the tinder of a general conflagration was there, someone provided the spark, and others poured oil onto the flame instead of water.

Nor were the alliances that in 1914 confronted each other foreordained. Only France was committed to Russia, and Germany to Austria—both for good historical reasons. But in the Agadir crisis Russia deserted France, and in 1912 Grey tried a rapprochement with Germany. Had London given a clear warning in 1914, the warmongers might have drawn in their horns. Originally, Italy and Rumania had been in the German camp; during the war both switched over to the Entente. Italy would have liked to stay out of the war, and Austria was prepared to yield to her the contested city of Trieste in payment for neutrality. To accept the offer would have been wise. But Italian chauvinists wanted martial glory. Mussolini, paid by the Entente, and Marinetti—the futurist writer—eager for destruction, led patriotic mobs to force the government's hand.

The only countries that needed the war were Austria and Russia, because both were afraid of appearing weak, afraid that revolution might overtake any course of safety. But both, as the outcome was to show, hastened their disintegration by this very decision to "flee forward."

Depending on one's inclination, one might quarrel about the relative shares of responsibility that may be assigned to various nations, classes, and persons. But one cannot doubt that all persons in responsible positions during the crucial weeks of July 1914 were gambling with the possibility of war, and that the diplomats were playing their routine poker game without understanding the elemental force of nationalism—which they themselves had called into being.

5

War as Revolution

*At this time thousands and hundreds of thousands felt what they ought to have felt in time of peace: that they belonged together. A city of 2 million, a country of 50 million, in this hour felt that they were experiencing world history, a moment that would never return again, where each of them felt called upon to melt his minute ego into the glowing mass, to purge himself of all selfishness. At this moment, all differences of origin, language, race, class, and religion were drowned in overflowing brotherliness. Strangers talked to each other and shook hands. Each experienced a heightening of self; he was no longer an isolated person but embedded in the mass; he was nation; his otherwise insignificant person had received a meaning. . . . He was a hero. Whoever wore a uniform was wined and dined by the women. . . .**
— Stefan Zweig

This war is the greatest democratic wave that ever swept the planet.
— General Wilhelm Groener

SERBIA ONCE HAD BEEN AN AUSTRIAN PUPPET. Now, after a bloody coup and two victorious wars, it called on all the southern Slavs to unite under the crown of King Peter Karageorgevich. The Hapsburg monarchy included many Slavic minorities: Poles, Czechs, Slovenes, and the recently annexed Bosnians. They looked to Belgrade for support, and Belgrade looked to St. Petersburg. Serbian agents fomented subversion among the Hapsburg Slavs. A clandestine group, popularly known as the Black Hand, was directly controlled by Serbia's police.

On June 28, 1914, Archduke Franz Ferdinand, crown prince of Austria-Hungary, and his wife visited the provinces of Bosnia-Herzegovina, which had been added to the Hapsburg crown only in 1909. It was a deliberate provocation, for that day was sacred in Serb history. At Sarajevo a Serb student, Gavrilo Princip, a member of the Black Hand and in league with Serbian officers, shot the couple and killed both.

Europe stood aghast. What would the "old emperor," Franz

Joseph II, decide to do? He was clearly entitled to amends and firm assurances; moreover, he had a unique opportunity to isolate and pillory the Pan-Slavic activists in the eyes of the civilized world, most of which was ruled by relatives of the assassinated couple. It was known that Czar Nicholas II was unhappy with the commitments to Pan-Slavism which his foreign minister Sazonov had made. With very little subtlety, Franz Joseph II might have obtained the banishment of his enemies from the St. Petersburg court. Instead, the militarists in Berlin and Vienna decided to teach the Pan-Slavists a lesson—but succeeded in making Serbia the martyr, uniting public opinion in Europe against themselves. Austria's foreign minister, Count Leopold von Berchtold, a bon vivant and gambler, took three weeks to think up his demands, and then gave Serbia forty-eight hours to accept them. Serbia's reply was so conciliatory that Wilhelm II was afraid it might elude the deserved punishment. But it rejected the key stipulation: that Austrian police should search for conspirators on Serbian territory. Given a free hand by its German ally, Austria declared war on Serbia on July 28th and thereby set off the chain reaction of alliances.

The moment the Austrian declaration of war became known through "extra" newspaper editions, patriotic crowds began to parade their hatred in the Vienna and St. Petersburg streets, shouting, "On to Belgrade, down with St. Petersburg!" or "Down with Vienna, hit the Huns!" Flags, songs, passionate speeches whipped up the mob's aggressiveness.

Only then, on the 29th, did Bethmann-Hollweg forward to the Austrians a suggestion that they might occupy Belgrade—just across the border and the Danube—and then negotiate. But Berchtold ignored the belated warning and let his generals go ahead.

Now at last Grey warned that England would stand by France in case of a continental war. Would Bethmann-Hollweg have refused to give Berchtold a free hand if Grey had taken his stand earlier? Grey believed, according to diplomatic textbook routine, that the opposite was true: by withholding his support from France, he hoped to restrain Russia and keep himself available for mediation. His ambiguity encouraged Austrian intransigence. The years of "normal" diplomacy were past; in both Vienna and St. Petersburg the forces that wanted war were strong. Neither emperor could yield an inch— certainly not the aggrieved Hapsburg, nor the much-humiliated Romanov. Both were afraid of their jingoes, and neither was any longer in a position to heed the warnings.

It is a myth believed by historians and statesmen that an order to mobilize, once given, cannot be reversed at will. Austria's declaration of war on Serbia was followed by partial Russian mobilization; on the 31st, Germany declared a state of "alert for war." Having agreed that he could not allow Serbia to go down, the czar now was told by Sazonov that his clumsy war-horse could not be partially harnessed but—in the face of a German ultimatum—must be allowed to prance on the field in full armor. At the Crown Council, he was warned that his armies were in no shape to fight Germany, that in fact he was risking his reign and realm; but he could not be held back any more than King Croesus marching out to destroy a great kingdom.

Feeling threatened by the Russian mobilization, the German generals pressed their chancellor to lose no time. Both Germany and France mobilized on the first of August; simultaneously, Germany declared war on Russia.

The shortest road to St. Petersburg was via Paris. The nefarious Schlieffen Plan required Germany to violate Belgium's statutory neutrality. On August 3, Germany declared war on France and invaded Belgium. If this bold strategy was designed to keep England off the turf, it backfired. Carried out in defiance of the British pledge the day before, it was the most effective alarm possible for getting England to join the defense of France. On August 4, England declared war on Germany. "I did not want that [war]!" the kaiser exclaimed. German war propaganda reflected genuine disappointment that "perfidious Albion" was meddling in the affairs of the continent. Until the last moment, Bethmann-Hollweg had believed that the British were bluffing; his entire diplomatic maneuvering in July had been an effort to lay all blame for the outbreak of the war on Russia. The czar was thoroughly unpopular in the west, especially among German working-men. August Bebel (see page 30), now dead, had said: "If it's against bloody czarism, I'll shoulder a gun in my old age."

Until August 4, Germany had been defending "civilization" against the "cossacks"; suddenly, after that date, it was defending "soul" and *Kultur* against the cheap *Krämergeist* (commercialism) of England and the shallow "civilization" of decadent France. Not since the Thirty Years War had ideology played a similar role in a German war. Troeltsch, a specialist in the teachings of the Christian churches, contributed the idea that the German concept of freedom was "organic" and hence superior to the "abstract" ideals of 1789. Thomas Mann wrote his infamous *Reflections of a Non-Political Man* (he later repudiated the book but used its arguments as evidence in *Doctor Faustus*). He acclaimed the "German War" as an uprising of *Geist* against western democracy, and thanked Providence for "this great storm" which was to sweep away "that horrible world which no longer exists and will not return. Did it not crawl with all that vermin of the intelligentsia?"

Many saw the war itself as an act of liberation. The young composer Alban Berg wrote to a friend: "If the war were to end tomorrow, we would be back in the old rut. . . . However fervently I wish for peace, I cannot pray for it now." Bethmann-Hollweg's assistant, Kurt Riezler, reports that the chancellor "shared the authentically German belief that the German people needed a war." Rudolf Binding, the poet, felt that the German people "have been seized by a great religiosity" and were basking in this great new experience of community. Carl Zuckmayer, who volunteered for active service after an "emergency graduation" from high school, later reported that "the spirit was not militaristic but revolutionary"; in the trenches "class walls would break down"; as the 1871 war had brought German unity, so this war would "bring German justice. Our victory would mean a united Europe under the auspices of German *Geist*." In the same spirit the young socialist deputy Ludwig Frank volunteered, saying, "In the trenches we shall lay the foundations of a new fatherland."

Many of Germany's greatest, including some who had been critical of the regime, joined in the Tyrtaean chorus: Gerhart Hauptmann, Richard Dehmel, Engelbert Humperdinck, Max Planck, Max Liebermann, and of course Friedrich Naumann and Ernst Haeckel. The patriotic paroxysm enveloped all classes; the workers in particular felt what they had never been allowed to feel: they belonged to the nation; they were needed and wanted. For too many people war did not mean that "the lamps were going out all over Europe" (Grey) but that a beacon into the future was being lighted.

From the balcony of his palace, the kaiser proclaimed: "For me there are no parties any longer, there are only Germans." The trade-union officials responded with a no-strike pledge for the duration. An official *Burgfrieden* (civil truce) was declared, and the chancellor proclaimed that unequal suffrage was obsolete. By this time the workers stood to lose much more than their chains: they had to preserve not only their organizations, their union halls and insurance funds, but also their share in Germany. The SPD was in an awkward position. It had provisionally transferred its treasury to Switzerland, and its organizers, deputies, and editors were not sure that they would not be arrested on the first day of the war.

More than arrest, they feared that they would be exposed to the wrath of patriotic mobs. The masses supported the war; the comrades across the Rhine had not given any indication that in their own countries they would oppose it. Only a small minority, internationally, stood by the solemn resolutions—adopted as recently as 1912 at the meeting of the Socialist International in Basel—that the socialist parties would not cooperate with their governments in case of war. In all western countries, socialists and trade union officials did not hesitate to take cabinet posts.

On August 4, 1914, the Social-Democratic Party of Germany likewise declared: "In the hour of danger we shall not forsake the fatherland . . . [but] we condemn every thought of annexation. We demand that, as soon as the goal of security has been attained, the war be brought to an end." By a vote of ninety-two to fourteen, the party caucus decided to approve a war appropriations bill in the Reichstag; no one dared abstain. The action inspired the socialist poet Karl Bröger to the lines: "This great emergency has shown / Your poorest son is your truest son / Remember it, Germany."

The community of the trenches was real enough. The horrors they experienced separated front-line soldiers from those in the supply lines and from the homeland. The deep class cleavages of society were evened out in the bomb craters and foxholes. Since proportionally more officers were killed than men, commoners were promoted to ranks that had heretofore been held mostly by the noble.

On the home front, too, new elements surfaced: the war profiteer, the draft dodger, the adolescent who took the place of an absent husband, the defense worker who did not need to risk his skin, the shirker who somehow had arranged to be certified "indispensable for the war effort"—cartoonists' types all who were to live on in the folklore of anticapitalism. While the bulk of the people suffered many deprivations, and eventually hunger, a few prospered enormously. Krupp's earnings rose fantastically—not only from the shells the Germans fired but also on patent licenses for products which the enemy used to kill Germans. General Paul von Hindenburg, the commander of the eastern front, wrote his wife (and the papers naively quoted it) that "the war feels like a stay at a spa." It was also rumored that the crown prince made most of his conquests in French boudoirs.

To equalize sacrifices, to assure a fair distribution of supplies, to prevent hoarding, and to allocate resources, governments in all the warring countries had to introduce rationing. Rathenau saw that the German economy was in no way prepared for the kind of war it was supposed to sustain. Raw material and food supplies might last for three months; unless a military decision was reached by Christmas, the German government would be faced with a totally new kind of war—a protracted siege in which the entire nation, with all its human and material resources, would have to be mobilized to keep the front supplied with ammunition. Only an organized economy, Rathenau reasoned, would permit the war to go on indefinitely. Eventually bread, meat, milk, butter, shoes, and clothing could be obtained only with stamps. Raw materials were allocated through the so-called war companies, industrywide pools that outlined a system of industrial planning so complete that a socialist theoretician, Karl Renner, the future Austrian chancellor, exclaimed: "Socialism, wherever we cast our eyes!" To him, the organization of a war economy proved that a state-directed economy could do the job better than private enterprise.

In 1917 an "Auxiliary Service Law" froze workers to their jobs and subjected labor disputes to compulsory arbitration by boards on which employers, trade unions, and the state were represented. The idea suggested itself: if the government could conscript thirteen million men for war, there might be even better reasons for conscripting money and equipment; and after the war it would be incumbent upon the state to lead all those people back from war work to peaceful occupations. In his pamphlet *Of Things to Come*, written in 1917, Rathenau, though far from being a socialist, drew the most radical conclusions from his experience with state-planned capitalism.

Worry about supplies also played havoc with the Schlieffen Plan, which ought to have won the war. The strategy required all the German forces to make a supreme effort to reach Paris as quickly as possible. This meant abandoning the eastern provinces to the Russians for the moment. But when the "Russian steamroller" approached, the German high command panicked and sent two divisions to defend East Prussia. The kaiser did not dare abandon to the enemy the eastern provinces, where most of the grain and potatoes came from. At Tannenberg General Paul von Hindenburg won a brilliant victory: he stopped the Russian advance, annihilated several Russian armies, took 92,000 prisoners, and drove the enemy into its traditional arsenal of defense—space. The Germans occupied a large area of Lithuania and Poland, which contributed to their food supply but was of no military consequence.

The victory in the east, against the Slavic "hordes," was immensely popular; its titular commander became a hero overnight. His oversize statue was raised before the Reichstag. People did not know then that the real strategist was General Erich Ludendorff. The German armies also helped the less warlike Austrians hold the Russians at bay; but their victories in the east were not decisive, and throughout the war the invariable "We are still holding on to Lemberg" (Lvov) made the Austrian army look ridiculous.

The truth, then unknown, was that Ludendorff's conquests in the east cost Germany the decisive victory in the west. For the Schlieffen Plan was a total failure by being only half successful. Schlieffen had reportedly died pleading, "Make the right [northern] wing strong!" His successors weakened and denuded that wing. Although it pushed through Belgium swiftly, it became overextended in northern France and had to be shortened when the troops were totally exhausted. They still had to march on foot all the way. At the Marne River, fifty miles from Paris, fresh French reserves were brought into battle by quickly requisitioned taxis—a first in war history—and stopped the German advance. Both sides now dug in. The trenches were soon extended north and south until there was one long front from the Swiss border to the English Channel. Schlieffen's heirs had not reached their strategic aim.

At the end of September, two months after the war had started, the German chief of staff, General von Moltke, told the kaiser that he had lost the war. Germany found itself in an iron ring of hostile forces; although it was deep in enemy country, it had no realistic hope of a military victory.

Moltke's successor, General Erich von Falkenhayn, then designed a monstrous new strategy: to attack a specific point with such an enormity of shells that the enemy had to exhaust its resources in its defense. Bogged down in the mud of Flanders, in the casemates of Verdun, in the bomb craters of the Somme, brave but helpless soldiers gave their lives to conquer, defend, abandon, and reconquer a few hundred feet of terrain; millions of shells were fired to make a breach, and the enemy had to cover the gap with corpses. Had the body count decided the victory, the Germans would have won. They killed a million British and 1.3 million French soldiers, 1.7 million Russians, and a half million Italians, while they and the Austrians lost 3 million dead on all fronts. But neither side broke through.

The stupid, headlong assault, grandiosely called "battles of matériel," really meant that tactics had been substituted for strategy. Instead of beating the enemy, one tried to wear it down, exhaust its resources, fray its nerves. This concept was called "war of attrition." In 1915 the Germans began using poison gas. In the summer of 1916 the Allies achieved tactical surprise with a terrifying new weapon, the tank. Both sides had used airplanes from the first week on—but only for reconnaissance and psychological effect. Neither of these mechanical weapons was decisive yet, nor used strategically; nevertheless, the contestants felt that this was the first total war and the first where matériel was more important than men.

An entirely new notion of the hero emerged from the dogfights between airplanes, and from the commando raids in trench warfare. This tragic perversion of the warrior image was the man-machine, the dehumanized destroyer god, superman with hand grenade and gas mask. The Germans trained special shock troops, the bravest of the brave, who infiltrated enemy fortifications to open a breach for the infantry. These specialists in destruction, activists dedicated only to the job and desensitized to human feelings, later on were glorified in the war literature of fascism. Ernst Jünger (himself a shock-troop officer) exalted the heroic automaton gone berserk, the hero of the totalitarian age. Many returned from the war as human wrecks, unable to find their way back into civilian life, and hired themselves out to political adventurers.

Meanwhile, Ludendorff took over in the west and developed his conception of "total mobilization," the transformation of the whole nation into one military camp. Instead of seeking a political solution, he proposed collective suicide. He not only dominated military decisions but forced the government to impose further sacrifices on the homeland and to escalate the hunger warfare against the enemy.

From the first day of the war, the British had blockaded the sea-lanes; the German counterblockade was expected to starve Britain of war matériel. Zeppelin attacks too were tried to scare the British into peace. At no time before had the civilian population been held hostage with such deliberate intent. In both countries clergymen prayed to God to let the other side starve to death. *"Gott strafe England!"* ("May God punish England!") screamed the posters that admonished Germans to buy war bonds.

By the third winter, the Germans were indeed starving. With more and more bran in it, bread grew blacker and coarser. Marmalade was made of turnips; unappetizing margarine replaced butter; the pig and cattle populations were decimated for lack of feed and care. The winter of 1917 is engraved in survivors' memories as "turnip winter" because little else was available. Ersatz substances had also been invented to take the place of leather, rubber, fibers, sugar, honey, milk, matches, and other articles of daily use. The familiar gold and silver coins had long since disappeared from circulation, and the government brought pressure on jewelry owners to sacrifice it on the altar of the fatherland.

This was no longer a heroes' war. It had turned into the brutish inertia of "holding out" (see page 3) because there was nothing else left to do. The alternative was surrender to an enemy who had every reason to be vengeful in victory. There was no longer any cause except sheer "survival." That word for the first time appeared as a war aim: to outlast the enemy, to outdestroy it.

Sullenly, people "held out" and hoped for a miracle. Ludendorff deployed the most ruthless, most terrible weapon: unrestricted submarine warfare. Any boat approaching England, whether or not carrying contraband, would be sunk without regard to the fate of its crew or passengers. But the political backlash of submarine warfare was far more damaging to Germany than the submarine warfare was to England. The sinking of the Cunard liner *Lusitania*—which carried 1,198 persons, among them 139 Americans (though also contraband goods)—aroused public opinion in the United States and helped that country's decision to join the Entente. The submarines, having provoked the coming of fresh American troops (April 1917), could not prevent their landing, and the American reserves finally became decisive. Although Germany "won" the war in the east (see Chapter 6), people now were saying: "We will victory ourselves right into the grave." ("*Wir siegen uns zu Tode.*")

Ludendorff's 1918 offensive in the west did indeed bleed the German armies to death. By August they were on the defensive; in September they retreated to the prepared "Siegfried Line," and Ludendorff pressed the civilian government to seek an armistice "urgently." In November he told the kaiser that there was no hope—the front was breaking—and left under the protection of a Swedish name and dark glasses.

It had been the most exhausting war of German history, fatal to the further predominance of Europe in the world. It could have been ended four years earlier had not both sides been determined to win decisively, to annihilate the enemy's power. Thus, from its second year, it no longer was a war for limited gain but a new war, a total war in both senses: totally engaging the nation and aiming at total power. It was the first war fought with propaganda arms, with mechanical arms, with economic arms, fought by land, by sea, and in the air. It was the first war since Napoleon in which ideologies confronted each other. It wrought irrevocable changes in the social and political fabric of the warring countries.

The revolutions that ended the war in the eastern monarchies changed the map of Europe; but, most important, the war itself had produced new attitudes of man to man and of man to society. It had created new forms of business and a new relationship between individual and nation. For the first time, people came home from the war determined never to permit its repetition, and to build a new society different from the one they had left. Collectivism was seen for the first time as a realistic alternative in modern industrial society; the question was only whether it would be collectivism of the socialist or the fascist, of the democratic or the totalitarian kind.

6

The End of the Old Order

Prince Max von Baden: *I put into your hand the fatherland's fate.*
Fritz Ebert: *I have given two sons to that fatherland.*
(Dialogue on November 9, 1918)

After the great war comes the great debacle.
—August Bebel

IN ALL COUNTRIES THE WAR UPSET THE STATUS QUO, socially and politically. The aristocracy, decimated, lost control. New leaders emerged and class lines broke down. Women took their husbands' places in business. Children grew up without models of lawfulness and authority. Ernst Glaeser has movingly described the war as seen from the perspective of those "born in 1902." War profiteers upset social manners and made their presence felt in postwar society. The value system changed almost imperceptibly; "survival," at first a patriotic slogan, became every family's motto. To deal on the black market, to "go hamstering" for a few eggs or a pound of butter, to have "connections" no longer provoked opprobrium but, at worst, the neighbors' envy. In manners and morals, the war brought on such a decisive breakthrough that one might count the twentieth century from the year 1914.

Likewise in politics. National unity called for an opening up toward the left, which soon changed the mode of governing in England and France. Lloyd George's coalition government and Clemenceau's leadership were democratic dictatorships that considered war "too serious a business to leave to the generals." In Germany, by contrast, the war emergency led at first to an almost undisputed dictatorship by General Ludendorff.

Meanwhile, however, the dissenting Social-Democrats in the Reichstag had grown bolder. In March 1915, the fourteen (see page 69) abstained on a war appropriations bill; in December, twenty voted against and another twenty abstained. They established contacts with left-socialist groups in the enemy countries. Two international meetings (at Zimmerwald and Kienthal, Switzerland, in 1915 and 1916) called for an immediate peace without annexations. Expelled from the SPD in 1917, the dissidents formed the Independent Social-Democratic Party of Germany (USPD). On May Day in 1916, the radical leader Karl Liebknecht, the fiery son of one of the SPD's cofounders, marched in Berlin at the head of a few dozen young socialists shouting: "Down with the war! Down with the government!" He was arrested and indicted for giving aid and comfort to the enemy. With Rosa Luxemburg, a native of Poland who had long been the spokeswoman of the left in the socialist camp, he issued letters signed *Spartakus*, which were widely distributed among the soldiers. From these letters the group took the name Spartakus League. It felt that no reconciliation was possible with the hopelessly compromised SPD.

Liebknecht's trial aroused sympathies far beyond the small circle of his political friends. It even provoked a protest strike in Berlin—the first political strike in defiance of party and trade union policy. This was soon to be followed by economic strikes, as griping about the hardships of war increased on the home front, by job actions even in the war industries (actions for which a man could be sent from his "safe" job to a punitive regiment), and eventually by strikes directed against the war, annexationist war aims, the system of government, and unequal suffrage in Prussia. In several industries, notably in the building and metal trades, a new organization grew up, defying the trade union bureaucracy—the *Obleute* or shop stewards, an organ in many respects like the soviets that were arising in Russian war factories. Soon it used the German equivalent of that term: *Räte* (councils).

In the spring of 1917, the war acquired a new political dimension. The czar's regime collapsed, but the republic that succeeded it continued the war. Now the Entente powers could say that democracies east and west were fighting the obsolete empires: Germany, Austria, and Turkey. In April, the United States entered the war, and Wilson's idealism gave new hope to the captive nations. In January 1918 he published his "Fourteen Points," which promised self-determination to all nationalities—an appeal to them, of course, to rise against the Hapsburg monarchy. Czech soldiers, indeed, deserted by the thousands, as described in Jaroslav Hašek's masterly novel, *The Good Soldier Schweik*, or surrendered to the Russians.

The same explosive idea, national self-determination, had, however, occurred to Ludendorff. The ex-socialist Joseph Pilsudski was encouraged to organize a "Polish Legion" and to declare Poland's

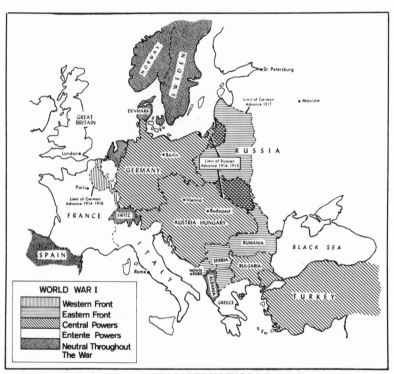

FIGURE 1. GERMANY IN WORLD WAR I

independence from Russia; the Baltic provinces were promised independence under a Hohenzollern prince; even "my dear Jews" were addressed in Yiddish—they had nothing to lose in changing masters. The great coup, however, was the transfer of Russian socialist leaders—mensheviki as well as bolsheviki, who now called themselves communists—from their Swiss exile, via Germany and Sweden, to their native land, where they immediately began to organize the second revolution. The German staff was aware of Lenin's promise to make peace and distribute the land; expecting the revolution, uniformed peasants deserted by the thousands so as not to miss the land reform at home. In November 1917, after a heroic offensive which tied the German armies down, the Russian republic collapsed, and Lenin was in a position to redeem his word.

But meanwhile, important changes had occurred inside Germany. Hard pressed by worker unrest, the kaiser, in his "Easter Message" of 1917, promised equal suffrage. The SPD, the Center Party, and the Progressives now submitted to the Reichstag a "peace resolution" suggesting a return to the status quo ante bellum—with certain ambiguities, however, requested by the chancellor. But instead of helping Bethmann-Hollweg, the resolution precipitated his dismissal; his successor, Georg Michaelis, was a nonentity who took orders from Ludendorff.

In September the Reichstag leaders used their power. For the first time in German history, they overthrew a chancellor and wrote a program for the incoming government. They wanted reform of the franchise, labor-management councils in industry, the abolition of censorship and of military interference with politics, and assurance of a peace without annexations. But the new chancellor, seventy-four-year-old Count Georg von Hertling, was no match for Ludendorff and Tirpitz either. The admiral founded the Fatherland Party, a high-pressure instrument of annexationist policies. Its program was to fight against "the enemy within"—liberalism, democracy, and socialism.

All too soon the Pan-German energies found employment abroad. At Brest-Litovsk on March 3, 1918, the Russians accepted the humiliating, revengeful terms of the dictated peace: dismemberment of the minority areas, separate peace with the Ukraine, six billion marks of indemnity to be paid, oil and wheat to be delivered. But in practice the Germans had to collect the tribute themselves and to shore up puppet governments in the Baltic areas, the Crimea, and the Caucasus; they were drawn deeper and deeper into Russian affairs and, as a result, could not transfer as many troops from the eastern to the western fronts as they had hoped.

If Brest-Litovsk brought no military relief, politically it was a disaster. Philipp Scheidemann, the new socialist spokesman, told the Reichstag that the treaty might set an example for the Entente when they came to deal with a beaten Germany. It also encouraged Austria's teeming minorities to demand self-determination. It made Lenin a martyr and bolshevism an alternative. Moscow was broadcasting its message of peace by revolution.

But the revolution did not come from below. Ludendorff himself, at his wits' end, suggested to the kaiser: perhaps a parliamentary government would obtain a more lenient peace? Hastily, the party leaders were informed—at last, on October 2, 1918—that the war was lost and that it was up to them to retrieve the wasted opportunities. Now they shouted hypocritically: "We have been misled!" But how could the members have been ignorant of stories that had been told by every soldier on leave and even been printed in the papers?

With the imperial establishment paralyzed, the Reichstag had to take responsibility for liquidating the war. The Germans had a vague idea (actually mistaken) that Wilson's Fourteen Points called for a democratic peace with a democratic German government. So the constitution was changed to allow members of the Reichstag to be ministers (October 4); the kaiser appointed Prince Max of Baden, a reputed liberal, as chancellor, and he invited socialist, Progressive, and Center politicians to serve as state secretaries. For the first time a government was formally presented to and approved by the Reichstag. It immediately asked for an armistice and accepted the Fourteen Points as the basis for peace. When Wilson replied that he would not negotiate with the kaiser, the Social-Democrats told the prince-chancellor that he could not save the monarchy any longer. The reluctant revolutionaries who had been waiting in the wings for over a year were Matthias Erzberger of the Center Party, a Swabian schoolmaster of indomitable energy and craftiness who had switched from annexationism to peace; Fritz Ebert and Philipp Scheidemann, two not very colorful secretaries of the SPD, both of modest origin and proud of having grown up to be responsible statesmen; Progressive intellectuals like Hugo Preuss, who had a plan to disestablish Prussia and make Germany democratic; Max Weber; Friedrich Naumann; liberal businessmen like Rathenau and Robert Bosch; General Wilhelm Groener, Ludendorff's successor as general quartermaster who had previously, as munitions minister, shown consideration to labor unions and had warned early on that Germany could not win the war (to him also had fallen the chore to tell the kaiser that he had to go); trade-union leaders like Carl Legien (ADGB; see page 30) and Adam Stegerwald (Christian labor union); Dr. Wilhelm Solf, a civil servant, who served as foreign minister.

This was essentially the coalition that was to emerge from the war; and even before the war was ended, it came to be underpinned by a "working agreement" between trade unions and employers. The outlines of a new order became visible as the old order went into its bankruptcy.

Militarism did not go down without a last gesture of defiance, however. While army morale was flagging, the admiralty decided to put out to sea and challenge the British navy for a last confrontation. Even if it had been successful, the expedition would not have saved anything but honor—and for that the sailors refused to risk their lives. On October 28, disobeying the wanton order, the coalmen stopped firing the steam engines, the guards put their officers under room arrest, and the red flag flew from the masts of the battleships.

The next day, the entire navy in all ports was on strike. Their demands were modest: they wanted nothing but an honorable discharge; they had no intention of making a revolution. But once on shore, they found themselves acclaimed as heroes. Spartakus and the *Obleute* had their trusted contacts in the navy. Sailors' *Räte* were formed, which fraternized with soldiers' and workers' councils. The Social-Democrats and the Independents sent their emissaries— the former to control the mutiny, the latter to spread it. For the first week of November, mass strikes and demonstrations were being planned in nearly all cities as sailors came to rouse the movement, which swelled every day and struck panic in the administrative bodies. The socialists were forced to withdraw their representative from the government lest they lose contact with the masses, which by now demanded the kaiser's unconditional abdication, the dismantling of the general staff, and an immediate end of the war. Revolutionary workers' and soldiers' councils were formed in all big cities. In Bavaria Kurt Eisner, an Independent Socialist, took power at the head of a "Workers', Soldiers', and Farmers' Government"—although the farmers' councils were somewhat shadowy. Army units began to elect councils, and officers had to surrender their epaulettes. The princes fled with the least ceremony and noise possible. The king of Saxony, famous for his informality, told a delegation of mutineers: "Go and clean up your mess yourselves." Wilhelm II went to Holland; his friend Albert Ballin, the shipowner, shot himself. Only a young captain offered to march, at the head of his company, against the revolution; his name was Heinrich Brüning. (Later he was a chancellor of the republic.)

In Berlin, the masses invaded the imperial palace; from the palace window Karl Liebknecht, liberated from prison, proclaimed the "German Soviet Republic." Not to be outdone, Scheidemann proclaimed from the Reichstag window the "German Republic," but was berated by Ebert for that unauthorized action. For Ebert had meanwhile received the chancellor's office from the hands of Prince Max—a procedure not foreseen in the constitution; the Reichstag alone could choose a chancellor, but it did not muster the courage to proclaim its sovereignty.

Actually no constitutional authority existed. Sovereignty had returned to the people which, at that moment, November 9, 1918, were represented only by the councils—elected, self-appointed, or hastily put together by the Social-Democrats and Independents, trade unionists, and revolutionary shop stewards. No other organ could assure the citizens' safety and their supply of food: none could authorize public expenditures or issue passes, could adapt itself to the unusual and unforeseen emergencies and yet retain its constituents' confidence. In Berlin the councils formed an Executive Council of rather radical composition; it was the only body capable of ensuring law and order, of maintaining essential services, and of providing legitimacy for a government. Its first order was that "all administrative bodies must function as usual"; its second act was to appoint a government—not from its own ranks but one that the two socialist parties had agreed to form, composed of three Social-Democrats (Ebert, Scheidemann, Otto Landsberg) and three Independents (Hugo Haase, Wilhelm Dittmann, Emil Barth, the latter representing the revolutionary shop stewards). The Independents also installed one of their men as police commissioner of Berlin.

The government called itself "Council of People's Deputies"; Saxony and Bavaria, via their stationery and stamps, declared that they were now "People's States"; Brunswick, under the Independent Sepp Oerter, styled itself a "Councils' Republic." For at least a month, the new order was revolutionary in the sense that all options were open and that none of the old powers had standing, legitimacy, or function.

Meanwhile the Hapsburg monarchy had come apart. By October the Czechs and Slovaks had established their state, and the southern Slavs had joined Serbia to form the kingdom of Serbs, Croats, and Slovenes that later became Yugoslavia. Rumania acquired the large area of Transylvania; Galicia went to Poland. The young Emperor Karl, who had succeeded his uncle only two years before, abdicated on November 12th. Rump Austria and rump Hungary separated; the newly founded Republic of German Austria declared its intention to join the Reich.

Russia, Turkey, Austria-Hungary, Germany: four empires had disappeared. Chaos ruled in central and eastern Europe; the nations Engels had called "unhistorical" emerged with claims to greatness, and new rivalries were added to the old ones. The heritage of the war was nationalism—the disease that had started it.

PART TWO

The Republic

7

The Founding of the Republic

*The German Reich is a republic. State power emanates
from the people.
The national colors are black, red, and gold.*
—Articles I and III of the Constitution

WHAT KIND OF REVOLUTION? Was it to be a total revamping of the
social, economic, and political structure? Or, as Rathenau said
cynically, "a change in the supervisory personnel"? Ebert considered
his interim government a trusteeship, with Germany's future constitution to be decided by a National Assembly. To Liebknecht, on
the other hand, nothing but surrender of all power to the *Räte* (councils)
deserved the name of a revolution.

But revolution is not a scheme one can impose from above. It becomes necessary whenever the old powers are no longer able to govern,
and possible if new powers are able to assume control. Had the councils
been strong enough and willing to usurp management functions in the
factories, to occupy the offices of cartels and war companies (see page
70), to depose and replace county presidents, police officers, and
administrative bodies at the local level, no one could have stopped them.
But they took none of these measures and refrained from any revolutionary despotism. Either they did not have the personnel or they lacked
the courage to provide a new kind of government. They did not dislodge
the Junkers from their privileged positions on the big estates east of
the Elbe nor the monarchist judges from the courts. They waited for
legal processes to devise a new constitution and for expert bodies to
advise on the future economic structure. A Socialization Commission
was created to determine which concerns or industries should or
could be nationalized; although it met for two years, it made no
recommendations. As foreseen, it foundered on the problem of compensation. Paradoxically, the nonsocialist Rathenau was for outright
expropriation but the Social-Democrats were afraid of it.

More accurately, the plan which Rathenau and his second-in-
command, Wichard Moellendorf, worked out with Social-Democratic

Minister of Labor Rudolf Wissell, was rejected by the cabinet. They had designed a corporate structure of regional and industrial control boards, where management and labor would be represented equally by elected delegates. A Central Economic Board, defined later in Article 165 of the constitution, was to supersede the Reichstag. The model for Moellendorf's plan was the war economy over which he had presided after Rathenau's resignation. It was to find application in April 1919 over a limited sector when the Reich Coal Association was created as a public corporation with power to set maximum prices, divide the market among firms, assign production quotas, inspect accounts, and rule on discount policies. Similarly the Potash Cartel was sanctioned by law. The minister of economic affairs had veto power over its decisions but labor relations were free from state interference.

Moellendorf's conception of *Gemeinwirtschaft* was based on a mixed form of public ownership with private investors holding non-voting stock; stiff taxes were to force the owner of utility shares to sell their stock to the state, for which purpose a special Reich fund was to be created with capital levied from excess industrial profits.

The Social-Democrats preferred a slow-motion process. Their strategic hope was that progressive state governments would expand the public sector of the economy. Railways, postal service, telephone, and telegraph were already Reich property; the Reichsbank was a public corporation charged with managing the money supply. When aviation and radio became available, they were monopolized by the Reich government. Under Social-Democratic leadership, the Prussian state created power dams and developed a policy of public ownership, especially in the fields of energy and public utilities. Socialist municipalities too were eager to take over bankrupt companies or to create new ones in the fields of urban transportation and utilities. The Reich government, however, developed no conception of public ownership and went on favoring private enterprise and cartels.

The socioeconomic framework of the republic, therefore, was not socialist and not even mixed; commentators described it as an industrial democracy, with equal rights enjoyed by employers and trade unions. The foundation of this system was laid in a "Working Agreement" signed (on November 15, 1918) by the trade unions and the employers' associations. It was to be the economic charter of the German republic for the next thirteen years. The agreement recognized the trade unions (Social-Democratic, Christian, and Democratic) as workers' representatives and allowed the election of shop stewards in factories employing more than fifty workers. It also established grievance procedures.

In its first decree, the Council of People's Deputies announced restitution of all civil rights, amnesty for all political prisoners, and the abolition of compulsory labor, of the hated Regulations for Servants, and of all special laws for farm laborers. For the near future, the council promised the eight-hour day, unemployment compensation, and the election of a constituent assembly under equal, free, direct, and secret suffrage for adults. For the first time, women were to vote.

Thus, the two socialist parties laid the groundwork for a pluralist, parliamentary democracy and a welfare-state economy, but did not seize power for themselves. Although the council was composed of three Social-Democrats and three Independents, the levers of power fell soon into the hands of Friedrich Ebert, a former harness maker and labor organizer, a patriot and democrat who rose in the SPD through his ability to negotiate, mediate, and organize rather than through any great ideas or leadership qualities. He belonged to the right wing of the party and was able to communicate with middle-class leaders. In office he lost contact with his own party's rank and file and sought to ingratiate himself with the former ruling classes. He hoped to convert them to the republican order by converting the republic to the old order. He hated the idea of revolution and used all his influence to contain it; he considered the council movement a rival to his party and to the trade unions. In the critical November days, his first concern was to bring the troops home in good order. He obtained assurance from General Groener, at army headquarters, that the army would support the government; in return he agreed that the officers were to retain their ranks, insignia, medals, and command. Both men may have felt that they were saving the fatherland from disorder and civil war. Ebert was most anxious to return to a rule of law and to legitimatize the new regime by election. The chief of staff, Hans von Seeckt, directed this appeal to the officers: "No matter whether or not we like the present form of government, whether or not we think it is the right one—what matters is to save the Reich and the state itself."

The revolution did not penetrate into the administration and failed to build up its own organs. No effort was made to create a republican army and a republican officers' corps. Instead, Ebert authorized the recruitment of "free corps" under the command of the kaiser's officers. These were mercenaries, unsettled front soldiers who had fought against bolshevism in the east, adventurers who loved nothing better than to smash the revolution of working men—their social antipodes. By employing these bandits to protect it, the government put itself into their hands.

Citizens' militias were also formed to defend property and to break strikes. Ebert had freed himself from the council movement which had been his first legitimation. Henceforth, the republic and the revolution went different ways. The councils were no longer the supplement of parliamentary rule, but its rival.

In mid-December, a national Congress of Workers' and Soldiers' Councils (*Rätekongress*) was convened in Berlin. The disorderly mode of electing revolutionary organs usually favors extremists; so the reporter of the *Vossische Zeitung* trembled:

> Representatives of the Workers' and Soldiers' Councils—dozens of them, wild men, with war-frayed nerves—foam at their mouths, babbling with excitement. Demagogues emerging from obscurity, full of evil thought, wild desires, all in stormy moods, in perpetual tension. The only enduring power in this country resides in men in soldiers' uniforms and workers' shirts, sturdy seamen, colliers, voiceless only yesterday, serving an alien will, now released, masters of our destiny. . . .

Actually, only one-fifth of these delegates were Independents or Spartakists. When Karl Liebknecht tried to speak, the majority shouted him down and hastened to divest themselves of the power they held: by 400 to 50 votes they decided elections for a constituent assembly should be held on the first day possible, January 19, 1919. They did, however, also vote to reconvene as a watchdog body and to demand early socialization. Moreover, they showed more wisdom than the government by calling for a republican militia.

Yet they had abdicated their power. The revolution reached its high tide at the councils' congress; thereafter it never reached the government level again. Soon the political councils on the local level atrophied, confined themselves to supervising supply services, or turned into mere public-relations channels for the administration. Only the economic councils in the factories retained their vigor for a few years, within their strictly economic function. Political soviets on the Russian model were never a realistic alternative to parliamentary government in Germany. The Independents, who had placed their hopes on the expansion of council power, were losing influence; their departure from the government was hastened by the following incident.

The "People's Marine Division"—a thousand sailors and as many of their friends—had installed itself in the former royal stables, on the pretext of "protecting" the government but also keeping an eye on it. It was considered a power position of the Independents.

Shortly before Christmas, the sailors were asked to evacuate the building, and they mutinied. Ebert did not hesitate to call the troops and use artillery against the well-liked division. Thousands of demonstrators came to its rescue, and the troops had to withdraw.

After that it became impossible for the Independents to remain associated with Ebert. Under rank-and-file pressure, their three leaders resigned from the government, leaving all power in the Social-Democrats' hands. More resignations followed on the provincial and local levels, with Emil Eichhorn, the Independent police commissioner of Berlin, the only exception. He resisted his dismissal and called on the workers to demonstrate for his tenure.

In January, great numbers of protesters marched in the streets. Liebknecht formed a Revolution Committee, which declared the government "deposed." Strangely, however, instead of storming any administration offices, the demonstrators seized the newspaper buildings and barricaded themselves there, waiting for the troops to dislodge them. This was the so-called Spartakus Uprising. The Spartakus League had recently constituted itself the Communist Party (KPD) under the leadership of Karl Liebknecht and Rosa Luxemburg. At the founding congress, Rosa Luxemburg had warned the ardent revolutionists that Germany was not ripe for a socialist revolution, and that they would have to gain a majority of the workers before they could think of overthrowing the government by force. Behind the scenes, the party tried to liquidate the ill-considered uprising; publicly its paper, *Die Rote Fahne* (*The Red Flag*), supported it.

Not surprisingly, the government panicked and gave full powers to Gustav Noske, whom it had co-opted. In assuming responsibility, he said: "I guess someone has to be the pig," and sent the bloodthirsty Free Corps to storm the occupied buildings and clean up Berlin. They executed hundreds by drumhead justice; the red scare was followed by white terror. Liebknecht and Luxemburg were apprehended and slain by the troopers.

The vile deed was abhorred by many good republicans who hated to see the image of the young republic bloodied. Having considered Liebknecht a sectarian, they now looked at him as a martyr; "Red Rosa," once an object of derision (as, for example, in Gerhart Hauptmann's *The Fool in Christ: Emanuel Quint*), soon came to be recognized as a great thinker and woman, worthy of love and respect. The murders were to haunt the Social-Democrats, who had not desired them but had to answer for them. The killing of 1,200 workers in the subsequent eight weeks cut the umbilical cord between the republic and the revolution.

On January 19, 1919, the peaceful citizens quietly elected a National Assembly, while the military was still rampaging in Bremen, Brunswick, the Ruhr valley, and Saxony. The result was a vindication of Ebert's policy: the SPD polled 38 percent of the vote, the Independents only 8 percent. Neither then nor at any time later did the workers' parties between them achieve half of the total vote. They might have won more than half of the seats under the old one-man-constituency suffrage; but the middle-class parties had insisted on the proportional system.

In the center of the political spectrum, a great bloc of middle-class parties had emerged; 20 percent had voted for the Center Party and 19 percent for the Progressives, who now had adopted a new name, German Democratic Party (DDP). Both parties were then tilting slightly to the left. Erzberger had taken some risk with his anti-patriotic peace policy; Naumann was still an inspiring leader of social liberalism, attracting the freethinking bourgeoisie and the progressive intellectuals. His new program called for abolition of classes, reparation of old injustices, redistribution of wealth and incomes, and replacement of the old master of the factory by a producers' community: "Instead of subjects, let us have citizens in the shops." In the Center Party, too, the labor wing under Adam Stegerwald had gained influence. The right was so ephemeral that left-center majorities might have adopted a decisive transformation of German society. Instead, the Social-Democratic, and Center parties formed the "Weimar Coalition," which contented itself with establishing a formal democracy.

The National Assembly was convened not in the Reichstag nor in the venerable St. Paul's Church in Frankfurt (see page 5), but in the National Theater in Weimar, where Goethe had staged his plays—far away from the turmoil of the revolution. The choice of the location was a hint to the middle class: this republic is to be built on the tradition of German *Bildung*, not on the ideas of revolution. At the opening, Ebert declaimed: "The idealism of our great poets and thinkers must fill the life of our new Republic." The assembly had three major assignments: to give Germany a legitimate government, to write a constitution, to make peace with the former enemies. After these tasks were completed, the capital was moved back to Berlin; but the sleepy Thuringian town had given the Weimar Republic its name.

Ebert was elected provisional president by acclamation, and Scheidemann was named chancellor. He formed a cabinet with six Social-Democrats, three Democrats, three Centrists, and Count Ulrich von Brockdorff-Rantzau as foreign minister. This coalition then commanded three-quarters of the assembly but was never again to get even 50 percent of the vote in a national election.

Elections were also held in the individual states, many of which had middle-class majorities. But in Prussia, on two-thirds of the Reich's territory, the Weimar Coalition was able to rule for twelve years, a stronghold of republicanism.

Up to then, republicans had clamored for Reichsreform, i.e., the dismemberment of the dynastic artifacts and the establishment of a unitarian republic. Now only some tiny Thuringian states were merged, while republican Prussia opposed all plans to diminish its power. So did Bavaria; there, however, the voters disowned Eisner's Council State. (His USPD received only 3 percent of the vote.) On his way to the legislature to submit his resignation, he was shot. A Social-Democratic premier, Hans Hoffmann, succeeded him.

Eisner had been an idealist, and his rule had a touch of Schwabing—Munich's "Left Bank." His assassination unleashed that self-propelling radicalization which is typical of revolutions elsewhere. Anarchists, Independents, and literary rebels seized power in Munich, armed their followers, severed relations with Berlin, planted freedom trees, composed Jacobin songs, and filled a week with libertarian rhetoric. The word strained to become deed, but reality eluded these brave dilettantes. The communists overthrew them and raised an army, only to speed the repression and white terror that now came to Bavaria. The Free Corps, called by Hoffmann, suppressed the revolution and, in retaliation for twelve hostages shot by the communists, killed 557 rebels. Among those executed were the communist leaders Eugen Leviné and Karl Levien, and the anarchist philosopher Gustav Landauer. Among the 2,000 who were given prison terms were the playwright Ernst Toller, the cabaret poet Erich Mühsam, and a forerunner of Keynesianism, Sylvio Gesell. B. Traven, later to become an internationally famous novelist, escaped to Mexico.

By now, the center of political activity had moved away from the revolution—far enough away to permit the Weimar parties to write a constitution. The draft submitted by Professor Hugo Preuss, a Democrat, borrowed from the 1849 model, from Bismarck, and from the American and Swiss systems. It provided the framework of a pluralistic state that was intended to be democratic without being weak. The list of "fundamental rights" made it the most liberal of all constitutions. It guaranteed equality and freedom for all, freedom of speech and assembly, and, for the first time in constitutional history, "a living worthy of a human being"; it proclaimed that "ownership obliges one . . . to serve the common weal."

Sovereignty was vested in the Reichstag, elected by direct, equal adult suffrage. But the Reichsrat, or upper chamber, with a limited veto, represented the states' governments, and a Reich Economic Council was supposed to represent the interests of labor, business, and the consumers. It failed to develop power, however, and served only in an advisory capacity.

The National Assembly had wisely elected a president. But when it wrote the constitution, it decided that future presidents were to be elected by direct popular vote. The office of the president was conceived as ordinarily ceremonial (as in France) but equipped with strong emergency powers. The president could dissolve the Reichstag and call new elections; Article 48 gave him the power to suspend the constitution, including civil rights, and to rule by decree. These emergency powers, however, were limited in time and subject to the Reichstag's approval. Their use by Ebert was controversial; their misuse by his successor was contrary to the spirit and letter of the constitution.

In a parliamentary system of government, the administrative branch is accountable to the legislative, and its policies reflect the program of its majority. Since all administrations were constituted by coalitions, the government's program had to be carefully negotiated among the partners. In practice, this meant that policies were designed by the majority leaders; "government by the bosses" was the feature most resented in antirepublican propaganda. The electoral law strove to give each voter and each philosophical nuance proportional representation. To achieve this, the parties presented lists of candidates; for each 60,000 votes received by a list, one candidate, from the top down, was elected. The voter could not cross out any candidates, or change their order. He voted for the party, not for the man; in the same way the candidate was dependent on the party organization. (The communist deputies even had to assign their Reichstag emoluments to the party.) The constitution did not recognize these realities but stipulated that the deputy must vote his conscience; in practice, party discipline was well enforced.

A prerequisite for parliamentary government is vigorous participation by the masses in party life. Local meetings were held weekly or monthly; dues were paid by placing stamps in the membership book; cashiers made quarterly rounds to collect from delinquent members. Each party had its local and national newspapers, its illustrated magazines, its sports clubs, its chess clubs, its book clubs, its bands, its paramilitary squads, its trade union, its flag—the leftists had red, the center had the colors of the republic, the rightists those of the monarchy, the Nazis a black swastika on a white field surrounded by red. Parties of the right received subsidies from industry and big landowners, but on the whole dues were the major source of political finances. It can be shown that voters responded to strong propaganda efforts.

Many small parties were local, ephemeral, or fronts for other parties, and held only a few seats in the Reichstag. There were seven major parties, which we enumerate from left to right:

1. Communist Party (KPD). After its merger with the Independents (USPD), the party had 900,000 members. In the 1920-1930 period, its vote fluctuated between 2.5 and 5.9 million. Its military organization was the Red Veterans' League (RFB), its trade union had the initials RGO, its youth group was the KJVD.

2. Social-Democratic Party (SPD). At peak, 1.5 million members. 6.1 to 9.1 million votes. Military organization: *Reichsbanner Schwarz-Rot-Gold.* Trade unions: ADGB (blue collar), ADB (white collar), DBB (government employees). Youth: SAJ.

3. Democratic Party (DDP). At peak, 800,000 members, rapidly dwindling. After 1930 it joined with the paramilitary *Jungdeutscher Orden* to form the *Staatspartei.* Its vote fell from 2.3 million in 1920 to 1.3 million in 1930, and 334,000 in 1933. A small trade union organization survived locally.

4. Center Party (*Zentrum*) and its Bavarian counterpart, Bavarian People's Party (BVP). The latter was more conservative, more agrarian, anti-Prussian, and dedicated to the "Bavarian Idea"; both were Catholic. They participated in nearly all government coalitions, nationally and locally. In Prussia the party was republican, in Bavaria monarchist. Combined vote varied from 4.6 to 5.8 million. Christian trade unions and apprentice associations.

5. German People's Party (DVP), the former National-Liberals, party of big business. At peak, 800,000 members. Vote fell from 3.9 in 1920 to 1.5 million in 1930 and 432,000 in 1933. Under Stresemann's leadership the party evolved from monarchism to "republicanism of convenience."

6. German-Nationalist People's Party (DNVP), the former Conservatives. Monarchist, representing agrarian and mining interests, but having a wide following among civil servants, petit-bourgeois, and white-collar employees. At peak, 1 million members. Vote rose from 2.5 to 6.4 million (1924), then declined to 2.2 million (1932). It supported many militant organizations such as the *Stahlhelm* (Steel Helmet) Veterans' League, *Kyffhäuserbund*, Bismarck Youth. Between 1 and 3 million votes were also polled by a number of small "Christian,"

"Peasant," and "Middle-Class" parties, whose representatives generally voted with the German-Nationalists. German-Nationalist Salesclerks' League. A front organization: *Landbund* (Land League).

7. National-Socialist German Workers' Party (NSDAP, popularly called Nazi). In 1932, 1 million members. Vote rose from 0.3 in 1920 to 6.4 million in 1930, and doubled that in 1932. Storm Troops (S.A., also called Brown Shirts), SS (Protection Squad, in black uniforms). Hitler Youth (HJ), League of German Girls (BDM). Trade union: NSBO.

None of the other parties ever got as much as 4 percent of the vote; in 1930 the DDP and DVP fell below 5 percent, which twenty years later under the Bonn electoral law would have denied them any seats.

Since no single party ever received 50 percent of the vote, coalitions were necessary. Disregarding coalitions that would have been impossible, the following combinations were realistic:

1. "Weimar Coalition": SPD, Center, and DDP (1919-20, 1921-22).

2. Middle-class bloc: Center, DDP, DVP (1920-21, 1924, 1926-27, 1930-32).*

3. "Broad Coalition": The same plus SPD (1923, 1928-30).

4. "*Bürgerblock*" (enlarged middle-class bloc): Center, DDP, DVP, DNVP (1922-23, 1925, 1927-28).

In Saxony, Thuringia, and Brunswick, there had been SPD-KPD coalitions, but only briefly. For some time, in Thuringia and Brunswick, Nazis ruled in coalition with the *Bürgerblock* parties.

Election results from 1919 to 1932 are summarized in Table 1.

Had the National Assembly breathed the spirit of 1789 or 1848, it would have launched a bold program of republican reforms: dismantling the states, distributing land in the east, seizing the properties of the former princes and of war profiteers, laying down guidelines for the nationalization of basic industries, rewriting the civil service code, and replacing the Wilhelminian judges, administrators, and army officers with men from their own ranks. The constitution, however, contented itself with formal determinations. It permitted nationalization, but the assembly did not order any; it recognized the workers' councils as a necessary structure for economic democracy, but it gave them no power; it declared the state's independence from

---

*Such minority government had to be "tolerated" either by the SPD or by the DNVP, which alternatingly prevented its fall by abstaining on a vote of confidence (see page 192).

TABLE 1. ELECTION RESULTS, 1919–1932 (PERCENTAGE OF TOTAL VOTE)

	1919	1920	1924 (May)	1924 (Dec.)	1928	1930	1932 (July)	1932 (Nov.)	1933[a]
NSDAP	—	1[b]	7	3	3	18	37	33	44
Nationalists (DNVP)	10	15	20	21	14	7	6	9	8
Conservatives[c]	1	2	5	6	11	11	2	4	2
DVP	4	14	9	10	9	5	1	2	1
Bavarians	{20	4	3	4	3	3	3	3	2
Center		14	13	14	12	12	13	12	12
Democrats[d]	19	8	6	6	5	4	1	1	1
SPD	38	22	21	26	30	25	22	20	18
Communists and Independent Socialists	8	20	13	9	11	13	15	17	12

a Election in March 1933 was no longer entirely free.
b Includes *Völkische*.
c Various right-wing parties (later supporting Brüning): Hanoverians, *Landvolk*, Peasant Party, Small-Business Party, Christian-Social People's Service.
d In 1932–33: *Staatspartei*.

Note: Because of rounding and splinter parties not included in the table, totals may not add up to 100.

the church, but it gave the states the right to institute denominational schools.

Instead of creating a republican army, the new Reichswehr was to be organized by officers of the former, imperial army. The republic thus was placed under the protection of generals who tolerated it only as long as it served their purpose. The test came in March 1920, when the government at last tried to disband the Free Corps. Two of these brigades, under the command of Captain Hermann Ehrhardt, refused to obey the order and allied themselves with General Walter von Lüttwitz, an army commander near Berlin. Defying the government, 5,100 armed guards with swastikas painted on their helmets marched through the Brandenburg Gate in Berlin, where, by sheer accident (as he later testified in his trial), at 5 a.m. General Ludendorff was walking his dog. They occupied the government buildings, declared the constitution abolished and the government deposed, and installed as head of state one Dr. Wolfgang Kapp, an East Prussian monarchist and Pan-German whose name most Germans heard there for the first time. The only memorable act in his brief administration was the seizure of matzos, which prevented the Jews from observing their Passover diet.

The National Assembly and the government fled to Stuttgart and asked the army to beat down the insurrection. General Walther Reinhardt, the commander, agreed; but General von Seeckt, speaking for the staff, gave the preposterous answer: "Reichswehr does not shoot at Reichswehr." Other generals took the side of the rebels. The republic had no army.

Now the government called on the unions to stage a general strike. Never has a political strike been so effective: it paralyzed traffic, public utilities, and other services for five days. Significantly, even the higher civil servants supported the strike, and nothing was left for Kapp but to pack his luggage and go into hiding.

Having defeated the counterrevolution, the government might have asserted the authority of the republic with an iron hand and revived the dynamism of the revolution. This was indeed the intention of Karl Legien, head of the free (socialist) trade unions. He offered to form a new cabinet with SPD, USPD, and trade union backing; for this project he had also won the Christian and Democratic labor unions. It would have been a new departure in political philosophy and might have injected new dynamism in the young republic, filled its formalistic shell with socialist content, and rallied all progressive forces under the black, red, and gold banner. The Independents, however, whose most dynamic wing by now was headed for a merger with the communists, absolutely would not share responsibility with the SPD "murderers." Thus the left lost what might have been its last chance to retrieve the revolution.

The miners of the Rhine-Ruhr valleys did not accept this outcome. After General Watters had declared for Kapp, communists and Independents hastily summoned the workers from the factories, formed "Red Hundreds," occupied town halls and other strategic places, took hostages, harassed the troops, and forced them to retreat from the area. They were determined not to permit a return to the status quo, but they were obviously too weak (and too disunited) to force revolution on the rest of the country. A truce was negotiated, but the militias were betrayed. As soon as they had surrendered their arms, treacherous and vengeful troops came back and visited white terror on innocent villages; "order" was restored to the Ruhr.

In Bavaria the Kapp putsch was completely successful. The Social-Democratic government was compelled to resign, and a right-wing coalition under Gustav von Kahr, a Bavarian monarchist, took power. He was supported politically by the Bavarian People's Party and militarily by the Free Corps and "Home Protection Leagues," which by then had begun to give legitimacy to patriotic pyromaniacs from all over the Reich. The "Bavarian idea" manifested itself in a display of yahoo manners so uninhibited that hotel owners petitioned the government to discourage Jew-baiting during the tourist season. Bavarians also liked to refer to their system as "the nucleus of order" in the midst of the republican *Sauwirtschaft* (pigsty).

In Berlin, too, the Kapp putsch was eventually won by the losers: the government recognized that it did not enjoy the confidence of its generals. It allowed General Reinhardt, who had stood by the republic, to resign, and gave the command of the Reichswehr to none other than Seeckt, the monocled aristocrat who had remained "neutral" between law and mutiny. A brilliant organizer, he was to build up the Reichswehr as "a state within the state." Noske, whose policy of pampering the generals had so clearly led the republic to the brink of disaster, was replaced by Otto Gessler, a democrat who was even more subservient to the generals.

On balance the Kapp putsch had brought about a noticeable nudge to the right. This became painfully clear in its juridical aftermath. Out of 712 civilians indicted for participating in the putsch, only one was punished: he served three years in honorable detention (fortress), with full rights to his pension as a civil servant. Of the 775 army officers involved, only 19 were disciplined. But thousands of years in jail were meted out to their opponents. The German judiciary resumed that class bigotry for which it had been famous under the monarchy. A young officer who had shot and wounded Erzberger got away with eighteen months in jail because "he had acted from patriotic motives."

Since the government was no longer representative of the real distribution of power in the country, the National Assembly was dissolved. In the election of June 1920 the Weimar Coalition lost 9 million votes; the nonrepublican parties on the right gained 3.5 million, those on the left 2.5 million. The German republic had become a republic without republicans. The parties of the Weimar Coalition were forced to fight now against antidemocratic ideologies both on the right and on the left.

Who was to blame? It is easy to argue that the republic had been born under an unlucky star. But its policies had been far from incisive; its ideology had not been clear and certain. It had not fulfilled the hopes of its friends; it had not won over its enemies. It lacked authority and a will. Its poor image did not reflect its immense merits: it had preserved the nation's unity and identity; it had involved the masses in the process of democratic decision making. For the first time all classes were participating; its political turmoil was itself a great educational experience for the masses. Political initiative had passed from the administration to the Reichstag, and from a small coterie of courtiers and generals to the parliamentary parties. Germany had the freest of all existing constitutions, which gave all social forces the greatest chance to develop. But of course, as Rosa Luxemburg had said, freedom is tested when it is demanded by unpopular and wrongheaded agents. The Weimar Republic gave not only freedom but influence to its enemies. Its political structure was empty of social content—or rather, it was waiting to be filled with social substance.

The revolution had been made by the workers, but they had not pressed for a socialist economy. They had broken the power that had held all classes in subservience to the state; but they had not dislodged from power the officials, judges, and teachers who were still beholden to the old concepts of the authoritarian state. They had won bargaining rights, unemployment insurance, minimum wages, and the forty-four-hour week; but they had not wrested economic power from the owners and managers of private concerns and large estates.

Nevertheless, the former ruling classes no longer ruled absolutely and no longer felt that they owned the state. The state no longer ruled over all classes; its decisions were subject to bargaining. This was pluralism—a notion that was little understood in Germany, and certainly not by the former ruling classes. They were not prepared to share power, and they considered "red" everything that was not monarchical. They campaigned not against the left parties but against the republic, its functionaries, its institutions. Thus, the "People's Party" screamed its promise to "free you from red chains" from a black, white, and red poster. Floods of anti-Semitic literature, including novels and near-pornographic smut, attacked the "Jew Republic" and the "bosses" in government. Reactionary papers pilloried, ridiculed, and calumniated republic politicians like Erzberger, Preuss, the Prussian Prime Minister Paul Hirsch, Ebert, Scheidemann, and Noske, always suggesting that "party government" was intrinsically bad.

However, these bitter expressions of deep hate, financed lavishly by big industrialists and agrarians, legitimatized the republic in the eyes of the workers and of democrats who might have liked to see a stronger, more Jacobin republic. No matter what mistakes the governing parties might have made, the republic stood for principles of tolerance, peace, reason, freedom, equality, social justice. Neither the snobbish sneer at Hugo Preuss's "screwdriver trousers" nor the invidious insinuations about Erzberger's carelessness in financial affairs, neither the anecdotes about Scheidemann's vanity nor the anger over Noske's betrayal, could silence the testimony its enemies' hate gave to the republic.

8

From Versailles to Rapallo

National Socialism was born not at Munich but at
Versailles. —Theodor Heuss

ON NOVEMBER 11, 1918, THE GERMAN ARMIES were still on French soil, although by then their positions had become untenable. The German people did not learn that the General Staff had been suing for peace for a month. Instead, a civilian, Matthias Erzberger, had to sign the severe armistice terms, and the generals spread the myth that "an unconquered German army" had been "stabbed in the back" by treacherous politicians, the "November criminals." The myth served two purposes: it laid the blame for Germany's postwar miseries on the shoulders of the republic and in addition blamed it for the loss of national honor. It also flattered the German pride and persuaded the Germans that the Allies had won the war merely by a dirty trick; since history had been cheated of a just ending, Germany need not pay reparations.

On May 8, 1919, at Versailles, an elaborate treaty was presented to the German delegation—and received with an outcry of protest. Its harsh terms seemed designed to humiliate Germany, irreparably ruin its economy, and reduce its future generations to servitude. Social-Democratic Chancellor Scheidemann said:

> What honest man can sign such a capitulation? Would not the hand wither that put itself into such bonds? [The phrase was to cost him his career.] This treaty will make a corpse not just of Germany but of the right to self-determination, of faith in treaties. It will be the beginning of a general process of barbarization.

Likewise, in a pamphlet at once famous, John Maynard Keynes predicted that "the economic consequences of the peace" would be disastrous not just for Germany but for all Europe. If reasonable men were aghast, we need not wonder that chauvinists and demagogues responded with hysteria and even paranoiac symptoms.

The treaty was indeed severe—though no more so than the Treaty of Brest-Litovsk, which Germany had not yet renounced. It was intended to make Germany a second-class nation and to hamstring her postwar recovery. Some of its clauses were humiliating and provoked precisely that German nationalism which the treaty was supposed to tame. "Versailles" became the political stereotype of the right which convinced a majority of the German people that they were being held in colonial bondage and that their republican government was a mere commissioner of the Allies.

There are several submyths to the main theme. One says "world Jewry" or "the elders of Zion" had systematically planned the destruction of Germany. Another asserts that German and French capitalists, in cahoots, imposed the crushing burden on the German workers in order to break bolshevism's neck.

We must distinguish justified grievances from irrational demagoguery. The Germans had hoped that a republican government would be given credit for ending the war, that Woodrow Wilson's Fourteen Points would establish a fair new world order, and that the peace treaty would not merely exact reparations from Germany but, through them, would open for her the way back into the family of nations. Instead, the vindictive and fearful Clemenceau had dominated the Paris conference, Lloyd George had been bound by his wartime promise to "make the Germans pay," and Wilson was tied down by two premises: his idea of building a permanent framework for international peace, and the United States' loans to the Allies.

To obtain consent for his plan for a League of Nations, Wilson had to make concessions at German expense. In order to ensure that American bankers got their money back, he had to agree that the Germans must pay reparations to the Allies. These were hard facts that no American president could have disregarded, and it is unhelpful for understanding them to psychoanalyze Wilson's relations with his mother.*

To recognize these realities, however, is not to say that the Treaty of Versailles and the other Paris peace treaties were either wise or just. Their territorial dispositions were not based on reliable information; the crazy quilt of nationalities along the Danube did not permit "self-determination" for every minority; the power-hungry demands of some new nations were allowed to override economic common sense. Natural units were willfully destroyed; irredentist

---

*Regrettably, Freud has lent himself to this exercise in psychohistory—a pseudoscience at best.

problems were left unsolved to create military borders. Danzig and Trieste were deprived of their economic hinterlands to be made "free cities." Poland incorporated Ukrainians, Byelorussians, Germans, and Lithuanians, and had a strong Jewish minority. Czechoslovakia retained Hungarians, Bohemian Germans, and Carpatho-Russians. Not all southern Slavs were happy under Great-Serbian domination. Rumania annexed Bessarabia and Transylvania. These new states were joined by alliances and constituted a French satellite system, designed to defend the new borders and to prevent a return of the Hapsburgs. In the Treaty of St.-Germain, reneging on the promise of self-determination, rump Austria was forbidden to join either Germany or any other combination that might have made her able to survive. The other successor states were not viable either and had to be subsidized by French loans.

Germany was deprived of 13 percent of its territory and 10 percent of its population—not to mention its colonies. It lost half of its iron ore, one-fourth of its coal deposits, 15 percent of its rye and wheat potential. It also had to surrender its merchant fleet, a good part of its railway rolling stock and other equipment, and many head of cattle and horses. To be sure, it ceded mostly those territories that its rulers had taken from other countries: Alsace reverted to France; Poznan and West Prussia to Poland; small border zones with non-German populations to Belgium, Czechoslovakia, Denmark; and Upper Silesia's Polish districts to Poland. The coal basin of the Saar was to be administered by France for fifteen years; various zones of the Rhineland were to be occupied for five, ten, and fifteen years. Austria had to yield Alto Adige (the South Tyrol) to Italy, whose borders thereby extended to the Brenner Pass. To give Poland access to the sea, a "corridor" had to cut East Prussia off from the rest of Germany (and the Poles harassed travelers in transit instead of making the border acceptable to Germany).

If all this was painful, the financial clauses of the treaty were oppressive. The German economy was mortgaged to pay installments on a reparations debt whose total was still unspecified. It was only in 1921 that the Reparations Commission fixed this sum at $28 billion (132 billion marks, including interest), to be paid over forty-two years. (The German gross national product then was about $15 billion.)

Finally, the Treaty of Versailles contained a number of articles that deeply affected German pride. The army was to muster no more than 100,000 men, and Germany was not allowed to produce or own tanks, battleships, or military aircraft. Control commissions were to watch over Germany's ability to pay reparations, and over the fulfillment of the disarmament clauses; German war criminals were to be extradited for trial by the victors; Germany admitted "war guilt" (responsibility for having brought about the war) and assumed liability for war damages. For decades, even to this day, German historians have tried to disprove this "war-guilt legend" and soon pass from defensive arguments to an offensive for revision of the treaty. "Versailles" became the symbol of German degradation and the source of German righteousness.

A stable peace can be built either on total justice or on total injustice. A witty Frenchman stated, "For a harsh treaty, this one is too mild," and Clemenceau insisted that there still were twenty million Germans too many. The treaty, as a German history book sums it up, was severe enough to fan German nationalism into white heat, but not severe enough to contain that flame inside the German border. French fear of German revenge provided the incentive for that very revenge.

Again, as with the Armistice, the question was who would sign the treaty. The Democrats resigned from the government; but they had neither an alternative policy nor a strategy to offer. Some hotheads spoke of "national resistance," perhaps in alliance with the Soviet Union. In his prison cell in Berlin, Lenin's emissary, Karl Radek, had received staff officers like Major Kurt von Schleicher, the future gray eminence of the Hindenburg regime, and businessmen like Rathenau. The wildest schemes were being aired. Count Harry Kessler, an aide in the Foreign Office, noted in his diary:

> It is possible for old Prussian discipline and new socialist discipline to merge to form a proletarian master class, which could assume the role of the Romans propagating, arms in hand, a new culture. Call it Bolshevism or whatever; the impoverished Prussian Junker has always been a proletarian. If sometime these German masses, brought up on discipline, become inspired by a faith, by a Liebknecht or whomever, then woe to all our enemies!

"National bolshevism" was to become a Third World ideology thirty years later. It was not a practical alternative for Germany. A European civil war on German soil? Groener told the government that he had no army to wage resistance; the socialist ministers knew that the people were in no mood to renew the war. Instead, Bavaria would secede and seek shelter under the French umbrella; Upper Silesia would fall to Poland, which even then was organizing guerrillas in the area; in the Rhineland, a separatist movement was likely to gain strength if the Reich was powerless. Only three years later the Ruhr war was to show the utter futility of guerrilla tactics in a highly industrialized country.

No matter how "bad" the peace was, it was better than national death. Again, Erzberger had the courage to tell the Germans that they had to sign. Having already been shot at and wounded, he knew that it also meant signing his own death warrant; an ex–minister of finance, Karl Helfferich, launched against him a vicious campaign of calumnies, meant to discredit both the republic and a policy of reconciliation.

In the National Assembly, 138 deputies of the Democratic Party, the German People's Party, and the German Nationalist People's Party voted against signing the treaty; 237 Independents, Social-Democrats, and Center deputies voted for signing. They assumed responsibility for a peace that all Germans called shameful.

When the treaty was ratified in January 1920, few Germans were aware that it was a blessing in disguise. It limited the army to 100,000 men and prohibited the spending of unconscionable sums on hardware, navy, air force, tanks, etc. It forced the Germans to concentrate on civilian production, especially on export goods; it deprived them of obsolete equipment and afforded them the most advanced technology. As long as reparations were paid in kind, they turned out to be good business for German industry. French concerns finally insisted that reconstruction of their devastated country should be their own patriotic privilege.

General von Seeckt, making best use of his 100,000 men, forged a professional army of highest caliber. The military clauses of the treaty were circumvented in a number of ways: athletic training in the schools, state sponsorship of sports activities, paramilitary training by "patriotic leagues," the Steel Helmet, a right-wing veterans' league, and the Bismarck Youth. Under various names, like Protection League and Civilian Guard (*Einwohnerwehr*), vigilante organizations were tolerated or, in some states, encouraged. Large estates in Bavaria, East Prussia, and Silesia became sanctuaries for illegal Free Corps groups. Finally, the Reichswehr conducted or delegated training camps for underground recruits or seasonal volunteers, known as Black Reichswehr. Although their existence was an open secret, publication of details could send an editor to jail for several years—or even bring death to the informant: the infamous *Feme* murders horrified Germany. (The medieval *Feme* was a secret court of justice, which condemned and executed traitors without a hearing.)

And soon help was to come from unexpected quarters. The Soviet

Union permitted Germany to produce war matériel, to develop new designs, even to train personnel—clandestinely, of course—on Russian territory. Cooperation between the Reichswehr and the Red Army had begun when both countries were fighting Poland in 1920. At the end of that year Grigori Zinoviev, president of the Communist International, addressed the congress of the Independent Party (USPD), inviting them to merge with the KPD. The right-wing Fehrenbach government made no move to prevent him from entering the country; it was steering toward a showdown with the western Allies over the reparations problem. Many felt that the two "pariah" powers were bound to find each other. Ideological differences rarely played a role in Lenin's foreign policy. His overtures occurred at the very moment when German police had beaten down a communist uprising in central Germany.

Just then western pressure for reparations was growing unbearable. The Reich had paid eight billion marks instead of the twenty billion which had accrued and were due by then. In May 1921 England and France declared that German payments were in arrears and occupied three Rhine ports as "sanctions." The Fehrenbach cabinet resigned, and once again the republicans had to take the responsibility for a dismal decision. Joseph Wirth, a genial Swabian schoolmaster who belonged to the left wing of the Center Party, formed a minority government of the Weimar Coalition. His foreign minister was Walther Rathenau, who felt that Germany must try to obtain easement of the treaty by making an effort to "fulfill" it. This became the magic formula for republican foreign policy in the coming years; but "fulfillment policy" also became the hate phrase with which the nationalists denounced the Republic.

As bad luck would have it, however, the French voters returned to power Raymond Poincaré, the wartime president and spokesman for France's *petit épargnant* (small depositor). His aims were to recover the czarist loans and to prevent the resurgence of Germany. At the World Economic Conference held at Genoa in April 1922, he succeeded in linking the question of Russia's prewar debts with German reparations, and Rathenau felt isolated. There were rumors that the Russians might be prepared to pay their French creditors if they were to receive reparations from Germany. The German delegation was near despair when suddenly, at 2 a.m., the Soviet foreign minister Grigori Chicherin called to invite Wirth and Rathenau to a private talk. The scene has often been described: how the German delegation, in pajamas, decided to accept the invitation, at the risk that this would blow up the conference and ruin German relations with England. The next day, April 16, the Russians and Germans met in a village nearby, Rapallo, and there signed the famous treaty which seemed to reorient German policy toward the east.

The coup was stunning, although the text of the treaty was innocuous enough: mutual renunciation of reparations, exchange of embassies, most-favored-nation treatment. But a commercial treaty followed which barely camouflaged the clandestine cooperation of the German and Russian war industries.

General Seeckt commented in a memorandum:

> Poland is the nucleus of the Eastern problem. . . . Her existence is incompatible with ours and even more so with Russia's. If Poland falls, the eastern pillar of the Versailles Treaty falls. Our aim, to break the predominance of France, is attainable only through Russia. . . . Politics must be based on power. . . . We want a strong Russia, strong economically, politically, and militarily. . . . We shall be stronger if we help Russia build an arms industry.

Wirth agreed with his chief of staff; but Rathenau, who was essentially western-oriented, expected to use the eastern connection as a mere counter in future negotiations with England.

The Rapallo Treaty has often been interpreted as an alternative; it was, rather, a complement of German policy toward the West. By taking this first independent postwar step, Germany freed itself from one-sided dependence and carved out a space for a foreign policy of its own.

9

From Bankruptcy to Stabilization

The form of government, the freedom that thanks to the fatherland's defeat had fallen into our laps, could not for a moment be taken seriously as the framework for a new nation.
—Thomas Mann, *Doktor Faustus*

WE MUST NOW GO BACK to the defeat of the Weimar Coalition. In the election of June 1920, the center of gravity had shifted to the right. The German People's Party, lavishly financed by manufacturers, had polled nearly four million votes. But its leader, Gustav Stresemann, once a monarchist and an annexationist, had seen that in order to govern, the right had to shift its action toward reality and to accept the republic as its "territory of operation." He joined the cabinet of Chancellor Konstantin Fehrenbach, the first to be composed solely of middle-class parties.

In the beginning, the administration seemed to be favored by good luck. Reconstruction and rising exports stimulated employment so that throughout 1920 less than 1 percent of trade-union members were out of work.

It is true that the prosperity had been financed by increasing budget deficits and that the value of the mark was declining. The deficit rose from 155 billion marks in 1920 to twice that much in 1921, and to 55 trillion marks in 1923. In 1919 a paper mark was worth half of a gold mark, in 1920 only one-fourteenth. In 1921 it was worth five old pfennigs and in 1922 only two pfennigs; thereafter it went tobogganing. This was partly the legacy of wartime financing: the government had recklessly placed its IOUs in the hands of its suppliers, who were able to exchange them for money at their banks, which in turn discounted them at the Reichsbank, which ordered mark bills from the Government Printing Office. The same technique was used to finance the reparations deliveries and the social services. The government was spending four times as much as it took in.

It was profitable for business, but a fool's paradise for the treasury. Joseph Wirth, the minister of finance, was a mathematics teacher used to dealing with figures on the assumption that they did not change their intrinsic value. His director of the Reichsbank, Havenstein, cynically stated that he would keep on printing money until the Reich was rid of its debts. He did not say that in the same process he was relieving the middle classes of their savings and pensions.

The public had not yet grown wise to the hoax. During the war they had patriotically exchanged their jewelry and their gold for paper money, and they could not believe that they were becoming paupers. In voting for right-wing parties, they hoped to restore the mark to its gold value and to shake off the new burdens: unemployment compensation, pensions, aid to refugees from Poznan, but, above all, reparations. Hence they were pleased to see the new government take a strong stand against the Treaty of Versailles and refuse to pay reparations or welsh on the figures. Nationalism and the gold mark were two faces of the same symbolism.

Patriotic phrasemongering, however, was no substitute for diplomacy. The government's brave posturing failed to impress the Allies. Fehrenbach, rather than come down from his high horse, resigned and handed the reparations problem back to the Weimar Coalition. The new chancellor was the folksy Wirth, an upright republican who believed in reconciliation with former enemies. He also brought into the cabinet Rathenau, known for his expertise and his wide international connections. Colleagues have reported that the two men complemented each other.

But Wirth kept the incompetent Havenstein and continued his former financial policies. When he took over in May 1921, the dollar fetched 70 marks, in October twice as much, a year later 320 marks; when he left office in November 1922, the dollar was worth 4,500 marks, the paper mark 0.1 old pfennigs. Capitalists were expatriating their money or buying up real estate; foreigners were acquiring apartment houses and businesses in Germany, which caused enormous resentment and fed chauvinistic, racist radicalism. Whoever had merchandise held on to it or sold it for foreign currency. Everyone's motto was: seek safety in real values.

But not everyone caught on while there was time. Some prospered; but others fell into unspeakable misery, and public morality decayed. Honest, respected families were reduced to eating herring and potatoes while hitherto unknown people with neither *Bildung* nor manners feasted ostentatiously in resort places, displaying their recently acquired jewelry.

The working population suffered most grievously. Wages could not keep pace with price increases. Union contracts—the proud achievement of the republic's first day—turned into shackles. In October 1923, a day's wage would buy a pound of butter, a week's wage a pair of cheap shoes. One-fourth of all Berlin children were underweight; one-third of the graduates of a Pankow grade school were too weak to take regular jobs, and 15 percent of them had tuberculosis. Fortunately, American charities provided a lunch of soup for children who came to school without breakfast, and in winter they distributed underwear too.

Miraculously, there were no hunger marches and few spontaneous outbursts. The Communist Party (recently merged with the majority of the Independents, and half a million members strong) tried in vain to win the blighted and underfed workers for an "offensive strategy."

The few communist uprisings that occurred in March 1921 reflected the factional strife in the Kremlin rather than the German workers' mood. Max Hölz, a Robin Hood character with a few hundred followers, made the roads unsafe in central Germany for a week; the Mansfeld copper miners staged a repeat of the Peasants' War; 10,000 workers occupied the Leuna chemical works—Germany's biggest and most modern—for a week. But their action remained isolated, and the police overpowered them. Thereafter, the unrest petered out in bombs placed in public toilets—clearly the tactics of a desperate minority.

Quite a different revolution affected the status of the middle class. They were being expropriated—not by socialism, as they had feared, but by their own financial ignorance. This staid class, which had lived by the rules of Polonius, now saw it clearly demonstrated that borrowing pays, and that selling one's country short is prudence. What hurt it most was the loss of pride and of the ethical standards on which it had been brought up. It saw the triumph of a morality which its folklore had always associated with shady characters, Levantines, Jews; now "everybody did it"—a harsh blow to self-respect.

Society was being polarized. On the one side was loss of status— nice old ladies selling their family heirlooms; fathers losing their sons' respect; staggering suicide rates; despair and ruin. On the other side were adolescents wallowing in luxury, nouveaux-riches spending their money as fast as they could and discovering new styles in living it up. A hit song of the year said, "*Wir versaufen unsrer Oma ihr klein Häuschen/und die zweite und die dritte Hypothek*" ("we are drinking up our granny's little cottage, and the second mortgage, and the third"). Just a few years earlier, most people had hardly known what a mortgage was. Crime and vice, cocaine use and prostitution were on the rise. To get even with the newly rich, the "better people" told jokes about their lack of education and table manners or stigmatized them with the epithet *Raffkes* (lowborn go-getters, successors of the uncultured, nouveau-riche "Piefke Family," whose deportment at fashionable Riviera resorts had been the butt of cartoonists before the war). The *Berliner Illustrierte* ran a competition asking, "What does Raffke say when he sees the Colosseum in Rome?" The prize went to the answer "Don't start building if you can't finish the job." The irony of it was that the most ruthless profiteers were not the newly rising, but some old families; not the Jews, but the cream of the national bourgeoisie, led by the patriotic Hugo Stinnes, who bought himself a multimillion dollar conglomerate of shipping, iron and steel, newspapers, and other ventures. He used his vast resources to prevent the stabilization of the mark and to finance vociferous attacks on the republic because it was unable to stop the inflation.

The middle classes had become thoroughly demoralized and alienated. The government had been a partner to the most gigantic heist in history; it had lost all authority. Vis-à-vis a regime that has destroyed all sense of value, anything is permitted; the trust in public order, offended and betrayed, is converted into rebellion. The German middle class, once so famous for its loyalty to its sovereign, now rose against a state that failed to protect property and security.

Petit-bourgeois radicalism is at one and the same time authoritarian and rebellious, monarchist and anarchist, traditionalist and modernist; it preaches law and order but applauds assassins. When Eisner's murderer, Count Arco, was released from prison, Munich society lionized him. When the Independent deputy Karl Gareis, who investigated the Free Corps crimes, was fatally shot, the right had openly protected the murderers. On August 26, 1921, Matthias Erzberger was killed after an intensive campaign of vilification led by Karl Helfferich. The murderers belonged to the infamous "O.C.," a successor to the Ehrhardt Brigade (see page 96), which was allowed to agitate and recruit openly in Bavaria. *Die Christliche Welt* wrote: "It is unbelievable how many so-called Christians have greeted this deed with relish; this mentality is freely displayed in streets and on tramways."

Undisturbed by the effect of his words, Helfferich now selected a new target for his smear campaign, Dr. Walther Rathenau, who had the additional blemish of being Jewish. In the streets of Berlin, loutish gangs were singing: "Death to Walther Rathenau, the God-accursed Jewish pig!" On June 23, 1922, in the Reichstag, Helfferich pointed to the minister, declaiming that he was responsible for the devaluation of the currency and the destruction of the middle class. The next day, Rathenau was assassinated by three members of the O.C.

This time, the republican reaction was strong. The trade unions called a twenty-four-hour strike. Angry demonstrators stormed the offices of the German-Nationalist Party. Two German-Nationalist deputies, deeply ashamed, resigned from their party. Chancellor Wirth, in his funeral oration, vigorously denounced those who had directed the hand that pulled the trigger. "The enemy is on the Right!" he exclaimed. The government issued a Decree for the Protection of the Republic—soon to be converted into law—which threatened severe punishment for desecration of the national flag, vilification of the republican form of government, incitement to murder, and expression of approval for violent acts against members of the government. A Special Court for the Protection of the Republic was set up. Police were authorized to ban meetings that might result in violence.

Liberals were not quite happy with this legislation, since it could be used against the left as well as against the right, and German judges were not known for their love of civil liberties. Special Prosecutor Ludwig Ebermayer was probably loyal to the republic, but to the communists he became a symbol of "class law." (Militants of the labor movements were indeed prosecuted with more vigor and sentenced to longer terms than were terrorists of the right.) Although he did prosecute Free Corps and *Feme* murderers, the judges usually let them get away with nominal penalties.

The republic was in danger, and republicans felt the need to close ranks. Those Independents who had not joined hands with the communists in 1920 now forgot their wartime quarrels with the SPD and returned to the fold of their old party. The communists, too, underwent a remarkable mutation. After their defeat in 1921, they lost half of their members, and some of their most capable leaders returned to the SPD—among them Paul Levi, the titular head of the party, and Ernst Reuter, the future mayor of Berlin.

For Wirth, however, the socialist consolidation was bad news. His cabinet represented only a minority, and he would have liked to enlarge its base. But right now the Social-Democrats could not afford to sit down with the People's Party—the party of Stinnes and the other inflation profiteers. Wirth had other troubles, too. He could not stop inflation. His "fulfillment policy" was unable to move Poincaré. It was like a curse: the conciliatory Aristide Briand had not been able to communicate with Fehrenbach; Wirth was faced with a French premier who meant to bleed the Germans to death, to humiliate them, to make any future comeback impossible, to dismember Germany. Wirth resigned rather than face that music.

The administration that followed in October 1922 was introduced as a "government of experts," which in the language of the German right meant no Social-Democrats and no Jews. Its leader was Wilhelm Cuno, the president of the Hamburg-America Shipping Line and a conservative of suave manners. Within three months, the dollar had leaped from 5,000 to 20,000 marks.

Cuno made reasonable proposals for a solution of the twin problems of reparations and world monetary relations. But, to show his bargaining power, he delayed the shipment of a few hundred telegraph poles to France. Not since the Trojan horse has a piece of wood had such historic significance. Poincaré, of course, was not interested in getting deliveries and reparations but in finding Germany in default; on January 11, 1923, without even consulting with England, he marched into the Ruhr valley and seized the coal mines.

The response in Germany was indignant righteousness. Cuno at once declared "passive resistance" against the occupier: not a morsel of coal was to issue from the mines' heads; not one barber should serve a Frenchman. The German government paid the Ruhr workers for striking and the employers for losing business. Saboteurs, trained by the Free Corps with the government's secret blessing, wrecked bridges and trains, endangering the lives of thousands. Alfred Krupp von Bohlen, accused of conniving with the resisters, was jailed; his workers revered him as a martyr. One Albert Schlageter, who had been caught sabotaging, was shot by the French; he immediately became a national hero in Germany.

Once more, as in August 1914, a patriotic truce enveloped all parties. Even the communists, seeing an opportunity to tie Germany closer to Russia, vigorously supported the national resistance. Karl Radek gave a funeral oration for Schlageter at a meeting of the Executive of the Communist International. He offered the German government gratuitous advice on making the resistance more effective; he reminded it of the great age of the Liberation War against Napoleon, when the Prussian king and the Russian czar fought side by side; and he denounced Stinnes, the hypocritical patriot who was codirector on the board of the Alpine-Montan Company with Schneider-Creusot, who had forged the gun that shot Schlageter. He also wrote editorials for *völkische* (German-racialist) papers; *Die Rote Fahne* ran editorials by Count Westarp and Reinhard Wulle, two notorious racialists.

The *völkische* movement had been smoldering in the German cauldron for some time; it had denounced the "Jew Republic" and its founders, the "November criminals," as carriers of alien philosophies. Now for the first time this bastard offspring of crass ignorance and pretentiousness grew politically virulent. A few ultrachauvinist deputies had seceded from the German-Nationalist Party and given parliamentary standing to the racialist ideology. The movement was divided into many sects—one of them headed by General Ludendorff, who had gone paranoiac; another by a gifted orator, Adolf Hitler, who had ample money to spend and drew large audiences in Munich. He was subsidized by the Bavarian army command, and his lieutenants were frequent guests of Munich's police commissioner.

Like the communists, the *Völkische* predicted that the patriotic front would not risk the merry war with France. They declared that they would not join that united front unless a reckoning had first eliminated the traitors and Jews. This was the spirit of National-Bolshevism, of the national and social revolution. But it was vain to call for a Carnot. The year was not 1793. Workers did not like to go to jail; capitalists could not afford to let their facilities lie idle; nor could either overlook the fact that British miners were doing overtime. (The German miners paid them back three years later during the British mine strike, when they literally shipped coal to Newcastle.) The truth is that the patriotic strike was less than total, and the French were able to seize increasing quantities of coal.

Meanwhile the Ruhr conflict cost the government 40 million marks a day; 152 people died; thousands had to leave their homes; the economy lost 3.5 billion marks in damages. Cuno pushed patriotism to the limits of madness. Insisting that Germany was right, he preferred to let it starve rather than submit. In his eagerness to prevent the rape of a few tons of coal, he would rape the savings of the German middle class. Within a few months, the dollar jumped to 100,000 marks, to a million, a billion, a trillion marks. An inverted Shylock, he exacted the pound of flesh from his own people. Hundreds of government presses spewed out new notes in ever-increasing denominations—hundred-mark, thousand-mark, soon one-million-mark bills, and in 1923, one-trillion mark bills: "1 000 000 000 000 Mark." People needed a shopping bag to carry their daily allotment of cash; workers, paid twice a day, would rush from the payroll window to get to the stores before the price tags were changed. By the fall of 1923, the dollar was worth 4.2 trillion marks—and then a new government stabilized the mark by simply stopping the printing presses and issuing carefully controlled amounts of new money.

The unity of the Reich was in serious danger. In Saxony and Thuringia, socialist governments were arming the workers. In Bavaria, the Free Corps and Black Reichswehr were preparing their people for an uprising against "Berlin" and the "Reds." In the Rhineland a separatist "government," subsidized by the French, threatened to secede. In Küstrin a Major Buchrucker, organizer of the Black Reichswehr, attempted a coup. The *Feme* executed people who were not patriotic enough. Fear of assassins alone held the government together. The Bavarian army command openly fraternized with the Free Corps.

It was clear that the Ruhr resistance would have to be broken off before winter forced the miners back into the pits. Even earlier, the workers lost patience and went on strike, this time against their own government. "Cuno must go" was their only demand. In September the Social-Democrats mustered the courage to overthrow him.

Gustav Stresemann formed a "Broad Coalition" government (including SPD, Center, Democrats, Bavarians, and People's Party), which proposed to do four things: to stop printing money; to break off passive resistance; to depose the socialist-communist governments in Saxony and Thuringia; and to make the Reichswehr and the Bavarian separatists break relations with the Free Corps and take their orders from the national government. It obtained indictments against the racialist leaders who would not submit to the army command.

To do all these things, the government invoked Article 48 of the constitution and invested executive power in General Seeckt, making him practically the sole arbiter of the constitution (Enabling Act of October 13, 1923). Seeckt had no use for either the policies or the personnel of the Free Corps. Since he had presidential aspirations, he was anxious to use his powers constitutionally. He judged that war with France would be foolish, and he had no intention of striking an alliance with Russia, of fighting a Russian war on German soil.

By now the Russians were afraid that Stresemann might beat a retreat. The KPD began feverish preparations for a "German October" (the Russian revolution was still counted by the Gregorian calendar). Red Army officers were moving little flags on the "strategic triangle" in Saxony and Thuringia. In these two states, the KPD joined the SPD to form "workers' governments," and the police there trained "Red Hundreds."

Seeckt decided to march into Saxony first. The communists hastily put the question of resistance to a shop stewards conference in Chemnitz, but found that the workers were in no mood for revolution; the vast majority repudiated them. Not a single unit decided to go it alone. But one of the messengers who was to call off the revolution arrived too late: in Hamburg, a few hundred communists mounted a barricade. They remained totally isolated and gave up soon. The government had won without much bloodshed; the KPD was driven underground. But the SPD, angered by the illegal, one-sided intervention against Saxony, withdrew its ministers from the Reich government.

President Ebert then turned to Bavaria and the danger from the right. Kahr had been proclaimed Bavarian commissar, and the commanding officer in Munich, General Lossow, supported him. Both were in uneasy league with the Nazis. Disobeying an order from Berlin, Lossow put Seeckt to the very test he hated: a confrontation with his own people. But Seeckt could not back down, because the issue now was whether he was in command.

By November, relations between Berlin and Munich were at the breaking point. Kahr suspended the national government's power in Bavaria; Lossow alerted the Free Corps to march on Berlin. But he, too, was afraid of civil war. He hoped to reach a tacit compromise with Berlin. A meeting was called in Munich's largest beer hall: Kahr and Lossow apparently hoped to play for time.

At that moment Hitler burst into the meeting, fired his pistol into the ceiling, and herded the occupants of the dais into a side room. He could not wait and look on while others were negotiating his opportunity away. He had hoped to win as their partner; now he proclaimed himself Reich chancellor, with Ludendorff, Lossow, and the Bavarian Police Minister Seisser as his assistants.

Kahr and Lossow somehow escaped the clutches of Hitler and made peace with Seeckt. Next morning, when Hitler and Ludendorff marched at the head of a small band of Free Corps men, they faced a hail of police shots, threw themselves to the ground, and were arrested. Fifteen of their followers were dead. A Bavarian jury could not avoid sending Hitler to honorary confinement—but only after they had been promised that he would be released nine months later: it was enough time to write the book nobody read, *Mein Kampf.* Lossow was deprived of his rank, but nothing happened to Kahr and Ludendorff.

Stresemann had shown extraordinary courage throughout this month. He had given up a fight that had become a sacred symbol to his friends on the right. He had preserved the unity of the Reich. He had fought the adventurists on left and right. In a country deeply torn by ideological strife, he had remained realistic. When the Munich usurpers threatened to march on Berlin, he wrote in his diary:

This week it will be decided whether the national leagues will dare to fight. The government has concentrated enough Reichswehr. But should the Reichswehr fail us, the rebels will win and we will have a nationalist dictator. I am fed up with this dog's life. If the gangs come to Berlin, I'll sit right here in my office where I belong. They can shoot me but I'm not going to flee to Stuttgart.

Just as from a monarchist he had turned into a republican politician, Stresemann now became a great statesman. Spurning appearances, he always went for the substance of power; he jettisoned all ideological luggage to achieve, methodically, one of his goals after the other. Now he turned to the currency problem. The plans had been worked out by Social-Democratic Finance Minister Dr. Rudolf Hilferding; but now a rightist, Dr. Hans Luther, became minister of finance, and Dr. Hjalmar Schacht, a banker of austere persuasions and with a symbolically stiff collar, was made currency commissar and then president of the Reichsbank. For psychological reasons, the new currency was called *Rentenmark* (*Rente* suggests mortgage) and supposedly was based on the value of Germany's real estate—which was merely a way of stating that it was based on the government's taxing power. The value of the new mark was fixed at 1 trillion paper marks, and the dollar at 4.2 new marks, or 4,200 billion paper marks.

The question now was whether the owner of a savings-bank book in the amount of 1,000 marks in 1914, who had not touched it, should receive 1,000 or one one-billionth of the new marks. The Reichstag decided that "mark is mark"; all old marks were to be exchanged at the exchange value of November 20, 1923. The middle class thereby was expropriated; more than one commentator has called this verdict the greatest robbery in history. Stresemann, whose government was responsible for the decision, later deplored its consequences:

Historians may see above all the lost territories, the lost opportunities in colonization, the loss of wealth for the state and the people. They overlook the most painful loss which Germany sustained: the loss of the intellectual [*geistige*] and professional middle class that had been the pillar of the traditional state. It paid for its total dedication to the state with the total loss of its material resources and was proletarianized.

He was exaggerating. Creditors received the right to sue for up to 25 percent of the original value, so that those who had held on to their savings accounts lost no more than their French counter-parts, while those who had sold their assets for a song had no claims. But industry, farmers, municipalities, and utilities now sailed into the period of stabilization and prosperity virtually free of debts.

If Stresemann deserves most of the credit for overcoming the crisis, his contemporaries did not appreciate it. He had antagonized the nationalists by breaking off the Ruhr resistance, and he was negotiating a reasonable solution of the reparations problem. He had antagonized the Social-Democrats by intervening in Saxony and Thuringia. He was unpopular in his own party. After three months he faced a vote of no confidence in the Reichstag.

His successor was Wilhelm Marx, a former judge who belonged to the right wing of the Center Party; his minister of the interior was the mayor of Duisberg, Jarres, close to big industry and to the right wing of the People's Party. But Marx also retained Stresemann as his foreign minister; for indeed Stresemann's stature was now such that no government could do without him. Stresemann died in 1929.

The crisis of 1923 was the republic's turning point. It was composed of a foreign-policy crisis, a financial crisis, a monetary crisis, a crisis of the basic political structure of the Reich, and a constitutional crisis. It was overcome by the stubborn cleverness and courage of three men: the president, the chancellor, and the commander of the army. They overcame it by suspending the con-stitution, by grossly misusing the extraordinary powers they had—but also because the enemies of the republic made grave mistakes, and because the republicans made sacrifices of power and even graver sacrifices of ideology. To maintain the republican form of government, the Social-Democrats allowed their enemies—the military and big capital—to usurp all power. In the course of the crisis, the republic assumed the shape of capitalistic normalcy.

The crisis had been resolved at the expense of the majority of the people. The workers had to make immediate and temporary sacrifices; the middle class had lost status. When elections were called in May 1924, the lingering resentment was reflected in substantial losses by the moderates and unexpectedly high gains by the extreme right: four million who formerly had not voted or had supported Stresemann marched off to the Nationalists, Racialists (*Völkische*), and National-Socialists.

There existed now three blocs of about equal strength: the two labor parties (SPD and KPD), the moderate middle-class parties, and the extreme right. Since no workable coalition could form a majority, the Reichstag was dissolved once more in December. By that time the stabilization of the currency and the return to normalcy had taken hold sufficiently to strengthen the center and to weaken the extremes. The moderates won twenty-four seats and the SPD thirty-one, and the Nationalists regained six seats from the Racialists.

This result called for new alignments, a break-up of the opposition blocs to the right and left. The communists now followed an ultra-left course of organization, building outside the mainstream of politics; and the Nazis took a similar stance on the far right. Meanwhile the SPD and the Nationalists took turns "tolerating" governments of the center right. In terms of social policies this course of action benefited the classes whom these parties represented; the farm lobby obtained subsidies and tariffs; the workers saw their standard of living rising as never before. For the first time wages exceeded the prewar level; public employees received substantial increases in their salaries; the unemployed enjoyed larger benefits; and while the eight-hour day was not restored, overtime pay now became the legal norm. The pluralistic system began to become practical and made sense for those who knew how to use it.

10

Back to Normalcy

*If the old, warlike Germany is to disappear, we repub-
licans must wish that the new Germany can prosper.*
—Edouard Herriot, French Premier

FROM NOVEMBER 1923 UNTIL JUNE 1928, Germany was ruled by the
Bürgerblock—a succession of six coalition governments of the middle-
class parties. Twice the chancellor's name was Hans Luther, four
times Wilhelm Marx—both rather colorless, conservative politicians,
the former identified with the People's Party, the latter with the
Center. Twice the (monarchist) German-Nationalists were part of the
coalition; twice the Social-Democrats "tolerated" the government by
abstaining in votes of confidence. In March 1924, when the Enabling
Act of October 1923 expired, the army surrendered its special powers
to the civilian authorities without hesitation. The Steel Helmet and
the German-Nationalists, eager to participate in power, declared
themselves prepared to accept the Weimar constitution as "the basis
on which we operate."

An American president's promise of "normalcy" had come to
Germany, too. The currency had been stabilized; political unrest had
subsided; the Reichstag had workable, though not stable, majorities;
business was picking up; and fortunately, England and France had
governments that did not cater to wartime resentments. Stresemann,
who was foreign minister in every cabinet, hoped to negotiate a
reparations settlement that would prove Germany's good will without
ruining her finances, and President Coolidge contributed the advice
that the problem of Germany's debts should be dealt with as "business,
not politics."

In May 1924 the experts acknowledged the principle that
reparations would have to be linked to Germany's ability to pay and
to transfer the payments without unsettling the international balances.
The American banker Charles Dawes proposed that Germany should
pay between 1 and 2.5 billion marks yearly (between 2 and 5 percent
of her national income); a reparations agent was to determine these

amounts, as well as those which it would be safe to transfer. The revenue of the German railways and industrial income was to be pledged to produce the payments. In return, Germany was to receive a loan of 800 million marks and insurance against arbitrary sanctions in the future. Although no link was explicitly admitted, it was also hinted that return of the Ruhr and an earlier evacuation of the Rhineland depended on acceptance of the plan. And it was further anticipated that once Germany was again creditworthy, American capital would be heavily invested in German industries. This proved to be true and, with the help of American loans, German industrial production reached its prewar level in 1927 and surpassed it in 1928.

Although the burden Germany assumed was heavy, economists have argued that in reality it never paid. During the six years that followed adoption of the Dawes Plan, it received twenty-five billion marks in foreign loans, of which ten were used to pay reparations, ten were re-lent to other nations, and five were used to cover the foreign-trade deficit. The loans, invested in industry, farming and municipal bonds, were supposed to produce revenue, so that a public debt had been shifted to profit-producing enterprise. The communists therefore charged that German workers had to produce surplus for their own as well as foreign capitalists.

The government used its emergency powers to impose the necessary taxes and to suspend the eight-hour day. However, it was not the left that led the fight against Germany's exploitation but the right. The German-Nationalists added the catchword "Dawes" to "Versailles" and used it as a stick to beat the republic with. The plan, however, had so many advantages that German industrialists lobbied for it; when the needed legislation came to a vote in October 1924, enough German-Nationalists voted for it to provide the required two-thirds majority.

The Social-Democrats were the champions of Stresemann's policy of reconciliation, and they attached to it a pacifist ideology which he did not share. For Stresemann, rapprochement was a way to restore German sovereignty in the west and to free his hands against Poland in the east. For the Social-Democrats fulfillment was a step toward European unity, and they believed that in this endeavor French Foreign Minister Aristide Briand was their ally.

In 1925, using the favorable climate, Stresemann made a gesture that must be called a masterstroke in diplomatic history. He proposed a pact of collective security guaranteeing the status quo in the west. Germany would voluntarily renounce any claim to Alsace-Lorraine, agree to submit all disputes to international arbitration, and accept a guarantee of the existing borders by England and Italy. In return, Stresemann expected an early evacuation of the Rhineland.

After careful preparation, a pact was concluded at Locarno, Switzerland, in October 1925. It was hailed as Germany's first step toward equality and as Europe's first step toward a system of collective security. Briand insisted that Germany join the League of Nations, an event held up by technicalities for a year. As immediate rewards of his policy, Stresemann could count on the return of the Ruhr in July 1925 and of the Rhine cities in August 1925, the evacuation of Cologne in January 1926, and finally the recognition of Germany as a big power. In September 1926, when it joined the League of Nations, it was given a permanent seat on its council.

The Locarno Pact was equally distasteful to the German-Nationalists and to the communists. The former left the cabinet because, to their mind, Germany must never recognize any part of the Versailles settlement or count on the western powers' good will. The communists considered the pact as a further step toward Germany's integration into England's anti-Soviet front. To allay Russian fears, Stresemann signed a new pact with Chicherin in April 1926 promising not to take part in any interventionist coalition, and in view of that treaty, Germany was exempted from the League's Article 16, which obliged members to participate in sanctions against nonmembers. Stresemann intended to stay neutral in the developing Anglo-Soviet conflict, perhaps even to mediate. Together with Briand, he received the Nobel Peace Prize in 1926. In 1928 they joined the U.S. Secretary of State, Frank Kellogg, and fifty-six other nations in signing the Kellogg-Briand Pact in Paris, renouncing war as a means of national policy.

Stresemann stated that he would not use force against Poland but refused to sign an "Eastern Locarno"; the Corridor, Danzig, and parts of Upper Silesia remained German irredenta. Right and left extremists continued to denounce "fulfillment" as the symbol of foreign domination; the Social-Democrats had to take the blame for its painful features. They earned little thanks for renouncing demagoguery, but were harassed by character assassins.

A bizarre lawsuit illustrates the climate of vilification to which leading republicans were subjected. Back in 1918, Ebert had led a munitions workers' strike; now an obscure journalist called this an act of high treason, and the Hugenberg press gave him such wide publicity that Ebert felt forced to sue for libel. Instead of arguing that the strike might have helped to end the senseless carnage a day sooner, Ebert swore that he had joined the strike only to end it.

Despite this kowtowing to nationalist opinion, the court ruled that Ebert had been guilty of high treason. Ebert had 150 such suits pending; moreover, a Reichstag committee was investigating silly allegations concerning his typist.

The republic had its share of petty scandals. A Dutch merchant, Barmat, had supplied food for Germany during the first postwar months, and then had used his connections to obtain credit he was not entitled to. He was sentenced, on technicalities, to a mere three months in jail; but once the involvement of republican politicians was established, the Reichstag majority ordered an inquiry into the president's part in the affair. Having delayed a necessary appendectomy to answer the absurd charges, Ebert died on February 28, 1925.

To the enemies of the republic, Ebert was a symbol of the revolution. Yet if one man can be considered responsible for steering the republic away from revolution, it was Ebert. His policies had alienated him from the rank and file of the party in which he had risen so high. He had won the respect of many of his former enemies, but the mass of the bourgeoisie had no thanks for him. An exception was Stresemann, who paid him this tribute:

> The word "national" has been misused for partisan purposes lately. But if he who gives his best for the fatherland is rightly called patriotic, then the President was of a thoroughly patriotic nature. The sincerity with which he fulfilled his duty was born of the German character. His intentions may have been different from ours, his philosophy not the one that unites us. But love of country is not the privilege of any one party. For our national anthem he chose the chord of Unity and Justice and Freedom.

In the first presidential election by popular vote, six candidates ran. None could muster a majority on the first ballot. On the second ballot (which was not a runoff), the republicans united behind Chancellor Marx. The parties of the right rolled out a symbol of past glories: Field Marshal Paul von Hindenburg, then seventy-eight years old and totally inexperienced in politics. The communists supported the candidacy of Ernst Thälmann, a longshoreman from Hamburg. The Comintern later declared this to have been a mistake, but few radical workers would have voted for Marx even if Thälmann had withdrawn, and many Protestants denied him their vote, too. Paradoxically, the Bavarian People's Party endorsed the Prussian marshal, and so Hindenburg was elected by a plurality of 14.6 million votes over 13.7 for Marx and 1.9 for Thälmann.

Though Hindenburg was a minority president, the nationalists had won a great victory; foreign diplomats now had to shake hands with a man who was still on the war-criminals list. But Hindenburg swore to uphold the constitution and, with the patient guidance of sometimes exasperated protocol officers, served the republic as a loyal figurehead president during his first five years. He disappointed many who had hoped for grand gestures of defiance. One small such gesture was his order to hoist the marine flag (black, white, and red) over German consulates abroad, which provoked a cabinet crisis; another was his attendance, in full military regalia, at an anniversary of the Tannenberg victory, on which occasion he read a repudiation of the "war guilt" thesis—which almost provoked an international crisis.

Nevertheless, he maintained a dignified posture even where the demands of duty ran against his personal taste. When Seeckt allowed a son of the ex–crown prince to take part in army maneuvers and a scandal threatened, Hindenburg let the general go. When schemes to circumvent the disarmament clauses of the Versailles Treaty were exposed, Hindenburg replaced Defense Minister Otto Gessler with General Wilhelm Groener, a man strictly opposed to the Patriotic Leagues, the Black Reichswehr, and other adventurers' games. In a certain way Hindenburg's limitations helped the republic, for his name commanded great authority on the right and especially in the army. He shielded the office of the president from the manifestations of disrespect it had suffered under Ebert.

Amateur psychoanalysts have suggested that the Germans are in special need of a father figure at the head of state. To his voters, Hindenburg represented authority, law and order, the good old days, and unity. Other republics have turned to generals to save them from partisan discord. Ebert was, despite all his efforts to forget it, a Social-Democratic president; Hindenburg, for all his obvious ties to the monarchy and to the Junker class, was a symbol of unity behind whose bulk the string pullers were able to hide their divisiveness. His tenure softened the right's irrational hatred of the constitution; he proved that no constitutional change was needed to bring the old order back to the top. His friends, the German-Nationalists and Agrarians, served in cabinet posts during 1925 and again in 1927-28.

The old order walked as a ghost. A certain Harry Domela, who resembled the kaiser's grandson, had used the obsequiousness of high society to live off them for years, and then published a book holding them up to ridicule. A visiting card with a crown, or even a simple "von," was still the best recommendation in republican Germany. The constitution had abolished nobility, but a law allowed the use of the title as part of the name. Now the former princes were suing the republic for restoration of their palaces (which had been converted into museums). Outraged victims of inflation proposed a referendum to "expropriate the princes without compensation." The proposition polled 15.5 million votes—more than Hindenburg had obtained in his election—but that was not enough to win; inept wording had deterred many property owners, and since not voting counted as "no," the vote was not secret.

Although respectability won, the left was on the offensive again. In the Reichstag, the Social-Democrats fought against the government's tariff bills, against its tax gifts to big estates and big industry, against its favors to the 2,500 cartels. They also exposed the army's secret installations in Russia, its shady dabbling in industrial ventures, its underground contacts with the Patriotic Leagues, its amateurish attempts to beat the restrictions of the peace treaty. They opposed the vainglorious plan to build a series of battle cruisers or "pocket battleships" (since Germany was not allowed to have battleships, highest-efficiency features had to be squeezed into small space at great expense). And they held up to ridicule the cabinet's attempt to control "smut" in print or immodesty in swimsuits.

The left now had its defense leagues, too, which gave its parades a certain militancy. The Reichsbanner was basically composed of SPD people but was open to all republicans; the Red Veterans' League was Communist. Marching in uniform behind bands, protecting meeting halls, and generally being visible, these groups, though unarmed, checked the uninhibited displays of the Steel Helmet and of Hitler's S.A.

Social-Democrats and republicans also had established strong beachheads in some state and city administrations. Prussia, Hesse, and the Free City of Hamburg were governed by Weimar coalitions, which provided progressive welfare programs, used patronage to republicanize police and civil service, and expanded public ownership in the utilities. Aided by four years of prosperity, they were able to increase the services of state and municipal agencies and to win respect for republican institutions. As a result, the 1928 election brought gains to the Left. The SPD polled 9.2 million votes, the KPD 3.2 million—between them a gain of 2 million votes for labor. The middle-class parties between them declined from 11.2 million to 10 million votes. The German-Nationalist and parties still farther to the right between them declined from 8.5 million to 6.6 million. Moreover, they were badly split as a result of dissension in the government.

This election marks the high point of pluralistic democracy. It indicates a healthy trend in German politics only ten years after total disruption and five years after impending dissolution; and only three years after the Hindenburg election, the majority of Germans seemed to have settled into the routines of a new *Rechtsstaat*—government by law.

Since no ideology had prevailed at the polls, Hindenburg called on Herman Müller to form a cabinet of the Broad Coalition, ranging from the Social-Democrats to the People's Party. No better symbol of the new sobriety could have been found than this uninspiring party bureaucrat, who was no match for the grave crises that lay ahead. Hindenburg said of him: "Mr. Müller is a good man; too bad he is a Social-Democrat." He retained Stresemann as foreign minister.

The National Association of Industrialists and the big steel cartel, however, were not happy with the Broad Coalition. They withdrew their support from the People's Party and encouraged Hugenberg's campaign against Stresemann's policy of reconciliation. They tried to undermine the government's authority in dealing with problems of the economy. In the winter of 1928-29 they locked 100,000 metal workers out after the state arbitrator had granted them a six-pfennig increase; they obtained a reduction of the increase, but a Reichstag resolution forced them to recognize the government's right to make arbitration compulsory.

In foreign affairs, the trend was toward normalization. Stresemann, with the help of the American banker Owen Young, was able to negotiate a new reparations agreement which reduced the total of Germany's debts from 137 to 37 billion marks, to be paid in fifty-nine yearly installments which could be reduced but no longer increased. Moreover, the Military Control Commission and the reparations agent were to be retired, and the Rhineland was to be evacuated within a year. Stresemann was not to live to see this happen, but meanwhile he was subjected to a furious propaganda campaign; its targets were the Young Plan and the government that had accepted "two generations of slavery." Hugenberg initiated a referendum to prevent adoption of the plan. Only 5.8 million voters supported this initiative—fewer than had voted for the right parties one year earlier. It was obvious that people no longer believed in defiant gestures and patriotic rhetoric.

But Alfred Hugenberg drew a different conclusion from the defeat of his party. The nationalists, he felt, had been too cooperative as part of the coalition. Wresting the leadership from the advocates of realpolitik, he placed his considerable skill—and the vast resources of his newspaper and movie empire—at the service of one idea: to foil every success of the republic; to organize militant resistance against its institutions; to make the constitution unworkable. In his own words, he was pig-headed (*stur*). His minions fanned the flames of xenophobia and militarism, and he allied himself with Hitler, who was to destroy him after he had destroyed the republic.

At the same time, unfortunately, Prelate Ludwig Kaas emerged in the Center Party as a strong challenger of its republican course. He was bigoted in his views and jesuitic in his ways. He hated both the secular state and socialism in all its shapes. His special project was a school law that would force parents to send their children to denominational schools.

A third man was soon to join the enemies of popular government. Hjalmar Schacht, the president of the Reichsbank, originally a Democrat, turned more and more to the right. Late in 1929 he directed a strong attack on Hilferding, the Social-Democratic finance minister. Both had to resign; but the conflict between capitalistic and labor interests in the coalition was now coming into the open, and the one man who could have restrained his colleagues was no more. Stresemann had died in October 1929—just a few weeks before the failure of Hugenberg's referendum could have reassured him, and six months before the early evacuation of the Rhineland was to vindicate his policies. He was not a man anyone loved; he could not have been elected president. He was an effective politician who did the right thing not from conviction but out of craftiness; his own term for his methods was "finessing." He was a republican of convenience, and perhaps he and Rathenau symbolize the tenuous symbiosis of the enlightened bourgeoisie with the republic—an association that could never become a union but that, a year after his death, even ceased being an accommodation.

Class war was also polarized by Stalin's adoption of the "General Line" in 1928 and by the Sixth World Congress of the Communist International. Earlier than anyone else, the Comintern economist Eugene Varga had predicted that capitalism was headed for a major depression (*Krise*). The German communists concluded that they would have to win the workers away from the Social-Democrats, whom they considered "the main support of capitalism." Consequently, they split the trade unions and branded the Social-Democrats "social traitors" or even "social-fascists." Since the SPD was in the government again, it was on the defensive. Exasperated, the Social-Democrats tried to use state power to stop communist propaganda.

On May 1, 1929, the Prussian minister of the interior, a Social-Democrat, prohibited the customary May Day parade. Communist demonstrators defied the ban, and thirty-two of them were fatally shot in Berlin. Many voters showed their disapproval in the 1930 elections, and the two workers' parties could not forge a united front when one was needed in the depression years. Instead, in 1931, the communists joined their worst enemies, the Nazis and the German-Nationalists, in a referendum to unseat the Prussian government. They lost; but a year later they were once again united with the Nazis in a wildcat strike against the Berlin subway. Their strategy was to expose parliamentary democracy as a sham and to force the republicans, especially the SPD, to expose themselves as enemies of freedom. The tactic worked, and brought disaster to both socialists and communists.

The Social-Democratic program of "economic democracy" was losing both its glamour and its foundation. The idea had been that capital, labor, and a benevolent state should form a concert in which the balance would gradually be tipped toward the common weal. Hilferding had spoken of "the political wage level." Now, however, the state was becoming a bone of contention between warring interests; the benefits of prosperity were distributed unevenly, and when prosperity came to a stop in 1929, the disposable pie grew smaller and the fight about the distribution grew fiercer. Economic democracy never lasted long enough to become an institution, and in the Great Depression that was to follow, the ground on which it was supposed to be built crumbled away.

11

From Prosperity to Depression

The twenties were gone before they had really started.
—René König

THE BROAD COALITION CAME TO POWER in the midst of a commercial boom. Germany was expanding its industrial resources, renewing its manufacturing and transportation equipment, and introducing new materials and consumer articles that had not existed before. Acetate fiber (rayon), the movies, cosmetics and other pharmaceutical preparations, radio, electric household appliances, and photography created new markets. Many of the new materials improved the quality of life. What had been ersatz now became a glorious achievement. Household utensils assumed a modern, streamlined look. The fashion industry provided Paris models for the masses. Highly organized department stores pushed cheap articles and ruined many small craft shops. Escalators and Christmas shows, white sales and bonuses were attractions that stimulated sales.

A dozen manufacturers were making automobiles. One car was so small that it became the cartoonists' laughingstock, but automobile races were occasions for national excitement. Modern houses required elevators, warm water, and central heating. There also was the new suburban development, the garden city or "settlement." The cities built playgrounds, stadiums, and swimming pools; they also needed additional utilities, and the states had to build power stations, while the Reich was responsible for expanding the railways and the mail, telegraph, and telephone networks. To finance all this, the predicted dollar invasion materialized. In the four years after the Dawes Plan, American banks invested 5.2 billion dollars (twenty-five billion marks) in German enterprise and government securities—not always wisely, for some of these investments did not generate profits. Building swimming pools, playgrounds, and stadiums may be desirable as an investment in health but is unsound financially, especially if some of these municipal bonds are short-term loans whose renewal is not assured. Germany was building new cities and paying reparations with borrowed money. Stresemann warned:

> We must distinguish more sharply between essence and appearances. Foreigners judge us by the latter, and this creates misunderstandings. The whole world is up in arms because the Prussian government has authorized 14 million marks for reconstruction of the opera house; the full price may be nearer 20 million. Even the victorious countries cannot afford such a luxury. The world must think we are wallowing in gold. Does Mayor Adenauer have to have a wonderful fair building? Does he have to boast that [Cologne] has the biggest organ on earth? The Rhenish Museum in Cologne, the Press Exhibition in Cologne, are the most luxurious in their fields. Frankfurt had a 2.5-million-mark deficit in its Music Exhibition; Dresden is building a hygiene museum at national expense.

Similar attacks on "public spending" were voiced by the conservative president of the Reichsbank, Hjalmar Schacht, who established himself as an independent, veto-wielding branch of government. His criticism may have been sound from the narrow viewpoint of the financial community and foreign creditors. But it was partisan; it was hostile to public expenditure and to expansionist techniques of money management. Had public authorities not provided jobs, industrial production would not have reached even the prewar level, and unemployment would never have dropped below the million mark, as it did in 1927-28.

New markets and products, public expenditure, and foreign financing provided the backup forces for the brief prosperity of the middle 1920s. But its most powerful generators were two catch-up needs of the industrial system: new housing construction and "rationalization," which meant modernizing industrial equipment, plant, and machinery. War-worn and obsolete machines were replaced by technologically advanced devices; the assembly line triumphed over older methods of manufacturing. Highly sophisticated labor-saving machinery was taking over what men had done before or were unable to do with mere muscle power. Industry proudly showed off the million-mark blast furnace that needed only four men to service it, or the thousands of spindles operated by one worker. The making and replacement of all this new equipment gave jobs directly to many, and by its snowball effect to many more—until the new machines began to spew out excess quantities of goods and the market became glutted. For five years, though, the expansionist forces were stronger, and the boom was aided by a downward trend of prices for food and raw materials.

With advanced technology came concentration of business. Sixty-five percent of all shares represented large concerns; consolidations and mergers were the order of the day. Giant corporations were founded, such as I. G. Farben (chemicals and dyes) and Vereinigte Stahlwerke (steel). The largest concern, Vereinigte Stahlwerke, employed 182,000 blue-collar workers and 16,000 office employees—with their families, that amounted to half a million people. Its product, which included that of satellite concerns, exceeded two billion marks. Some industries were effectively cartelized—the Rhenish-Westphalian Coal Syndicate and the Potash Syndicate, for example, controlled all of their respective markets. The merger of the Deutsche Bank and the Disconto-Gesellschaft resulted in the DD-Bank. The Darmstädter Bank merged with the Nationalbank.

Despite the great number of new industries and the shift in production and consumption patterns, however, the old families still dominated the industrial establishment. The names of Kirdorf, Stumm, Röchling, Krupp, Borsig, Siemens, Thyssen, Vögler, Wolff, Flick, Bosch, Duisberg, and Silverberg were well known before the revolution. Rathenau had been shot; Albert Ballin had shot himself; Stinnes' heirs were unable to hold his empire together—but that was an inflation conglomerate anyway.

The leaders controlled their industries through business associations and cartels. Twenty-five hundred cartel agreements supervised prices, production, and trade practices of farmers and manufacturers, and the big business associations—especially the General Association of German Industrialists and the Land League—were powerful in political councils. Their policies prevented necessary adjustments when the depression came.

In the ten years following the war, yearly per-capita income rose from 740 marks to 820 marks. Savings-account deposits, which had been wiped out in 1923, had risen to nine billion marks by 1929. Rayon production, which had been 1,000 tons in 1913, was 91,000 tons in 1927. Consumption of electricity had doubled; the number of motor vehicles tripled.

Mark wages increased; even real wages increased considerably. Although the emergency legislation had eroded the eight-hour day, skilled workers were doing well. Between 1924 and 1928, a metalworker's weekly income increased from twenty-eight to thirty-seven marks, a construction worker's from twenty-seven to sixty-two marks, a printer's from twenty-six to fifty-four marks, a textile worker's from twenty to thirty-seven marks, while the cost of living rose only from 142 to 152 percent of prewar levels. In 1927 civil servants received a raise of 20 to 25 percent, over the protest of the austere Reichsbank president and also of the reparations agent, who charged that the additional expenditure amounted to a year's debt service. Yet rationalization kept unemployment high. Even at the peak of prosperity it exceeded one million. In 1927 the Reichstag adopted a law on unemployment insurance. It recognized the right to financial support for all workers who lost their jobs involuntarily. Agents were no longer allowed to investigate the need or worthiness of the beneficiary. The law made insurance payments compulsory for sixteen million workers. Benefits varied from six marks (for workers earning ten marks a week) to twenty-two marks (for workers earning sixty marks); and they could run for thirty-nine weeks, after which "crisis support" (welfare) took over (after a humiliating investigation into beneficiaries' financial means) with lower benefits.

While much of this pointed to a stronger economy, there were a few serious flaws. Manufacturing exports were never to regain their prewar level, while imports rose and the balance of trade was negative. Farms that had gotten rid of their debts were heavily mortgaged again; despite protective tariffs they could not compete with overseas producers. Rationalization of industrial production led to better productivity, increased output, and sharp competition; but eventually it would have to come to a stop, and then millions of workers would be structurally unemployed. By January 1929, the official count of unemployed was three million. Finally, the commercialized reparations debt hung over German borrowers.

Each of these factors might have been tolerable by itself. But when credit became scarcer, the boom collapsed.

There had been early warnings. Nearly a year before "Black Friday," Stresemann had told newsmen that

> we have been living on borrowed money. Should a depression occur and the Americans withdraw their short-term credit, then we will be bankrupt. . . . Statistics show how much the industrialists have borrowed, how much the cities, how much we have borrowed just to stay alive. We are disarmed not only militarily but financially. We have no means.

And as early as fall 1927, the reparations agent, Parker Gilbert, had said:

> Four years have elapsed since[the Dawes Plan]. In that time Germany has made enormous progress. It has restored its domestic and foreign credit, reorganized its industry, and renewed its production capacity. Its stock of raw materials and its capital have been replenished; the

general standard of living has been rising. It would be regrettable if all that were to be endangered by a short-sighted and unsound game of politics. The rising level of public expenditure has given the economy an artificial stimulus that threatens to undermine the stability of public finances. [retranslated]

Although many had spoken of an impending recession, no one had anticipated the power with which it struck. Soon after October 1929, the American banks began to recall their short-term loans, and the jerry-built structure of European finances came tumbling down like a house of cards. Since the German economy was geared for a rapid increase more than others were, it was hit hardest by stagnation. Its export markets were lost quickly. Those industries that were strongly cartelized refused to cut prices but curtailed production and employment; those that were competitive cut prices and wages ruthlessly. Farm prices, which had been declining for a few years, now dropped so abruptly that peasants could not meet their tax and mortgage obligations.

There had previously been uprisings by comparatively wealthy grape growers in the Rhine area. Now in Schleswig-Holstein foreclosures set off unrest among dairy farmers, and under the leadership of Claus Heim a radical *Landvolk* movement arose. Targets of its wrath included the banks, the cattle dealers, the tax collector, and the bailiff. It bombed public buildings and resisted foreclosure auctions. Its despair has been movingly described in Hans Fallada's novel *Peasants, Bosses, and Bombs.*

The middle classes, barely recovered from the shock of inflation, now faced the threat of bankruptcy. They searched desperately for some scheme that might insulate them from the danger, and the most popular one was the idea of *Stände*—estates or guilds, reminiscent of the all-too-pretty picture that German schoolteachers had painted of the medieval crafts system. They would have liked to abolish the cutthroat competition of big, capitalistic department stores and chain stores, along with usurers, trade unions, taxes, and lawyers. One-third of the middle class was threatened with "proletarianization."

By 1930 many unemployed, too, had lost their status as workers. They had used up their unemployment benefits; they had forgotten their skills; they had lost contact with their colleagues; they had lost hope of being hired back because their unemployment had become "structural," irreversible. Pitifully inadequate welfare rates were paid to those who permitted social workers to search their closets for valuables. Men went around the courtyards singing melancholy romances to get a few pennies dropped for them from tenants' windows—but that trade soon became competitive too.

The government offered neither hope nor policy. Instead of fighting unemployment, its factions fought over who should make the "sacrifices." For with three million unemployed to support, the compensation fund was empty. The Social-Democrats proposed to raise both the employers' and the workers' contribution from 3.5 to 4 percent; the People's Party proposed to decrease the benefits. Hilferding warned: "For the sake of 30 pfennigs, you place the Republic in jeopardy." But Müller, thinking of the next election, used the issue to resign (in March 1930) and allow the bourgeois parties to assume responsibility for the unpleasant decisions that had to be taken. He was playing politics as though this depression were not of an unprecedented nature.

The "crisis," as the depression was called in Germany, demanded bold economic innovations; but conventional wisdom considered belt tightening the proper remedy for hunger. The then-current prescription for depressions was that prices and wages had to fall until the inefficient producers were weeded out and the system found a new balance. The government, too, was expected to practice austerity—which of course cannot be done while parties resist sacrifices. Enemies of the republic used this impasse to unleash a campaign against those "interestmongers," and against the "parties' state" in general. Instead of facing the economic problem, the propaganda focused on "the bosses."

Despite the dismal Cuno experience, therefore, Heinrich Brüning was asked to form another nonpartisan—or "presidential"—cabinet. He belonged to the right wing of the Center Party and was a jesuitical type who passed for an enigma. The picture that emerges from his diaries is that of a narrow, subaltern mind that stood in awe of the old marshal and aimed to fulfill his restorative wishes. He had been introduced to Hindenburg by Kurt von Schleicher, a "political general" and a schemer who had become influential in the president's inner circle. He assembled a "Cabinet of Experts"— in fact a *Bürgerblock* government, with the president of the Land League acting as expert on agriculture and two directors of I. G. Farben acting as experts on finance and commerce.

The program of this "crisis administration" was austerity. Lacking a majority, however, the cabinet could impose the necessary economy measures only by emergency decree, using the president's powers under Article 48. Under the constitution the Reichstag could suspend such a decree. But when an ill-assorted majority of Social-Democrats, communists, and German-Nationalists did so, Brüning dissolved the

Reichstag. The framers of the constitution had certainly not meant to give the president the power to maintain laws rejected by the majority. Arthur Rosenberg, in his *History of the Weimar Republic*, suggests that the dissolution of the Reichstag was unconstitutional and the republican parties should have declared a state of revolution. By accepting Brüning's action they had, for all practical purposes, abdicated their power. This was precisely the crisis of parliamentary government: the parties left to the executive a responsibility they were loath to shoulder.

The election of September 14, 1930, came as a shock to all—not only because it gave the radicals a majority but because it focused the klieg lights on the crisis of the traditional parties and the pluralistic state. The Nazis polled 6.4 million votes, the communists 4.6—a gain of 7 million between them. The KPD gained roughly what the SPD lost; the Nazi gain was attributed to three components—they had won over, from the German-Nationalist and other middle-class parties, a million voters; they had won a large proportion of the young first voters; and they had mobilized two million people who had never voted before. Brüning's Center Party held, but his allies, the middle-class parties, were crushed; together they held only 205 seats. Hugenberg's own German-Nationalists were almost halved. When the 107 Nazis in brown shirts came marching into the Reichstag, everybody knew that a new age was upon Germany.

For the SPD, the election presented a problem of a new kind: with 77 communist, 69 Nationalist and allied, and 107 Nazi deputies to oppose him, Brüning had no majority if the Social-Democrats merely abstained; they had to support him positively, not just "tolerate" him, as they claimed they were doing for want of a policy.

Brüning used his precarious position cleverly. By threatening to yield to a new government that would include Nazis, he had the SPD over a barrel. Either they could refuse cooperation, and be responsible for ending parliamentary government for good; or they could give him their cooperation, and be responsible for the unpopular measures that he had to decree. His diary reflects the pleasure with which he followed the fascinating opportunities his electoral blunder had opened: he might create a bourgeois republic with a strong executive even without appearing to subvert the constitution; he could reduce the Social-Democrats to impotent flunkeys; he could reduce the power of the trade unions and restore the discipline of a former age. The communists mistakenly characterized his government as prefascist; it was strictly restorative and counterrevolutionary, but had none of the "populist" features of fascism and national socialism.

It had no appeal to the masses and did not even conduct its campaign against the reparations by means of emotional appeal. It merely pointed to the threatening stance of the Nazis when talking to Germany's creditors, just as it did when blackmailing the Social-Democrats.

Brüning was successful on one count. In June 1931 President Hoover announced a general moratorium on all international debts, and Germany has never paid a red pfennig since. The continued decline of all economic indices through 1932, therefore, cannot be laid to the reparations. But the nationalists continued to campaign against "Versailles" and Owen Young.

In need of a propaganda victory, Brüning announced in March 1931, without any diplomatic preparation, the plan of a customs union with Austria—which the Hague Court promptly declared illegal. It caused such displeasure among French bankers that they withdrew their money from Austria's Creditanstalt, which failed and pulled into its ruin the Darmstädter & Nationalbank in Berlin. Brüning had to declare a general bank holiday in July, or the crash would have become general. Even after this crisis, he continued to pursue his deflationary course, cutting civil service pay without, however, balancing the budget, ordering wage decreases without preventing massive failures of businesses, subsidizing farm prices without helping the farmers. In May 1932, when Brüning left, the unemployment figure was almost six million.

In *Fabian—The Story of a Moralist* (1931), Erich Kästner draws up an indictment of the capitalistic economy:

> The state subsidizes the big estates and heavy industry. Products are dumped on the world market but sold at monopoly prices here. . . . The entrepreneurs depress the wages and reduce purchasing power. The state taxes the little man but does not burden the rich. Capitalists send billions across the borders. . . . In America they burn wheat and coffee to keep the prices from falling. In France the peasants deplore the good harvest. Too much wheat and we have nothing to eat.

12

From Boom to Bust
Popular Culture in the 1920s

Das gibt's nur einmal,
Das kommt nicht wieder,
Das ist zu schön, um wahr zu sein. . . .

This happens once in a lifetime,
This will never come back again,
This is too lovely to be true. . . .

—Hit song

THE 1920S HAVE BEEN DUBBED "roaring" or "naughty" or "the jazz age" or "the age of Freud." Once the anxieties of war, revolution, and inflation were over, the new permissive morality remained and proclaimed itself as liberation. Its ambivalence toward lust and crime can best be documented in its hit songs, its detective stories, its B movies (and even some great ones), its popular dances.

Superficially, it was all fun. One had to catch up with the lost opportunities to enjoy life; one had a right to be uninhibited, a duty to get away from the straitlaced Wilhelminian and the uptight bourgeois conceptions of life. It had been proven scientifically, it had been revealed by philosophy, it was practiced by numerous sects which combined calisthenics with Oriental wisdom: western man must untie his knots, live by his instincts rather than by his head, say yes to his body.

A hundred years earlier, after the Napoleonic wars, the waltz had whirled society away from its worries; it was then considered lascivious and forward. The new dances that swept through Europe after World War I came from the United States, a country hardly touched by its horrors. The Hiawatha, the foxtrot, the Charleston—whose jagged, nervous gyrations contrasted so significantly with the sinuous, flowing rhythms of traditional dances—were eagerly taken up as expressions of defiance, or at least as extravaganza, as frolic or irony, as mocking the solemnity of the ball routine. Some people went further: wild parties and bohemian manners no longer were

139

confined to the low life on the fringes of society, but became something to boast about in good company. In fact, the pillars of society were seen at some of the slummiest affairs, and at least one nude party, occasioned by Josephine Baker's visit in Berlin, appears in the memoirs of several writers.

Eroticism was allowed to exhibit itself, literally, more naked than ever before. The Tiller girls danced topless in the Berlin *Admiralspalast*; Cecilia de Rheydt offered nude dances without much pretense that they were art. One hesitates to cite these goings-on as signs of "modernity," let alone "freedom." They were simply the reverse face of a commercial culture that has to provide more and different kicks every decade.

An analysis of popular music will show deterioration in the quality of the material, but no change of direction: we still find the old sentimentality. The great age of the operetta was over, as Franz Lehár, Emmerich Kálmán, and Leo Fall were no longer producing. But Künnecke's *Der Vetter aus Dingsda*, Paul Abraham's *Blume von Hawaii*, and Ralph Benatzky's *Im Weissen Rössl* ran to hundreds of performances. Some of the hit songs of the period have folksy tunes: *"Das ist die Liebe der Matrosen," "Ich hab mein Herz in Heidelberg verloren,"* and *"Es war einmal ein treuer Husar,"* are good examples of this kind, while others, like *"Valencia"* and *"Ramona,"* had more sophisticated, somewhat erotic tunes and stimulated people to invent pornographic parodies.

Some hit songs of the period reveal a totally alienated attitude toward sex. There is no more sighing after love, but only a record of fleeting affairs: *"Wer wird denn weinen, wenn man auseinandergeht, Wenn an der nächsten Ecke schon 'ne andre steht?"* ["Who's going to cry if we have to split up, since another is waiting at the next corner?"]. A witty Munich cabaret number exposed the desentimentalizing of love: "At Werther's time, when you wrote of love, you wrote with tears on blue parchment. . . . Now it's simply [sound of a typewriter clicking]: 'I am having a sale in love and invite you to bid.'" An old play by Arthur Schnitzler, *La Ronde*, which illustrates serial love, aroused a scandal; it seemed to sanction the fleeting encounters. (It had waited twenty years to be performed, and it exposed the loss of depth in modern relations between human beings.) Nowhere has this frivolous attitude been expressed with greater precision than in Joseph von Sternberg's *The Blue Angel*. Siegfried Kracauer, the first to write regular film reviews in Germany, felt that that film owed its popularity to Marlene Dietrich's raucous voice and to Lola Lola's callous dealings with people.

Berlin had become the vice capital, the Babylon of the world. Innocuous amusements overlapped into underworld entertainment. The Kurfürstendamm and Lunapark, the cafes and the public balls, the bars and pubs, brothels, transvestite balls, nude parties, cocaine pushers, and prostitutes might have confused a provincial visitor. "The Germans," Stefan Zweig wrote,

> brought to perversion all their thoroughness and love of system. Made-up boys with artificial waistlines promenaded along the Ku-Damm. . . . In darkened bars one could see high officials and bankers courting drunken sailors. . . . Amid a general collapse of values, insanity seized middle-class people who so far had been orderly and rigid. To be suspected of virginity would have been considered a disgrace in any Berlin girls' high school.

This is absurdly exaggerated, and one wonders in just what crowd Zweig moved; but it was true of some crowds. Heinrich Mann had described the same mores in Munich long before the war, and a hedonist like Isherwood never met the millions of Berliners who worked hard to make a living and had no money for the cabaret, or whose lives were absorbed by some movement (social, political, religious, educational, etc.).

Nor should we forget that for every one person who sang sophisticated, frivolous, satirical, blasphemous, or jeering lyrics, there were a hundred who melted in schmaltz. If this was the age of Marlene Dietrich, it also was the age of Richard Tauber, the tenor of romantic love, and of Hans Albers, the happy prince conquering girls' hearts. Most Berliners would not even have known where to find the providers of vice. Yet the image of Berlin in the 1920s was made by its dandies and promoters, by the shimmy-dancing gigolos, by the short-frocked, cigarette-smoking girls, by the movement for sexual freedom and reform of the family laws. Bertolt Brecht summed it all up in *The Rise and Fall of the City of Mahagonny*, where the actors taking their bows carried posters reading "For Chaos in the Cities, For the Venality of Love, For the Honor of Murderers, For the Immortality of Vileness."

In *Fabian* (1931), his deeply pessimistic, lacerating mirror of decadence, Erich Kästner says of Berlin: "In the east there is crime; in the center the con men hold sway; in the north resides misery, in the west lechery; and everywhere—the decline."

The works of Broch, Kästner, Hermann Kesten, even of Fallada and Heinrich Mann, are full of disgust and contempt. They flailed the decadent society and its literary, political, legal, educational defenders, its hypocrisy, its indifference and complacency, its self-seeking, lust-seeking, profit-seeking immorality. Whether these writers were deliberate critics of the world into which they were born—war, capitalism, inflation and depression, depravity and crime—or whether they just expressed the "stranger's nausea," they make us feel that Europe was in danger. They were all moralists who thought that a society that has suffered the twentieth century's depravity must be doomed, that a different society will supersede it. But before that day, these writers were having a great day of judgment, indicting not men and their institutions, but God himself, who allowed these abominations to happen.

Many people were unable to see either the fun or the protest in this, and protested against the protest, calling it "cultural bolshevism." What the critics of Weimar culture (and even some of its admirers) failed to understand was this ambiguity. The incomparable chanteuse Claire Waldoff in each of her songs conveyed that cheeky Berlin brat who enjoys herself thoroughly and yet sees through it all with a "So what?" The satirical Munich weekly *Simplicissimus* had a similar attitude.

The concept of "Weimar culture" implies both its profanities and their critics—e.g., the cabaret with its good-humored satire of German nature and mores or its biting attack on German politics; the political weeklies—*Die Weltbühne* and *Tagebuch*—with their muckraking analyses of the establishment in the arts, in industry, in the army, or wherever; the stage, bursting with new energies, new moods, with more critique, with foreign imports, with experiments bolder than anything before. "All of this," said Gottfried Benn, "put Berlin in a class with Paris. That overflow of excitement, these artistic and commercial improvisations, were largely owing to the [Jewish] sense of quality."

The poetry of the 1920s betrays a freshness and brashness, a cool cynicism which, however, reflects upon itself and mocks that which it seems to accept. It all bore a certain resemblance to the poetry that accompanied the great French revolution of the eighteenth century; as Nietzsche had foretold, the idols of classical certitude were falling, and Berlin's society was titillated by the sense of dancing on a volcano.

It may not be easy to disentangle the breakdown of traditional morality from the striving for a new morality, the promiscuity of the smart set from the sexual freedom the life reformers had in mind. The sacred and the profane, the frivolous and the sincere, the cynical and the authentic, may have dwelled close to each other. However, while what was said may be ambiguous, the change in institutions like church and marriage, or in people's allegiance to such institutions, points up a clear trend.

The Weimar scene—or, more exactly, the Berlin scene—was rich with career people of a new type: the intellectual adventurers, those who lived by their wits without having specific skills and training. They might be entertainers, social thinkers, planners, politicians, managers in the new industries, culture tycoons, educators, consciousness raisers, prophets of new sciences or sects, liberators from sexual or other oppression, promoters—in brief, men and women whose rapid rise was achieved by relating to other people and whose real contribution was measured by the judgment of their peers. They were intimately related to the old bohemia, whose tastes they propagated and whose life-style they imitated, though considerably better heeled. They traveled internationally, and they picked up cultural trends. This highly mobile group adopted every new fashion, provided it was shocking; it considered mobility, newness, and progress the essence of living and would do anything to be "modern."

There was still a good deal to be liberated from. The pioneering works on sexology had been written before the war; slowly now their findings were being dispersed—first among the artists and theater people, then among the more sophisticated strata of the liberal upper classes, then in the education departments of labor organizations, and last but not least through the youth movement. The public's attitudes grew more relaxed. Unmarried couples were tolerated, "marriages of conscience" were respected in the more advanced circles of the bourgeoisie. Divorce, though still considered a misfortune, was no longer considered a disgrace. But the actual number of divorces rose only slowly, and the courts tried to make them difficult.

Sex education and sex clinics became available in the big cities. Books about birth control, the sexual plight of young people, "the biological tragedy of woman," homosexuality, and similar topics were freely sold in bookstores. Two murder cases, one involving lesbians, the other a male homosexual student, were widely discussed in the papers and opened the way to a more sympathetic understanding of the issue.

The left parties fought valiantly to abolish Articles 218 and 175 of the criminal code banning, respectively, abortion and homosexuality. Dr. Magnus Hirschfeld, a professed homosexual, headed an "Institute for Sex Research" in Berlin (which used to be cited as an example of the capital's moral decline). Friedrich Wolf, the communist playwright, staged a moving tragedy about Article 218, and a best-selling book proclaimed that *My Body Belongs to Me*—all to no avail. Birth control was still the privilege of the rich, while thousands of poor women died of nonprofessionally induced abortions.

Although one-third of the labor force was female, women were rarely seen in leading positions. By now, they were 15 percent of the university enrollment; a few were in the Reichstag; and Gertrud Bäumer, a Democrat, was *Ministerialrat* (assistant secretary) in the Department of Welfare. But for most women, careers were not a matter of choice or of pride, nor were they remunerated equally for comparable work where they competed with men. They tended to go back to the home as soon as their husbands earned enough for both. Bourgeois homes had sleep-in maids, which, it was felt, made it all the more necessary for the wife to be at home.

Even so, the new woman strove to be companion rather than matron. The ideal of beauty changed abruptly and reflected the changing status of women vis-à-vis men and the family. Instead of the old hourglass figure, the lean, boyish figure of the gamin was envied and imitated; those who did not have it tried by doing Mensendieck (a famous calisthenics school) exercises to get it. What had been considered feminine was denied; corsets and falsies were discarded. The "natural look," of course, favored youth over maturity and looks over wealth. Such was the temper of the democratic age: let every girl compete!

The fashion revolution announced the emancipation of women. They cut their hair, they used makeup, they smoked, and they raised the hemline—to the ankle first, then to the calf, and finally to the knee. For a long time, bobbed hair and makeup were frowned upon by employers as distractions to male colleagues.

The new look reached the working girls last. It had begun in bohemia and was spread by society ladies; salesgirls then rushed into the act, showing more and more leg clad in the new, beautiful rayon stocking. If this was emancipation, men liked it, too.

The men, meanwhile, shed the patriarchal handlebar mustache and tried to look rakish, boyish, sporty, adventurous, or intellectual, with horn-rimmed glasses and hair brushed back instead of parted. The starched collar was replaced by the soft collar or, among workers, the turndown collar. Here, too, a suggestion of nonconformity was a sign of being modern. But the breeches, knickerbockers, trench coats, and similar nonbourgeois vestments of the early 1920s later yielded to the more traditional business suit—though vests did not return and stoutness was never again viewed as proof of prosperity or respectability.

In the middle 1920s, some domesticity reappeared in women's fashions. Tight-fitting skirts once again emphasized the repressed female curves; high-heeled shoes in which she could not run after a bus suggested woman's frailty. Fashion designers treated women like dolls again; having once stressed equality, they now created evening dresses with plunging necklines for high society—a style the office girl could not afford and also found impractical. Ironically, fashion seemed deliberately to deny the depression which threatened the middle-class family and made such luxury doubly expensive.

The emancipation of women had not gone very far, and it had been creeping rather than demonstrative. When Hitler took over and the Nazis established an all-out men's society, women apparently were not losing enough to voice resentment. It is noteworthy that more women than men voted for the parties of the "national revolution."

Youth, on the contrary, took its emancipation seriously. Both the youth and school-reform movements were based on the premise of self-education; both recognized youth as a stage of human life in its own right, not mere preparation for maturity. Learning was to proceed *vom Kinde aus* ("from the child's potentials"), and the life of young people was to be shaped by peer groups under their own responsibility.

But neither the school-reform nor the youth movement changed the power structure in society or in education. The authoritarian "learning school" remained untouched; some attitudes within it, however, changed. High school students were allowed to debate, to have opinions. Learning was made easier by new materials and methods. In a few cities where socialist mayors worked with democratic educators, high schools for workers' children or "add-on" schools for graduates of the "people's school" provided new avenues to university studies. "Gangway for Talent!" was the SPD's slogan; in practice it was a device to co-opt talent into the elite. Though school tuition was nominal on all levels, education was not democratic even under the republic. Adult education and the efforts of the KPD, SPD, and trade unions to provide higher education for their members did not lead to any certificates or degrees.

The youth movement continued to play out the father-son conflict of the Wilhelminian era. It strove for a new style in living, a new community, and a new authenticity; although it did not have the word "alienation" yet, it struggled against its reality in its own stammering language. It wished to restore man's wholeness to him. But in trying to do so, it left out a good deal of recent human experience. It worshiped nature, the Gothic Middle Ages, and Romantic poetry. It went back to the folkloristic sources of art and reintroduced forgotten crafts. It read Hermann Hesse, Stefan George, and Rainer Maria Rilke, but also sentimental Romanticists like Waldemar Bonsels. And finally, it read Julius Langbehn and Paul de Lagarde, Hans Grimm's *Volke ohne Raum* and Ernst Jünger's frontline experiences. It was patriotic, full of idealistic devotion, ready to die for a community—and hence became an easy prey for nationalistic seducers who were expressing similar nostalgias.

Nudism was another way of defying the establishment. It was popular with the youth movement and among socialist and anarchist sects, but for many it was a cult in its own right. Related movements in calisthenics, in music, and in dance claimed to liberate the body from the strictures of the industrial-capitalist society. As frequently happens with cults and fads, practice did not always guarantee what theory promised; but these clubs or schools kept a Platonic ideal of total man before the public eye. Dance was not conceived as entertainment but as fulfillment of human spirituality. All life-reform movements were interested in calisthenics, eugenics, and environmental protection as necessary for renovating the human condition.

Traditional gymnastics and sports were less ambitious and well within the framework of industrial society—in fact, were its health-promoting complement. Participatory sports had wide appeal and were officially encouraged to make up for the lack of universal military training (banned by the Treaty of Versailles). That does not account, however, for the proliferation of athletic and sports leagues and for the millions who practiced every day. Competitive games were the most democratic of all pastimes, and the forty-four-hour week made it possible for many to devote care and time to their leisure occupation. Leisure and pleasure came to be regarded as every citizen's inalienable right. The philosophy of *Homo faber* (man the maker) was attacked simultaneously by the Roman Catholic theologian Romano Guardini at Berlin University, the anthropologist Leo Frobenius at Frankfurt, and the Dutch art historian Johan Huizinga in his *Homo ludens* (playful man). The idea that man is most himself when playing came down from Friedrich Schiller, the classical playwright and idealist thinker, and it was eventually taught to high-school seniors.

However, Germans would never equate leisure with idleness. Twentieth-century sports were hard work—truly the mirror image of industrial society. One fought for prizes and records; one admired the champions. Crowds were beside themselves when they saw a real hero's feat: Lindbergh crossing the Atlantic in a nonstop solo flight; Gertrude Ederle swimming the English Channel; Nobile in his dirigible flying over the North Pole; the Zeppelin's trip across the Atlantic; the attempts to climb Mount Everest.

It has been charged that our age surrendered the soul of man to the idols of machinery. Yet it reserved its most enthusiastic moments for the test of man against machine, or for man as master of the machine—the air pilot "riding" the storm; Professor Auguste Piccard ascending to the stratosphere or diving to unbelievable depths. Like centaurs, brave men were riding fast motorcycles, automobiles, and airplanes as though they had become one with their machines. This was the spirit of the age as it understood itself.

In spite of all their conflicts, westerners had in common the striving for the impossible, the obsession with man's ability to overcome the limitations of his physical nature. This is what people understood and what they were proud of.

Yet the masses took part in these conquests only vicariously. Worse, spectator sports and sensational reporting more and more took the place of actual participation in sports activities. Spectator sports certainly were the one "activity" most characteristic of the period that interested practically the whole nation. Watching the championship fight between Max Schmeling and Jack Sharkey or hearing it reported over the radio point by point, seeing the amazing Paavo Nurmi run away from a field of competitors, rooting for the favorite soccer team, following the six-day bicycle race—these were the leisure-time occupations of blue-collar workers. Automobile races provided excitement for all ages and classes. The winners in these contests were far better known than Einstein and Thomas Mann; their pictures hung over every boy's bed, and their names emerged at the top of the list when pollsters asked people to name their idols or their role models.

Movie actors and actresses also appeared on such lists; for obviously, the movies were the second most important entertainment. The average young couple might have seen a dozen pictures a year, or perhaps ten films and a popular operetta or revue. Most of these shows were low comedy, adventure, Wild West, schmaltzy love stories of the *Student Prince* variety, sensational peephole scenarios with titles like *The Maharaja's Favorite Wife*, Sad Sack or Sergeant Bilko–type barracks humor, and patriotic gore like the sequence of ten films about Frederick the Great directed by Czerépy (most German filmmakers came from Vienna or Budapest). If pageantry and schmaltz could be combined, as in Eric Charell's *The Congress*

TITLES THAT HAVE MADE HISTORY

1918
Spengler, *The Decline of the West*
Karl Barth, *The Letter to the Romans*

1919
Hofmannsthal, *Die Frau ohne Schatten* (libretto to Strauss opera)
Hesse, *Demian*
Ernst Bloch, *Spirit of Utopia*

1920
Pinthus, *Twilight of Mankind*
Kafka, *The Castle*
Kaiser, *Gas* (part 2)
Werfel, *Not the Murderer*

1921
Toller, *Man and the Masses*

1922
Hofmannsthal, *Das grosse Salzburger Welttheater*
Kraus, *The Last Days of Mankind*
Brecht, *Drums in the Night*
Thomas Mann, *The Confessions of Felix Krull, Confidence Man* (first version)

1923
Rilke, *Duiniso Elegies*

1924
Thomas Mann, *The Magic Mountain*

1925
Kafka, *The Trial*
Brecht, *A Man's a Man*
Hofmannsthal, *The Tower*
Zuckmayer, *The Merry Vineyard*
Heinrich Mann, *The Chief*

1926
Hans Grimm, *Volk ohne Raum*
Hendrik de Man, *Psychology of Socialism*

1927
Brecht, *Manual of Piety*
Hesse, *Steppenwolf*
Heidegger, *Being and Time*
Arnold Zweig, *The Case of Sergeant Grischa*

1928
Wassermann, *The Maurizius Case*
Hauptmann, *Till Eulenspiegel*
Stefan George, *The New Reich*
Brecht, *Three-Penny Opera*
Ernst Glaeser, *Jahrgang 1902*

1929
Karl Mannheim, *Ideology and Utopia*
Remarque, *All Quiet on the Western Front*
Döblin, *Berlin Alexanderplatz*
Ferdinand Bruckner, *Illness of Youth*
Werfel, *Barbara*
Friedrich Wolf, *Cyankali*

1930
Musil, *The Man Without Qualities*
Brecht, *The Measure Taken*
Lion Feuchtwanger, *Success*
Zuckmayer, *The Captain from Köpenick*

1931
Hermann Broch, *The Sleepwalkers*
Erich Kästner, *Fabian*
Karl Jaspers, *Man in the Modern Age*

1932
Hauptmann, *Before Sunset*
Ernst Junger, *The Worker*
Fallada, *Little Man, What Now?*
Joseph Roth, *Radetzky March*
Karl Jaspers, *The Contemporary Condition of Mind*

1934
Thomas Mann, *Joseph and His Brothers*

Dances, so much the better.

Ernst Lubitsch had started the German film on its career of great tableaux, where history was seen from the boudoir and the camera was allowed to show the world from stunning, bold perspectives. He directed *Madame Dubarry, Anna Boleyn*, and *The Loves of Pharoah*. Lavish decorations and cruel, almost sadistic characterizations assured him of a big box office; but he certainly did not explore (nor did he mean to) the nature of tyranny or history in any depth. He used an ultrarealistic technique and, for the first time, a mobile camera which totally transformed the screen's image of reality.

More serious attacks on tyranny were intended in Carl Mayer's *The Cabinet of Dr. Caligari*, Paul Leni's *Waxworks*, and Friedrich Wilhelm Murnau's *Nosferatu*. They all represent power as mad—but somehow uncontrollable, mystical. The style is expressionistic, the terror of the irrational brought home in the ghostly scenery.

Turning away from expressionism, Murnau directed (from Mayer's scenario) the most famous and perhaps the best of all silent films; *The Last Laugh*, with Emil Jannings as a liveried doorman who has been demoted to men's-room attendant. Murnau tried to give his films a Joycean quality of inner dialogue, a haunting subjectivity of perception.

Fritz Lang, too, started his career with dream and horror films; *Dr. Mabuse, the Gambler* was the high point of his incantations. Then he turned to the saga of the *Nibelungen* and built it into a heroic epic for the German people (school classes were taken to see it). Expressionism here had an aftermath of stylized, symbolical sequences. The scenario was written by Lang's wife, Thea von Harbou, long associated with nationalistic causes. *Metropolis*, a giant production conceived by the couple and superbly staged, showed men enslaved by the machine age. There were gripping scenes of mass rebellion and anguish, and a silly, corny fantasy of salvation through love. The final conciliation of the tycoon with the workers was not seen at the time in the perspective of the fascist and technocratic analogies that strike the viewer today.

In a sequel, *The Last Will of Dr. Mabuse*, Lang claims to have made a deliberate statement against Nazi terrorism. But Kracauer wrote: "Lang is so concerned with highlighting the magic spell [or power] that his film mirrors [its] demonic irresistibility rather than the moral superiority of its opponents." In his first talking film, *M*, Lang was also obsessed with an uncontrollable power—one that drives a man to child murder. The monster is a petit bourgeois, a meek person except in his moments of attack. The underworld is seen, as in Brecht's *Three-Penny Opera*, as a replica of bourgeois society.

As Carl Mayer was characteristic of early expressionism, and Fritz Lang brought out the romanticism of the middle of the decade, so Georg W. Pabst represents the new objectivity of the late twenties. He said: "What good is romanticism today? Life itself is romantic enough—or ghastly for that matter." *The Joyless Street* shows with pitiless honesty the ruin of the Viennese middle class and of its moral values. The film, which brought together Greta Garbo and Werner Krauss, was banned in England. In his next film, *Secrets of a Soul*, Pabst followed the psychoanalysis of a man who has been drawn to murder. *The Love of Jeanne Ney*, based on a story by Ilya Ehrenburg, introduced a Russian commissar as a human being. In these three films, Pabst used his incorruptible eye to reveal the truth about people and things, but seemed much less interested in plot and lesson. However, he also made two moving films in a realistic style which served the ideas of pacifism and international solidarity: *Westfront 1918* and *Comradeship*. Later, though, he served Hitler.

The best-known German film, *The Blue Angel*, was based on Heinrich Mann's novel *Small-Town Tyrant*, a cutting indictment of bourgeois hypocrisy. Joseph von Sternberg transformed it into a story of cruelty and pitiful humiliation. Mann protested at first, but perhaps Sternberg was right: the age no longer wanted left-wing analysis of tyranny, but indulgence in its manifestations.

The program notes for *Dr. Mabuse the Gambler* said: "Mankind, swept about and trampled down in the wake of war and revolution, takes revenge for years of anguish by indulging in lusts . . . and by passively or actively surrendering to crime." This urge accounted for the immense popularity of detective stories and films. What had been "penny dreadfuls" to the previous generation became a more or less sophisticated genre of literature. The English practitioners of this trade were far more skillful: Sir Arthur Conan Doyle, Edgar Wallace, and Agatha Christie outsold any German author. The action in German thrillers usually took place in London or New York; in a few cases the detective story carried a left-wing message.

The detective story not only tells us that crime does not pay; it also shows that it has its satisfactions. More and more, during the 1920s and early 1930s, interest switched from the upholder of public order to the criminal. The policeman often is shown to be stupid, venal, and overly assiduous, while the detective is a loner and a gentleman. The criminals are no longer the scum of the earth but gamblers, gentleman blackmailers, almost heroes. In a true story that became famous, two underworld brothers foiled all efforts of the police to obtain a confession—and soon were so popular that the plot was used in a film and in cabaret skits. Two best-sellers, Jakob Wassermann's *The Maurizius Case* and Franz Werfel's *Not the Murderer but the Victim Is Guilty*, dealt with the ambiguity of justice and morality. So of course did Brecht's *Three-Penny Opera.*

Inadvertently rather than by design, a film often shows the motives, the problems, the way of looking at the world that may be characteristic of an age. German films of the 1920s testified to the perplexedness of the little man in a world full of cruelty and ambiguousness, a world where rationality itself had been put into the service of irrationality, a world of conflicting forces and uncertain allegiances. Even where the little man was the protagonist, as in Heinrich Zille's drawings of Berlin's workingmen or in his film *Mother Krause's Journey into Happiness,* in Brecht's film *Kuhle Wampe* or in Alfred Döblin's novel and film *Berlin Alexanderplatz,* he was still bewildered. The world of his fathers had enjoyed the certitude of knowing what was up and what was down, what was good and what was bad. That was not so clear any longer—since the revolution, since Freud and Einstein and all that.

Without knowing much about relativity and psychoanalysis, everyone used words like "relative" and "subconscious" and wise-cracked about them. Of course it was not Freud's fault that he was misunderstood, and that people deliberately overlooked his warning against irrationality. They overlooked his consideration that those dark drives were dangerous and his anxiousness to preserve that "thin crust of civilization" that saves us from chaos.

But chaos was precisely the experience of the age. Its great writers tried to face it honestly; its popular culture tried to deny it or to gloss over it, to flee from it, to abandon itself to it. Weimar culture was the heroic attempt to cover and sublimate, to acknowledge and glorify it. As Freud has explained, humor minimizes a danger, devalues that which is too precious, debunks tragedy. Denizens of the 1920s had a lot to be humorous about. Satirical magazines flourished and folded; so did the political cabaret. The world was crumbling; but the Berlin smart aleck still knew how to quip about it. The Nazi salute of the raised arm was interpreted as meaning: this is how high the mud has risen.

13

The Periclean Age of Europe

Jede dumpfe Umkehr hat solche Enterbte,
denen das Frühere nicht,
noch nicht das Nächste gehört.

In time of change
Some are left disinherited.
They do not belong to the past,
But not to the future either.

—Rainer Maria Rilke

MORE THAN ANY OTHER PERIOD, the 1920s was a time of transition, experiment, and debate. More than any other country, Germany seethed with innovation and variety: the expressionist painters in Munich and Düsseldorf; the Bauhaus in Weimar—later in Dessau— whose functional style has been called the hallmark of Weimar culture and has made it internationally famous; the dance school in Dresden-Hellerau, pioneering in modern expression as against the formalism of traditional ballet; the State Theater in Berlin under Leopold Jessner's direction, introducing rebellious plays by young authors and staging classical drama in startling, media-oriented interpretations; the National Gallery, exhibiting modern painters; the *Hochschule für Politik* in Berlin, the first to give a degree in the political sciences; and the social sciences faculty in Frankfurt, the first to pierce the rigid four-faculties scheme of the German university.

To these public institutions one might add many private circles with special purposes: the Psychoanalytical Institute in Berlin; the Warburg Library in Hamburg; the informal but closely ruled circle of Stefan George, forging the leadership of a "secret Germany." Erwin Piscator imaginatively directed plays of social significance. The Comedians' Cabaret was a constant gadfly to republican politics and middle-class inanity.

Many magazines built up a community of readers. Herwarth Walden's *Der Sturm* published expressionistic poetry. Franz Pfempfert's *Die Aktion* was avant-garde and anarchist. Every week a faithful constituency eagerly awaited *Die Fackel*, written, edited, and published by *Totae Germaniae Praeceptor*, Karl Kraus. There were the great taste-setting publishing houses, S. Fischer, Insel-Verlag, Rowohlt; and the galleries, Cassirer, Flechtheim. There was also the Kant Society and, on the other side of the philosophical spectrum, the offshoot of Moritz Schlick's Positivist Circle in Vienna: the Society for Scientific Philosophy. Social reformers gathered around the magazine *Die Hilfe*, life reformers around *Die Tat*. There were the Rosicrucians and the Anthroposophical Society; the Institute for Social Research in Frankfurt, developing Marxist theory (and, vulgarizing it, the Marxist Workers' School, run by the Communist Party); the Internal Mission and various Catholic institutions, such as the Görres Society. These circles did not communicate with each other but merely listened to their own lectures in their various coffeehouses or academic meeting places. What united them all was the conviction that intellectual issues mattered and that their private or public debates were essential to the life of the nation.

Deprived of participation in the big-power game, Germans found their national redemption in cultural achievement; and they might well be proud of their contributions to the arts and sciences of Europe. Gerhart Hauptmann—for all practical purposes the poet laureate of the republic—and Thomas Mann received Nobel Prizes in literature; Albert Einstein, Werner Heisenberg, James Franck, Gustav Hertz, Max Planck, and Erwin Schrödinger in physics; Walther Nernst, Fritz Haber, Wilhelm Ostwald, Adolf von Baeyer, and Carl Bosch in chemistry; Paul Ehrlich and Albrecht Kossel in medicine. There were also state prizes and state academies to honor the nation's spiritual leaders.

One might speak of an intellectual establishment; but it was an odd assortment. A photo of the Academy of Writers shows two poets of the prewar generation—Theodor Däubler and Alfred Mombert— each represented in modern anthologies by one entry; ditto Max Halbe and Ludwig Fulda, two older novelists who even then had hardly any readers left. On the left and modern side the academy included the worker-poet Oskar Loerke and the expressionist radicals: Alfred Döblin (*Berlin Alexanderplatz*), Georg Kaiser (*Gas*), and Fritz von Unruh (*Ein Geschlecht*). Also on the left were Heinrich Mann, Hermann Hesse, René Schickele (*The Rhineland Heritage*), and Leonhard Frank.

In the center were the solid and safe middle-of-the-roaders: Thomas Mann, Ricarda Huch, Jakob Wassermann (*The Goose Man*), and a then-popular novelist who has dropped out of survey textbooks,

Bernhard Kellermann. Likewise forgotten are a very patriotic writer of historical pageants, Walter von Molo, and two other conservatives, Wilhelm von Scholz and Eduard Stucken.

All in all, it was a truly "broad coalition," from which were absent only a very few of those who are still well known: Stefan George and Gottfried Benn. But at that time, the right might have asked for the inclusion of Hans Carossa, Ernst Wiechert, Rudolf Binding (*Ein Opfergang*), or Hermann Stehr. Brecht and Klabund were too young. The circle of immortals would certainly have been larger, had natives of the Danube monarchy been eligible. Of the older generation were Arthur Schnitzler and Stefan and Arnold Zweig; then Rilke and Kafka, Franz Werfel, Robert Musil, Hermann Broch, and, above all, Hugo von Hofmannsthal, who wrote librettos for Richard Strauss—to name only those who are still well remembered. They are all part of a history of German letters.

The cultural life of the Weimar years was not confined to the borders of the German language; its interests were cosmopolitan in scope. The drama was still under the impact of Ibsen and Strindberg; Pirandello, Gorki, Čapek, and Shaw were performed in many cities. The old and new Russian authors were avidly read; Dostoevsky had just been translated by Moeller van den Bruck (the author of *The Third Reich*). Every new volume of *The Forsyte Saga* was a literary event in Germany. *Die Neue Rundschau,* the prestigious magazine of the S. Fischer publishing house, exchanged contributions with *La Nouvelle Revue Française*. François Mauriac, Paul Valéry, Romain Rolland, Anatole France, and André Gide were well known.

America was represented by Upton Sinclair and Sinclair Lewis, then Hemingway. Rabindranath Tagore made a triumphant tour through Germany; Buddhism and Hinduism were studied; Hesse and Waldemar Bonsels set their stories in India. Döblin had written *The Three Leaps of Wang-lun*; Brecht, too, liked India or China as scenes of action. Weimar's problems were indeed those of Europe and the world; its literature was part of worldwide trends. Vice versa, Berlin was a center which stimulated many intellectual movements abroad. Stephen Spender, W. H. Auden, and Christopher Isherwood lived there for a while. So did Vladimir Nabokov and Eugene Zamyatin, author of the first counter-Utopia. Germany gave refuge to the victims of persecution, and its cultural life benefited greatly from its generosity. Thus, Karl Mannheim and Georg Lukács introduced the sociology of knowledge; László Moholy-Nagy taught at the Bauhaus.

As usual, many celebrities of the period are now forgotten, and

some who were then known only to a few became famous posthumously. Much of what belonged to Weimar culture was neither
specific to it nor even original. Most of its achievements were
founded on developments that had begun before the 1920s, and much
that was tried during the 1920s did not survive. The same is true
of the sciences; the 1920s produced few breakthroughs that matched
Planck's quantum, Einstein's relativity principle, or Freud's descent
into the subconscious. And yet what had been just a seed with an
uncertain potential now showed its full stature and significance.

The mere process of dispersion was bound to change the new
insights. Expressionism spread from painting and poetry to the film.
Philosophers and theologians found it necessary to point out the
implications of relativity and of psychoanalysis. The new thinking
about space and time—abandoning the concept of an absolute space
and an absolute time—had a profound, revolutionary effect on the
understanding of history and confirmed the purposes of the expressionists.

The public gradually accepted and digested the new views as
elements of a general change in attitudes toward reality, and in
the process the new views changed their physiognomy, too. Freud
himself found new uses for psychoanalysis in *The Future of an Illusion*
and *Civilization and Its Discontents*, and his followers studied its
implications in art history and related fields. Einstein developed
the general theory of relativity and the general field theory. Schrödinger
worked out wave mechanics. Heisenberg established the indeterminacy
relationships which permit a link of the old Newtonian with the
new nuclear physics. Philipp Frank spelled out the meaning of causality
and determinism in light of the newest discoveries.

Certainly it was not easy to accept as "truth" theories that were
at odds with common sense and appearances, or to integrate them
into any of the prevailing views. How should the layman understand
that light could be explained as waves or as corpuscles, depending
on the particular occasion, and yet that both aspects were mere poetic
similes anyway? Or that Newton's laws were all right for the realm
of his everyday experience but had to be modified for very large
and very small bodies? Or that matter was not of this or that nature,
which the scientists had been debating for two thousand years, but
an intellectual construct that needed constant reconfirmation and
redefinition? When the Max Planck Institute in Berlin was once closed
for repairs, a wit attached a note to its door, reading: "Beware of
falling matter! Temporarily closed for radical alterations." Once-solid
matter had become "a convention about something that is not there."

To cope with all the conflicting theories, Einstein in 1929 offered a "general field theory"; until the end of his life he tried to find means of saving the notion of causality and of restoring to physics the certainty it had enjoyed in its classical period. He could not bear a disorderly universe; he was convinced that "God does not throw dice." But among his colleagues he remained a minority of one. They abandoned the unified world view with an astonishing lack of regret.

Classical physics had gone, with its optimistic belief that the true secret of nature can be known—if not by man, then by God. Rejecting all "metaphysical" assumptions, twentieth-century science found itself without eternal principles that might give its endeavors the foundation of certainty. If a theory was to be considered a "policy" rather than a truth, if a law was a pattern of behavior rather than a directive ordained by the Creator, then no imposing systems of science, no great structures of philosophy could be built on such moving ground. Philosophy was no longer the mother of all sciences but a catalogue of heuristic procedures. Each science was free to develop its own methodology and logic. The unity of man and world was in doubt if the unity of the sciences could no longer be taken for granted.

In his inaugural thesis, therefore, Theodor W. Adorno questioned the ability of philosophy to answer the cardinal questions of philosophy, and Max Horkheimer (both authors were the leading minds of the Frankfurt School for Social Research) asserted that the previously assumed harmony between reality and reason had been broken—or, rather, differing philosophical schools had been forced to deal with one aspect of reality and sacrifice the other. The neo-Kantians had emphasized the formal aspect; vitalism had renounced any claim to making sense out of empirical reality; positivism had accepted the reality without giving the human mind any power to derive an ethics from knowledge. Nikolai Hartmann and Max Scheler tried to reconstruct a system of material values, though on rather shaky ground. The solution that phenomenology and, after it, existentialism offered, was really a pseudosolution; for, as Karl Jaspers said: "Genuine philosophy is the questioning appeal for man to come to himself; it exists only where someone strives for it. . . . But it must remain without object and therefore without result. Clarity of consciousness implies the claim but does not bring fulfillment."

It was a situation of crisis that was thus characterized: not uncertainty about any special results of scientific investigation, but doubt about fundamental assumptions, about the proper approach to questions of value and of ethical behavior. The situation brought forth new attempts to define the problem of man's existence and gave the intellectual life of the republic a flavor of Enlightenment. At no other time has the old been rejected so lightly for no other reason but that it was old, or the new been accepted on the ground that it lacked age. Nowhere else has the outcry of man's impotence been cheered so loudly as an achievement, or has rebellion been hailed as salvation itself. What was problematical was declared profound; the unfinished was admired as perfect, while perfection was suspect. No certainty was left unquestioned, no doubt unuttered.

The generation that came out of the Great War had fallen into the habit of distrusting authorities and traditions. It had survived by breaking most rules of civilized behavior, and it found most ideologies unhelpful in finding a new compass. The grand ideas of the previous age were dead—mere metaphors, said the expressionist writer Carl Sternheim. "No more worlds to experience, no more realities to feel, no more truths to believe," complained the poet Gottfried Benn. Hermann Bahr, a critic and novelist, put it this way: "Never has man been so shaken by anxiety and horror. Never was the world so silent, man so small, or freedom so dead. Need cries out into the darkness. Art, too, cries out into the darkness. That is expressionism." Such stammering confessions were echoed a thousandfold in the distressed pages of Kafka and the early Döblin, or in the anguished canvases of Paul Klee, Max Beckmann, and Max Ernst.

The certainties of the prewar era lay in ruins. But why complain? These were precisely the fortresses against which this generation had rebelled: family, career, academic aesthetics, and bourgeois life-styles. Now it had been liberated and was searching for a different order. This was the basic problem of a republican order which was not yet and was never to be, the culture of the Weimar Republic. On the contrary: the intellectual community, artists, thinkers, scientists, scholars, and a large part of the educated public were in opposition to social and political reality. The word "alienation" had just been introduced into the debate by the neo-Kantian philosopher Emil Lask, whence it migrated into the neo-Marxist literature. But the condition it describes had been known under various names. Max Weber had spoken of the world "losing its magic" (*Entzauberung*), and he put special stress on two symptoms: the bureaucratization in both state and business, and the subjection of all human action to the standard of "purposeful rationality" (*Zweckrationalität*).

This "discontent of civilization" manifested itself in neoromantic poetry or in expressionistic protest, in the yearning for "wholeness" or in the desire to smash everything that seemed whole, in the father-son plays that pervade German literature or in the cult of barbarism, in the call to return to the old values of blood and soil or in the urgent drive to create new gods. "Moribund is that nation whose gods die," said Stefan George. "War on metaphors!" said Sternheim. Ernst Bloch published *Spirit of Utopia*. Historians and ballad composers celebrated the great iconoclasts and outlaws of German history: Thomas Münzer, John Huss, Erasmus, Schinderhannes. The State Theater staged Schiller's *Brigands*; Max Reinhardt deployed rebel masses of peasants and sansculottes in Goethe's *Götz von Berlichingen* and Georg Büchner's *Dantons Tod*. Peter Martin Lampel wrote *Revolt in the Reform School*. The time was out of joint; poets, ascetics, beggars, and thieves felt they had been born to set it right. Ludwig Rubiner, who was one of them, wrote in *Die Aktion*: "Our comrades are prostitutes, poets, pimps, collectors of lost items, occasional thieves, do-nothings, couples embracing, the religious demented, drunkards, unemployed. . . . We are the rejects, the dregs of society, the despised, the shirkers."

The cast of Brecht's *Three-Penny Opera* includes only lumpen, no real proletarian. The youth movement, in its own songs, extolled the highwaymen and mercenaries of the Thirty Years War. The cabaret, too, impersonated marginal people who loved to live off the bourgeois, to rip off, to defy or destroy middle-class society or to laugh at its destruction. Arnolt Bronnen made a point of exhibiting sexual cruelty, cynicism, and insensitivity; Hanns Johst warned that humanism would destroy the soul; Ernst Jünger confessed to a certain lust in seeing the spirit destroying itself.

In its beginning, expressionism was not political. Its fleeting alliance with the November Revolution was based on an illusion which was soon disabused; its flirtation with communism ended in disaster. Georg Kaiser, who often sounds "left," really thought that poetry can be a counterreality, freeing man from a world that makes no sense. Ernst Barlach, the sculptor, wrote plays of medieval piety in opposition to the greed and selfishness around him. Poetic integrity was considered the enemy of bourgeois stupidity and insensitivity. Hence the gestures of defiance and carelessness, the shows of contempt, the ecstasies of style and expression which pass for authenticity in the face of hypocrisy. "Style is superior to truth," said Gottfried Benn. For the expressionists were not united by any idea of truth; they were confident that their language would cut through the false reality of everyday routines and reach out toward the "new man." Kurt Pinthus published the famous anthology *Twilight of Mankind*, with contributions by all the young poets of the war decade:

Georg Trakl and Georg Heym, the mystic Else Lasker-Schüler, Rubiner, the ecstatics Yvan Goll and Johannes R. Becher, the nihilistic Gottfried Benn, the sweet, melodic Franz Werfel, the desperate Walter Hasenclever, and, of the prewar generation, Theodor Däubler.

Later, the new writing was often referred to as an "*O Mensch* poetry"; but at the time it meant the commitment to give birth to the "new humanity." It is true that these poets often confused their new style with the revolution, and that no two of them saw the revolution in the same way. But they all agreed that new energies were bursting forth, and that they were the messengers of liberating forces. "If, man, you decide to be good, you will give birth to a new earth," said Max Brod, Kafka's friend and editor. Pinthus had four words as an epigraph to his anthology: "Man, Brother, World, God."

Expressionist poets found it difficult to maintain the pitch when they saw that the revolution had failed. Goll, Heinrich Mann, Döblin and others have indeed accused the Weimar politicians of having betrayed poetry. The poets lost their audience. Only those who changed their style and dealt with postrevolutionary problems gained a more enduring fame: Döblin, Werfel, Brecht. Those who tried to maintain a more anarchic stance lost themselves in the irrelevancies of Dada and surrealism.

Strangely enough, the situation was quite different for the expressionist painters. Many of them became famous *as* expressionists; their canvases were bought by the National Gallery. They did not have to change, and they went on to paint easily recognizable Noldes, Beckmanns, Pechsteins, Klees, Kandinskys, etc. It must be admitted that some of them grew repetitious and empty or formalistic. Surrealism gave a new direction to Klee's black humor and to Ernst's powerful imagination: they projected the horrors of their experience on canvas. Beckmann continued to struggle with mythological figures. But Vassily Kandinsky's later abstractions or Oscar Kokoschka's later portraits are tired imitations of a fire that no longer burned high.

All of this made it possible for the avant-garde culture to be absorbed by its enemy, the main culture. Artists and critics concerned themselves with problems of form and style; but once explosive problems such as the conflict between father and son became manageable. Jakob Wassermann's treatment of that issue in *The Maurizius Case* is no longer revolutionary and expressionistic.

In fact, writers and painters now took up a new style. Called "new objectivity" (or, to humor poets' vanities, "magic realism"), it fits the conditions of bourgeois stabilization. Problems were dealt with, no longer as though they were deeply puzzling and affected the author's and reader's existence, but as episodes in the writer's and the nation's life. The psychological novel and the historical novel became fashionable.

Musical culture even more than painting was dominated by the old masters. The Bach renaissance pointed to the same "returning to the innermost soul" (*Verinnerlichung*) as the romantic revival. The neoromantics—Mahler, Debussy, Sibelius—were performed more often than Stavinsky, Hindemith, or Schönberg. The opera house played nineteenth-century works by Verdi, Puccini, Moussorgsky, and Richard Strauss. Only occasionally did one hear contemporary operas like Ernst Křenek's *Jonny spielt auf*, which used jazz rhythms, or Alban Berg's *Wozzeck*, which used twelve-tone techniques. To the general public they seemed unpleasantly sensational. The great surviving rebels of the preceding generation—Arnold Schönberg, Igor Stravinsky, and Paul Hindemith—found audiences only among the connoisseurs; like their painter colleagues, they turned from expressionist to more formal styles.

Expressionism was a stage, a transition. Among its devotees, some continued to use its devices, like Unruh and Benn; others began to mine different veins. Some turned to the right, like Benn, others to the left, like Brecht. Some grew disillusioned, like Toller. Others became pamphleteers, like Kurt Hiller and Kurt Tucholsky; their *Weltbühne* came to be the organ of disgruntled intellectuals and antimilitarists—free and often irresponsible critics of the republic who were congenitally and professionally out of step with everything and each other. Arnolt Bronnen and Hanns Johst became Nazi commissars, Johannes R. Becher a communist commissar.

Some also turned "right" or turned "left" by sheer accident, or because of their antagonists' stupidity. Carl Zuckmayer meant to provide nothing but fun with his bawdy comedy *The Merry Vineyard*, but he found himself, much against his will, the center of a cause célèbre. The left alone defended him, and he became its most popular author of critical plays in the folk manner. Nor had Erich Maria Remarque expected to become famous. His title—*All Quiet on the Western Front*—was taken from the daily army report, which of course concealed much suffering and thousands of deaths. Remarque, no pacifist, aimed only at being an honest reporter. Then Hugenberg decided to denounce the novel as a symbol of "the Ullstein German" (Ullstein was the great liberal-Jewish publishing house, Hugenberg's rival). The scandal of white mice at the movie premiere brought world fame to a mediocre novel. In the case of Hans Fallada's *Little*

Man, What Now? the clever choice of an appropriate title for a topical theme guaranteed world success to this somewhat mawkish reportage, after the author's sympathetic report on the peasants' revolt (*Peasants, Bosses, and Bombs*) had almost landed him in the fascist camp.

Partisanship on the left or right often decided where a play would be staged or how long it could run. The social drama, or *Zeitstück*, of the period is usually built on a famous trial (Dreyfus, Bullerjahn) or a current problem like birth control or juvenile delinquency. In a special class were the many war books, of which only Arnold Zweig's *The Case of Sergeant Grischa* was noteworthy. Likewise, of the many books that were now written about "ordinary people," only Alfred Döblin's *Berlin Alexanderplatz* stands out as a work of literature. The "proletarian novel" was usually as spurious as its counterpart, the patriotic novel, and both were written in the same style.

Quite a different approach was taken by Tucholsky, Toller, Walter Mehring, and Brecht, who used the cabaret style to criticize, denounce, and deride the bourgeoisie. Just as George Grosz found an outlet for his rage in the cartoon, Brecht developed the didactic play or "epic theater," in which he tried to avoid two vices of the bourgeois theater: a sentimental identification with the hero and a "consumer attitude" in the audience. Instead, he strove for the "estrangement" effect, which forces the audience to judge the characters rather than to feel with them. Fortunately, his joy in inventing stories kept the poet from following his theories. *The Good Woman of Setzuan* and *Three-Penny Opera* are superb entertainment even though they teach. His ultra-Leninist oratorio, *The Measure Taken*, advocates the utmost abnegation of personal feelings in the service of the cause; yet his lyrics still betray cultural despair rather than concern for the workers.

The problem of the artist in bourgeois society appears throughout the work of Thomas Mann. Interestingly, he never sees it in terms of symbiosis, but only of incongruity; the demonic forces, he knows, are destructive, but they are fascinating and, even in their compulsive drive toward death, they make life interesting and worth living. Stefan Zweig, too, was attracted by the demons, and knowledge of psycho-analysis may have helped him and many other writers to define the problems of the individual in acquisitive society. In *The Magic Mountain*, Thomas Mann provides an allegorical pageant of Europe's sickness; after long and necessarily inconclusive debates between spokesmen for the liberal and totalitarian philosophies, the protagonist eventually chooses "life"—by going to war.

Robert Musil, too, in *The Man Without Qualities*, tried to paint a pageant of decadent culture, with more biting irony than Mann's against the bourgeoisie and more realistic presentation of the horrifying alternatives; but his debates are even less conclusive, and the novel remained unfinished. The hero of Hesse's *Demian*, beloved of the youth movement, belongs to a race that has risen beyond good and evil; he, too, goes off to the war. In the deeply confessional self-lacerating *Steppenwolf*, Hesse returned to the theme of ambivalence between bestiality and saintliness; in *Narcissus and Goldmund* he projected a dreamworld of freedom. At the end of his career, Hesse for the first time turned the theme around: in *Magister Ludi*, from their sacred aerie the servants of the mysterious "glass bead game" (the German title) descend to the world—only to die. Hugo von Hofmannsthal, too, opposed the soul to a world without mystery; in his last play, *The Tower*, he tried to "show how the Soul, out of a dark, mythical realm, stumbles into the merciless reality of our life," and again he hoped for an aristocratic brotherhood to save beauty and goodness.

Even more esoteric was Stefan George's endeavor to build an aesthetic cult and an order of leaders who would select themselves by their response to his noble verses—those verses sculptured as in marble. It was perhaps not George's fault—though certainly a measure of his eccentricity, or of the unworldliness of the German *Geist* in general—that several of his disciples mistook his prophecy of a Führer to mean Hitler. The master himself had to flee the (Third) Reich which he had conjured up. (Another disciple, Count Claus von Stauffenberg, atoned for them all in his attempt to kill Hitler.)

For all writers, the cleavage between bourgeois society and the artist was problematic; but different writers drew different con-clusions. Thomas Mann expected the contest between life and death, bourgeois and artist, reason and the demon, to go on indefinitely and sought a humanist detachment for himself to describe it. In his late work *Joseph and His Brothers*, he retold the old myth "in the face of the new barbarians who fight against *Geist*." Hofmannsthal and Hesse, too, spoke up for the civilizing, humanist creations of the mind—Hofmannsthal revived the medieval play *Everyman* and re-enacted *The Great World Theater* at the Salzburg Festival.

By contrast, Stefan George and his disciple Ludwig Klages went back to the telluric forces in search of the lost unity. Their hate of the bourgeois led them to despise the work of the Enlightenment and the advances of modern science; blood and soil, the instincts of the tribe, were what counted for them. Klages—otherwise a gifted psychologist who wrote a sensitive guide to graphology—entitled his book *The Intellect* [*Der Geist*] *as Antagonist of the Soul.* Another great psychologist, the Swiss doctor Carl Jung, also sought comfort and healing in the archetypal structures, sharply diverging from his former teacher Freud.

Finally, the theme was developed scientifically by sociologists, anthropologists, psychologists, and philosophers. Max Scheler, the sociologist, saw modern civilization as a misfortune: "This mechanism in which mankind is being caught, and which threatens to choke it to death, is its own civilization, which is exploding the boundaries of will and intellect and gets more and more difficult to manage, more and more subject to its own law."

The great novelists of the Weimar era were moralists, parodists, ironists, critics of their society and of their fellow men, rebels against God or at least their fathers; they were doubters, ruminators of thoughts. They often lapsed into romantic and baroque moods; they viewed their creations with a detached smile; they could not believe in what they desired most to believe in. They were all *Aufklärer* who were skeptical of the Enlightenment. Ideals were held high but at the same time scrutinized with skepticism, or even parodied.

All through German literature in the twentieth century, the villain is the middle-class. Whether the writer is a conservative or an anarchist, whether he opposes to middle-class morality his own high ethics or his freer mores, whether he despises the bourgeois for their lack of morality or exposes their spirituality as hogwash, he always looks down on his cousins the moneybags and their materialistic culture. He always feels he belongs to the elite whose merits and values are insufficiently appreciated by the "masses." Thomas Mann in his ironical and Bertolt Brecht in his ribald way see the bourgeois as a con man, gangster, parasite, but never as a working man.

Nor do they see the worker as a proletarian. In the entire works of great German authors one never passes by, let alone enters into, a factory. The poor, "the people," are prostitutes, thieves, vagabonds, waiters, boatmen, woodcutters at best, but usually lumpen proletarians, just as the bourgeois are lumpen bourgeois, the nobles lumpen aristocrats, and the intellectuals themselves lumpen bohemians. German literature has no Balzac, no Zola, no Tolstoy, no Dreiser, not even a Galsworthy.

Confrontation with the bourgeois and with rationality, and rejection of modern industry and technology, are traditional themes of European romanticism. We find similar tendencies in Maurice Barrès, Miguel de Unamuno, D. H. Lawrence, George Bernard Shaw,

Gabriele d'Annunzio, and others. What was specifically German in this ideology was its antiforeign accent (as it had been characteristic of its Pan-Slavic model in the previous century). Rilke complained that "something infinitely trustworthy and human, which had continued to reside in our grandfathers' houses, clothes, in every fountain, etc." had been replaced by "indifferent things, pseudothings, coming from America." Franz Werfel warned that "Europe is being ground to death in the deadly mortars of America and Russia." It was new also for scientists to chime in: Max Born, the atomic physicist, condemned both "Marxism and . . . American thought, which is based on superficial pragmatism and confuses utility with truth." Oswald Spengler, who was not hostile to technology as such, nevertheless warned the Nordic peoples not to allow a mechanical civilization to endanger their life force, not to forget their own warrior values, not to betray the secrets of technology to the inferior nations: "Faustian man, who alone can master technology, perishes, and the parasitical races, who can only utilize what others invented, will rule."

Thus the 1920s reveal themselves as an era of conflicting attitudes and philosophies, of perplexities and experiments, of exuberance and despair—always exciting and vibrant, even where the impulses were neither very new nor very profound. The significance of "Weimar culture" is the dispersion of earlier initiatives, the broadening of the popular base for cultural innovations, the breadth of cosmopolitan influences, the variety of tendencies, the participation of large audiences in vital debates. Above all, it is the feeling that intellectual issues were relevant to the life of the nation and vice versa, that the life of the mind does not float in a social vacuum but receives its impulses from public issues. Few other periods have seen a similar involvement of the arts and sciences with every aspect of the national life. One thinks of the eighteenth-century Enlightenment and of the fifth century B.C. in Athens. But in making such a comparison, one must remember that the Periclean age was not one of tranquillity and harmony but of strife, crisis, doubt, and anxiety. These were periods of rapid change and of disbelief, domestic and foreign wars, dangers that tested the values, the attitudes, the entire frame of reference of the prevailing culture.

Certainly, attempts were made to find a new philosophy of values or a new "system." Nikolai Hartmann and Max Scheler are the most notable examples. But Scheler's search ended in the cry of despair: "We are the first people who do not know what man is, and know that we don't know it." He asked: "Does the increased awareness of man's nature mean that he knows better where he stands? Or is it merely an ever-growing illusion?"

Scheler became the founder of a new science, the sociology of knowledge, which led him to a radical relativism. Ernst Cassirer tried to save a Kantian approach in his *Philosophy of Symbolic Forms*. This was a cultural anthropology with epistemological concerns. He wrote: "The critique of reason becomes the critique of culture"—an almost Copernican turn, for it led to the radical critique of western ideologies that was then undertaken by Marxists like Georg Lukàcs, Karl Korsch, Walter Benjamin, and Bertolt Brecht—or by their opponents on the far right (Spengler, Jünger, the writers of the monthly *Die Tat* under its new editor Hans Zehrer, and the existentialists). Among them, they brought the crisis of the 1920s to a head.

We shall now have a closer look at these adverse tendencies, which Fritz Stern has aptly called philosophies of cultural despair.

14

Failure of Nerve and Revolution from the Right

"WEIMAR CULTURE" IS USUALLY ASSOCIATED WITH the notion of freedom, or even of leftism. But just as it included Brecht, it also was host to Oswald Spengler, Carl Schmitt, and Othmar Spann, who deprecated this freedom. Simultaneously with writers who spoke up for man, the decade produced confessions of total dehumanization. Ernst Jünger, E. E. Dwinger, and Franz Schauwecker recorded the "front experience" of World War I in cool, steely, crystalline language that left no room for rhetoric or emotions. They used not even the terms of patriotic gore; they knew neither fear nor pity; their only passion was destruction of an enemy who remained equally dispassionate. Even the word order in their novels suggests that men have no will. And even comradeship appears to mean the feeling of the unit's identity rather than the "I-thou" relationship between men. Monstrous abstractions, mechanical organizations substitute themselves for human agents.

This reified language also found its way into newspaper clichés. Men were "sucked into the breach"; people's aims were "determined by their destiny." In his study *The Worker*, Jünger projected his ideal of totally mechanized soldierlike robots who may not even be either man or woman. Not meant to be a satire, it could be read as an anticipation of *1984*.

Freedom and the individual, the "ideas of 1789" and democracy, equality and, above all, "the mass" were the targets of this literature, which denies humanism and humanity the grounds of principle and history. The Austrian political philosopher Othmar Spann, in *The True State* (1921), advocated the corporate state; Hans Freyer proclaimed *The Revolution from the Right* (1931).

167

In contrast to the optimistic philosophies of liberalism and socialism, the new conservatives did not believe that man could save himself by his wits or that the west should be proud of its achievements. Nor did they like the development of urbanism, democracy, and cosmopolitanism. Instead, they called for "roots" in the national or racial "soil," for trust in the instincts of blood and the tribal culture, which was opposed to technological "civilization" as the "organic" was opposed to the "mechanical."

The attack on western values was spearheaded by a philosophy of history which turned all previous notions upside down. Instead of causation it asserted "destiny," instead of progress "eternal return"; instead of humanization it preached nationalism.

Spengler's *Decline of the West*, which appeared in 1918, remained the most influential work of historical philosophy in the 1920s. It sold 36,000 copies in five years. Although professional historians have found fault with its scholarship, its prophetic style and enormous vision assure it a place among the seminal books of this century. Spengler challenged the traditional view of history which looked at Europe as the center and its culture as the pinnacle of progress. For the first time, he showed that a true "world history" must recognize the coming and going of many civilizations; each of them has produced values of its own which we may not be able to appreciate but which are in no way inferior to ours. Moreover, he revealed that those achievements of industrial development which are the object of our greatest pride may be indications of stagnation and decline. He claimed that these insights amounted to a "Copernican revolution," removing western man from his self-centered fool's paradise and placing him before the dire alternative of a new ice age: byzantinism, syncretism, stagnation, and Caesarism.

In contrast to Marx, who had promised all nations a better future, Spengler taught his own nation "tragic heroism"; happiness, peace, harmony, progress, humanism are so many illusions of the ascending phase. Now it behooves the Nordic races to look their destiny straight in the eye and to fulfill its grim verdict with cool determination. If they will not be the executors of destiny, destiny will doom them. *Pace* Clausewitz, politics is but another form of war.

Like Stefan George, Spengler meant to write for an aristocracy and was surprised when the plebeians took hold of his philosophy. But unlike George, he must be held responsible for the wayward interpretations of his doctrines. His exaltation of war, his "decisionism," his contempt of humanism, his very method of historical classification were designed to negate science as it had been known in the preceding two thousand years. His famous "morphological method" gave him easy excuses for assigning positive and negative labels to nations and institutions as he needed them for his political purposes.

"Engaged science" became a trend now on both the right and the left. Professor Rudolf Smend, writing on political philosophy, labeled "organic" all institutions he liked—such as monarchy—and "inorganic" those he disliked, such as pluralism. Likewise on the right, Professor Carl Schmitt declared that all politics is based on the distinction between "we" and "they," and he had no difficulty in proving that pluralism, or a multiparty state, is incapable of properly defining "them." He worked out an ideology for the Brüning government, then another one for the presidential dictatorship under Papen, and finally one emphasizing "the concrete order and Gestalt" for Hitler, who booted him out—deservedly, too, for Schmitt was trying to save a place for traditional institutions, such as the army and the bureaucracy, next to the party.

On the left, engaged science was advocated by the neo-Marxists of the Frankfurt Institute for Social Research. They doubted that a bourgeois could understand or use Marxian dialectics, just as the racists maintained that Jews could not understand the new race science. Needless to say, the mixture of Galtonism and nationalistic mysticism that was taught at some German universities had little to do with science, and it was taught not for the sake of eugenics but for political purposes.

The climax of partisan philosophy was reached in the philosophy of existentialism, which simply used epithets like "*das man*" (everyman). "inauthentic," "sophists," "*Entscheidungslosigkeit*" (lack of decisiveness, a synonym for tolerance), "the mass" to discredit democratic theories, or "nobility," "heroism," and "authenticity" to recommend its own attitudes. These are, frankly, the same that had been developed by Spengler and Jünger as "tragic heroism." The aristocratic and openly antidemocratic ideal is here transformed into the language of "authenticity," which shields the individual from the demands of the public.

Existentialism seemed to be a philosophy that once again spoke to man about himself and about his relationship to his world and to other men. It turned the tables on all previous philosophy since Plato, which had sought to rise from the particular to the general, the universal, the essence. Heidegger analyzed man's condition by descending into the interior of the individual. He found worry (*Sorge*), anxiety, fear and trembling—it was not given to him to find love and friendship. To him, all being is defined by its being-unto-death. Returning to the pre-Socratic philosophers, he built on these premises a new ontology—an undertaking which students applauded after the dry skepticism of academic neo-Kantianism and positivism.

Of course Heidegger was aware that in each heart, the "authentic" and the "inauthentic" struggle—a dichotomy we found under different names, such as soul and intellect, in Hofmannsthal, Klages, Rathenau, and George. But in practice, acceptance of the philosophy came down to the self-selection of the elite: of those who would not "minimize death by trying to manipulate it. In being-unto-death the expectation must be trained [*ausgebildet*: Heidegger loves military terms] and endured [*ausgehalten:* the 'stick it out' of World War I]." By contrast, "the worrying [*Sorge*, his key existential word] of the mediocre person reveals an essential trait [of mankind] which I call the leveling down of all possibilities of being."

No wonder this philosophy has been called "an appeal" (*Appell*). Irrespective of any merit which professional philosophers may find in its method of reopening an approach to ontology, its popularity seemed to derive from its ability to segregate the "new" from the "old," those who strive for "being" from those who persist in rationalist routines.

Heidegger made for himself an archaic language to express what is truly beyond reach. His idiosyncrasies make it difficult to assess his real contribution. At his death in 1976, *Le Monde* called him the greatest philosopher of this century. But here we can concern ourselves only with his public impact.

Heidegger met Ernst Cassirer, the neo-Kantian, in a famous debate at Davos. Cassirer came away from this experience suspecting that he had been lured into a sectarian rite where no rational dialogue was possible; Heidegger's disciples came away with a claim of "victory" over an old-fashioned pedant: their master had liberated philosophy from the dictatorship of reason. Actually, existentialism's intuitive, subjectivist method opened the door to the debasement of scientific methods in research. On the pretext of purging the universities of what Karl Jaspers called the "nineteenth-century superstition of scientism," the method of empathy (*Verstehen*) was now introduced into fields where even Dilthey (supra page 49, *Lebensphilosophie*) would not have used it. Werner Sombart, the veteran historian of capitalism, who had started out as a socialist and ended as a national socialist, now made a distinction between "economics that explains" and "economics that understands." Even more urgently, of course, such empathy was recommended in fields like sociology, anthropology, and psychology.

Older philosophers had tried to separate value judgments from the pursuit of truth. Max Weber had laid down the distinction in his famous lectures *Politics as a Vocation* and *Science as a Vocation.* Now the direction was reversed; judgment was subject to engagement. Scheler and Jaspers admitted that existentialism could be understood only by him who surrendered to it and suspended his skepticism. Philosophy is replaced by intuition or introspective meditation. An act of faith, an inner experience, a gift of grace, may be required to enter into the spirit.

Heidegger, following Sören Kierkegaard, made the important discovery that man is indeed possessed of irrational fear, and may act out of the wanton desire for nothingness. He also took from Freud (or from St. Paul and St. Augustine) the insight that in admitting original sin we may be able to live with it, and even to go out into the world and act without being inhibited any further by guilt feelings. Existentialism here reveals itself as a Manichaean religion, recognizing that man must do evil in order to live.

Whether or not Heidegger was a Nazi when he published *Being and Time*, Nazi intellectuals hailed his philosophies as an instrument for destroying the ideologies of liberalism. Heidegger, in turn, hailed Hitler's movement as the embodiment of that "being-unto-death" which was to "liberate" western man from the shackles of the Enlightenment. In seizing the presidency of Freiburg University, Heidegger dedicated it to "science service" (*Wissensdienst*), which he placed in a highly suggestive parallel to labor service and military service. Truly too much "engagement"!

Jaspers' personal kindness, his honesty, and his Jewish wife saved him from falling into the Nazi trap; but intellectually he belongs among the philosophers who were not content to look at democracy with dispassionate skepticism. In all his publications before 1933 he leveled vicious, often demagogic, attacks against "the masses" and "democracy." This is especially true of his summary of contemporary philosophy, *The Contemporary Condition of Mind* (1932). The negative traits of what Jaspers derisively calls "the world" he always finds in a democratic society.

Shocking as such pronouncements may sound coming from the lips of a philosopher dedicated to the pursuit of pure being, they were not isolated occurrences. From the beginning of the century, many western literati had debased their art in the service of nation, race, state, monarchy, or church. Thought did not direct action but was at its command. In neighboring France Julien Benda wrote the searing attack *The Treason of the Intellectuals.*

Could religion offer a way out of the crisis? Liberal theologians rested contentedly on their theoretical and practical achievements early in the century. Adolf von Harnack's popular *The Essence of Christianity* was influential far beyond the borders of Germany and Lutheranism. He spoke with humility and tolerance, disregarding the churches and their institutions, and reaching out to all who recognized the dignity of man, the immanence of God, and the humanity of Christ. A companion in arms was Ernst Troeltsch, who showed the historical nature of the Christian teachings, denied revelation, and abandoned the old claim that Christianity was unique and universal.

The liberal view of a mild Jesus who cared for the poor agreed well with the efforts of liberal pastors and social scientists. Engaging Christianity in a dialogue with the working class was also the concern of the "socialists of the lectern," Christian socialists like Paul Tillich, the periodical *Die Christliche Welt*, the Settlement Movement under Friedrich Siegmund-Schultze, and the Internal Mission under the leadership of the Bodelschwingh family, which later was to play a role in the anti-Nazi resistance. Both in theology and in practical works, these liberals were optimistic; they believed that each of us carries the divine spark within. While not denying that man is weak, they tended to minimize the distance between him and God, to forget original sin, and to secularize religion. They would not believe that a crisis had seized the European consciousness and denied that their own work was meant to forestall a crisis of Christianity.

There were others, however, whose religious needs sprang from a deep consciousness of man's insufficiency, and whose Christ was not a model for men but a judge whose wrathful countenance they would face on judgment day. Albert Schweitzer, the doctor, missionary, Bach scholar, and organist, first made a name for himself as a theologian of anguish and crisis. His reputation as a great humanitarian and apostle of peace won him the Nobel Peace Prize, and many Europeans revered him as a Protestant saint, worthy to be named, in our century, with Tolstoy and Gandhi. His follower was the Swiss professor of theology Karl Barth, whose interpretation of St. Paul's *Letter to the Romans* (1918) marks an epoch in modern theology. Based on Kierkegaard's experience of man's depravity, it was rightly called "crisis theology." Though fundamentalist, Barth's faith set his mind free to seek radical solutions in man's worldly affairs. Obedience to God and humility before men enhance the soul's righteousness in doing God's work on earth. Again and again in the course of western history, puritans of this type have seen themselves in the image of God's soldier-priests; this trait was to preserve the orthodox from the blandishments of Hitler's secular church in the 1930s.

Karl Barth was a socialist and often took positions close to the communist line; his coreligionist Friedrich Gogarten inclined to conservatism. In this group we also find Barth's disciples Rudolf Bultmann and Martin Niemöller, who as conservative churchmen resisted the totalitarian claims. The right-left scale in politics is not congruent with the orthodox-liberal scale in theology. A radical theology cut across party lines and prepared a position of extreme distrust vis-à-vis the mundane affairs of the age. It had nothing to say to people who had not experienced the collapse of that liberal, optimistic, scientific, or idealistic philosophy.

Tillich reports that one night on the battlefield where many of his friends had perished, "I walked along the rows of dying men, and much of my classical German philosophy broke down: the belief that man could know the essence of his being, the belief in the identity of essence and existence. The traditional concept of God was dead."

The harsh theology of Kierkegaard which these dialecticians accepted leaves man in the position of an absurd freak, and offers no hope that he may understand God's arbitrariness. It is the theological counterpart to existentialism.

In contrast to crisis theology, which demands faith, liberalism led many among the educated to a mystical view of man's relationship with the divine. The study of Paracelsus, the Cabbala, of Jakob Böhme and Angelus Silesius, permitted scholars like Martin Buber, Ernst Troeltsch, Gershom Sholem, and Bodo Sartorius von Waltershausen to conceive of a God who grows and fulfills himself through man. It is not through man who needs a savior, but through man who creates one, that God can live.

Esoteric religions, anthroposophy, and Bahaism were for the educated; Christian Science and Jehovah's Witnesses made proselytes among the lower classes. Socialists either had no church affiliation or belonged to the "Free-Religious Community" which held marriage and "youth initiation" ceremonies but no other services.

Times of crisis bring forth heretical sects, mystics, faith healers, miracle workers, and other saviors, some profound and others very superficial or even ridiculous. In the early 1930s, when the depression struck hard, astrology became a fad. It was said that big financiers, and also Hitler, consulted astrologers. A "shepherd" diagnosed diseases by examining patients' hair; another charlatan, who cured appendicitis and psychosis by applying cottage cheese, was able to found a sect and to publish a weekly paper. One could easily exaggerate the significance of such occurrences, had they not happened at the same time people were also looking for a political "savior."

No doubt these developments signified a crisis of European culture, for they had parallels in other countries. Lukács recorded them in a three-volume book, *The Destruction of Reason*, and, of course, related them to the decadence of the bourgeoisie. Max Weber's brother Alfred examined them under the title *The Fourth Man*, asserting the rise of a new age. Ralf Dahrendorf rather feels that these perplexed reactions were resurrections of traditional attitudes, especially among the lower middle classes. Peter Gay and Walter Laqueur seem too quick in assigning "right" and "left" labels to cultural tendencies and in therefore assuming that one is a response to the other. The excerpts here assembled suggest that all the intellectual trends were manifestations of the same crisis.

Moreover, parallel phenomena appeared in other countries of Europe, so that Ernst Nolte and other historians speak of an "age of fascism." Since economically, intellectually, politically, and socially the crisis was deeper in Germany than elsewhere, the "fit" between the fall of the republic and the ideological breakdown of western values seems to be closer. Society offered fewer avenues to satisfaction, fewer assurances of mental peace, less legitimation. On the evidence of its outlook on history, it no longer believed that progress was irresistible. On the evidence of its moral philosophy, it had no assurance that problems could be resolved without creating new ones. On the evidence of its religion, it had more faith in the endurance of evil than in the goodness of God.

It is not surprising that in such a situation people should turn to faith healers and Pied Pipers, looking for a savior or leader. Others see the way out of their despair only in total revolution. Failing to solve their problems by dealing with them directly, positively, and day by day, they seek to abolish the entire system of human relations from which they arise. They look to some kind of other-worldly solution—a totalitarian *Weltanschauung* that transposes the practical problem into a totally different system of coordinates. National Socialism and communism were such alternatives to reality.

15

The Rise of National Socialism

Whoever overturns us is strong.
Whoever lifts us up is godly.
Whoever gives us presentiment is profound.
　　　　　　　　—Friedrich Nietzsche

DURING HIS BRIEF INTERNMENT at the Fortress of Landsberg—after the Munich putsch in 1923—Hitler wrote *Mein Kampf*, a document which his contemporaries mistook for a snarling mountebank's ravings. They failed to see that it was full of shrewd observations on their own weaknesses, which its author was determined to exploit. Adolf Hitler had no bag of tricks, no special powers or mystical gifts, as his defeated enemies were to claim later; but he had a one-track mind that brooked neither doubt nor contradiction. His rather simplistic philosophy reduced every problem to yes or no, white or black, German or Jew. Hence his intransigence, the rejection of halfway solutions and of "bourgeois politics." Neither in Germany nor in the world would he share power with anyone.

In negotiations, that attitude permitted him to hold out for just that one second longer than his opponents, and often forced them to save him from doing something desperate. He would let a project founder rather than allow his partner even a face-saving advantage. For him, a truce or compromise was merely the launching stage for further demands, and any temporary arrangement was acceptable only if it helped to destroy the enemy.

> The bourgeois parties want only electoral victories; they never envisage the enemy's destruction. [*Vernichtung* was one of his favorite words.] We know that when the Marxists win they will destroy us; we expect nothing else. But when we win, the Marxists will be destroyed. We know no tolerance; we shall not rest before the last of their newspapers has been destroyed, their last organization has been destroyed, their last educational agency has been destroyed, and the last Marxist either converted or liquidated. There is no middle ground.

As a speaker Hitler held the masses in thrall. He told them what he would do to the Jews, to the French, to the Russians, to the international conspiracy of capitalists. He promised the Little Man total revenge for the humiliations of the Versailles Treaty and the lost war. His credential was the simple fact that he had made no deal with anyone and appeared to be pure in a world of corruption.

Hitler was neither just the miserable fool—flophouse resident, drifter, house painter, sex pervert—nor the genius of evildoing whom some of his biographers and friends have described. He was an ordinary mountebank of some pluck who found extraordinary circumstances permitting him to play a role in history. His skill was to discern those favorable conditions and to exploit the weakness, and especially the cowardice, of those who could have stopped him.

There is a myth about "the demon" Hitler who was able to capture his people's soul. Thus Michael Freund, a conservative scholar, writes in his *Deutsche Geschichte* (Gütersloh: Bertelsmann, 1960):

> There was something superhuman and inhuman in the man, a trait of devilish sanctity. He lived for himself, simply and in veritable purity. In direct contact one could see nothing extravagant or pathological in him, and he was free of ordinary egotism; he consumed himself in what he held to be his mission. He was a genius, the purest example of a crippled genius. He was possessed by larger-than-life forces and inspirations, impulses of genius, superhuman or subhuman, divine or demoniac, which may lead to sainthood or madness, enlightenment or bestial cruelty.

Hitler himself had promoted this legend:

> Providence has called me to be the greatest liberator of mankind. I free man from the fetters of the intellect which has made itself master; from the dirty and humiliating torment of morality; from the pretensions of freedom which only a few can stand. To the Christian doctrine of the significance of the individual I oppose the ice-cold logic of . . . the immortality of the nation.

To his judge he shouted, in the manner of revolutionaries of all times: "It is not you who will pass judgment on us. The last word will be spoken by the eternal court of history."

Self-serving memorialists and codefendants at the Nuremberg trial lent credibility to the legend of the new Genghis Khan; their testimony was gobbled up by sensation-hungry court reporters and newspaper readers in the west. Even thirty years after the tyrant's death, books continue to be written and films are shown to mass audiences who still try to solve the mystery of his fascination.

Since we know his success, we may overestimate Hitler's charisma or his cleverness. His contemporaries were apt to make the opposite mistake: undervaluing the emotional force of Nazism and under-estimating the perverted ambitions of its leaders. Hannah Arendt has spoken of "the banality of evil"; before the Nazis seized power, their enemies often shrugged their shoulders: Hitler seemed a mere German philistine, a most common face, a vulgar speaker, a mercenary, a clown, just an imitator of Mussolini.

Unfortunately, all this was beside the point. Hitler knew how to play on the fears and idiosyncrasies of the German people. He expressed their feeling of having been shortchanged by geography and history; he perpetuated their conviction that all the world was conspiring to make them miserable and humble. Unlike other agitators, he did not persuade; he summoned his audience to participate in a hunt, a ritual of death, a vociferation of hatred. He expressed the secret fantasies of the German Cinderella: dreams of revenge. Max Scheler called this propaganda "the politics of *ressentiment.*" Brecht has called its flavor in "Pirate Jenny" from the *Three-Penny Opera*: a song of a lowly girl who will be avenged by mighty brigands. Even for Brecht this dream was a lumpen-proletarian rather than a Marxist symbol.

Hitler turned the *ressentiment* into a conspiracy; he organized the fear. *Mein Kampf* sold 100,000 copies in three years. It included hardly anything that had not been said by other anti-Semitic writers. But it moved decisively away from *völkische* lunacies, from nostalgic medievalism, sectarian rituals, romantic life reform, and religious Teutonism. Hitler was modern and political. When he was released from Landsberg Prison, he reorganized the party and also gave it a new strategy. Like the communists, who had come to a similar decision earlier, Hitler recognized that the time for putsches was past. To win power, the party had to win votes, using the legal means of the parliamentary state. The S.A. (*Sturmabteilungen*) were severed from their original Free-Corps connection and trans-formed into a party militia. With funds from the anti-Semitic Thule Society, Franz Eher bought a Munich newspaper and converted it into the large-format *Völkischer Beobachter*; in Berlin Dr. Joseph Goebbels published *Der Angriff*; in the Rhineland Gregor Strasser established an organization that helped the party to break out of its Bavarian provincialism.

The National Socialist German Workers' Party (NSDAP)—or

Nazis, just as the Social-Democrats were called Sozis—had 200,000 members in 1928; partly overlapping with these, the S.A. had 100,000 members. By 1930 the party had grown to half a million members. What distinguished them from other parties of the right was their militancy and intransigence. The *Stahlhelm* also marched but rarely engaged in brawls. The S.A. was highly visible everywhere. Its weekly parades, its attacks on Jewish passersby, its frequent raids on Reichsbanner or Red Front hangouts, its busting of socialist and communist meetings, attracted those who liked to be on the side of the bullies rather than the victims.

Red Front and Reichsbanner men were as brave as the S.A.; but they were poorly backed by their parties. Their newspapers, on the day after a battle, would not celebrate them as heroes. Nazi goons, by contrast, were cheered by high society, police, and courts when they went out "fighting bolshevism," and Hitler stood by plain murderers (see page 195). He bluntly asserted that "heads will roll," and Hermann Göring, the popular air ace of World War I, added a sardonic touch: "polite to the very last rung [of the gallows ladder], but the rope at the top."

Terror was their propaganda. In *Mein Kampf* Hitler stressed his contempt for the masses and asserted that they must be "raped like a woman." His agitation frankly addressed itself to the killer instinct of the human animal. It is not even correct to say that he exalted military values and deprecated "philistines"; more precisely, he praised banditry.

Meanwhile, the social radicalism of the early party program was muted. It still called for "breaking the thralldom of interest," for nationalization of large corporations, profit sharing in industry, and settling homesteaders on the big estates. But Hitler now distinguished between "creative" (Aryan) and "greedy" (Jewish) capital. Nationalization was to be the penalty of only those who had appropriated land by speculation; for settlement he proposed, instead of German soil, the wide spaces of Russia, temporarily owned by unworthy Slavs and waiting to be conquered by "the right of the stronger race." To dominate, to rule over others, was the dream of the "little Nazi." The S.A. sang: "Today Germany, tomorrow the world."

The movement remained plebeian, rural, and marginally academic. But it dropped the dogmatic and sectarian locals and, instead, gained the support of conservatives such as piano maker Bechstein, steel king Fritz Thyssen, coal barons Carl von Stumm and Hermann Röchling, and above all of Alfred Hugenberg, the newspaper tycoon, who directed his editors to play the Nazis up. Of course these gentlemen meant to use Hitler. He was supposed to win votes away from the labor parties. This failed. But in September 1930 he won two million first voters, two million "unpoliticals" who had never voted before, and two million defectors from the traditional right. The middle-class leaders now were at the mercy of their "drummer boy." Companies rushed to offer Hitler insurance money. Even a foreign firm, Philips, a Dutch rival of the "Jewish AEG," and Sir Henry Deterding of the Royal Dutch and Shell Co. supported the antibolshevik crusade. Not to be left out in the cold, Jewish financiers like Jakob Goldschmidt of the near-bankrupt Darmstädter Bank chipped in. The American reporter Hubert R. Knickerbocker wrote a book asking whether Germany should choose the hammer and sickle or the swastika.

Hitler could now envisage the legal way of winning power. He expelled some S.A. leaders who considered the parliamentary tactics a surrender of principle. He personally assumed leadership of the S.A. and appointed as its chief of staff Captain Ernst Röhm, an adventurer but not a revolutionary. Posturing as a radical patriot, he took part in the big rally of all rightists held in Harzburg in October 1931 with an odd assortment of participants: Hitler and Hugenberg; the leaders of the *Stahlhelm*, Franz Seldte and Theodor Duesterberg; General Seeckt; ex–Reichsbank president Hjalmar Schacht; assorted Hohenzollern and other princes; the German-Nationalist Salesclerks' League; and even some defectors from Stresemann's People's Party, who were all sniffing the auspicious breeze of a new season. The proclamation of the "Harzburg Front" is worth quoting at least in part:

> We demand the immediate resignation of the Brüning [see end of Chapter 11] and Braun [see page 196] governments, the immediate suspension of the dictatorial powers of these governments, whose composition is contrary to the will of the people and who maintain themselves only by emergency decrees. We demand new election of the obsolete representation of the people [sic; the grammar is Hitler's]. In the coming upheavals the nationalist organizations will defend the life and property of those who side with us for the nation, but will refuse to protect the dominant system with our blood. [Chancellor Brüning had challenged the S.A. to volunteer for border patrol, as relations with Poland were tense.] We demand restoration of German sovereignty of defense and armament. Cursed be he who tries to separate our unity. We implore the President, whom we elected, to yield to the impassioned demand of millions of patriotic men and women, veterans and youths, to nominate a truly nationalist government.

These words obviously were meant to keep Hitler in line. His allies, who tried to harness the populist horses to their own chariot, were his prisoners already. Joachim Fest has pointed out that they had done him the invaluable service of legitimatizing his illegitimate methods of political warfare, of making his unsavory person and his S.A. goons acceptable to polite society.

In January 1932 Hitler spoke to the exclusive Industrialists' Club at Düsseldorf. In March and April he ran for president, forcing his allies to decide either for him or for their former idol, the old Marshal Hindenburg. He speculated—correctly—that no matter how many or how few votes he could get, in the end he would have established himself as the only alternative to the 85-year-old president. He polled eleven million votes on the first and thirteen million on the second ballot, trailing Hindenburg by six million votes.

In July 1932, coinciding with the trough of the depression, the Nazi wave crested. The NSDAP slate for the Reichstag received 13.7 million out of 36.9 million valid votes—37.4 percent of the total. But when, only four months later, the last free election was held, the NSDAP had slipped down to 33.1 percent. It was still declining and its treasury was heavily in debt when, surprisingly, Hindenburg handed the power of the chancellorship to Hitler. Under the beginning S.A. terror, the Nazis then whipped up 17 million, or 43.9 percent of the vote. They never polled a majority in a free or semifree election.

Political analysts and historians have asked the obvious question: what made so many millions of Germans listen to the raucous voice of this Austrian corporal who offered no solutions to real problems like unemployment and declining incomes but harangued about illusory goals like racial purity, tearing up the Versailles Treaty, conquering space in the east, even war? His followers were not simply victims of the depression. There were more women among them than men, more people who had jobs than who did not, more members of the upper and middle classes than of the working class. Even to those who were unemployed, Hitler offered no program of work relief.

A theory popular at the time stated that the Nazis were simply "running dogs of capitalism." This was begging the question—which is precisely why so many allowed themselves to be swayed. Many big corporations, like Krupp and I. G. Farben, supported other parties; what must be explained is why their money was spent in vain. Hitler complained that business gave him less than it gave to the small People's Party. But millions of "little men" were generous.

Thyssen has estimated that he and his corporate friends contributed two million marks a year, while the budget of the party—10,000 local offices, S.A. supplies, newspapers—may have been fifty to seventy million marks, much of it from small contributions.

Another theory that seemed plausible in the 1930s and 1940s starts out from the psychoanalytical insight that man shuns responsibility and would rather surrender his freedom than make critical decisions for himself. In *Escape from Freedom*, Erich Fromm tried to show that the Germans as a nation have a long history of subjection to authority. This theory had already been used to explain Hindenburg's election in 1925—as it could be used to explain Maurice MacMahon's in 1873 and Philippe Pétain's in 1940, or Ulysses S. Grant's in 1868 and Dwight D. Eisenhower's in 1952. But it cannot explain the subversive activity of pseudosocialist S.A. troopers against the venerable authority of Hindenburg. If psychoanalysis is indeed to serve, Hitler was a brother figure and posed as a martyr. He aroused the darkly murderous instincts of the crowd and transformed rebellion into a quasireligious rite. Heinrich Mann, representing the old generation, vented his exasperation at their subversive activities:

> They are the opposite of democrats. They want everything to change, even if the majority thinks differently. They want the Absolute, and they are full of hatred. . . . All threats, protests, and actions are directed at those over thirty and their ways of life. They go to the theater and applaud parricide.

Let us now turn to the sociological theories. The Nazi movement was recruited among small businessmen, students and professors, petty officials, shopkeepers, former army officers, and almost all rural classes. Among industrialists it was supported by those who were bankrupt rather than by the prosperous; among workers by few who had a skill, but more often by white-collar employees. The German-Nationalist Salesclerks' League came increasingly under Nazi influence.

It was a movement of all who were losing status, a desperate reaction to the threat of social decline. But it also included some of the new elites, the technocrats, the workers' sons who hoped to be co-opted into the elites, and the ideologists of a new age. Especially the students thought of themselves as idealists, often as revolutionary. They believed in the patriotic uprising of a German folk community that would throw off all the foreign elements and bring justice to all Germans. They also hoped that it might restore them, the flower of the German elite, to their rightful place at home and in the world.

Theodor Geiger has estimated that in 1932 about 18 percent of all German families belonged to the old middle classes (those who still owned businesses) and 18 percent to the "new middle class" (technical and commercial employees, people who were seeking more elbowroom than their fathers had enjoyed, but who suddenly found their way blocked). Finally, 13 percent were losing their fight to remain independent. They were the first to flock to the new savior's colors; since there was no hope for them within "the system," they expected a great political miracle, an apocalypse, of which they would be the instruments.

Even worse was the condition of the farmers. They were being outproduced and underbid by overseas producers, exploited by domestic middlemen, oppressed and foreclosed by tax collectors and bankers, threatened by unionized labor. The powerful farm lobby obtained tariffs and subsidies, which helped the big grain-producing estat s but not the small dairy farmers. In several areas, such as Holstein, Hesse, and among the Rhenish winegrowers, revolts had erupted to prevent foreclosures. The *Landvolk* and the Nazis provided leaders for these protests.

All this was the basis of a populist movement—anticapitalist, anti-industrialist, antimodern, antiliberal, anti-Jewish, antiforeign, antigovernment, antilabor; intensely nationalistic but in its own mind revolutionary or at least seditious, feeling alienated from the web of government. The small Nazis were resentful of "bosses" and officials who seemed to be protected from the ravages of the depression; they all looked toward a more stable order, in which they would be protected from the storms of competition, from usury and taxation. This order was seen as *Stände*, the corporate order, guilds guaranteed by a strong state that would protect their kind against foreigners and Jews—in particular the small shopkeeper against department stores, the craftsmen against big industry, the peasant against middlemen, the "Aryan" lawyer and doctor against Jewish immigrants.

But the NSDAP was not one of the parties representing interests. It was a "movement." It did not propose this remedy or that, but called for abolishing "the system." It was neither right nor left but used a confusing blend of all propaganda slogans. The Nazis asked: "Where is the social republic? Where is the end of capitalism? Where has militarism been overcome? Where are the blessings of freedom, equality, and brotherhood, and all those pretty phrases with which the revolution has befogged our brave nation? Bourgeois nationalism and international Marxism divide our people, but the manipulators of those ideas are chums under the skin." Cutting across all special interests, a national uprising, culminating in a dictatorship of the German soul, would abolish all divisive ideas of 1789, all foreign domination and alien institutions. Restoring Germany to herself, it would transcend those grievances to which sociologists paid primary attention.

Millenial movements need a devil. The propagandist's art consists in reducing all enemies to the same elusive, ubiquitous symbol. In *Mein Kampf* Hitler explained that "the Jew" (always in the singular!) assumes as many shapes as the devil. He is foreign but right in our midst, liberal but for that precise reason oppressive, capitalist as well as bolshevik. Goebbels warned his readers not to be taken in by the poor Jew next door, who looks so innocent but is a relative of one of the big conspirators who huddle on Wall Street hatching their evil designs for world domination.

Whatever social anti-Semitism existed in Germany was no more than the reflection of normal communal clannishness; racial segregation was much less visible than in Austria, Russia, or America. Prussian nobility had married Jewish bankers' daughters; Bismarck had used Jewish brokers, lawyers, politicians, and writers for his purposes. A substantial number of Jews—more than their share in the population—had been decorated or killed in the wars of 1870-71 and 1914-18. The German-Nationalist candidate for president in 1932, Duesterberg, leader of the *Stahlhelm*, had a Jewish grandmother.

Although the Zionist movement was gaining ground, Jews did not claim the status of a national minority. They were assimilated, and closely identified with intellectual movements in recent history, such as Bismarck's *Kulturkampf*, neo-Kantian philosophy, and modern art and criticism. They had won Nobel prizes for Germany. But intellectually few of them had progressed beyond the period of emancipation, of liberalism and individualism. They tended to be concentrated in small business and the professions and therefore believed in Adam Smith's doctrine of free trade; they naturally supported the secular state and freedom of thought. As a group they represented the spirit of 1848, from which the rest of the middle class was turning away so decisively. Except for the working class, they were the only group that was republican by conviction, and anti-Semitic propaganda was simply antirepublican propaganda. The Nazis spoke of "the Jew republic." Jews were urban, cosmopolitan, intellectualistic, and critical—or in Nazi language, corruptive (*zersetzend*).

There were economic conflicts, too. Jewish middlemen, moneylenders, rent collectors, and cattle dealers were unpopular with the peasants. In retailing they dominated the furniture and ready-to-wear business. They also were identified with banking and department stores. In the professions, Jewish lawyers, doctors, scientists, artists, actors, conductors, and writers reaped more than their share of honors, which anti-Semites attributed to Jewish preponderance in the press. Students asked for a quota to limit the number of Jewish candidates, and they acclaimed professors who advocated a "German science," "German law," "German anthropology" (race science), even a "German mathematics." Only at the universities and some high schools were there open manifestations of anti-Semitism; elsewhere Jews lived unmolested among their neighbors—until 1931, when S.A. troops began to stage attacks on isolated pedestrians. Perhaps it was not anti-Semitism that resulted in Nazi violence but, on the contrary, rowdyism that created a need for anti-Semitism as its alibi. Thus, William S. Allen writes in *The Nazi Seizure of Power* (in the Hanoveranian town of Thalburg), "[people] were drawn to anti-Semitism because they were drawn to Nazism." Goebbels was indignant to find that German beaches were open to Jews while American Jews were segregated.

Political anti-Semitism must be distinguished from the social-economic and cultural varieties. Its intellectual fathers were mostly non-Germans: Dostoevsky in his Pan-Slavic writings, Count Josef Gobineau, and Houston Stewart Chamberlain (Richard Wagner's son-in-law). Baldur von Schirach, the perennial Hitler Youth leader, claimed that a book by Henry Ford had converted him to anti-Semitism. Hitler in his Vienna years had been impressed by Georg von Schönerer's Pan-German agitation, which was both anti-Catholic and anti-Jewish, and by Christian-Social Mayor Karl Lueger, who specifically denounced Jewish influence in the imperial capital. Incidentally, it has been noted that many National Socialist leaders were "elective Germans," born or reared abroad—Hitler in Braunau (Bohemia), Göring in Haiti, Hitler's personal aide Rudolf Hess in Cairo, his ideologist Alfred Rosenberg (author of *The Myth of the Twentieth Century*) and Joachim Ribbentrop in the Baltic area, his "farm estate" leader Walther Darré in Argentina, and Schirach in the United States.

In Germany, political anti-Semitism began with Richard Wagner and Heinrich von Treitschke, the Prussian historian, supported by the socialist Eugen Dühring and the liberal and much-loved novelist Gustav Freytag. As in France, petit bourgeois socialism had an anti-Semitic tinge, while the labor movement, founded by Marx and Lassalle and humanitarian in its impulses, considered anti-Semitism its worst enemy. Stoecker's efforts to substitute race war for class war had failed. In the pre–World War I Reichstag, anti-Semitic parties were represented by three, or five, or at best sixteen deputies, all elected in conservative districts. The Conservatives, their successors the German-Nationalists, and the Land League had "Christian" and "German" planks in their platforms; Theodor Fritsch's *Manual of the Jewish Question* and Dietrich Eckardt's racial theories were influential on the right; "race science" was taught at many universities.

In the early 1920s a flood of anti-Semitic literature, some of it lurid or even pornographic, inundated Germany. Its political effect simmered down as soon as the republic seemed safe and prosperous, but some corruption scandals fed anti-Semitism. When the depression came, Nazi propaganda turned its biggest guns against the Treaty of Versailles, the reparations, and the bolshevik danger; but it attacked "the Jew" as a symbol of evil rather than as a person—no less violently, to be sure, but not as though equal conviction could be assumed among the audiences. The antiphonal chant "Germany, awake! Judah, croak!" was a ritual, a sort of exorcism. The metaphysical entities of Germany and Judah were fighting—the children of light and the children of darkness. Germans were called upon to align themselves with the forces of light.

On the whole (Upper Bavaria and much of Austria were regional exceptions), the majority did not approve of Jew-baiting; but one further exception must be noted. During the early 1920s, Germany had received an influx of Jews from territories that had been ceded to Poland, and also refugees from religious persecution in that country. Some of these, uninhibited by ethical standards and customs of the west, exploited the opportunities of the inflation ruthlessly and displayed their new wealth indiscreetly. They were unpopular even among German Jews; many who tried to be law-abiding citizens still remained "eastern" in their speech, manners, and mentality. They had "opted for Germany" but offended their hosts' sensibilities. The novelist Hans Carossa, a conservative of impeccable character, claimed to be no anti-Semite but felt that "eastern Jews" should not be allowed to buy property. He believed that Hitler would punish those S.A. men who were guilty of "excesses." Allen found many respectable citizens of Thalburg who voted for the "good Nazis" because they discounted the violent language of the local leader and trusted that, once in positions of responsibility, the Nazis would behave like other politicians and maintain law and order.

Still, they expected Hitler to create a different kind of state, to talk tough to Germany's neighbors, to rebuild an army, and to restore the pageantry that Germans associated with their memories of greatness.

In Germany, politics was hardly ever "who gets what"; it was always the struggle between angels and devils, Siegfrieds and dragons. Any analysis of the Nazi syndrome that restricts itself to sociological terms leaves out the mythical component and the psychology of resentment. The "little man" presented in somewhat sentimental hues by Fallada in *Little Man, What Now?* is forever perplexed because he does not understand the world that shapes his fate. He does not ask simply, "What next?" He also wants to believe in something and in someone. He looks for the strong man who will rescue him from the snares of Judah's gold and Welsh treachery, and restore him to his due dignity. He sees himself and his rescuer in many shapes: he is Cinderella waiting for the prince, or for Siegfried, the dragon slayer, or for Superman, the Avenger of the Disinherited.

He also sees Germany as a Cinderella among nations, disinherited and likewise waiting for the strong man who will raise her to the rightful place of which she has been deprived. The myth of the Aryan race supports the belief that a better fate should be reserved for the worthy, those whom Nature and God have so clearly marked out as eminent among the races. But what does the Little Man see? Those who should be the masters are being humiliated by the dwarf-nations and dwarf-people, by money powers and world conspiracies.

All observers who have studied the myths of German nationalism during the 1930s agree that even without a depression to drive the lesson home, the imagery of revisionism would have exerted its strongest attraction on millions who had been brought up in a highly status-conscious society. "National socialism may have been as much a cause of the Depression as its consequence" (Graml); it was the politics of *ressentiment* in a world whose values had broken down.

So deep a crisis of consciousness called for quasireligious responses. The fervent belief in the leader, the brother figure who will reverse the vicious order of the world, is only one facet of this utopian myth. Another is the total rejection of "the system," the refusal to cooperate with any part of it, the denial of any possibility of improvement, and hence the belief in a total revolution, the purge of all devils. A third element, which foreign powers overlooked to their regret, is the expectation of continued fight: in a permanently Manichaean world ever-new enemies demand a permanent revolution.

Thomas Mann has described the link between the cultural despair of the declining middle class and the Nazi ideology in this analysis, which he found confirmed in many student meetings at German universities:

> The economic decline of the middle class was accompanied by the perception of a historical crossroads, the end of the bourgeois epoch and its intellectual universe which dates from the French Revolution. A new situation of the soul of mankind, which turns its back on the bourgeois principles of freedom, justice, education, optimism, progressivism . . . expresses itself in an irrationalistic backlash . . . which celebrates as truth the dark underworld of the soul. . . . Alimented by such pseudospiritual streams, this National-Socialist movement amalgamates with the wave of eccentric barbarism and . . . mass-democratic primitivism. . . . The eccentric disposition of a truant humanity finds expression in Salvation-Army style politics, the dervishlike repetition of empty formulas. Fanaticism becomes the principle of salvation.

The question for the republicans was whether they would be able to counter this "flight from freedom" with a better ideology and to give hope to the bewildered masses.

PART THREE
Hubris and Eclipse

16

The Suicide of the Republic

What kind of a republic is this which is defended by its enemies?

—Karl Severing,
Prussian Minister of the Interior

AFTER THE ELECTION OF SEPTEMBER 1930 (see Table 2), the government of "Sad Heinrich Brüning" was no longer parliamentary, but relied more and more on the sole authority of the president. The only truly republican minister in the cabinet, Joseph Wirth, was fired, and his post was given to General Groener, Hindenburg's old man Friday, who now held both the Departments of Defense and of the Interior—an unusual situation in a republic.

Brüning had two aims. At home, he strove to replace the parliamentary republic with a "presidential government," embodied in the old field marshal, whom he worshipped. In foreign affairs he was determined to abrogate the Treaty of Versailles, notably the reparations and disarmament clauses. To achieve both aims he used two instruments: the world economic depression and the threat of a Nazi revolution. He refused to take any measures to alleviate Germany's economic distress. Instead, he decreed severe belt-tightening measures, which enabled him to declare to the Allies: we are too poor to pay one more penny. Testimony from Brüning's closest collaborators reveals—and Brüning's letters and diaries confirm it— that he deliberately looked the other way as the depression was deepening and the masses turned away from the republic.

Brüning's simple recipe was to reduce prices, wages, social services, and capital taxes, while imposing a head tax. To promulgate the necessary measures, on the authority of Article 48 he issued emergency decrees. Motions to repeal them received the votes of communists and rightists; to offset them, Brüning needed the votes of the SPD. But he made no concessions in return. He told the republicans: if you fail to uphold the government, you will have more elections, more Nazis, eventually a dictatorship; and he presented himself as the last rampart of republican government.

TABLE 2. THE REICHSTAG ELECTIONS, 1930-1932
(PERCENTAGE OF TOTAL VOTE)

	September 1930		July 1932		November 1932	
Socialists	24.5		21.6		20.4	
Communists	13.1		14.6		16.9	
Labor combined		37.6		36.2		37.3
Middle-class parties		32.6		19.8		20.0
NSDAP	18.3		37.4		33.1	
Nationalists[a]	11.5		6.6		9.6	
Extreme right combined		29.8		44.0		42.7
Percent of electorate not voting	18.6		16.6		20.1	

a DNVP (Hugenberg), *Landvolk*, Peasants' Party, *Landbund*.

The SPD leadership accepted this logic of the "lesser evil" and agreed to "tolerate" the Brüning government. It also created an extraparliamentary force, the Iron Front, with uniforms resembling those of the Prussian police. Had the Social-Democratic leaders known that two more years of depression lay ahead, their course might have been different. They had no antidepression strategy—Keynes' book was not to appear until 1936—and proposed no structural reforms, but claimed to be acting as "the physician at capitalism's sickbed"—a strange place for a socialist party to be. They hoped that Brüning would keep the Nazis at bay and thereby save the republic and the freedom of the labor movement. In retrospect, it can also be said that they saved the appearances of a state of law for another two years.

This theory did not go down well with the rank and file. Many saw no virtue in saving the empty shell of the republic. To the activists, the greatest of all evils was sharing with Brüning responsibility for his disastrous deflation policies; they did not believe his republican protestations and correctly perceived that his true purpose was to destroy the labor movement. The dissidents were unable, however, to rekindle the class struggle or to persuade the labor parties to form a united front against fascism. A similar appeal by Trotsky was unavailing. The KPD's theoretical monthly, *Die Internationale*, asserted that "democracy and dictatorship are only two forms of the dictatorship of the bourgeoisie"; its Central Committee reported confidentially to Stalin that "a Nazi dictatorship would destroy the SPD and leave us as the only workers' party."

Blinded by party egoism, the communists did not mind acting in tandem with the Nazis. They joined the rightist propaganda against the Treaty of Versailles and supported the Nazi referendum against the Prussian government; they split the trade unions and led wildcat strikes. It is true, however, that the workers were becoming increasingly exasperated with the immobility of the SPD, and that the KPD at least seemed to be doing something. No one on the left seemed to have a strategy for the crisis.

Brüning used compulsory arbitration to reduce the wage level, and decrees to lower the civil servants' salaries. When industrialists proposed measures of economic expansion, he refused on the grounds that Germany must not look prosperous before the reparations problem had been settled. When the French government offered him a billion-dollar loan in return for an "eastern Locarno" (see page 123), he rejected it. In June 1931 he deliberately induced flight of capital to diminish German assets, and he told his finance minister that he had to "impose a measure of misery on the German people." He knew that this policy would increase chauvinist radicalism, but he considered the S.A. a stick to scare the Allies with. A vest-pocket Machiavelli, he was eventually caught in his own tricks and rewarded with a Harvard professorship.

Throughout 1931, the number of bankruptcies, of unemployed, of new recruits for the S.A., increased. The old politicians of the right had to eat the fruits of demagoguery they had sown. Ever since the Harzburg rally (see page 179ff.) they had been tied to Hitler, who now demanded the presidency. Someone had granted him German citizenship so that he could be a candidate in the election of March-April 1932. Brüning then persuaded Hindenburg, now eighty-five years old, to stand for a second term, and the republicans had no choice but to support him. Hence a bizarre alignment: Hindenburg was the candidate of those parties that had ridiculed him as too old and hidebound seven years earlier, and whom he hated or did not understand. By contrast, those who had elevated him on their shield in 1925 as protector of property and tradition now, on the second ballot, had to support the foreign-born corporal, the protagonist of the rabble. Everything was perverted in this election. The republicans hoped to ensure their future by voting for a senile marshal whose campaign managers hoped to get rid of them; Hitler, who openly aspired to dictatorship, campaigned for a majority mandate.

Hindenburg won by a margin of six million votes (see page 180), but resented owing his second term to "reds" and Catholics. Hitler, who had obtained more than one-third of the vote, established himself as the only alternative to "the system." Ernst Thälmann, the communist, polled five million votes but failed to draw any Social-Democrats away from Hindenburg. The Social-Democrats, in nominating Hindenburg, lost their identity and ruined whatever fighting spirit was left in the Iron Front. Brüning, who thought that a Hindenburg victory would give him clear sailing, found out all too soon that he was the real loser. He had built up the presidential dictatorship; instead of being grateful, Hindenburg fired him, just six weeks after the election.

Brüning was a victim of his prejudices. He believed that by paralyzing Parliament and parties he could rule as a bureaucratic manager, with the venerable marshal's charismatic figure behind him. He felt that the time had come to dampen the noisy, noisome, and sometimes embarrassing Nazi antics, their insolent terror, their affronts to authority and good sense, not least their socialist demagoguery. He prohibited the S.A. and SS. To his surprise, the ban aroused a revolt among the generals; they clamored for the head of General Groener, who had signed the decree. Perhaps they had never forgiven him for telling the kaiser the truth on November 9, 1918 (see page 79). He had been a dedicated servant of the republic; his dismissal should have been a warning signal to the republicans. But they trusted Brüning's vain and blind assurance that the constitution was safe since he had the old marshal's ear. He forgot that he himself owed his position to the camarilla that ruled the senile president.

This was his undoing. For Hindenburg's heart was on the other side, and his intimate adviser, General Kurt von Schleicher, was negotiating with Hitler, hoping to find a base for a government that would be more popular—and farther to the right. Hitler demanded new elections and the abrogation of the S.A. ban.

Hindenburg's son Oskar, a totally gullible individual, was selected to guide his father's course. His friends had given Hindenburg an estate in East Prussia, and he listened to his good comrades' and neighbors' complaints: the Junkers had been asked to make a sacrifice. The government had proposed to settle a number of unemployed people on bankrupt big estates—almost the only measure it ever thought of to alleviate the pains of the depression. Oskar von Hindenburg found it easy to convince his father that such a government had to go. One morning late in May 1932, Hindenburg received his chancellor with the notice, which he read to him, that he would not sign any more emergency decrees for "this cabinet of bolsheviks." Stupefied, Brüning had no resources to challenge his idol.

The masses certainly had no reason to rise in defense of a chancellor whose hunger decrees had become a symbol of republican ineptitude. In his last speech before the Reichstag, he had appealed to the parties not to let him down "a hundred yards before the goal," and there was some justification to his appeal. The depression was about to touch bottom in mid-1932; the forthcoming reparations conference promised a favorable settlement; a scheduled disarmament conference was to recognize, at least in principle, Germany's claims to equality. Brüning's fall denied the republic all credit for the fruits of its patience; the subsequent governments reaped the benefits of Germany's improved position.

But Brüning did not fight. Instead of remaining as head of a caretaker government, he handed the office to the man whom Schleicher had selected to succeed him: Franz von Papen, a courtier type, an amateur jockey, a member of the most aristocratic clubs—but a signal failure in everything he had done except a rich marriage. Schleicher served as defense minister, and more members of his aristocratic club, picked by Hindenburg, served as ministers. Most of them were to retain their posts in the Hitler government.

As promised, Papen lifted the S.A. ban, dissolved the Reichstag, and called new elections. To no one's surprise, the Nazi strength was doubled. But the communists, too, increased their vote. The middle-class parties were further pulverized. Now Hitler demanded the chancellorship and, rebuffed, ordered his minions to be on their worst behavior both inside and outside the Parliament. He went so far as to express undying solidarity with a group of S.A. men who had murdered a farm laborer in his bed and been convicted.

Papen served entirely by virtue of Article 48; only 10 percent of the Reichstag supported his administration, which was never confirmed and therefore exercised its power in flagrant violation of the constitution.

The same situation in reverse prevailed in Prussia. The twelve-year-old coalition government under the Social-Democrat Otto Braun lost the election. Communists and Nazis between them had a negative majority which prevented the formation of any new government. The Weimar Coalition, therefore, stayed on as caretaker government; but it was spiritless and ineffective. Since the S.A. felt that the federal government was behind them, they committed murders right under the noses of the Prussian police—giving Papen a pretext for charging that the caretaker government was incapable of maintaining order. With utter contempt for logic, decency, and constitutionality, he deposed the Braun government on July 20, 1932—on the grounds that it did not enjoy a majority! This time the trade unions could not call a strike, the state police were not reliable in case of a showdown with the army, and the SPD leaders had no stomach for a civil war. Nevertheless, the street battles went on. A hundred dead and many hundreds of wounded were the harvest of the Papen government.

True, that government took initiatives which, for the first time, helped the economy to recover. Tax vouchers were given to companies that scrapped old machinery and bought new. Papen also organized a labor service to siphon unemployed youths off the street—and, incidentally, to militarize them.

He seemed to succeed politically, too. He dissolved the Reichstag, and new elections were held in November. For the first time the total turnout decreased, and the Nazi vote declined even more. The Nazi tide was turning.

But Papen still had only 10 percent of the Reichstag behind him. He therefore proposed to Hindenburg a coup d'état. Professor Carl Schmitt, Germany's most influential teacher of political philosophy, who also had argued Papen's case against Prussia before the Supreme Court, provided the ideology: the parties that had "owned" the state were nothing but pressure groups. Instead of the social-economic interests penetrating the web of government, the state should "politicize society." The Nazis had grasped a particle of truth, but their anarchic movement had to be channeled and directed so as to politicize the nation from the top down, to integrate every activity into state activity, and to "nationalize" business, labor, and mass movements. Political decisions would have to be arrived at not by compromise—a noun that in German is usually preceded by the adjective "foul"—but by domination.

Professors Schmitt and Smend and other critics of the Weimar system may have been right in their diagnosis. People were tired of the parties, of new elections every few months, of governments that were unable to act decisively. The elections had failed to provide majorities that could cope with the kind—and magnitude—of crisis the world and Germany in particular were facing. The republic had not known how to earn the people's allegiance; it was unable to call on their citizen spirit, to unite them, to demand sacrifices from them.

But that distrust extended to Papen a fortiori: Schleicher refused to back his coup and still hoped to put together a majority government with NSDAP and the Center Party. When Hitler stubbornly insisted that he had to be chancellor, Schleicher conceived a bold new project, ostensibly inspired by the corporate-state idea of Schmitt and the magazine *Die Tat*. He flattered himself, as a "social-minded general," that he would succeed in rallying various elements—socialist and nationalist—that were disenchanted with their parties. He saw straws in the wind: the impatience of some trade union leaders to get job-creating projects under way; the desperation of top Nazis over Hitler's reckless go-for-broke strategy. Gregor Strasser, the Nazi organization chief, was ready to split, and talked about a "coalition of all anticapitalist forces." At the same time, trade union leader Theodor Leipart saw the dwindling membership rolls and decreasing effectiveness of his organization; he was tempted to dissociate it from politics in order to save collective bargaining—an exciting possibility. The traditional parties were breaking up in disarray. Hans Zehrer, editor of *Die Tat*, wrote about the two last years of the republic in enraptured language:

> Never has there been so much thinking and planning. It was as though the ice had been broken; the old powers resigned themselves to abdication. Inspired minds had overcome the old differences of jargon and began to communicate in a new language; the meaningless old concepts of Right and Left disappeared. . . . We were in a trance; everything seemed possible; everywhere there were forces on the march. None of the conventional truths were applicable any more; everything assumed a new meaning. But in every debate there was a silent guest who, though invisible, dominated the discussion and asked the questions, dictated the answers, and imposed the method. This silent guest was Adolf Hitler.

"*Weimar Dämmerung*" said Stephen Spender—the end of the alleged "boss rule" and the promise of a state "above the interests." But the republic could not be overthrown by a military coup. Only a mass movement that imitated democratic forms could supersede the system of democratic procedures. Schleicher's conception was derived from the ideas of Lassalle, Moeller van den Bruck, and Max Weber: a dictatorship of trustees, a "people's emperor," a Jacobin dictatorship, a "third party" that would cut across the old right-left scale, or the "corporate state"—a strange mixture of medieval guild mystique and Mussolini's straitjacket for modern capitalism.

Schleicher was prepared to adopt a new economic policy—bold tax rebates and public works to prime the pump of recovery, a labor service, and generous land distribution to absorb the unemployed. He also hoped to found his government on broad social movements instead of parliamentary majorities. With that concept in mind, he overthrew Papen and offered himself as chancellor. Could the general achieve what Wilhelm II had dreamed—the social-Caesarian government? Alas, he had no experience of mass movements. Hitler beat the Strasser revolt without effort, and the SPD forbade Leipart to deal with Schleicher. Thus the general appeared empty-handed before the president and had to ask him for the same powers which he had denied Papen.

The ex-chancellor, meanwhile, vengeful and wily, had been busy. To get even with Schleicher, by now he was prepared to accept Hitler as chancellor. In the house of a Cologne banker, Kurt von Schroeder, he reconstituted the Harzburg Front and agreed on a cabinet that would include Hitler as chancellor, Göring as Prussian prime minister, and Wilhelm Frick, who had been a ruthless minister of the interior in Thuringia, for that same position in the Reich. Dr. Goebbels was soon to be added as propaganda minister—the first and last ever to bear that title. The defense minister, General Werner von Blomberg, was also sympathetic to the Nazis: they would be in possession of all means of coercion. But they would be contained (or, as it was styled, "framed") by ten conservatives, including Hugenberg, Papen, and, as foreign minister, Konstantin von Neurath.

The arrangement had the backing of industry and Junkers. The latter were in a hurry because new disclosures about the misuse of farm subsidies were threatened in the Reichstag, and some of the charges pointed to Oskar von Hindenburg. The latter and Papen went to work on the old man once more. On January 30, Hindenburg dismissed Schleicher and made Hitler chancellor.

A low backstage comedy had brought the republic down; even before the newly elected Reichstag could meet, it was dissolved and a new election was to be held under the impact of the newly proclaimed "national revolution." The stunning news unleashed a wave of jubilant demonstrations. Torchlight parades celebrated the "victory." Hindenburg from his palace and Hitler from the window of the chancellor's office saluted the "brown battalions of the German uprising." The republicans were paralyzed. That same evening, the persecution of the "enemies of the state" began. What had fallen was not a form of government but a conception of law. Mob violence took the place of due process, and the new government encouraged it. Hugenberg knew that he was being overridden and confided to a friend: "I have committed the greatest blunder of my life."

What followed was a lesson for all who had kept their eyes shut for fourteen years. The republic had protected all, including its enemies and detractors. Its defense had been in the hands of faint-hearted legalists who had allowed the substance to erode while observing the formalities. Freedom, which had fallen into their laps by default, was defended neither by positive steps to enlarge it nor by militant attacks on its enemies. No republic can live if its officers are without republican conviction and its friends without republican virtue.

* * *

IN EVALUATING THE WEIMAR REPUBLIC, we must beware of the prejudice of hindsight. Its fall is not the judge of its worth. Were its institutions not adequate to its problems? Were the failures attributable to men? Or were outside forces overwhelmingly adverse?

One thing is sure: rarely has a state been founded on such calamitous premises. Rarely has one been pursued by such poor luck in foreign and economic affairs. But in that case we may ask whether so liberal a state should have been attempted under such circumstances. Its political heritage called for a stronger state—one that would have shown force against enemies who used force, and that gave new ideas and new symbols to the young. It failed to give inspiration and it did not develop economic instruments and policies to fight the depression. The disasters were used by its enemies to discredit and erode democratic processes. But could not, should not, the workers' parties have used these same disasters to propose and promote a better republic?

Here, once more, the past was too heavy a mortgage. For KPD and SPD to unite, they would have had to be different from the parties they were—the one totally dependent on Moscow and yet apocalyptic in its expectations, the other mired in the defense of a status quo which had little to recommend its preservation. To save democracy, it would have been necessary to defend both its form and its content, and to defend the latter it was necessary to expand it. In fact, the ultimate reason for the fall of the Weimar Republic was that both its friends and its enemies felt that to save it one would have to transcend it.

To explain the fall of the republic, we need not blame the mysterious "German character"—an explanation that explains nothing and accepts Hitler's type of reasoning. It is quite a different thing to say that the conception of a pluralist state ran counter to the ideas about state and society that had been developed historically in Germany. The traditional state had been a power beyond the parties. The Weimar Republic was a pluralist party state, while power was an idea traditionally connected with the right and with those forces that were opposed to the republic. The idea of a republic deprived of power was too advanced for its time. Society—the "pressure groups"—had not been able to develop a "general will" equipped with both a policy and power.

In the free-for-all of class wars that resulted from this unsolved political problem, the forces of the right, the traditional coalition of heavy industry and large estates, had the upper hand. Since they were quite unreformed and unenlightened, their policies aggravated the cyclical depression, and their conceptions were unsuited to dealing with the structural crisis of the German economy. As a consequence, not only did the working classes lose a good deal of the social gains they had chalked up in the early years of the republic; the middle classes, too, suffered losses of substance and of prestige. In the last years of the republic the upper classes themselves no longer felt secure in their positions. But since they had not acquired political maturity in the brief years of republican prosperity, they were now prepared to surrender the fate of Germany to anybody who promised to rule it—they had tried the *Bürgerblock,* the presidential government, the emergency decrees. Their best hope probably was an army coup—which, however, never materialized. In Italy they had seen that it paid to hand the reins of government to an adventurer (even the radical *Weltbühne* carried laudatory articles on Mussolini, and the popular historian Emil Ludwig published a book with his interviews). They hoped to get rid of the hated republic, the government of party bosses. They did not know that they had surrendered to a revolution of the disinherited.

17

The Nazi Seizure of Power

Whoever did his duty in the service of the state, obeying my orders and taking severe measures against the enemies of the state, whoever ruthlessly used his revolver when attacked, is sure of my protection. If anyone calls this murder, I am the murderer.

—Hermann Göring, 1933

ON THE MORROW OF THE TORCH PARADE, the Nazis had maneuvered their conservative partners into the defensive. The "framers" had been framed. Hitler had no intention of being Hugenberg's errand boy, and not even his chancellor. He wanted total power and the full Nazi program. Dr. Goebbels had given ample warning in good time: "We shall observe all the niceties of the law in order to get power, but we shall use it the moment we have it." S.A. men wanted not a change of government but a revolution—more than a "German uprising." They distributed jobs among themselves to replace the "card-carrying party officials." The "Fighting League of Small Business" hoped to transform the department stores into market stalls. The unemployed clamored for land settlement. The students claimed a share in the university administration. Nazi ideologists saw the day of the "corporate economy" coming. Anti-Semites were looking for Jewish businesses to expropriate. In the factories the NSBO (Nazi Plant Organization)—often just one man in a brown shirt—ousted the leftist shop stewards and proceeded to demand improvements of working conditions. "Old fighters" bounced Jews and republicans out of the civil service and revised seniority rights. Göring purged the Prussian police and civil service of republicans; all provincial governors were deposed; 40,000 S.A. men were put into police uniforms.

More ominously, the terror became official. An emergency decree "for the protection of the German people" gave the police power to arrest persons suspected of fomenting unrest, to ban public meetings, and to censure publications. The SS (*Schutzstaffel*, Himmler's elite corps in black uniforms and death's head cockades;

the SS rune [𝟒𝟒] used in Nazi publications was meant to say: they strike like lightning) was given the function of a special political police: the Gestapo (Secret State Police), which soon earned a reputation for utter ruthlessness.

On February 27, a week before the election, the Reichstag was set on fire. The Nazi leaders lost no time accusing the communists and unleashing terror against them. About 4,000 militants were arrested, including the party chairman, Ernst Thälmann (he was to die in a concentration camp). The party offices and papers were closed. The communist scare was used to justify arrests also of people who had no communist connections whatsoever; but the purpose of the campaign was obvious: to paralyze the Iron Front, to smother the recalcitrants with terror, to give striking power to the SS.

Of course the communists had no motive for arson. The Nazis had an interest, and they also had the opportunity: Reichstag President Göring controlled an underground entrance to the building. The police, however, arrested a Dutch anarchist, Marinus van der Lubbe, who confessed to having done it all by himself (i.e., carried inflammable material into the building and used the draperies to spread the fire, a feat not impossible for one person but not easily accomplished either). Lubbe was convicted by the court and decapitated. Two Bulgarians were arrested and tried with him, one of whom, Georgi Dimitroff, was actually Moscow's adviser to the KPD. His resounding speeches in his own defense and as accuser of the Nazis made him a worldwide hero of the left. After the trial he was exchanged with a prisoner in the Soviet Union and became president of the Comintern.

In 1933 most observers believed that the fire was the work of the Nazis. Subsequent research has provided no proof of this hypothesis, but it has revealed an additional motive: Hitler was afraid that the military might be planning a coup. His swift reaction on February 27 shows that he was prepared and that the patriotic allies did not trust each other.

Despite the terror, the election—on March 5—produced only a bare majority for the government coalition: 43.9 percent Nazis and 7.9 percent German-Nationalists. Two million who had never voted before had rallied to the victors by this time. Nevertheless, to obtain a majority in the Reichstag for the Nazis exclusively, Göring had to declare all communist votes void. KPD deputies were deprived of their parliamentarians' immunity. By March 8, Wilhelm Frick, the minister of the interior, could congratulate himself on the arrest of 10,000 "enemies of the state." Many were held clandestinely by SS goons in makeshift barracks. "Concentration camp" entered the political vocabulary.

A sumptuous ceremony was held in the Garrison Church in Potsdam, linking the new regime with the tradition of Frederick the Great. Royalty, church, army and brownshirts, Hindenburg and other spiked helmets, were united. Then, in its improvised domicile in the Kroll Opera, the Reichstag was told to commit hara-kiri. An Enabling Act, adopted by all against the 120 SPD votes, with the communists absent, authorized Hitler to pass laws by decree.

Two notorious gestures foreshadowed the spirit of the regime. On April 1, the S.A. picketed Jewish stores; in the same month, they began to burn books they considered un-German. More important for the moment, however, was seizing the spoils. Following Papen's precedent of July 20, 1932, Hitler moved to impose Nazi governments on all states. This procedure was called *Gleichschaltung* (homologizing the lower echelons with the Reich government). A law of April 11 purporting to "restore professional civil service" instead reserved government jobs for card-carrying Nazis. At the same time, "People's Tribunals" were created to expedite the load of prosecutions and to strike fear into recalcitrant office holders who were clinging to their jobs. These courts were not bound by the codified law but could render justice "according to sound popular feeling." They meted out 9,500 jail sentences in 1933, and thereafter averaged 10,000 sentences a year. Twenty thousand enemies of the state were formally executed in the twelve years of Nazi government, apart from the genocide victims (see page 255).

With the beginning of the academic year, after Easter, the universities more or less tumultuously dismissed Jewish and republican rectors (academic presidents). A new student law put vigilantes in charge of the classrooms. Among the new rectors were Ernst Krieck in Frankfurt, Alfred Bäumler in Berlin, and Martin Heidegger in Freiburg (the last was to fall out with Hitler a year later). They all made militant announcements promising that "German science" would take the place of the vile objectivity that had dominated traditional academic teaching and research. The historian Hermann Oncken was dismissed because he had published an essay on Cromwell, with pointed allusions to the year 1933. Jewish professors, like other Jewish civil servants, were given a Hobson's choice of resigning or risking unpleasantness. (Heidegger did show courage in standing by a Jewish professor who, moreover, had been guilty of criticizing Carl Schmitt.) Many world-famous scientists, scholars, artists, writers, and musicians found asylum abroad. Germany's famous "cultural life" became a desert, while the transfusion of German intelligentsia made great contributions to the cultural development of overseas countries.

After homologizing the university, the Nazis turned to labor. On

May 1, they purloined the Marxist "Labor Day" celebrations; one day later, they took over all trade unions and formed the "German Labor Front," which was to foment "folk community" in the plant. As "folk comrades," employers were members; beauty commissions were to clean and decorate the working premises; athletics and other entertainment were organized in imitation of Mussolini's *dopolavoro*; finally, group vacations were promoted under the motto "Strength through Joy." (Joy, in this Spartan state, must be justified by strength.)

If "revolution" means replacement of elites, rapid change in life-styles and ways of doing business, a shift of economic parameters, and a new legal and administrative system, then the Nazi takeover of power in 1933 was a revolution. The takeover at the top was smooth because the previous cabinets had paved the way. Hindenburg's friends had occupied the technical and economic cabinet posts, but they were no match for the dynamic, brutal methods of the Nazis, who held the real levers of power and now began to homologize business associations, political parties, youth organizations, the press, the theater, and of course the state radio, which was to become Goebbels' great weapon.

As minister of propaganda he saw to it that the Nazi presence overrode everything everywhere. His monopoly of information surrounded the Germans with a fabricated environment that withheld from their perception whatever was not favorable to the Nazi outlook on the world. Events were even manufactured for the sake of the proper "look" of the world. Everything had to fit into the proper structure. Minds were to be homologized, too. There could not be two different opinions in a totally structured world. "One Reich, one People, one Führer"—the formula leaves no room for parties, and not even for debate. The Reichstag would meet only to sing the national and party anthems; mordant Berlin humor called it the highest-paid chorus the Kroll Opera had ever had.

SPD leaders who were not in concentration camps went abroad; their party was dissolved. In July the Center Party—ignominiously abandoned by the Vatican in exchange for a concordat—agreed to disband, and so did the other middle-class parties. Only the German-Nationalists were allowed to join the NSDAP, while the *Stahlhelm* was absorbed by the S.A.; independent youth groups were ordered to merge with the Hitler Youth.

Hugenberg resigned from the government on June 27, and now Hitler could say that the party had become the state. But this was not the signal for that "second revolution" which the S.A. men were still expecting. On the contrary, the leadership was anxious to terminate the revolution. On July 14, the NSDAP was given the monopoly of all political activities. Neither "reactionaries" nor S.A. troopers were allowed to issue statements or agitate; irregular interventions had to stop; the brown cohorts had to come to order. Frick declared: "The glorious revolution has entered its stage of normal, legal construction. Any sabotage, illegal interference with business, violation of prevailing laws, must be suppressed. The appointment of commissions must be stopped."

In the fall, the Nazis assailed the old system in three fields where ideology was to be molded: the church, the press, and the arts. There had been no dearth of assurances that the spineless intellectuals were prepared to surrender lock, stock, and barrel. The liberal *Berliner Tageblatt* greeted the appointment of Goebbels to the ministry of propaganda by saying: "At last we have a professional!" Professor Eduard Spranger, for whom the republic had created the first chair on youth psychology, told the Academy of Sciences that Hitler was the charismatic leader whom Max Weber had expected. A sociology congress assigned to science the task of "helping to create the historical reality of the German state." The *Zeitschrift für Philosophie* devoted a special issue to "The Philosophy of National-Socialism." Julius Petersen, Berlin professor of literature, declared that Goethe and Schiller had been the first Nazis. Bäumler, the Nietzsche scholar, proclaimed that Hitler was "more than an idea, he is real" (which could not be denied). Needless to say, Carl Schmitt, only a year ago Papen's flunkey, now felt that "there can be no German state without a [National Socialist] movement"; being a teacher of law, he congratulated Germany for having overcome the principle of equality before the law.

In a famous oration, Gottfried Benn offered the new regime expressionism as its ideology. Old Gerhart Hauptmann placed his verse at the service of the regime. The conductor Wilhelm Furtwängler, deemed the most sensitive Beethoven interpreter, agreed to serve as "*Staatsrat*" in Goebbels' Chamber of Culture; like so many others, he hoped to "prevent the worst."

As it turned out later, all these abject accommodations were of no avail. Benn was rebuffed; Heidegger could not abide the official interpretation of Nietzsche; Furtwängler quit in disgust; Carl Schmitt had too many Jewish admirers. Emil Nolde, an ardent Nazi himself, was forbidden to paint, since Hitler had decided that expressionism was "cultural bolshevism." An exhibition of "decadent art" was staged to discredit all art that deviated from the neoclassicist style of Hitler's picture postcards. All arts were homologized by the creation of a

Reich Chamber of Culture presided over by Dr. Goebbels, which distributed favors and decided on matters of taste, on who was to be exhibited, and soon on whose play was to be staged and whose publisher was entitled to a quota of hard-to-get paper. Newspapers were controlled by a special decree of October 4 which subjected editors, publishers, and writers to severe licensing criteria. Only a few novelists managed to continue writing so as to convey a humanist message; Hans Fallada's *If You Ever Ate from a Tin Bowl* (about life in prison) is a moving example. Werner Bergengruen discussed the problem of dictatorship in *The Great Tyrant and the Tribunal.* One popular novelist, Oskar Maria Graf, a Bavarian Rabelais whom the Nazis liked because of his folksy themes, wrote an open letter to Goebbels: "Please burn me, too; don't separate me from my comrades." But the rest of Germany's famous forest of poetry did not even rustle. In fact, it had shed most of its leaves. The writers had gone into exile, even though their skills did not find a ready market there.

Homologizing the churches was a little more difficult, but only because of the totalitarians' insane claim to control, along with the citizens' bodies, their souls as well. The Catholic Church was more than prepared to give Caesar his due. Having concluded an advantageous concordat with Mussolini, it hoped to do as well with Hitler. In March the faithful were given permission to join the NSDAP or S.A. In April Pius XI received Göring and congratulated Germany on having "a government uncompromisingly opposed to communism." Although priests and leaders of Catholic lay organizations were molested by Nazi activists, although convents were searched and the Nazi press reported on their financial machinations to injure the fatherland, a concordat was signed in July—Hitler's first success in foreign policy. The church undertook to instruct the faithful to give unreserved support to the government, and Hitler promised to rescind previous orders to dissolve charitable institutions. The Pope failed to perceive that by shaking Hitler's hand he was helping him discredit the reports about Gestapo terror and atrocities that had been published abroad and whispered inside Germany.

Ungrateful, Hitler had no intention of keeping his part of the bargain. Church institutions were harassed; state institutions became increasingly anti-Christian; and in 1937 Pius XI was forced to publish an encyclical *Mit brennender Sorge* (With Burning Sorrow)—read from the pulpits in German but not published—in which he reaffirmed the Christian doctrine of natural right, rejected the profane idolatry of Führer, state, and race, criticized the regime's efforts to disrupt the family and indoctrinate youth, protested the closing of parochial schools, and deplored the anguish visited on the faithful who would not deny their consciences.

A different problem arose in the Protestant church. Traditionally a state-supported institution, as well as anticommunist, it kept silent when the Gestapo tortured trade unionists and the People's Tribunal sent innocents to concentration camps. But it was traditionalist also in matters of faith. It brooked no tampering with the catechism, and it wanted no S.A. uniform in the pulpit. The Nazis supported a "German-Christian" faction which proposed to aryanize the faith, to drop the Old Testament, and to reinterpret Christ in a more heroic vein. Hitler appointed their leader Ludwig Müller to be Reich bishop. But the majority of the pastors rejected him, and the strong-hearted among the traditionalists founded the Church Bearing Witness (*Bekennende Kirche*). About a third of the pastors, mostly in well-to-do neighborhoods, refused to swear allegiance to Hitler. Their leader was Martin Niemöller in Berlin-Dahlem, a former submarine commander of impeccably patriotic convictions. He volunteered for front service and was willing to give the state everything except his soul, and for that he was put in a concentration camp. Mere compliance, even abject surrender, were not enough. The regime insisted on voluntary, enthusiastic, dependable, total devotion.

Unlike a police state, a totalitarian regime needs the consent of the people, even if that consent has to be engineered. One method of thought control is the referendum. In November Hitler left the League of Nations with a bang and asked for the people's approval. They answered with an enthusiastic 92 percent "yes" vote and at the same time elected a Reichstag of his handpicked men. Thus began the series of demonstrations of unity that have given this type of Caesaristic regime the name "plebiscitarian." Merely authoritarian regimes either do not allow expressions of the people's will or do not succeed in making them sufficiently unanimous. The Caesaristic or plebiscitarian dictators represent the "general will" of the nation by virtue of engineered assent.

The Enabling Law and the referendum did not formally abolish the constitution (it never was abolished), but for all practical purposes Germany had become a state without a constitution. The Führer's will and the power of the ruling party were sovereign. Most institutions of the state and most private associations had been homologized; the army, which preserved its time-honored code, was in league with the dictatorship, and most respectable people, individually and collectively, had hastened to make their peace with the usurpers.

In January 1934, Hitler completed the revolution by abolishing the states and their parliaments as well as the Reichsrat, their representation in an upper chamber. Nazi *Gauleiters* (provincial leaders) took over the state governments. Ironically, unification of the Reich had been an aim of the left; now Hitler brought it about in defiance of the regionalist ideologies which had always been the province of the right. But the Nazi dictatorship was modern-minded and centralist. It readily sacrificed the romantic ideas of its early supporters when reality demanded a sober, forward-looking policy.

It is not surprising that the Nazis also had to disappoint the millions of small shopkeepers who had hoped for a corporate (*ständisch*) guild organization. Department stores and chain stores were "aryanized" but not abolished. Nor did the Nazis break up the big estates to settle the unemployed. The law of September 29, 1933, declared 700,000 farms of sizes between 50 and 125 hectares (122 to 310 acres) "hereditary." These farms—about one-third of the area under cultivation—were entailed, i.e. they could not be sold, mortgaged, or divided. Second sons had to go elsewhere to make a living. Four million small farms were not protected, although they may have accounted for as many Nazi votes.

One grievance of the farmers had always been the fluctuation of their prices, their dependence on a market that seemed to rule blindly. Here the Third Reich brought an effective remedy. A "Reich Food Estate" was created under Food Minister Walther Darré. It was to administer prices and production quotas, and it stabilized the grain markets. But farm income rose far less than other income, and farm technology did not advance because the entailed farms could not borrow capital. Other farms were once again heavily in debt at the end of the Third Reich. Conflicts among large, medium, and small farmers were reflected in sharp disputes between the Food Estate and the party organizations. Actually, fewer new farms were settled under the Nazis that under the republic, while a million people left the farms under the government of "blood and soil."

In the manufacturing industries it was even harder to conceal the gap between Nazi ideology and practice. The law of January 20, 1934, decreed that every enterprise was a "community" with a "leader" at its head. Grievances were not to be fought over but adjudicated by a "trustee." Independent unions (including the NSBO) and strikes were prohibited. The "leader" was to join the Labor Front, which took over many functions of personnel relations.

These measures helped large companies but did nothing for the small businessmen who had been the first to vote for the Nazis. After a year of Nazi government, the craftsmen, small shopkeepers, peasants, and workers were asking what had happened to the "socialism" in the party's name; some were once again talking of a "second revolution." Of the S.A. it was said that many members were "pink grapefruits"— red inside, yellow outside.

It is doubtful, however, that anything would have come out of this grumbling had not the S.A. leaders had personal ambitions. Heinrich Himmler had been clever enough to reserve the police functions for his SS, while the S.A. had no function. Röhm wanted to merge it with the army and to get for himself the military rank he had never earned. But in the interest of efficiency, Hitler rejected such proposals. With the social rise of the goons blocked by the army, the frustrated S.A. men got out of hand; their lawlessness grew so intolerable that Papen gave a speech criticizing their excesses. There is no proof, however, that Röhm or anybody else plotted against Hitler, and he certainly would have been a fool to plot against the army. A falling-out between Hitler and Röhm—the only man with whom Hitler used the familiar "thou"—definitely had occurred in mid-1934.

On June 30, when S.A. leaders were assembled in Wiessee, the SS suddenly struck, arresting hundreds there and in other places. The shabby pretext that they had been caught in homosexual acts fits poorly the charge of conspiracy; and, incidentally, some of their executioners were homosexuals, too. Hitler, who personally directed the operation, used the occasion to settle accounts with others who had betrayed him: Schleicher, Strasser, Gustav von Kahr, and Papen's speechwriter, Edgar Jung. Papen himself, unassailable thanks to his Vatican connections, was placed under house arrest and then dispatched to Vienna to prepare the murder of Austrian Chancellor Engelbert Dollfuss (July 25). Over two hundred persons, among them Röhm, were executed without judgment or defense.

The deed remains unexplained. The amalgam of victims to the right and left of Hitler shows a typical feature of totalitarian dictators— they do not swing from right to left, or from left to right, as democratic governments do, but spin off the unusable elements and concentrate the rest around the center. In this process the dictatorship rises above the factions and gains a new level of popularity; it unites the people for new goals. This sounds paradoxical; but Nazi authors and propagandists came to the absurd conclusion that by his arbitrary act the Führer had proven himself as the true protector of the law.

While the world stood horrified at seeing "a Chancellor who names and shoots his ministers in person," Stalin immediately recognized that Hitler had shown his mettle as a dictator who was likely to stay, and began to maneuver toward a rapprochement. More strangely, the 30th of June also earned Hitler the appreciation of true conservatives. Schacht now became his minister of economics and Carl Goerdeler his price commissioner. The inevitable Carl Schmitt declared that "the National-Socialist state is perhaps more constitutional than most other countries." To complete the logic, all files relating to the event were burned.

Five weeks after the bloodbath the old marshal died and his office was abolished. Hitler proclaimed himself "Führer and Chancellor of the Reich" and had the army swear allegiance to his person. Once again the people were called on to ratify what had been done, but only 84.6 percent did so. The 15 percent who dared to stay at home were heroes, and some urban districts, especially in workers' towns like Bielefeld, wealthy neighborhoods like Berlin-Wilmersdorf, and Catholic places like Aachen, produced more than 30 percent "no" votes.

After that, the ballot counting was controlled more effectively, and all districts always produced the same unanimity of support for the regime. Resistance was no longer permitted to show; it was all underground and, being without short-term hope, withered away. Europe had entered the age of the totalitarians. After 1934, Italian fascism, Hungary's and Rumania's racist movements, the military dictatorship that was to install itself in Spain, and the GPU dictatorship in Russia all point in the same direction: Europe was going into a decade of totalitarian conquests.

18

The Command Economy

*With spinning wheels and folk dances one cannot
produce guns and airplanes.*

—Schacht

IT WAS HITLER'S GOOD LUCK that unemployment was declining. The
worst of the slump was over; Papen's scheme for industry was beginning
to work; Franklin D. Roosevelt had broken up the World Economic
Conference and thereby given European protectionism a good excuse;
there was enough slack in the German economy to allow a quick
recovery; and Hitler could guarantee labor peace. The mere fact that
the insecurity and anxiety of the previous year had yielded to a stable
regime encouraged investment.

In September 1933 the great "labor battle" was begun, a program
of public works on a gigantic scale: the autobahn, barracks, arms
production. As a master technician at the head of the Reichsbank,
Schacht financed all this with shrewdly designed bonds, so as to avoid
the creation of new consumer demand. He also reduced interest rates
from 8.8 percent to 4.4 percent in four years, and he increased the
public debt from seven to forty-two billion marks—contrary to the
doctrines he had professed in a popular book.

Many unemployed were whisked off the streets by a universal
labor service (followed in March 1935 by universal military training);
numerous jobs were created through rearmament and in the new
bureaucracy of the party and the "estates" (*Stände* or corporations).
There were chambers and estates for almost every industry and business
category. Fifty-two Guild Associations were formed to satisfy the
ideological yearnings of the romantic Nazi followers who had expected
salvation through the *Ständestaat*. This was different from Mussolini's
"corporate state," which applied to industrial labor relations only.
The German guilds were meant to help small business. But they had
little power, and when the self-sufficiency program was put into
practice, they soon turned into government instruments for allocating
materials and other controls.

This was also true of the big agricultural estate. The idea was to protect peasantry as the healthy foundation of the German race. In practice, Nazi farm policy was motivated first of all by the aim of self-sufficiency. Instead of an organ of peasant self-administration, the agricultural estate was an instrument for administering the peasants.

The agrarian law of September 1933 had two sides: it gave peasants an incentive to consolidate small holdings and thereby forced many people to seek employment in the cities; it also stabilized farm prices. While it eliminated the uncertainties of the market, it also removed the incentive to modernize the farms. Thus, one goal of Nazi philosophy was in conflict with the other. The genuine concern for the family homestead contradicted the drive toward self-sufficiency.

However, the self-sufficiency program was pursued with vigor. Its aims were to save foreign exchange and to prepare Germany for the eventuality of war. Both goals were also set for industry: to create substitute materials, to develop sources of raw material, to invent processes that would make it unnecessary to import foreign goods. A feverish search for oil, iron ore, and rare metals was begun, and the chemical industry was encouraged to experiment with man-made fibers. The most sensational inventions were the flexible perlon (related to nylon) and artificial rubber ("buna"), both based on coal derivatives (Germany has an ample coal base). Oil could also be made from hydrogenated coal.

Although these processes might have been expensive, in a closed economy this did not matter. All the government had to watch was the consumer price and the balance of foreign exchange. Since wages were frozen for some time, the new money that was being pumped into the economy went largely into investment. Building construction, which had slumped to 2.3 billion marks in 1933, within four years went up to 9 billion marks, surpassing the Weimar figures; steel output rose from 7.2 million to 19 million tons. The Reich's revenue increased from 6.6 billion to 17 billion marks. Consumer goods production rose only moderately; excess wages were siphoned off the market through frequent collections (Winter Aid, National-Socialist Welfare, Germans Abroad, etc.) and through savings schemes—for a Volkswagen, a house, etc.—financed in advance by wage check-offs. When consumers complained about empty shelves, Göring answered coolly: "It's either guns or butter." Long before there was any actual threat of war, the German worker and the German economy were on a war footing. Families were supposed to eat a frugal one-pot meal once a week. The Sanitation Department ran separate collections of waste paper, aluminum, and tin, and later also of fats. Neighborhood control and "block wardens" enforced those household economies.

TABLE 3. INDEX OF INDUSTRIAL PRODUCTION (BASE YEAR 1932 = 100)

	Production goods	Munitions	Consumer goods
1935	206	950	113
1938	291	2,600	129
1941	ca. 400	3,000	125
1944	ca. 500	8,000	110

Food prices rose steadily, and imports were curbed as strictly as possible. Consumers received less foreign fruit, less meat and fat, even less bread than before the Nazi regime, but more potatoes and vegetables. They were, however, well supplied with household appliances; cars and other former luxuries rapidly became articles of more common use. Because of full employment, family income rose by 10 to 20 percent, while the cost-of-living index rose by only 8 percent. It is true that fund raising, compulsory loans, payroll savings, and higher taxes reduced take-home pay; and of course that Volkswagen was never delivered—except in the shape of an army jeep (See Table 3).

In 1932 Germany had spent only 1 percent of its gross national product on defense. Then, although the gross national product rose, defense rose even faster: to 6 percent in 1934, 13 percent in 1936, and 27 percent in 1938, not counting autobahn and other defense-related expenditures. In 1939-1941, despite the war, the percentage did not increase, but it jumped to 61 percent in 1943. Of sixteen million tons of concrete used in 1938, half was put into the Westwall and other military installations, one-tenth into the autobahn system, and one-tenth into housing. German industry produced 5,000 military and 3,500 civilian aircraft in 1939. I. G. Farben's sales soared from 876 million marks in 1932 to 1,990 billion in 1939.

The promises to small shopkeepers were forgotten. Only Jewish department stores were shut down. But up to 1939, 10,000 stores had to be closed in Berlin alone for want of merchandise.

In industrial enterprises, the leader principle was carried out rigidly. Under Gustav Krupp, the president of the Reich Association of German Industry, each branch or trade had its leader; within each firm, one leader was responsible for output and discipline. The workers elected "trustees" from a list provided by Labor Front and management.

The Labor Front also provided a shop steward and ran the program "Strength through Joy," which provided all kinds of entertainment, recreation and education: theater, concerts, cruises, sports, etc.

With labor service and military service, and with the feverish drive for increased production, the labor supply grew tight. Plants were luring workers away from low-paying jobs. The regime reacted with characteristic rigidity, and employees were frozen to their jobs or even commandeered to where they were needed. By 1936 it became necessary to place the whole economy on a mobilization footing. At the party rally of September 1936, while taking a sharp anti-Soviet propaganda line, Hitler stole the greatest bolshevik slogan and announced a Four-Year Plan. It was to be a four-year crash program of preparation for war.

Far from being a plan in the sense that all factors of the economy were harmonized for best performance of the whole, the "plan" existed only for the development of resources and arms supplies, while the rest of the economy had to adjust to that purpose. Traditional industries had to become suppliers of the munitions industry; other industries were starved of supplies and manpower needed elsewhere. Ad hoc regulations and special requisitions topped each other. Göring was made plenipotentiary for the Four-Year Plan, and he pushed his pet projects so vigorously that Schacht's Ministry of Economics was totally overshadowed. Late in 1937 Schacht resigned; but he retained his post as president of the Reichsbank.

We may therefore divide the course of Nazi economic policies into roughly four periods: (1) 1933, the initial "pump priming," concerned with reducing unemployment; (2) 1934, the "labor battle" with big public works, and the "grain battle" for self-sufficiency in foodstuffs; (3) 1936, the Four-Year Plan, with accelerated rearmament and special development programs such as the costly Salzgitter ore search; and (4) total mobilization for war, coinciding with other measures of war preparation (see Chapter 19). When the private sector did not adequately respond to the hectic demands of the government, the Nazis set up their own enterprises—either under state sponsorship or, in the cases of Göring and Goebbels, as their own, party-supported venture. They even created a Bank for Public Works (*Öffa*). One-third of all incomes now was derived from government business or subsidies. A free market no longer existed, and most industries could be expanded, or shut, by fiat. In a perverse way, "socialism" had been forced upon the Nazi economy. But it was the socialism of the barracks. Labor Front leader Robert Ley could say that the private citizen was a thing of the past.

To finance this huge enterprise, Germany's neighbors and creditors were ransacked. Less developed economies and small countries were drawn into the German economy of scale (*Grossraumwirtschaft*). This design developed first out of the voracious appetite of the arms industry; other industries had to earn *Devisen* (foreign currency). Imports had to be vigorously controlled to prevent currency from leaving. Money transfers out of the country were made nearly impossible. And if someone should think of evasion—buying a valuable stamp and taking it abroad could be punishable by death! The whole scheme was possible only in a dictatorship of this most ruthless type.

A most important source of *Devisen* was the control of foreign trade. Schacht's stratagems to improve Germany's foreign-exchange balance were legendary. Importers had to deposit their payments, and exporters their earnings, with the Reichsbank. By manipulating these accounts, Schacht created various kinds of "frozen marks" originating from different kinds of transactions, which could be bought at different discounts. Thus, he had the benefits of a devalued currency without its inconveniences.

He also used strong-arm techniques to force German merchandise on reluctant neighbors. To cite one example, he bought the entire raisin harvest of Turkey, then told the Turks they could use their credit account only to purchase certain items that happened to be available—e.g., this lot of harmonicas, sure to last Turkey for a generation. *Grossraumwirtschaft* was nothing but grand larceny for the benefit of the German economy. Germany's creditors were made to pay not only for Germany's armament but also for their own enslavement; their dependence was used to force on them barter agreements which converted partners into satellites. Referring to Denmark's need to export eggs, Berlin wits said that Schacht had grasped Denmark by the "eggs"—slang for testicles.

The tight controls brought strong interference with the operation of the enterprise. But did all this alter the basically capitalistic structure of the economy? Employers had to join the industrial estates that allotted orders and raw materials; but no company was expropriated or nationalized. Can the profit principle be reconciled with the principle of planning—especially the extent of planning that became necessary in the later stages of the war when the most minute details of allocation and production came under public control?

Obviously, this was not socialism; but it could no longer be called capitalism either. Franz Neumann called the system that developed in the last years of the war "command economy"—an economy which does not follow its own laws but the orders of the party or the state. Price movements no longer indicate the balance of demand and supply. Decisions on investment are made by the state, and not for the sake of profit. Profit is not eliminated; but it is no longer the motor, just as price is no longer the regulator but is regulated. The road to success lies not in providing service to people but in fulfilling the government's or the party's desires.

Nor does this mean that the organization of production and distribution is perfect. On the contrary, various claimant agencies—and in fact conflicting fiefs—may fight over jurisdiction and appropriation. Thus, Göring's Four-Year Plan authority may fight with Göring's *Luftwaffe* Ministry over the allocation of aluminum, and both may be disputed by Walther Funk's Ministry of Economic Affairs, by the governor of conquered Poland (a high-ranking party official), by the Organization Todt (later Speer) in charge of public works and defense projects, and by the procurement office of the army. Also, the structure may be very inconsistent. In one case, the traditional industry "leaders" are also the administrators of industrywide assignments; in another, prominent party men may be given the means of carrying out a crash program. These conflicts show that totalitarianism is not to be equated either with efficiency or with harmony. Corruption also plays its role: big orders go to those who contribute to Hitler's "special funds."

Even before the war forced them to subordinate their romantic and utopian ideas to the overriding rationale of efficiency, the Nazis had begun to favor big industry over small business, large estates over homestead farms, industrial organization over guild or corporate structures. Millions of small shops were "combed out" to recruit workers for factories. Millions of farmers were transplanted into the wide spaces of the east—though into the trenches, not as settlers. Once this high degree of state planning has been achieved, however, economic purposes depend on the kind of state that commands the economy. The Nazis could have decided to buy fewer guns and more butter. With *Grossraumwirtschaft*, a German empire in Europe could be largely self-sufficient and might give its citizens, including the satellite races, a better living. When the loot came in from all over Europe, consumers were satisfied. Unlike World War I, World War II did not begin to hurt the Germans badly until its last year, when the enemies were pressing in. Hitler seemed to have remembered the 1918 revolution: he did not tighten supplies as stringently as might have been possible and as was indeed suggested by Speer. He did not call on the women to do war work as much as, for example, the British did. (Of course, prisoners and conscripted foreigners were available; Himmler rented them out to I. G. Farben and Krupp.)

The thousand-year reich did not last long enough to realize its founder's vision; also, Hitler had little understanding of economic facts and theories. But even under the stress of war—and perhaps because of it and through it—the features of a totalitarian economy grew visible. At the bottom, prisoners or slaves, belonging to the inferior races, would do the menial work. Small-scale capitalism would supply the daily needs of the people under the supervision of the state. But the great tasks of the nation would be conducted by the industry leaders in conjunction with the party elite. Their task would be to direct and plan, to determine goals and policies. "Common weal goes before self-interest" was to be the guiding principle. Economic man had been replaced by the politically mobilized soldier-worker, the servant of his Führer and his nation, the master of the rest of Europe.

19

The Führer State

*Not theses and ideas are the laws of our being. The
Führer himself is Germany's reality.*

—Heidegger

NATIONAL SOCIALISM, FASCISM, and their various satellite regimes
in Croatia, Slovakia, Rumania, and Hungary had in common a
racist ideology and a political structure with three salient features:
a terrorist police organization, a movement or party, and a leader
whose personality and charisma demanded unquestioning obedience.
The means of domination was moral homogeny: the raised arm
and "Heil Hitler" greeting, "one Reich, one People, one Führer!"
Unlike a police state in the strict sense, which rules by brute force,
the Nazis could rule because the nation was on the Führer's wavelength,
and each citizen was involved, day in, day out, in the party's organizational network: S.A., Winter Aid, Labor Front, Hitler Youth, the
student organization, the professional leagues, etc.

To begin with the terror machine: the SS numbered 50,000 in
1933 and rose to 200,000 by 1939. It was first assigned the administration of illegal violence, then assumed the functions of a political
police and provided the personnel for Gestapo and concentration
camps. Later it received jurisdiction over the conquered territories
and the "Order Castles" (see page 225). The Waffen SS admitted
non-Germans of proper stock to service for the German fatherland.
Hitler used the SS to control the party; its leader, Himmler, reported
directly to him.

In the occupied countries the SS was the principal agent of
genocide. During the war, Himmler was able to build himself an empire
of slave laborers. Concentration camp inmates were exploited in
soil conservation projects or in the peat bog (where a defiant song—
though in minor key—was composed that went around the world).

The main purpose of the camps, however, was to break the inmates'
spirits, to humiliate them, and to "liquidate" them. The camps were
run in such a way as to ensure a high death rate. Their very name
inspired dread, and people referred to them only by the letters K.Z.

By 1937 the number of inmates had declined to 10,000, but at the outbreak of the war it was once again up to 25,000. Then it rose quickly to several million despite the heavy "turnover." This has rightly been described as a new phase in the Nazi revolution. The purpose of the concentration camps, then, was no longer deterrence but extermination.

To improve the race and to save food, mental patients and congenitally disabled persons also were put to death; but the killings were kept secret. The average German may have believed that the SS persecuted only enemies of the state; but he was afraid to test the borderline. He kept the window closed when listening to a foreign broadcast. He was careful not to speak his mind in the presence of strangers—and, alas! even in the presence of his children, who, he knew, had to report everything to their youth leader. Before voicing even a mild complaint or telling one of the many jokes about Göring's deficient sex life, he would "shoulder check" to see whether anyone was listening in; this was soon dubbed "the German look."

The Third Reich was a system of sycophants and spies. Behind the rhetoric of folk community, people were afraid of each other. The Nazis, who had been so bold in opposing the republic, had made the Germans into a nation of cowards; and as Hegel said, terror is usually spread by people who are scared.

Yet this is only half of the story. The Nazi Reich was held together not only through fear but also through the highly disciplined party and through the cult of the leader. He had been successful—which probably vindicated him in the eyes of many. He had been favored by Providence—Hitler's frequent boast—in both his economic and his foreign policies. He had, by merely coming to power, ended the strife and indecision that had plagued Germany. Now he was surrounded with all the paraphernalia of power which Goebbels and Speer knew how to display impressively at party rallies, over the radio, in the movies, in print. He was providing Germany with pride and glory; he had wiped out Versailles and ended the "shame." No doubt he had charisma, and he knew how to talk to the German people. He appeared to be doing for them what they were unable to do for themselves.

This "leader relationship" is what matters. Whether Hitler was "a genius" or just clever; whether he was the beneficiary of a myth or may have had psychic powers that enabled him to dominate people much his betters; whether he was a visionary or an actor; whether he was a relaxed conversationalist or dull in private gatherings (and all this conflicting evidence has been reported) is beside the point. At that time most Germans did not know any of the things that came to light later. The question is only this: what made an intelligent nation with a humanist tradition believe that this visibly hysterical mountebank had this exalted relation with them? Why did women kiss the fenders of his car? Could he "enchant" people more effectively than other speakers? He was assuming a role, or a number of roles, which most people were not ready to play themselves; they would have liked to be in cahoots with him, though, whenever he did assume these burdens.

It may therefore pay to study not Hitler's character, but his public roles. They had been prepared by mythmakers like Stefan George and Goebbels: the leader alone knows the destiny of the nation and in fact embodies it. His zigzag policies may not be comprehensible to the ordinary follower; hence faith in his superior wisdom alone guarantees the continuity of both ideology and policy. He may conclude a pact with Stalin while remaining antibolshevist, or a concordat with the church while remaining unrelenting in the pursuit of a secular, totalitarian state. This is the meaning of Hitler's oft-quoted remark about lying: the leader must be faithful to his ultimate purposes but not to his enemies or third parties. If he promises to make no further territorial demands (as he did at Munich) and then breaks his word six months later with the seizure of Prague, the true follower does not question his morality but rejoices admiringly that the clever Führer once more fooled his enemies.

The second function of the Führer is to hold the masses in thrall. A totalitarian regime is not simply a dictatorship over the masses, but it enlists their participation, even their enthusiasm. They feel represented through the person of the Führer; their acclaim gives the regime a pseudodemocratic facade. In contrast to a merely bureaucratic, military, and authoritarian dictatorship, the plebiscitarian variety receives its legitimation through frequent demonstrations of consent by the governed. The unanimity may be manufactured, but the tricks work; in the plebiscite a simple "yes" to an obviously desirable goal is linked to a manifestation of confidence in the regime. "Do you approve of the *Anschluss* of Austria with the German Reich?" elicited the predictable 99 percent "yes" votes. The masses chanted "Führer we thank you," and later on many graves bore the inscription "He died for the Führer."

The transmission belt between leader and masses is the party and its divisions—S.A., Winter Aid, Women's Auxiliary, Hitler Youth, Motor Corps, etc.—which keep the people in a constant state of participation. They must march, meet, collect contributions, and generally become absorbed in community work so extensive that all private affairs seem unimportant. The party is also the principal instrument of power which sees to the execution of the Führer's will in every activity, civilian or public, in the press, the theater, business, the law, the administration, etc. The party's power is absolute; it does not derive from the fact that, having conquered the government, it now mans all the desks. The party is above the government and gives instructions to it. It has its men in the administration and the estates, as in the press, in business, in the churches, etc., and it may also prefer to work through traditional agencies. In foreign policy, for instance, the leader may wish to depart from good practice even while the bureaucracy continues to work along with the conventional partners.

Thus, contrary to a widely accepted opinion, the party is not identical with the government. It considers the government its instrument, but it may often have to fight with it. A bureaucracy functions because it operates with more or less permanent rules and routines; it depends on credibility and predictability to deliver effective services. Its rigidity is a virtue in the eyes of those whose interest it serves. The party, by contrast, is constantly changing its short-term goals and even its methods; it has crash programs and whims; it follows the ups and downs in its mighty leaders' power struggles. Thus Göring quarreled with Schacht, Himmler quarreled with Frick. Joachim von Ribbentrop quarreled with Neurath—or rather, he conducted his own foreign policy until he had bounced him; but even then, high-ranking officials in the Foreign Office continued to counteract Ribbentrop's policies.

These instances of infighting are not exceptional but rather the rule, and nothing can be farther from the truth than the widespread belief that totalitarian regimes are more efficient than others because they are monolithic. They are neither monolithic nor efficient. If they achieve some selected aims, it is usually at the expense of others. The crash program benefits from the propaganda campaign that accompanies it; but under the monopoly of information the damage done elsewhere gets no airing either before or after it has occurred. Nor does anyone under the totalitarian regime ever hear about the many things it has failed to do.

After the Nazis were gone, their archives revealed the amazing amount of friction, frustrations, and miscarried plans in the regime. Not even the Gestapo lived up to its reputation of efficiency. For all its ruthlessness and thoroughness, thousands survived its persecution. Half of its effectiveness may have been owed to its reputation for being effective. The only advantage of a dictatorship seems to be that it can keep its scandals and failings from public scrutiny. The myth of totalitarian efficiency is largely based on a determined leader's ability to achieve a quick surprise effect (*schlagartig*—like a thunderbolt—was Goebbels' favorite word) while disregarding all other considerations. But some of these considerations may be vital, and the administrative bureaucracy was no longer capable of checking mistaken initiatives. Rather, it had become a mere tool of the party satraps who had seized command: a *Gauleiter*, a Führer or special deputy of some organization. There were no cabinet meetings. Hitler was in Berchtesgaden enjoying his private chalet, where he devoted himself to the main project of the year or, with his architect Speer, indulged himself in grandiose daydreams of the future world capital.

Thus the satraps were free to pursue their own daydreams and to commandeer the resources of the government for a sprawling multitude of special-purpose organizations, each pushing in its own direction with stubborn determination and creating new institutions that followed their rationale. These divergent drives did not result in a new legal order but in an irrational rivalry of fiefdoms. The regime has therefore been called polycratic (Martin Broszat) or dual government (Ernst Fränkel, emphasizing the duality of party and administration), or "a state of permanent improvisation" (Karl Dietrich Bracher). Franz Neumann denied it the character of a state altogether.

Misled by the evidence of disharmony and failure, some scholars have wondered whether the term "totalitarian" is appropriate. But undervaluing the totalitarian character is just as mistaken as overrating it. The characteristic quality of totalitarianism is not its effectiveness or its success but its despotic process of decision making, combined with that peculiar relationship between the ruling party and the organs of society of which we have spoken. In pluralistic societies, information and decisions by independent agents cause the government to make judgments about the problems it has to meet. In a totalitarian society, the preconceived view of reality, the problem to meet, and the solution are handed down from the policymaker to both the populace and the government. No independent check is possible; or if it is possible, the regime can deal with it in one of two peculiar ways. Since it holds the information monopoly, it can minimize a substantive difference of opinion into a personal scandal, as it did in the case of the generals (see page 234); or it can paint the dissidents with the brush of heresy and sedition, as in the case of the Röhm revolt.

There may even be a pattern characteristic of totalitarian regimes. Since the Führer moves freely from one opportunistic position to another, those who carry out a certain temporary policy may get attached to the attitudes or people favored by that policy—or, as Friedrich Meinecke said: "We Germans have the bad habit of making a philosophy out of every tactical position." Such sectarians to the right and left of the totalitarian center must be purged periodically. Even enemies of the regime often mistake the purge for a sign of strength. It is the result of frictions that cannot be solved.

The purge prevents a bureaucrat from acquiring a clientele, and the clientele from becoming a claimant group that might endanger the totalitarian view of the environment. But it also deprives the ruling party of a concrete link with some part of the populace and therefore forces it to escalate its totalitarian claims, its ideological view of the world, its challenge to those dark and abstract chimeras which it pretends to fight.

Why the regime needs concentration camps now becomes plausible: not to put real enemies behind barbed wire but to prove that it has enemies who cannot be fought in any other way. They are at once very powerful (as the Wall Street Jews) and visibly reduced to impotence (as the concentration camp inmates). On the other hand, the terror troop is made highly visible, and whispering campaigns make it even more formidable; its existence is proof that the regime needs it. It is not the idealism of the regime that justifies the terror, but the terror that justifies the regime.

Every totalitarian regime receives its name primarily from this ability to monopolize and manipulate information, to surround its denizens entirely with a fake impression of reality—its own superiority or even omnipotence; the weakness—nay, impotence—of its enemies; the justness of its claims and the futility of all counterclaims. Recognizing this basic strength of the regime, we immediately see its vulnerable point: it cannot expose itself to any truth-revealing contact with reality. Once caught in its own web of lies, it must "flee forward" into more adventure, more risk, more emergencies. The greater the suffering and distress in the later years of the war, the more soulful were Goebbels' appeals to rise heroically to the occasion. The final *Götterdämmerung*, in Hitler's last message, sounds like a proud achievement of the inborn death wish. (The psychoanalytical dimension of death worship has been noted, and exploited by the Nazis themselves. The death's-head units of the SS and the lurid vocabulary of destructiveness in Nazi propaganda are only the forerunners of the final education for death and the rush to war.) War did not happen because somebody fumbled the ball. It came out of the logic of the system, both by the will of the Führer and by the compulsion under which he worked.

Even the language was twisted to convey the special Nazi meanings in common speech. The "battle for bread" and the "battle of work" may have been good propaganda slogans for a self-sufficiency program, but the monster coinage "battle of births" (*Geburtenschlacht*), breeding children for the Führer, says the exact opposite of what it is supposed to mean.

This was the climate in which German children grew up during twelve years of Nazi monopoly in education. Not only the school taught Nazi ideals; in addition, boys had to serve in the Hitler Youth and girls in the German Girls' League (*Bund Deutscher Mädchen*). And when they left school, they were further indoctrinated in the Labor Service and in the army. (During the war there were women's auxiliary services.) To get anywhere in their careers, people had to join the party, the S.A., or one of twelve other Nazi organizations. Newspapers, radio, movies, and books provided a one-pot meal for the mind.

All life in the Third Reich was declared a continuous battle; the Reich could not exist without fighting. University studies, of course, were meant not to enlarge a person's horizon but to help the state. Instead of improving standards, the pressure almost suffocated the famous German scholarship. Talent was shunted into the "National Political Schools," which placed emphasis on the education of party leaders, and onto the Adolf Hitler Schools. Selected, racially perfect boys would be received at Himmler's "Order Castles," where he hoped to breed a race of overlords.

"Domination" (*Herrschaft*) was the key word in the totalitarian universe. Each man had his place in the hierarchy. That is implied in *ständische Ordnung*—the corporate order. Nevertheless, the regime was egalitarian: every soldier carried the marshal's baton in his knapsack. The men at the top—with Göring and Speer the only exceptions— were from modest families, unspeakably middle-class and plebeian in their manners and education. Their mediocrity caused Hannah Arendt to speak of "the banality of evil"; no Cesare Borgia among them. Even Hitler was only a beer-hall politician, artificially inflated. Had the times been different, these men might have been drill sergeants or family sadists, collectors of odd objects or cultists, but not public monsters. The Nazi revolution gave them the means to act out their dreams. They became mass murderers because by their lights the world seemed disorderly. They thought of themselves as crusaders who had been selected to right the wrongs of world history. The Germans had been at the bottom; now they would be the masters.

For this fantasy they had to be prepared to kill coolly, without emotion. Jews were vermin and had to be exterminated—a dirty job, but necessary. Himmler, who fainted when he saw the corpses, admonished his men to be tough:

Whether other nations prosper or perish concerns me only inasfar as
they are usable as slave laborers to support our culture. . . . It is a
fundamental mistake to be sentimental and to let other peoples benefit
from our liberalism. . . . Most of you may know what it means to see a
hundred or five hundred corpses, or a thousand. Withstanding this and
remaining an honest man, that has made us tough. That is a leaf of glory
in our history that can perhaps never be written.

This is the madness of the Nazis. A murderer who hates his victim,
a killer who wants someone's money, is at least understandable;
Brecht would call them middle-class murderers. But to kill millions
because their skull measurements are wrong cannot be described
with the word "banal"; this is to sever a nation's link with civilization.

The Nazis' madness, which they tried to communicate to the
whole nation, was not of the raving kind. It was strictly controlled,
bureaucratized, and mechanized. There were no pogroms in which
the people's rage stormed against the Jews. When the time came to
smash windows of Jewish shops and synagogues, the S.A. assembled
in orderly fashion, at 7 a.m., to loot designated targets. The death
factories were run with cool efficiency. The victims were savaged as
much as the circumstances required but not with any expense of
emotion.

If Max Weber saw the charismatic leader as an alternative to
bureaucratic government, here was the combination of both: a totally
rational apparatus in the service of total irrationality. It is surprising
to find how modern and rational the Nazis were in the choice of
their means. Whenever necessary, they discarded their German folk
ideas. They certainly believed that women belonged in the kitchen; but
when Hitler needed babies, he discarded the sanctity of the family.
Without giving women any "rights," he actually made it easier for them
to get a divorce, and the Nazis did more for illegitimate children and
their mothers than the republic had done—their population policy had
a higher priority than their ethical prejudices.

Likewise, they quickly forgot their preference for worthy craftsmen
and put all their money into big industry. As we have seen, they did
not ask what system, capitalism or socialism, produced the goods, so
long as it was efficient. They were pioneers in the invention of industrial
systems analysis and of organization. All fascist systems—especially
those in underdeveloped countries—are "modernizing," no matter
how reactionary their ideologies may be. Liberals and humanists do not
readily admit that progressive policies in technological fields can go
together with political reaction. Europeans, however, need only

remember the experience of enlightened despotism and mercantilism in the seventeenth and eighteenth centuries. The Nazis freely spoke of Hugenberg and the industrialists as "reactionaries," and did not consider themselves conservatives. In practice, their totalitarian claims clashed with those conservative ideas that were entrenched in bureaucracy, army, and church: the purposeful rationality of Hitler's, Himmler's, and Göring's ruthless pursuit of power overrode the narrow, dogmatic interests of the churches and the professional judgments of the generals. As with the arts and with science, war and salvation were to be decided on by the Führer's intuition—or rather, since war was to be substituted for salvation, the specialists in both fields were pushed into a corner.

Was this deluded view really accepted by the German people? For a long time, the bulk of the population was prevented from noticing what was being planned for them. They accepted the higher incomes, the greater job security, and the cruises with "Strength through Joy." They enjoyed Hitler's successes in diplomacy. But they did not seem to take his further plans seriously. The Nazi leadership was badly shaken when people lined up in the streets of Munich to cheer Chamberlain as a peacemaker (see Chapter 22). When war did break out, people did not cheer the troops marching off as they had done in 1914, nor did they greet them with flowers as they came home from victories over Poland and France. They did their duty—grimly and efficiently, but unenthusiastically and unconvinced. They received the loot the soldiers sent home from the seven corners of Europe and Africa. But they kept asking why the government did not allow them to enjoy the fruits of all those victories, for which they had made so many sacrifices.

When Hitler could provide no more victories, Berliners began to refer to Göring as "Meyer" because he had boasted: "If a single British airplane gets through to Berlin, my name shall be Meyer." Pointing to the ruins around them, remembering that Goebbels had taught them to chant "Führer, we thank you!" they now said sarcastically, "For all this we thank the Führer." Or they asked what unit of measurement "one Goeb" was, the answer being: the energy required to shut off a million radio receivers.

Goebbels never succeeded in spinning his cocoon of propaganda around all of Germany. As long as one country remained independent, and one corner of the German experience remained uncontrolled, Hitler had not won and could not feel secure. And this is the ultimate reason he had to go from one war to the next. The totalitarian monster cannot digest unless it keeps eating.

20

The Road to Empire

*War is nothing more than the continuation of politics
with different means.*

—Clausewitz

HITLER'S REVOLUTION WAS DIRECTED AGAINST the prevailing distribution of power in the world. *Mein Kampf* had distinctly spelled out what his goals were: the liberation of all Germans not now citizens of the Reich; the settlement of Germans in the vast spaces of Russia; the domination of the Germans over the Slavs and other inferior races; the humiliation of France and the destruction of her system of security—Versailles, the League of Nations, the Triple Entente (Rumania, Czechoslovakia, Yugoslavia). Would the western powers resist those plans? Diplomats tend to discount radical confessions as mere propaganda for domestic use and try to housebreak the new regime. Perhaps a few concessions will integrate it into the system of power? Perhaps its revisionist aims can be deflected away from one's own country into a different direction? Or would it be better to teach it a lesson from the very beginning?

Marshal Joseph Pilsudski, the dictator of Poland, put the question bluntly to his French ally. By creating a border incident, he hoped to deflate Hitler right at the start. But when France failed to back him up, Pilsudski concluded that he had to seek safety on his own. In January 1934 he signed a nonaggression pact with Germany—the first dent in the French security system. Alarmed, French Premier Pierre Laval concluded a treaty of friendship with Stalin and invited him to join the League of Nations. Mussolini, for his part, offered Hitler an honorable way to join the establishment. He proposed a four-power pact (Germany, Italy, France, England) to channel treaty revisions and recognize Germany's right to rearm—a concession that had been considered inevitable since 1932. The powers granted Hitler what they had denied the republic. But he, seeing how much more room for maneuver all of this opened, rejected the pact and left the disarmament conference and the League of Nations.

This tactic of provocation, which conformed with the Nazi style in domestic politics, served Hitler well in dealing with the established powers. Knowing that they were anxious to have peace, he threatened war. This method, not any specific plan or "schedule," was the distinctive trait of Nazi and fascist action in world politics. In retrospect, it might seem that Hitler and Mussolini had a concerted timetable or "master plan"; their punches came in such well-spaced intervals that they kept the defending powers groggy. Closer analysis shows that both were merely using opportunities opened by the ineptitudes of British and French diplomacy. In the beginning Mussolini too was a defender of the status quo: of the Brenner border and of Austria's independence.

The Treaties of Versailles and Saint-Germain, it will be remembered, forbade the union (*Anschluss*) of Austria with Germany. After the abortive plan of a customs union in 1931 and the disaster of the *Creditanstalt*, the Lausanne Protocol once again brought Austria under the financial and political control of the West. But it also caused resentment and indignation in Austria; Nazi agitation took root and began to influence some nativist politicians who would have liked to establish their own type of fascism. The *Heimwehr* (Home Defense) was a right-wing, provincial militia, financed by Mussolini and local industrialists. Its leader was a playboy, Baron Ernst Rüdiger von Starhemberg, whose adventurousness might have made him another Papen. Some subleaders, however, were Nazis.

To steal a march on the Nazis, Chancellor Engelbert Dollfuss of the Christian-Social Party in March 1933 led a coup to build an Austrian and Christian kind of corporate state. He banned the socialist Defense League and the Communist and Nazi Parties. To win the *Heimwehr* back from Nazi influence, he founded the Patriotic Front. In February 1934 his bloody suppression of a socialist uprising in Vienna legitimatized him as an "Austro-Fascist."

Not for long, though. On July 25, 1934, he was murdered when Hitler's minions staged a putsch in Vienna, Styria, and Carinthia. But Mussolini marched his troops to the Brenner Pass, and Hitler had to call the adventure off. Germany seemed more isolated than ever.

Then, in 1935, Hitler met with an extraordinary sequence of lucky coincidences. By a mere whim of the calendar, the time had come for the Saarland people to vote on their return to Germany. Up to 1933, their decision had been a foregone conclusion, since the interim French administration had done nothing to ingratiate itself. Now antifascists conducted a hopeless campaign to prolong the status quo until the Nazis were gone. They could rally only 9 percent of the vote for the slogan "Home into the Reich, but not now."

The Saarland vote was a windfall gain in prestige. In March 1935, profiting from a weakness in the French government, Hitler introduced universal military training—his first open challenge to the Versailles Treaty. England, France, and Italy met at Stresa, where they lamely declared that they would oppose any further unilateral breach. But, almost on the morrow of that declaration, England agreed to a further dismantling of the Versailles system: Germany was to build sea power up to 35 percent of the British tonnage. This was followed, in March 1936, by the symbolic entry of German troops into the Rhineland, which so far had been demilitarized.

Hitler's generals had warned him that this was risky. If France were to claim her rights under the Locarno treaty, and were to march, Germany had no means to stop the invasion. Hitler answered: "If they march, I'll shoot myself." It was the first of many times that Hitler's intuition triumphed over his generals' expertise. His bold actions gained him the prestige he later used to beat down all counsel of moderation.

Meanwhile, Mussolini had tried to cash in his reward for keeping watch on the Brenner. He attacked the biblical kingdom of Ethiopia, but found himself confronted by a rising wave of antifascist indignation, fostered by the left-wing Popular Front that was being formed in many countries. The League of Nations condemned the Italian aggression, and "sanctions" were imposed against the attacker. These did not include oil, and therefore failed to deny Mussolini his victory. But he felt slighted by the "capitalist nations" and called on all "proletarian nations" to rise against "imperialism." (Here begins the fascist-Nazi perversion of political terms—an important aspect of the totalitarian attempt to restructure the appearance of the world.) Mussolini demanded Nice, Savoy, Corsica, and Tunisia from France, fomented Arab revolts, and began to draw closer to Hitler, who of course had been happy to negate the League's sanctions.

The following year, the two dictators jointly supported the uprising of the Spanish generals, led by Francisco Franco, against a Popular Front government. Mussolini, who had a hand in preparing the *pronunciamento,* intervened with massive infantry divisions, and Germany with the "Condor Legion," an air unit that collected valuable experience in dogfights with Russian MiGs and brought shame on the German name by its savage attack on the open city of Guernica. (Picasso's famous canvas pilloried the deed.)

German intervention in Spain was carefully limited to avoid a general war. But it was conspicuous and determined enough to make the Popular Front government in France equally circumspect, and to assure Franco's victory.

In October 1936 Germany and Italy formed an "Axis" around which world politics was to revolve; they recognized Franco's usurper government and agreed on spheres of influence in southern Europe and Africa. As a present to Mussolini, Hitler sacrificed the Tyrolians of Alto Adige—heroes of German folklore—but promised someday to give these mountaineers better land in the Crimea. "They will just have to take a boat down the German Danube," he was to say. "German self-determination" never meant, for him, the self-determination of Germans; it meant *his* determination of German destiny.

A month later, Germany and Japan concluded the Anti-Comintern Pact; it was celebrated with great fanfare. Germany's new ally belonged to the "racially inferior" nations; but like Germany, Japan was on the prowl to dismember older empires. A gang of revisionist dictators was formed to disrupt the international order and establish themselves as masters in an imperial area. Hitler's method of revisionism differed from that of the Weimar Republic. He did not negotiate or try to erode the Versailles Treaty but faced the world with the fait accompli of a breach, an independent act of defiance, a unilateral coup accompanied by threats. Even where no substantial gains were visible, the challenge in itself was a blow against the diplomatic system. He meant to prove that collective security did not work, and that the great powers were unable or unwilling to prevent unilateral moves, to unite on a common policy, to punish infractions of the international law.

Inaction on the other side was Hitler's success. Again and again the German conservatives were proven wrong. Their warnings and objections were overridden by deeds, and Hitler's psychological insight won out: the democracies are soft, scared, not sure of their right, and stupid. In Rome as well as in Berlin, the conservative diplomats were pushed aside by the happy warriors. Joachim von Ribbentrop, a former wine salesman, replaced Neurath; Count Ciano, Mussolini's son-in-law, turned Italy's alignment from England to Germany.

Traditional diplomats were indeed not prepared for the fascists' revolutionary attack on their world. They were used to seeking accommodation, compromise, or, as it is sometimes called, appeasement—pacifying a claimant by piecemeal adjustments and revisions of the existing order. They were even prepared to make large concessions—as England's agreement to Hitler's naval program was—provided they had been arrived at by negotiation. Threats, blackmail, high-handed coups were seen only as means to a deal, as signals of danger. The diplomats failed to perceive that brute force aimed to assert itself independently of any substantive aims that might be sought.

Soviet Foreign Minister Maxim Litvinov alone warned that by its very nature the beast could not be appeased; that every new concession would only elicit new demands; that the virulent nationalists had reversed the famous maxim of Clausewitz. Politics had come to be the instrument and preparation of war.

Whether the rationalization by the aggressors themselves is racial, economic (Hitler used both), or historical (as Mussolini preferred), imperialism is essentially a manifestation of power for its own sake, the pursuit of power by power, the leap from one position to the next. Thus, the *Grossraumwirtschaft*—in itself a rational, even necessary concept—was justified not by its instrinsic merits but by the needs of the German war machine, which in turn was justified by the absence, in Germany, of those war matériels that the German war machine needed. As early as 1936 Hitler began to tell his intimates and his generals that by 1939 the country would have to be ready for war. Its armament race, he said, had a head start; but once the others woke up, they would overtake Germany—most likely in 1941. Moreover, Hitler believed in the prophecy that he would die in his fifty-fifth year, so he had only nine years left to build the Pan-German empire, nine years to satisfy his fantastic dream—which Albert Speer has revealed in his memoirs—of remodeling Berlin to become a grandiose world capital, with giant arcades leading to monumental buildings.

In 1937 Mussolini paid Berlin a state visit and joined the Anti-Comintern Pact. The crusade was announced with great fanfare while Hitler developed his plan of world conquest at a secret meeting of his military and political aides. A memo of this speech, by the hand of Colonel Friedrich Hossbach, his military attaché, was submitted to the Nuremberg court; its authenticity has never been challenged. However, the detailed scenario which Hitler unfolded, according to Hossbach, was totally different from that which materialized two years later. He thought that Italy might engage France in the Mediterranean and Germany might use the occasion to invade Austria and Czechoslovakia simultaneously, in 1938. Two of the generals present, who had already voiced apprehensions when Hitler reoccupied the Rhineland, raised serious objections on the realism of the plan, and Foreign Minister Neurath thought it premature. They were proven right two years later; for when Hitler decided to invade Poland he was allied with Russia, while the Italians were not at all ready to go to war.

But meanwhile the three dissidents had fallen into disgrace. Neurath had a conveniently timed nervous breakdown and was replaced by the reckless Ribbentrop. War Minister Field Marshal

Werner von Blomberg was trapped by his marriage to his secretary. (Göring had been a witness to the wedding, and then revealed that she had a police record.) General Werner von Fritsch, the army commander, was framed on a charge of homosexuality; and although a military court acquitted him, he had to go. With the decks cleared of pessimists, Hitler could launch into his adventurous course of world conquest. (As we saw in Chapter 18, Schacht resigned because he would not take responsibility for a change to a war economy in time of peace.)

In November 1937, British Foreign Secretary Lord Halifax told Hitler that England would not object to the *Anschluss* or to the dismemberment of Czechoslovakia and Poland, provided—and this was essential—that Germany would not use the kind of force that would set in motion the infernal machine of alliances and would once again obligate England to fight in Europe. The offer was based on the idea that England would disengage herself from the continent and seek closer "union now" with the English-speaking countries. This was the policy of Lady Astor's antibolshevik "Clivedon Set," of the London *Times*, the Rhodes Trust, the Royal Institute for International Affairs, Sir Henry Deterding and Sir Basil Zaharoff, the munitions merchant, and of Montagu Norman of the Bank of England.

In France, too, class war determined foreign policy. The traditionally patriotic right was insensitive to the Nazi danger, while the Popular Front had accepted the Soviet Union as a partner in the defense of collective security. Some would rather have been ruled by Nazis than by Léon Blum. Nor would they "die for faraway countries."

Strange bedfellows of these new pacifists were the genuine pacifists of the left and those labor groups that would not give up their antimilitarism even when confronted with a Hitler. The British Labour Party voted against the defense budget; the Oxford Union of British Students voted "not [to] fight for king and country." The same circles that only a few years earlier had vetoed a customs union between the republics of Germany and Austria offered Hitler the triumph of the *Anschluss*.

It was in this atmosphere that both Halifax and Mussolini warned the Austrian chancellor (Kurt von Schuschnigg had replaced Dollfuss) that he could not count on their support. Hitler summoned him to his aerie in Berchtesgaden on February 12, 1938, and ordered him to appoint the Nazi leader Arthur Seyss-Inquart as minister of the interior. At once riots broke out, and while Schuschnigg tried to put the question of Austrian independence to a popular vote, Hitler ordered his army to invade (March 11, 1938). Abandoned by everybody—not even the socialists would fight as long as Schuschnigg was in power—Austria did not offer resistance. Hitler made a triumphant entry into Vienna, followed by the predictably unanimous plebiscite.

The world thinks of Austria only as the country of Strauss waltzes. But Pan-Germanism and anti-Semitism were more rampant in Hitler's home country than in Germany. The jubilation on Vienna's Ballhausplatz in March 1938 exceeded everything that had been seen in any other city. Even proven antifascists were moved by the fusion of the German tribes and by the end of the Austrian rump state. More ominously, spontaneous violence against Jews and functionaries of the old regime and public humiliations of the beaten enemy—scenes of sadistic hate and popular fury which Goebbels had vainly tried to unleash in the north—now became commonplace in Austria. Dr. Goebbels announced "the rise of the Teutonic Reich of the German nation."

The day after his success, Hitler set October 1 of the same year as the date for the destruction of Czechoslovakia, which was now surrounded on three sides by the reunited German Reich. The instrument of that purpose was the German minority, which lived in the border areas along the Sudeten range in the east, the Ore Mountains (*Erzgebirge*) in the north, and the Bohemian Forest in the west of the Bohemian quadrangle. Under the Hapsburg monarchs, the Germans had been the masters in Bohemia. After World War I and the foundation of the Czechoslovak Republic, they had to take a back seat. Moreover, the German areas were the most industrialized and therefore had suffered most during the depression. It was not difficult for Goebbels to fan a strong movement for autonomy among the Sudeten Germans, as they were now called. A schoolteacher, Konrad Henlein, steered its ideology from communal grievances to Nazism. Hitler instructed the Sudeten German Party to make small demands first, then to escalate them and never to be satisfied with any offer—from autonomy to secession to *Anschluss*. He also formed, in Germany, a "Free Corps for the Protection of German Rights in Czechoslovakia."

In April 1938 he skirted war so closely that General Beck, his chief of staff, asked to be retired. The generals could not imagine that Czechoslovakia would abandon an area in which its fortifications were located, or that France would permit the dismemberment of her strategically most important ally. They also knew that their own armies were not ready to fight a global war; for the Soviet Union, too, was committed to the defense of Czechoslovakia.

So appalled were they by Hitler's reckless plans that they sent a young staff officer to warn the British prime minister—a most unusual thing to do for any soldier, but certainly unthinkable for a Prussian officer. Major Ewald von Kleist-Schmenzin told Neville Chamberlain that the generals were prepared to arrest Hitler should he order the invasion of Czechoslovakia; they asked the British cabinet only to stand firm against Hitler's demands. The German chargé d'affaires in London, Theodor Kordt, transmitted a similar request from a senior official of the Foreign Office, Ernst von Weizsäcker.

Chamberlain, however, thought he had a better plan. He brought pressure to bear on the Czechs to yield to the German demands. Armed with nothing but an umbrella (which gave the cartoonists a field day), he flew to Berchtesgaden. Mussolini remarked that the sight of the British premier must have affected Hitler the way blood affects a tiger. Indeed, Hitler at once escalated his demand: he wanted the area turned over to him without a plebiscite. Chamberlain was concerned only with assuring an orderly, peaceful, and agreed-upon procedure, and he told the Czechs to submit.

To receive a piece of land from Chamberlain's hands was not to Hitler's taste at all. Hence, when Chamberlain came back to Germany with the Czechs' surrender to the German demands, Hitler raised the ante once more: immediate occupation, and nothing less. Faced with an ultimatum the peaceful Chamberlain, humiliated by Hitler's provocative manners, flew home and ordered mobilization.

The world was holding its breath. Over a mere issue of procedure the powers were going to war. Gas masks were being distributed in the capitals. Parliament went into session, seeing before it nothing but the dire prospect of a chain reaction toward war—when, dramatically, a messenger arrived to tell Chamberlain that Hitler had agreed to a conference, at Mussolini's request.

At Munich, on September 29, Hitler received the heads of the French, Italian, and British governments. Mussolini submitted a text the Germans had prepared for him; it was abjectly adopted by Chamberlain and Daladier. All areas with more than 50 percent German population were to be occupied within ten days; Czechs were not allowed to remove property from those areas; the fortifications were to be surrendered intact.

It was a brutal dictate. The Czechs were not even asked to be present or to communicate their reservations. The Russians were bypassed. Chamberlain remained in Munich to obtain from Hitler a paper saying that he had no further territorial demands. Was Chamberlain so ignorant of the Polish Corridor issue? At the London airport he assured a cheering crowd that he was bringing "peace in our time."

"Munich" has since become a term of opprobrium. The conference had dismantled not only a bulwark of democracy in the center of Europe but the entire structure of Versailles and the French security system; the word of the western powers was no longer credible. Poland, Yugoslavia, and Rumania now knew that they would have to fall into the German orbit. Antifascists in all countries were discouraged. Stalin, too, would now seek an accommodation with Hitler. And finally, the dissidents inside Germany had lost their last ray of hope that Hitler would ever be stopped by outside opposition, or that he could be proven wrong.

Strangely, however, Hitler was not happy with his success. He felt cheated of the military operation, of earning laurels as a strategist. He told several people that Chamberlain had ruined the victory for him. Six months later he recouped the lost opportunity when on March 15, 1939, his troops marched into rump Czecho-slovakia, occupied the Hradšin, and severed the two nationalities from each other. Slovakia became a satellite state under the priest Josef Tiso; Bohemia-Moravia was made a "protectorate," where Neurath acted as governor and the murderer Heydrich as police chief.

Now Chamberlain saw that he had been deceived. In justifying his coup, Hitler had left out the one excuse that might have convinced the stock exchange: bolshevism. Instead, Berliners—accustomed to reading between the lines—noticed that for some time their daily papers had not vilified Stalin; and Stalin had responded by telling the Eighteenth Party Congress that the Soviet Union had no conflict with Germany and was not willing to pull other people's chestnuts out of the fire. Hitler had broken not only his spoken and written words but also his unspoken word. Instead of starting a crusade against the Soviet Union, he was opening negotiations with it.

Piqued, Chamberlain dealt out guarantees to Poland, Turkey, Bulgaria, and Rumania. Latvia and Estonia declined to be guaranteed and concluded nonaggression treaties with Germany.

On April 28, Hitler scrapped the Munich agreement, the naval agreement of 1935 (see page 231), and the nonaggression pact with Poland (see page 229). The world was on notice that appeasement had failed, that Hitler's "last territorial demand" was always his last but one, and that another crisis was in the making. The maneuvering for alignments began. The Soviet ambassador in Berlin stated to Weizsäcker that his government would not seek to exploit Hitler's difficulties with Chamberlain. And on May 3 the world learned with apprehension that Foreign Minister Litvinov, a Jew and a champion of collective security, had been replaced by Vyacheslav Molotov, whose name means "hammer" and who was Stalin's second in command.

Chamberlain sent a special envoy to Moscow to explore the possibilities of a joint defense. Molotov's answer was obvious: we have no common border with Germany; to be of any help we would have to march through Lithuania and Poland. These countries feared being rescued by the Russians even more than being raped by Hitler, and Chamberlain did not use his powers of persuasion in Warsaw the way he had done in Prague six months earlier. Fear of Russian preponderance in eastern Europe prevented the conclusion of an alliance that might have deterred Hitler.

To ward off the specter of a two-front war, Hitler was prepared to offer Stalin what England could not: the partition of Poland, and the possession of the Baltic coast. On August 2, Ribbentrop proposed to the Russian ambassador "talks concerning Poland"; ten days later Molotov replied favorably, and Ribbentrop insisted that Germany would have to act before winter set in. On August 18 a commercial treaty was signed: Germany was to give the Soviet Union a 200-million-mark credit.

Two days later, Hitler received a personal message from Stalin which sent him pounding the wall with glee: "Now I have the world in my pocket." Ribbentrop was dispatched to Moscow and on August 23 signed a "nonaggression pact," with secret articles dividing the Baltic area. Hitler was to get Lithuania and western Poland, Stalin the Byelorussian part of Poland and the northern tier of the Baltic states.

To make war an immediate certainty the conspirators limited the duration of the pact to a month. Stalin had deflected the Nazi thrust away from himself. If England and France were to honor their word to Poland, he could watch how the fascists and the imperialists destroyed each other.

Hitler hoped for a quick war in Poland, which would leave the western powers no choice but to recognize the fait accompli. On August 22 he had told his generals:

> The favorable conditions will not exist three years hence. We must act now. . . . Our enemies are worms; I have seen them in Munich. I was convinced that Stalin would not take their offer; Russia has no interest in preserving Poland. . . . Poland is now where I wanted it. We need not fear a blockade. The east will supply us with grain, cattle, coal. . . . The object is not to reach any particular line but to destroy the living sub-

stance of Poland. I shall provide propagandistic alibis. . . . The victor will not be asked later whether he spoke the truth.

And General Halder noted in his diary: "Y-day, Saturday, August 26. Final, no further orders necessary." Weekends were Hitler's accustomed days of surprise actions.

To avoid a two-front war, however, Hitler once more saw the British ambassador and renewed his offer to share the world with England, to guarantee the British Empire, and to confirm Locarno. He added that his real calling was to be an artist; once the Polish question was settled, he would retire from politics. This said, he called General Keitel and set the attack for the following day. He had used the year since Munich to build strong fortifications along the Rhine: the Siegfried Line. Would the French be so foolish as to take the offensive in 1939, if they had not dared to do it in 1938? He went through the motions of demanding the Corridor and Danzig, then offering the Poles a deal—but in the form of an ultimatum that left them no time to answer.

(To argue that an accommodation might have been possible had the western powers obtained a twenty-four-hour delay, Professors A.J.P. Taylor and John Lukacs must conceal from their readers Hitler's numerous declarations that he wanted to destroy Poland, not just to get Danzig. The genocide program, introduced into all eastern areas, leaves no doubt about his war aims. But Professor Taylor gives his case away when he suggests that Poland might have been compensated for the Corridor and Poznan with a piece of the Ukraine. Like his countryman Lord Balfour, Professor Taylor disposes easily of a country that does not belong to him.)

Instead of negotiating, Hitler dispatched his armies against Warsaw, saying, "I hope that this time no son of a bitch [*Schweinehund*] will propose another conference." Hitler was so afraid that Poland might yield up the Corridor peacefully that he provided a second provocation: S.A. men disguised in Polish uniforms attacked German fortifications. (All participants in the coup were sent to death battalions later.) As for that bumbling Mr. Chamberlain with his umbrella— after Poland was conquered, he would negotiate. Hitler was astounded when Chamberlain told him: "Negotiations only after the German army has returned to its bases."

It is no idle speculation to ask whether German irredentism might not have brought war under other leaders as well. The professional soldiers did not think it possible but prepared it well. The German people did not like it but supported and endured it. It can be stated confidently, however, that without the drive and fanaticism of this one man, Germany would not have been prepared psychologically, militarily, or economically. Hitler had become Germany's destiny.

Even though no war could possibly have been as popular as one against Poland, people went into it without enthusiasm. The small number of losses did not assuage the feeling that this war had been started wantonly, without necessity and reason. By year's end the police had to intervene against demonstrators.

21

The Second World War

We are the last Germany. Should we ever go under, there will be no Germany.

—Hitler

WHEN HITLER'S MECHANIZED ARMIES smashed Poland's meager defenses, even those who had never doubted the outcome were amazed at the precision and power of the German advance, the reward of careful planning and timing. Within two weeks, 500,000 Poles were incapacitated; the Germans lost only 45,000 men. On September 17, Stalin seized Byelorussia. Hitler annexed the parts that had belonged to Germany until 1918 and established a protectorate over the rest. Latvia, Estonia, and Lithuania were forced to sign nonaggression treaties with Stalin and to give him bases. Similar demands were tendered to Helsinki. On November 30, the Soviet army attacked the Karelian Isthmus. After a long, heroic winter campaign, Finland sued for peace. It had to yield territory, but it kept its independent government, with German support.

Though the two allies distrusted each other, the Soviet Union was of decisive value for Hitler's war economy. Without Russian grain, dairy products, soybeans, and animal fat he could not have survived the British blockade. He also obtained rubber and oil through channels made safe only by the USSR's compliance.

The administration of Poland was put into the hands of Himmler and Hans Frank, with instructions to reduce the country and its population to utter impotence, destitution, illiteracy, and helplessness. Intellectuals and potential leaders were abducted to concentration camps. Men between the ages of fourteen and sixty had to work in German factories, isolated from women. Farmers had to surrender their land to German settlers. Mass executions and sadistic orgies were a pastime of the SS.

In the west, the armies so far were confronting each other without doing anything much. The French spoke of a *drôle de guerre*, a phony war, the Germans of a *Sitzkrieg*. But Hitler kept his soldiers on the move. In a daring air and sea maneuver, he occupied Denmark and

241

Norway in April 1940. A British expeditionary corps failed to hold northern Norway. King Haakon VII went to England, while Vidkun Quisling ruled Norway as the Nazi satrap, introducing a new word into the political vocabulary.

The campaigns in Poland and Scandanavia confirmed the view of Colonel Charles de Gaulle that mechanized armies were strongest in offensive operations. The older French generals had learned the lessons of World War I all too well. Civilian by temperament, they had placed reliance on the Maginot Line, a continuous series of fortifications that would have been impenetrable to the armies of 1914-18; the politicians did not understand the significance of high mobility and concentrated firepower. They were afraid of airplanes carrying poison gas and fire into the cities; hence their concern was to keep this kind of terror away from the population. Hitler realized that modern aircraft and armored tanks had turned war once more into an art. General Heinz Guderian had invented the panzer unit—a massive thrust of tank power closely supported by special dive bombers (*Stukas*) which could pierce a defense line.

Once again, the battle was to be a great game of thrust and riposte. The campaign was conceived as the movement of a great mass toward strategic goals; war was liberated from the sterile doctrine that defense is stronger. In the war of movement the German technique achieved quick decisions—"lightning war," *Blitzkrieg*, struck terror behind the enemy lines. The German staff saw the chance of destroying the enemy army in a vast enveloping movement.

On May 10, 1940, Hitler's bombers attacked Rotterdam; airborne divisions landed at strategic points, paralyzing the unsuspecting Dutch. At the same time, led by dive bombers, the armored (panzer) columns swept through southern Belgium, annihilating opposing forces of the French, English, and Belgians near Sedan, then advanced toward the channel port of Abbéville in a great encircling movement. Lured into believing that this was a repetition of the Schlieffen Plan, the British expeditionary force was caught in northern France and Belgium between gigantic pincers; superior German forces squeezed it against the sea. With heroic efforts, mobilizing the entire air force and every available vessel, large and small, the British managed to extricate 340,000 men from the pocket of Dunkirk, but left behind them incalculable quantities of arms and ammunition.

Meanwhile, on May 10, Chamberlain had resigned and his opponent, Winston Churchill—the last Victorian, a lifetime defender of king, country, and empire—had assumed power at the head of a broad coalition determined to win the war. He promised not peace but "blood, toil, tears, and sweat." To a whole generation he became the living symbol of the west's will to survive.

Belgium's King Leopold surrendered on May 28, and Hitler's forces drove freely into France. There was no resistance. A month after he had launched his campaign, he entered Paris, from which the frightened populace fled in panic. A few patriots went to Africa to found the "Free French" army. The venerable—though senile—Marshal Henri Philippe Pétain formed a new cabinet for the purpose of surrendering to Hitler. General de Gaulle, catapulting from near anonymity, went to London and began a radio campaign summoning Frenchmen to resistance.

On June 21, a German general dictated surrender terms in the same railway car where twenty-two years earlier Marshal Ferdinand Foch had humiliated the German army. France was divided into an occupied part, encompassing Paris and Bordeaux down to the Spanish border, and a southern part whose capital was to be Vichy. There Pétain established an abject regime that tried to deny everything that had happened since 1789, while his Premier Pierre Laval sparred with Hitler about collaboration. Although Laval was a wily politician and schemer, his dangerous game dragged him deeper and deeper into the mire of subservience. He had to give Hitler material aid, had to extridite German antifascists, had to round up French laborers for shipment to German factories and Jews for the ovens in Poland; but somehow he managed to deliver fewer workers and Jews than Belgium and Czechoslovakia. In the beginning, the occupation was bearable. People had little to eat, fuel was scarce, and the prisoners of war did not return. However, few arrests were made, and fraternization was encouraged, especially with intellectuals. A new call for peace went out to England. But Churchill answered in the rolling phrases that were to be the signature of this war: "We shall fight on the beaches, we shall fight on the landing grounds. . . ."

Furious, Göring began intensive air attacks to prepare the invasion of England. The city of Coventry was razed; air bases and port installations were bombed; London was subjected to haphazard destruction. But the Royal Air Force defended the country; every night Spitfires and Hurricanes rose to meet the invading Messerschmitts. By October, Göring's Luftwaffe had lost 1,800 planes, the RAF 900. Germany was short of pilots and had lost the "Battle of Britain"—the last battle in which man-to-man fighting was still decisive.

After a year of war, Hitler's troops held the ramparts from North Cape to the Sahara and were plundering the stores of Paris, Copenhagen, Oslo, the Hague, and Brussels. They had an empire. But there was England—starved, but stubbornly alive. Moreover, Franco refused to declare war against England. Germany had to occupy the Vichy part of France, too. New troubles arose in the east. Disregarding the nonaggression treaties of the preceding fall, Stalin annexed the three small Baltic states.

In negotiations with Hitler, Molotov asked for a seat on the Danube Navigation Commission and for preponderant influence in Bulgaria. Hitler, trying to turn him away from the Balkans, offered Russia the Dardanelles, the Persian Gulf, and the Indian Ocean. (What irony! Sitting thirteen stories underground during a British air raid, Hitler offered Molotov the British Empire.) But as early as July 1940 he laid plans for an invasion of Russia; in September he strengthened the Anti-Comintern Pact militarily. In December he started military and diplomatic preparations for "Operation Barbarossa," the attack on Russia. The full measure of Hitler's madness appears in this design: to conquer England he had to conquer Russia; to forestall a two-front war, he had to begin the most gigantic campaign of all history in the east, while England's persistent air force was harassing him in the west and America stood ready to support all his enemies with its mighty resources.

In March 1941, Bulgaria and Yugoslavia were asked to join the Anti-Comintern Pact. When King Boris pledged that he would not take part in any war, German armies occupied Bulgaria. In Belgrade, Prince Regent Paul signed the pact; but anti-Nazi, pro-Russian army officers proclaimed young Peter II king and called on the nation to defend its independence.

Hitler quickly decided to expand his Balkan operation. German armies overran Yugoslavia and Greece in three weeks of April. A breathtaking air maneuver took Crete in May. Yugoslavia was divided up among Germany, Italy, Hungary, Albania, and Bulgaria. Croatia became a puppet state under the unsavory *Poglavnik* (Führer) Ante Pavelich.

The very swiftness of the German victory allowed parts of the Yugoslav army to hide out in the hills. Later they were joined by Serbs who did not care to be deported to German labor camps. General Draja Mikhailovitch, an ardent Serb patriot, collected them in a guerrilla force, the Chetniks; he prudently husbanded his forces against the day when an Allied landing would unleash a general uprising. Until June 22, 1941, the Chetniks received no help from the left; only after Hitler had invaded the Soviet Union did the communists launch their partisans. Their leader, Josip Broz, known under the name of Tito, had gained experience in the Spanish Civil War and in previous underground work. He appealed to patriotism and won the peasants' admiration, although they suffered from German reprisals.

The Balkan campaign delayed "Barbarossa" by a month. Later, too, guerrilla activities were to tie down Axis forces needed elsewhere. For the moment, possession of this bridge to Africa gave the dictators a decisive advantage. General Rommel was able to rescue the battered Italians in Libya and to push toward Alexandria. His zigzag war along the African coast earned him the sobriquet "Desert Fox"— another of those wartime exploits that lend themselves so readily to fictionalization.

With Europe his from the Dniester River to the Atlantic, Hitler was ready for the great blow which he hoped would convert the English to his anticommunist ploy. His panzer fist hit the unprepared Soviet Union hard, on June 22, 1941. One hundred fifty-three divisions with three million men took part in this furious onslaught. Within six months they conquered twenty million square miles, captured half a million Russian soldiers, and destroyed the central Soviet army, without accomplishing Hitler's strategic objective: the annihilation of the enemy's power of resistance. The bulk of the Russian forces simply retreated into the vast Russian space, as they had done 130 years earlier in the Napoleonic war. And while retreating, they destroyed everything the Germans might find useful. The savage "scorched earth" strategy slowed the German advance. Hitler might still have won a political victory had he pushed vigorously toward Moscow; for economic reasons, instead, he drove toward the granaries of the Ukraine, the industrial Donets Basin, and the Caucasus oil wells.

Winter that year came earlier than usual, and the Germans had wasted precious time. They were stalled in the Leningrad environs and a hundred miles from Moscow. They held a line from the northern tip of the Sea of Azov to the eastern tip of the Gulf of Finland; but the main Soviet forces were intact, even capable of counterattacking. Frostbitten, mired in mud and snow, the Germans first slowed down and then stopped. Their lines of communication were overextended.

In his occupation policy, Hitler made the mistakes inherent in his system and philosophy. The Germans had always looked down on the Slavs as inferior in mind and morals, hewers of wood and drawers of water. The war gave the SS a chance to plan genocide: to eliminate leaders, to decimate the male population and hold the women in servitude, to weaken them biologically, to loosen their hold on the land, and to replace them with Germans or others of Nordic stock. The children, Himmler held, needed to go to school for only four years and learn to count up to 500, to sign their names, to serve their masters honestly and obediently, and to praise God for allowing them to be ruled by the great German people.

The Nazi conception of the war was one of enslavement and extermination. Their cruelty reached its peak in the Ukraine. Had they been able to see the Russians as human beings, they might have perceived a great political opportunity; millions of Ukrainian and Russian peasants were prepared to welcome as liberator any enemy of the bolshevik regime. They were deeply disappointed when they discovered that Stalin had not lied. The Germans behaved like Tatars, murdering, looting, torturing, and raping. Alfred Rosenberg, Hitler's ideologist and a connoisseur of the eastern scene, said: "We do not come to liberate any Russians; we are carrying out German world politics."

German hubris dug Germany's grave. It aroused the Russian people to resistance. They left the invader no house wherein he could hide, no bridge he could cross, no food he could eat, no wood to warm himself by, no laborers he could press into service, no vehicle or machine, no horse or cattle, not a nail to fix a broken wheel.

The campaign failed, and the fault was entirely Hitler's. He had lost two precious weeks in his glorious conquest of the Balkans. In Russia he had pursued three goals at the same time: securing the necessary wheat in the Ukraine, conquering the political capital of communism, and exterminating the Slavic race. His armies, advancing in three prongs toward the Crimea, Moscow, and Leningrad, were entirely unprepared for the long, hard Russian winter. His racist blinders also caused him to underestimate the devotion and the anger of the Russian people.

Favored by nature and aided by the people's fury, sacrificing all for the fatherland's survival, the Soviet army was able to protect Leningrad and Moscow during two long winters. In the second summer, the Germans advanced to the foot of the Caucasus and laid siege to Stalingrad, the former Tsaritsyn, on the Volga. The defense of the narrow shoreline, the house-to-house fighting in the ruined city with the symbolic name, became another epic of this war (see Theodor Plievier's *Stalingrad*).

There, in November 1942, the Germans met their fate. A giant pincer of fresh Russian troops closed behind the attacker, annihilating twenty-two divisions. Whipped by Hitler's mad orders, 150,000 Germans died in two months of desperate fighting. On January 31, 1943, Field Marshal Friedrich Paulus surrendered with 90,000 men. At the same time, the Russians broke the siege of Leningrad and advanced on the entire long front. Also at the same time, Rommel had given up Africa, after being beaten by British General Bernard Montgomery at El Alamein.

The Soviet Union could not have turned the tide all by itself. The moment Hitler invaded it, Churchill had offered an alliance. He also met with President Roosevelt to proclaim the Atlantic Charter, which set forth principles of freedom and social progress for the postwar era, but above all ensured that no territorial change would be recognized. Russia and fourteen other governments also set their signatures to these principles.

* * *

AS EARLY AS SEPTEMBER 1940, England had obtained fifty American destroyers to guard the transports of supplies it had bought in the western hemisphere; in March 1941 the American Lend-Lease Act facilitated these purchases. In November Roosevelt extended a one-billion-dollar credit to the Soviet Union. A steady flow of convoys crossed the Atlantic, unloaded war matériel in England, and went on through submarine-infested straits to Archangelsk. Others went around Africa (the Mediterranean and the Suez Canal being impassable) to the Persian Gulf. By mid-1942 Russia had received 3,000 planes, 4,000 tanks, and millions of tons of other hardware, vehicles, and foodstuffs.

Naval engagements between German submarines and American transports had occurred all through 1941. On December 11—four days after Japan's attack on Pearl Harbor—Hitler compounded the mistakes he had made about England and Russia by declaring war on the United States.

Soon U.S. carpet bombing was to visit on German cities the same terror that Göring's pilots had wrought on Coventry and Amsterdam, and the American production potential spouted forth the essential war matériel that eventually was to decide the outcome of the war. German production facilities and transportation links were attacked from the air while German submarines sank allied supply ships (at the peak, in May 1943, as much as 500,000 tons, before countermeasures reduced the number and effectiveness of U-boats). Surveys conducted after the war established that the air raids had been unable to interrupt the production of war matériel significantly. But the manpower diverted to civil defense and repair, and the steady wear on nerves and energy, eventually began to tell on Germany, while the American war effort caused no hardship in this country. (No lesson can be drawn from these experiences for the future, because in case of a third world war, there would be no protected area of production.)

Eleven months later, American troops under Eisenhower landed in Morocco, joined forces with the British, ferried over to Sicily in July 1943, and worked their way up the Italian boot. On July 25 Mussolini was forced to resign by an angry *Gran Consiglio*; its members, his own creatures, now were anxious to save their skins, and applauded his arrest. The Fascist Party was dissolved. Marshal Pietro Badoglio, acting head of a provisional government, surrendered on September 3; but Mussolini, freed by a German SS squad, proclaimed a republic in the northern cities still under German control. From Milan he thundered edicts in the old spirit of radical revolutionary socialism, vainly trying to rally the Italian people to his drooping flag. When the German troops in Italy surrendered in April 1945, Mussolini and his mistress were captured by partisans and killed; their bodies were hanged head down in a public square in Milan. Having purged their criminals, the Italians did not have to suffer the ignominy of an inter-Allied court sitting in judgment of their war guilt.

Meanwhile, with Russia bearing the brunt of the war, Stalin demanded the opening of a "second front" that would divert more Germans to the western defense. The Allies had the choice of invading either France or the Balkans. The latter alternative might have allowed the western Allies to take Vienna and Budapest before the Russians did. Churchill personally reconnoitered the terrain and had a meeting with Tito, who flattered and probably fooled him; he came away with the impression that Tito might at worst become a little Balkan dictator. Therefore, when Tito voiced strong objections to an invasion of the "soft underbelly," he abandoned the plan. It was one of the most momentous decisions of the war: the western Allies were to land in France while the Russian steamroller overran eastern Europe.

All through 1943 the German army retreated slowly from Russia. Soviet forces reached the Polish border in January and the Rumanian border in April 1944. On June 6, 1944, the long-awaited D-Day, American and British forces landed in Normandy, secured a beachhead, and poured into France. At this moment, when defeat was staring them in the face, the German generals decided to seek peace by jettisoning Hitler. On July 20 Colonel Claus von Stauffenberg set off a bomb in Hitler's headquarters. He killed four officers but missed Hitler. The news of the blast was to be the signal for the arrest of all Nazi leaders. But the generals, who had planned foreign conquests so efficiently, now failed miserably. Instead of occupying the radio stations, they allowed Goebbels to proclaim, "The Führer is alive," and then protested that they could not break the oath they had sworn to him—who had violated every oath.

The resistance was suppressed in blood. Five thousand conspirators and suspected conspirators were executed, among them marshals, generals, high officials, clergymen, intelligence officers, bearers of well-known names, even SS commanders, the cream of the Prussian nobility. The popular Rommel was allowed to take poison and given a glorious state funeral.

Although the Allies had adopted a policy of "unconditional surrender," the conspirators might have surrendered under more favorable conditions. They might have saved German cities from destruction and they might have wiped the shame of Nazism from the German name. Since they failed, Germany had to go to her ultimate doom. Paris was liberated on August 24 by the French Forces of the Interior (FFI) and Allied troops; de Gaulle led the victory parade the next day. Most of France was free by the end of the year; but the Germans—strategically defeated—were still able to launch a strong counteroffensive in the Ardennes, the "Battle of the Bulge," in December.

Belying his pretended antibolshevism, Hitler defended his western positions most strongly while evacuating Russia and allowing the Russians to come closer to the heart of Europe. During the last months of 1944, while he still enjoyed the use of the channel coast, he launched 10,000 rockets against London—killing 2,500 people but failing to obtain the expected shock reaction. Far from grinding down the will of the English people, this new and terrible weapon stiffened their determination.

The rocket—or "V-weapon" as the Germans called it (V for Vengeance)—was Hitler's legacy to World War III. After the war the Russians and Americans quickly grabbed the scientists who had developed this instrument of terror in the installation at Peenemünde. Hitler had also recruited German physicists to explore the possibilities of an atomic bomb (see page 264), and Dr. Goebbels kept telling the Germans over the radio that a "miracle weapon" was being perfected in secret which at the last minute would turn the tide of war.

Up to the 20th of July, Hitler had not dared to impose on the people a regime of total mobilization. In the midst of many deprivations, he had allowed them diversions and food. Now Himmler was named commander of the reserve army, and Goebbels Reich commissar for total mobilization. Women were ordered from their households into the factories; theaters and other shows were closed; higher education, with the exception of engineering schools, was stopped; no one was allowed to take a vacation; men between fifteen and sixty who were not soldiers had to serve in the *Volkssturm*, an auxiliary troop without combat value but adequate for guarding bridges and railway stations.

But the war effort was faltering. The air force was no longer able to fend off Allied bombers, and the devastation Germany had to accept was unspeakable. In contrast to the brilliant victories by which Hitler had occupied entire countries within weeks, the Allied progress was slow, suffocating, submerging, grinding down the German defenses rather than winning any battles.

In the fall of 1944, the German armies were driven out of Rumania, Greece, Finland, Bulgaria, Yugoslavia, and northern France. On September 11 American units crossed the German border. On the twelfth anniversary of Hitler's ascent to power, he sat in his Berlin bunker, twenty-five feet below street level. Foreseeing his own doom, and perhaps remembering the prophecy of his death at fifty-five, he began to give confused orders to destroy public utilities, transportation facilities, bridges, mines, food stores, canal systems, communications installations, monuments, historic buildings, theaters, and castles— everything that might tell future generations of the great people that he was determined to take with him into his own Valhalla. Another order decreed death for any person found in a house that showed a white flag. Boys were ordered to sacrifice themselves in defense of lost positions; entire divisions of front troops were expected to "bleed to death"; a great orgy of destruction was to be staged. Resistance to the last man was madness—unless destruction had been his purpose all along. Goebbels, in his last speech, sent his pyromaniacal fantasy flying:

> Under the ruins of our devastated cities we have definitely buried the last glories (so-called) of the bourgeois nineteenth century. With these cultural monuments, the last obstacles to our revolutionary mission have fallen. . . . In the past, private property imposed on us certain hesitations. Now the bombs have razed the prison walls where Europe had been chained to her past.

On May 1, 1945, Hitler and Goebbels, completely isolated, killed themselves. Even their most faithful followers refused to follow them into death or to take all of Germany along into their doom. On May 7, a group of German generals went to Reims to sign the articles of surrender.

The man before whom Europe had trembled for ten years must be judged neither by his initial success nor by his ultimate failure. There can be no doubt he was a political genius who could galvanize his nation with his own mania. His vision was a Europe under German domination—a schoolboy's vision of a hierarchically ordered empire, with himself as the supreme king and each of his racial brothers permitted to see himself as a knight fulfilling a mission. For ten years, as long as Hitler's uncanny eye for the weaknesses of his enemies at home and abroad provided victories for the German people, Germany lived out the fantasy of a continuous festival of liberation. Based on hate, his delusion of power could be realized only in the pageantry of war and in the destruction of everything Europe had stood for in the preceding five hundred years.

Wholesale destruction of human lives, the killing of hostages, reprisals, and terror attacks on civilians with incendiary bombs and (in the last stage) with rockets and atomic bombs marked World War II as a turning point in history. War was now being waged for extermination and survival. Many of its actions were unrelated to military objectives and had turned into sheer acts of savagery. France remembers the killings of Oradour; Czechoslovakia, the destruction of Lidice; England, the bombing of Coventry; Holland, the bombing of Rotterdam; Germany, the burning of Hamburg and Dresden.

Hitler believed that his monumental buildings would remind posterity of his awesome grandeur. But he is remembered by the cemeteries and concentration camps, by the gas ovens and the lampshades made of human skin. The gruesome monuments of Lidice, Oradour, and Auschwitz proclaim that Nazism was anti-European, a lapse into barbarism. Some reverse Machiavellians now advise us from hindsight that the sacrifice of lives and happiness made in World War II was too high a price for eliminating this evil from European soil. They do not understand the contemporaries' revulsion, the bitter disappointment of all thwarted attempts to coexist with the monster, the failure of appeasement, the final insight that surrender would have meant the end of European history.

Leadership fell to the two nations that still believed in their mission: the United States in the west, and the Soviet Union in the east. Both assumed responsibility for a new organization of peace. But no longer did they conceive peace as a concert of powers. Rather, each saw itself as hegemon in its part of a divided Europe; each was armed with an idea; each was contemptuous of the European nations that had been unable to contain the aggressor in their midst. Europe had been the center of the world; it was now ruled by the two powers that had been on its periphery. It had generated attitudes and ideas which for centuries had revolutionized the world and conquered continents; now it received guidance from its onetime disciples.

22

The Balance Sheet of Death

Hitler has to lose this war. He does not belong in German history.

—Ernst Cassirer

GERMANY'S WAR HAD KILLED FOUR MILLION GERMANS, but almost ten times as many nationals of other countries—two-thirds of them civilians—were wantonly murdered in raids, retaliatory actions, or plain genocide. There were twenty-one million Russians, 375,000 Czechoslovaks, six million Poles, 1,680,000 Yugoslavs, 160,000 Greeks, 386,000 British, 810,000 French, 88,000 Belgians, 210,000 Dutch— and Jews, nationals of all these countries, whose number has been estimated at close to six million.

In addition to war actions and mercy killings, the Nazis carried out a viciously conceived demographic campaign against people whom they judged inferior or inimical to the German race. After the war, the United Nations was to name this crime "genocide"; its instruments were mass murder, starvation, and sexual deprivation. In the occupied countries they rounded up the young men and shipped them to Germany as "foreign workers." Two million Russian prisoners were allowed to die of hunger, disease, and exhausting drudgery. It was a devilish plan. Polish, Czech, and French men were kept in camps, away from women—withering leaves on the population tree. Even if Hitler lost militarily, he hoped to win the demographic war, decimating the hostile nations by direct and indirect methods of extermination.

That this was deliberate no one can doubt. Hitler and Himmler had announced their plans long before the war. These murders were not an incidental cost of the war which every general tries to hold down to the minimum. The purpose of the war was not the acquisition of a disputed territory, nor even supremacy over other nations, but the calculated extermination of other races.

So-called mercy killings of feebleminded Germans were begun first to get people accustomed to the idea that "useless" human beings ought not to survive. But the project met with unexpected resistance.

The churches, notably Bishop Clemens Galen of Münster, organized public protests, and the executions had to be translocated to Poland; in the later stages of the war, direct measures of genocide were kept secret. Tubercular Poles were killed and healthy ones arrested, abducted, expelled, manhandled. The country was deliberately put on rations below its accustomed living standard, and an SS order for the occupied area said: "The emergence of a Polish leadership cadre is to be prevented. All we want there is laborers." Any pretext was good for taking punitive action against entire villages.

Never before have people been punished on this gigantic scale—punished not for what they did but for what they were. Never before has a war been fought, systematically and methodically, against the existence of another nation. The most gruesome monument of that warfare was the extermination of the Jewish people in Europe.

In 1933, Germany had 550,000 Jews and another 180,000 lived in Austria. Up to the outbreak of the war 480,000 of these were forced to emigrate, but admission to western countries was increasingly difficult to obtain, and many were caught again by the German conquests. In 1935, on the occasion of the party convention in Nuremberg, a set of laws was passed that was meant to humiliate Jews. They could not employ non-Jewish maids under forty-five years of age, were prevented from marrying non-Jews, and were excluded from citizenship. They had to adopt Jewish first names, wear the yellow star, and avoid public facilities where they might mix with Gentiles. They could not teach, practice law or medicine, or perform in public.

In November 1938—*Reichskristallnacht*, the "Night of the Broken Glass"—S.A. units were sent to smash windows and loot 7,000 Jewish stores and synagogues. Thirty thousand Jews were arrested and urged to emigrate; Jewish communities were fined one billion marks and had to surrender all their jewelry and silver. On January 30, 1939, Hitler told the Reichstag: "The next war will bring the extermination of the German Jews." On July 31, 1941, Göring ordered Reinhard Heydrich, chief of security of the SS, to prepare "the final solution" of the Jewish question. The war made it possible to round up practically all Jews in western Europe and take almost all of them to concentration camps.

In Poland the Nazis captured three million Jews and had a disposal problem: they had no place to put these people. Adolf Eichmann claimed that he would have let them go to Palestine; they might even have been exchanged for tractors, as was done in one case. But on January 20, 1942, Reinhard Heydrich presided over a conference that decided to wipe out all European Jews by working them to death and "liquidating" those who survived. Some Germans knew what was going on. But Ernst Jünger did not dare name it even in his private diaries; he speaks only of "lemures doing their sinister work."

One comparatively peaceful place was Theresienstadt, in Bohemia. It was a camp for elderly people waiting to be shipped to their deaths. They had to surrender their valuables and write postcards to their friends at home—postdated, so that their disappearance would not arouse immediate suspicion of murder.

At first, people in camps were shot over open ditches. Later special gas wagons were sent to the camps. The gas killings took fifteen minutes; the dead were then found in cramped and fighting positions. After blood and excrement had been hosed away, the bodies were searched for gold teeth; their hair also was harvested for war use. Thus Oswiecim (Auschwitz), Treblinka, Majdanek, and many other places became names of infamy.

After the war the camps were opened, and there were gruesome revelations. Documentary films showed human wrecks—men and women reduced to the sheerest animal existence. German viewers were horrified. They could not believe that these crimes had been committed in their name.

But the outcry of indignation that was heard around the world evoked mixed reactions. Most Germans rejected "collective guilt"; they had been the first victims of the regime. It was unfair to identify them with the most heinous crimes, of which they knew nothing and which they could not have prevented. For their impotence, Karl Jaspers suggested, they might feel collective shame; but no man is guilty by association. On the other hand, many young idealists of the present generation have never forgiven their fathers for having participated in the horrors of the Nazi war.

An enormous literature has grown around the moral, legal, and political questions that arose out of the Nazi crimes. The only way, however, to make the problem manageable for the Germans would have been a purge—either a revolutionary reckoning with all who had held power in the twelve-year Reich, or an orderly court procedure conducted by Germans against those whom they would expunge from their nation.

Neither was permitted. Instead, the Allied powers instituted the war-crimes trials at Nuremberg—under a law that took effect retroactively, before a court on which sat a representative of Stalin—who was no less guilty than Hitler—and with a procedure where prosecutor and judges were on the same side. Although the defendants got a fair hearing according to British law, many Germans did not recognize this court as capable of rendering a final judgment. Above all, it could not do for German public conscience what a German court might have done—purge the community of the evil that had invaded it. In this trial, the two opportunists who were morally guiltier than the criminals acting from conviction—and also, probably, more representative of a majority of Germans—were acquitted. Papen became a papal chamberlain, and Schacht a much-sought-after consultant to dictators in underdeveloped countries. Albert Speer wrote two best-selling volumes of memoirs and diaries which revealed his enormous capacity for self-deception and the public's eagerness to be deceived.

Admiral Karl Dönitz, whom Hitler had named as his successor and who had signed the surrender, received a ten-year jail sentence. Longer terms were meted out to Foreign Minister Neurath, Hitler Youth leader Baldur von Schirach, and Arms Minister Speer. Economics Minister Walter Funk, Admiral Erich Raeder, and Rudolf Hess were given life sentences. Göring evaded hanging by taking cyanide. Martin Bormann, Hitler's adjutant, was sentenced to death but had disappeared. Adolf Eichmann, who had organized the mass killings, was tracked down fifteen years later, sentenced by an Israeli court, and hanged. Heydrich had been executed by a Czech patriot before the end of the war. Hitler, Himmler, and Goebbels had taken their own lives on the last day of the European war. Chief of Staff Field Marshal Keitel, General Jodl, Streicher, Frick, Rosenberg, Ernst Kaltenbrunner, Frank, Sauckel, Seyss-Inquart, and Ribbentrop were hanged. Alfried Krupp was jailed, but released after having served half of his term. Other courts sentenced 5,000 lesser war criminals—of a thousand death sentences, 600 were carried out. The German criminal code abolished capital punishment in 1949, but the statute of limitations was prolonged for certain crimes against humanity, so that persons like Bormann, should they be discovered, can still be tried. Responsibility for prosecution now lies with the German courts.

The judgments were received in silence, and the odious past is largely undigested. What remained was collective suspicion, which the conquerors cynically exploited. Both the Russians and, to a lesser extent, the Americans offered eager Germans an opportunity to exonerate themselves by services in the Cold War (see Chapter 26). There were, however, better ways of rehabilitating one's self-respect. The German Federal Republic assumed responsibility for those material damages that can be compensated for. It paid $3 billion to the state of Israel and a like amount to individuals, or their heirs, who had suffered loss of property, education, career; of freedom, health, and life. (The German Democratic Republic has no such restitution law.)

The Germans have another, moral defense. Germans were the first victims of Hitler's persecutions; Germans were in the concentration camps; Germans offered resistance even under conditions that became increasingly difficult and cruel. The heroes and martyrs who saved Germany's honor in her blackest hour are recognized in Chapter 23.

Unfortunately, Germans have also been able to cite atrocities committed by the Allies—the murder of Polish officers at Katyn, the air raids on water dams and open cities, the blockade, the rampage of Russian soldiers in German towns.

Incendiary bombs set the city of Hamburg afire; thousands died of asphyxiation. The Dresden raid, which has been described by Kurt Vonnegut in *Slaughterhouse-Five* was militarily unnecessary. It had been requested by the Soviet command but was executed by Americans. Surveys undertaken after the war have shown that the air raids, terrible though they were, failed to disrupt Germany's production and transportation sufficiently to affect the outcome of the war; nor did they seriously undermine the population's morale. Yet terror tactics were used as a weapon on both sides. Originally, "strategic bombing" had definable industrial targets; when it turned into "carpet bombing," the strategic purpose was lost, and blind fury was unleashed on the enemy population.

No war before this had uprooted so many people. Fifty million became displaced persons: rounded up, expelled, forced to flee, drafted for labor service, held as prisoners long after the war. Seven million foreign workers were conscripted into German factories. Millions of prisoners never returned home. Twelve million German-speaking people came "home to the Reich"—now much against their will— from the Polish-occupied zone, the Sudeten area, and other eastern European countries.

The material damage Germany had done to others was inestimable. Cities had been destroyed, communications disrupted, production facilities razed. The Soviet Union alone demanded $10 billion in reparations; the western Allies lost twenty-three million tons of shipping; England counted four million homes and $6 billion worth of plant, equipment, and transportation facilities destroyed in air raids.

More important were the moral consequences. European civilization was bankrupt; the white man's preeminence in the world was gone. European history was no longer world history. Technological leadership could no longer be equated with cultural superiority. The soldiers returned from the war brutalized, cynical, shorn of all illusions. In the beginning they might have believed in the ideas their leaders had invoked; in the end they were fighting for sheer survival— little cogs in a big machine of destruction.

World War II brought mankind close to the nightmare of 1984. Hitler had been defeated with the weapons he had chosen.

23

The Resistance

Just as God promised Abraham that he would spare
Sodom if ten just men were found in the city, so I hope
that for our sake he will not destroy Germany.
                                            —Henning von Tresckow

IN CONTRAST TO THEIR AUSTRIAN COMRADES who fought before
going down in 1934, the German Social-Democrats, and communists
in 1933 decided that they had no chance. Even before the Nazis
"dissolved" the German labor movement, it went underground. Many
of its leaders were in concentration camps or in hiding, or had to
seek asylum in the Saarland, Oslo, Paris, or Prague. They smuggled
information and underground papers to the militants in Germany,
who tried to maintain contact among themselves, preferably in small
groups and under new leaders. Some published their own little papers
in inexpensive mimeographed editions. Distribution, however, was
dangerous, and many arrests were made by the police. After 1936 it
became very difficult to continue any kind of political work that
could be visible outside a small circle. Contacts were reduced to
personal friendships. Moreover, the successes of the regime and Hitler's
increasing recognition by other powers seemed to put his opponents
in the wrong. All they could do was listen to foreign broadcasts;
communicating their information to others meant taking a risk.

One activity of the various labor groups in Germany and in exile
was ardent discussion of their defeat. How could it have happened?
Where did we make mistakes? Out of this came a change of heart in
both the Social-Democratic and the Communist Parties. In view of
the common danger, they were now ready to conclude an alliance,
even to form a Popular Front with non-Marxist, bourgeois-republican
parties. Thus in 1936 the governments of Azaña in Spain and Blum
in France were elected as antifascist coalitions, and German exile
writing reflected this mood of common experience and common hopes.

One place where solidarity was a matter of life or death was,
of course, the concentration camp. Political prisoners were there in

odd assortment with criminals, homosexuals, Jews, Jehovah's Witnesses, Gypsies, and "asocial elements." They had to mobilize all their strength and spirit to survive morally and physically. Postwar leaders like Kurt Schumacher and Fritz Erler were heroes in that community. When manpower shortages forced the Nazis to release prisoners, some were able to resume old associations or to conspire with new friends. Thus Julius Leber, a trade union leader, was able to build a bridge to former enemies, the conservative aristocrats.

The workers' resistance preceded by several years that of the military, the churches, and the bureaucrats. But the latter became more spectacular. Since Hitler had come to power with the conservatives' support and shared with them both the militaristic ideals and the hatred of the republic, their falling-out was a surprise to them. The Christian churches, as we have seen, had no objections to the Nazi state, or did not think it fitting to voice them. Only when Nazi thugs tried to become bishops, and to change the articles of faith, were churchmen compelled to reluctant resistance. In May 1934 Protestant leaders, gathered in Wuppertal, signed a declaration that established the Church Bearing Witness; among them were Unitarian, Reformed, and Lutheran church men including Professor Karl Barth, Professors Lietzmann and von Soden, Rudolf Bultmann, and Martin Niemöller. It read in part:

> Jesus Christ, as witnessed by Scripture, is the one word of God, which we hear and obey, and in which we trust in life and death. We condemn the false doctrine that the church must recognize, beside this one word, yet other forms of truths, facts, or powers as sources of its message. We condemn the false doctrine that the state should become . . . the sole and whole order of human life and therefore may claim that it fulfills the mission of the church.

Barth was soon expelled from Germany, and the leadership of the dissident church fell to Dr. Niemöller. The doctrinal points to which they all held fast were connected with the spiritual value of the individual: they fought for the right of converted Jews to be considered Christians; they defended the lives of retarded people whom the Nazis had condemned to euthanasia. They also published a few proclamations against arbitrary arrests, concentration camps, and anti-Semitism. Dietrich Bonhoeffer, Barth's student, protested against the anti-Semitic laws and went to his martyrdom; his prison letters have become one of the great inspirational books of Christianity. Great as the courage of these men was, they did not act on behalf of the church but out of their personal conscience. Only one clergyman, acting on his own, took part in the conspiracies that were to attack the system. Hitler therefore was wise to postpone the showdown with the churches to a time after victory. The Roman Catholic Church did not protest against the anti-Semitic laws, although they were in clear conflict with canon law. The Curia's trusted man in the ministry of the interior, Dr. Hans Globke, wrote the official commentary to those laws. In the Saarland, where the church had great influence, it supported Hitler during the 1935 plebiscite, and Cardinal Innitzer of Vienna in 1938 greeted the *Anschluss* with a warm proclamation.

Needless to say, the church blessed the fascist arms in the Spanish Civil War and in World War II. It never publicly censored the brutalities committed in the concentration camps and the mass killings—until a doctrinal principle was at stake: when the minister of the interior drafted a decree ordering "Aryan" women to divorce their "non-Aryan" husbands, Globke alarmed the bishops. They remonstrated that marriages could not be dissolved. The decree was not published, but the Jewish husbands were rounded up in Berlin on February 27, 1943, to be deported to concentration camps. Then something unexpected happened. Six thousand wives went to the station with their husbands and stood there, screaming and crying, for hours. The police, concerned about the secrecy of the operation, released the men. After this courageous act, Archbishop Bertram of Breslau asked all bishops to intercede with the minister, and for once the bishop of Berlin, Cardinal Preysing, appealed to his colleagues to "speak up, beyond the matter of non-Aryan Christians, about the atrocities committed against Jews in general." One Provost Lichtenberg, at the Hedwigskirche in Berlin, who had included in his sermons a prayer for the deported Jews, was arrested in 1941, and "died on his way from prison to concentration camp" in 1943.

Globke kept the top clergy informed about the mass killings, but the church was silent. It is true that the Pope granted asylum in Vatican City to a few hundred Jews, as a matter of Christian charity; but he has been rightly accused of gross failure to assume the burden of Christ's vicar. Rolf Hochhuth's play *Der Stellvertreter* (*The Deputy*) is based on a true episode in which one Kurt Gerstein, a high-ranking SS officer, tried to inform the Vatican but could not get a hearing.

The political failure of those who should have acted publicly stands in sharp contrast to the private decency of many good Christians who gave shelter to Jews, shielded their children from Nazi education, and defied or cheated the regime in many small ways which required more courage than the public acts that one was entitled to expect from unassailable dignitaries. That such action was indeed possible was shown in the case of the "mercy" killing of feebleminded persons (see page 253ff.) Often when the Nazis saw that the people were not with them, they stalled or retreated.

Nor can the generals' opposition be called political. Only a few officers opposed the Nazi regime on grounds of principle or conscience. Most quoted Seeckt's excuse: that as soldiers they had to be as unpolitical as the Pope was unworldly. Besides, they had every reason to be grateful to Hitler. When he destroyed Röhm, he relieved them of the threat that plebeian S.A. officers would join the army with the same rank. He had given them all the arms they needed, and finally placed every young German in their hands for training and indoctrination. In 1936, however, they had to differ with his judgment: they thought it risky to reoccupy the Rhineland and to intervene in the Spanish Civil War (see Chapter 20). And by 1938 they had grown so apprehensive of Hitler's reckless plans that they were casting about for an opportunity to arrest him. They had reason to worry. Hitler had revealed to them his plans for world conquest; they had sat in conference with him, listening to his endlessly raving speeches; they knew that Germany was ruled by a bunch of madmen and cranks. They had vainly tried to talk reason. In the crisis of September 1938 the chief of staff, General Ludwig Beck, proposed a desperate plan to undo Hitler and the Nazi regime; but the Munich surrender aborted the plot, and we shall never know whether Beck had any chance to sway his colleagues. His bold action—sending Major Ewald von Kleist to London with the plea for firmness—had no precedent in Prussian history; it amounted to high treason. Having been proved wrong and— from Hitler's point of view—fainthearted, Beck had to resign; but his successor, General Franz Halder, shared his fear that Hitler was leading Germany into ruin.

The center of this military resistance was Hans Oster in the counterintelligence office. Unbelievably, he was covered by his superior, Admiral Wilhelm Canaris. They had strong contacts in the Foreign Office and with other high civil servants who were defecting from Hitler. To show his seriousness, Colonel Hans Oster in 1940 informed the Dutch government of the exact hour when its country was to be invaded.

That same army honor code that had first made the officers Hitler's accomplices now compelled them to conspire against him. Ernst Jünger wrote the symbolic novel *On the Marble Cliffs* (1939), which denounced the Nazi atrocities in Aesopian language; the army shielded its publisher. Ernst Udet, a World War I air ace, was employed as an inspector by the Luftwaffe; he deliberately passed faultily constructed planes, hoping that they would be grounded—but Göring recklessly let them fly, killing many pilots. (The story of Udet's suicide has been immortalized in Zuckmayer's play and film *The Devil's General*. Indeed it was the tragedy of this class that they served the devil, and five thousand of the best were to pay with their lives for trying to live by a code that had lost all validity.)

The leader of the "bureaucratic resistance" was Carl Goerdeler, once mayor of Leipzig, price commissioner first under Papen and, after June 20, 1934, under Hitler—a man strangely combining professional competence with political naiveté, and personal decency with a total absence of sensitivity for the problem of the state he was serving. His office allowed him to travel widely and to make contacts with foreigners and with disgruntled German diplomats, army officers, and civil servants. A monarchist at heart, he planned for postwar Germany a society unanointed by any democratic or populist spirit. He thought he could serve Hitler, bombard him with memoranda for humanizing the terror, and plot against him; he designated himself as future chancellor and trusted that the Allies would let him keep the German borders of 1914, plus Austria and the Sudetenland. He hoped to save Germany by jettisoning Hitler.

His colleagues in that enterprise were other high officials, such as Johannes Popitz and Weizsäcker, who had conspired against the republic and then served the Nazi state. Their ideal was an administration of civil servants unencumbered by politics—whether republican or fascistic. By now those ideas are well known to historians. The diaries and memoirs of this circle—some indeed moving—reveal that those men could not have founded the second republic. If martyrs they were, it was not for the cause of liberty and equality. What they did was the expiation of their historical guilt, the penalty of their total misreading of history since 1914. They were the last of a dying breed.

Their amateurish conspiracy of July 20, 1944 (see page 248ff.), hinged on a few generals' willingness to break their oath to Hitler; it could not succeed because it was hatched without the people. Beck and Goerdeler had promised ministries to two former trade union officials, Julius Leber and Wilhelm Leuschner, who represented no organizations. They were arrested before the 20th of July. Another innocent victim of Hitler's revenge was Helmuth von Moltke, head of the Kreisau Circle, whose importance has been overrated. He refused to take part in the conspiracy because he felt that "Germany deserves to go to her doom." As he wrote in his last letter from prison, "I die because we were thinking together." Himmler had five thousand conspirators executed, and Hitler watched the films that were taken of the hangings.

Thus perished nobly the class that had once ruled Germany. Count Schenk von Stauffenberg, who had three times before tried to carry a bomb into Hitler's headquarters, was a deeply idealistic soldier, a disciple of Stefan George. Adam von Trott, Ewald von Kleist-Schmenzin, and Henning von Tresckow, who had carried messages abroad, were likewise animated by pure disgust at the regime. They had begun to act while Hitler was still winning. Their deaths had to be their monument.

Pure idealism also moved two students at the University of Munich, Hans and Sophie Scholl, to scatter leaflets from a balcony. They were arrested and executed. Little is known about "The White Rose" they claimed to represent.

In a somewhat different category were the generals whom the Russians captured at Stalingrad and then invited to form a "Free Germany Committee." It later proved useful in building the German Democratic Republic and linking it to the traditions of Potsdam. The national-bolshevik *Rote Kapelle* (Red Band) under air force Lieutenant Harro Schulze-Boysen was Russian-sponsored, too; he actually did intelligence work for the Soviet Union and was arrested and executed in 1942.

Finally, in this honor roll of brave Germans, we mention the atomic scientists who told Hitler that they could not make a fission bomb. Imagine what might have happened had they carried out their experiments sincerely and successfully. (American intelligence was aware of the experiments, but did not know that they had been given up. If the scientists at Los Alamos had known this, perhaps the atomic bomb would not have been invented in this country, either.)

Hannah Arendt has written the cruel words, "Only a dead German could be a good German." This brash judgment overlooks the millions who never accepted the regime but bowed before the superior power of circumstances. It presupposes a standard of conduct that has never been demanded of any large population. The number of martyrs is always small. The many small deeds—allowing a fugitive to get away, giving food or shelter to an escaped prisoner, aiding a foreign worker, passing useful information to enemies of the regime, failing to carry out an order, acts of mulish rather than heroic resistance—remain unrecorded. One such incident has been immortalized by Heinrich Böll in his prize novel *Group Portrait with Lady*—a monument to the survival of humanity in a humble, insignificant woman. The number of unsung heroes who were not conscious of making history but fulfilled a human duty to fellow men, hoping that their kindness would remain undetected, was quite large, and in each case the risk taken was quite high. But Hitler had maneuvered the German people into a situation where the choice was only between treason to one's conscience and treason to one's country. The slightest disregard of civil defense orders could draw the fire upon one's own family. By the yardstick of risks taken, the German people can be proud of the amount of resistance they offered at those times and in those places where it was feasible. It is all the more to be regretted, therefore, that the second republic has not made the 20th of July a commemorative holiday.

PART FOUR:

Divided Germany

GERMANY'S POSTWAR HISTORY

Germany's postwar history may conveniently be divided into the following periods:

1945–46   The occupation regime, with formal sovereignty vested in the Four-Power Control Council. Germany was to be treated as one country, although police power was exercised in four distinct zones.

1946–49   The Cold War; formation of two different states in East and West Germany.

For the German Federal Republic:

1949–55   The Adenauer era I: to the recognition, by Khrushchev and the Paris Treaties, of the Federal Republic.

1956–61   The Adenauer era II: to the Berlin Wall.

1961–68   The era of coalition governments with the CDU.

1968–   The era of coalition governments with the SPD and of détente.

For the German Democratic Republic:

1949–53   To the Berlin uprising.

1953–61   The Ulbricht era I: to the Berlin Wall.

1961–71   Economic reform to the end of Ulbricht.

1971–   The Honecker regime.

24

The Occupation Regime

*The Hitlers come and go. The German people and state
remain.*

—Stalin

THE GERMAN CITIES WERE IN RUINS, the railways disjointed, the
network of supplies destroyed, the storehouses empty, imports cut off.
Rations were half of what was considered the minimum. Families were
separated. Millions who had been soldiers were prisoners; many of
them were not to return for years. Famine was at the door; the
winter would be hard. Many people depended on CARE parcels and
American handouts. On the black market cigarettes became standard
currency. Chocolate and other food could be had by performing petty
services for the occupiers.

To these physical humiliations were added the dreadful revelations
about the regime that had acted in the name of Germany. But most
Germans were quick to balance the horrors of concentration camps
against the privations which German soldiers had to suffer as POWs.
Indeed, the horrors were now turned on the Germans. They had to
clean up the mess their war had left behind. Women were commandeered to carry the fallen stones from the ruins to some mound
(*Entrümpel-Frauen*), or to collect dead bodies.

Stunned by the enormousness of their defeat, the Germans stared
at the occupation powers and expected them to bring order into the
chaos, to provide food and administration, to do something with the
totally demoralized, soulless body of prostrate Germany. To the victor,
they felt, belonged not only the spoils but a paternalistic responsibility.

In February 1945, assembled at the Crimean resort of Yalta,
Roosevelt, Churchill, and Stalin had dealt out among them the future
of Germany. Their decisions were further detailed by the Conference
of Potsdam (July 17 to August 2) attended by President Harry Truman
and his Secretary of State James Byrnes—both of them new to foreign
policy. They were advised by persons either indifferent to a Soviet
victory in Germany or obsessed with the urge to take revenge on

all Germans. The Soviet Union was represented by Stalin and Molotov and England by the Labour men, Clement Attlee and Ernest Bevin, after Churchill lost the election.

Germany was to be divided into five zones of occupation for the time being (though nothing is as permanent as the provisional):

1. The area west of the Oder and Neisse rivers—24 percent of German prewar territory—to go to Poland.

2. The areas between the Oder and the Elbe to be occupied by the Soviet Union—another quarter of the old territory.

3. The area north of the Main River to be occupied by England.

4. The area south of the Main River to be occupied by the United States.

5. The United States and England to yield part of their zones to French occupation.

In the west, the pre-1935 borders were restored: France was to recover Alsace-Lorraine and the Saarland, Belgium and Denmark the areas annexed in 1919 and lost in 1941. In the east, Czechoslovakia recovered the Sudeten area; the Soviet Union was to take Königsberg (now Kaliningrad). A peace conference was to make final dispositions.

Reparations were to be taken by dismantling factories and transferring other stock; the Germans' standard of living was not to exceed that of their neighbors. Ceilings were set for the production of key materials. Steel output, for example, was reduced from 20 million tons (half of which had been for civilian use) to 5.8 million tons a year.

These provisions were a compromise among those who wanted to dismember Germany, those who wanted to convert it into pasture (U.S. Secretary of the Treasury Henry Morgenthau, Jr.), and those who wished to prevent chaos, starvation, and a power vacuum in Central Europe. The spokesman for the last policy was Churchill, who during the war had fanned the fighting spirit but never forgot that he would have to live with the Germans after the war. In the face of American idealism, which condemned power politics, he and Stalin already had made useful deals about "spheres of influence" in eastern Europe. These two imperialists foresaw that peace in Central Europe would be founded more securely on clear partition than on promises of collaboration. Truman rejected such propositions.

De Gaulle, too, felt that the more Germanies emerged, the greater would be France's security; and the Poles never considered their booty temporary—it was compensation for the eastern areas they had yielded to the USSR. Nevertheless, both for Austria and for rump Germany, a central administration was envisaged; it was vested in the two control commissions, in Berlin and Vienna, composed of the four powers.

Mainly economic considerations called for joint administration. Most of Germany's grain grew in the east; on the other hand, the USSR wanted to have a say in the Ruhr coal and iron basin. Twenty-five percent of Russia's reparations were to come from the western zones, in exchange for which the eastern zone would deliver food to the west. However, the Russians took what was due them but failed to reciprocate. They also organized a sort of "cold revolution"; under a slogan of denazification, they expropriated industrial firms and big estates, and put trusted men (communists emerged from underground or concentration camps, or flown in from Moscow) into key positions.

In the three western zones, the military government worked through traditional middle-class contacts, though with slight deviations—the French bringing their carpetbaggers, the new British Labour government giving socialists at least a chance, and the Americans preferring Roman Catholics. Despite the Central Control Commission in Berlin, therefore, the zones went different ways right from the beginning.

The treatment of the population by the various occupation troops was different, too. Americans and Britons kept a disciplined detachment, with orders against fraternizing, while the Russians allowed their soldiers to go looting and raping for a few weeks, deliberately destroying property and humiliating people. The agreement to root out Nazis from the administration was also carried out with different degrees of zeal: the British removed 150,000 from office, the Americans 300,000, the Soviet Union 500,000.

The Yalta and Potsdam agreements also gave the Czechoslovaks and Poles their revenge: German-speaking people were to be sent "home into the Reich." Twelve million of them poured into rump Germany. Nine million went to the western zones, boosting the population to 48 million and its density to 197 per square kilometer (1950). In addition, a million displaced persons from Russia, Poland, and Rumania could not go back to their countries. (After some had jumped from trains in desperation, the U.S. stopped the policy of forced repatriation.)

Other problems came to complicate the situation. Part of the U.S. food deliveries disappeared farther east—until the practice was discontinued. The western zones produced only half of the food they consumed and had to sustain three occupation armies. It soon became clear that to earn foreign exchange the Germans would have to be allowed, or even encouraged, to produce goods for export, and that the level of production had to be raised.

Originally, German industries were dismantled partly to reduce German industrial power and partly to pay reparations. But the beneficiaries could not make the best use of the surrendered equipment, some of which lay rusting along the railways as far as Vladivostok. The Germans fought doggedly for preservation of their technological assets, and eventually the western Allies stopped the dismantling. Fortunately, most of the plants were intact, and in some areas the Allied dismantling policy turned into a blessing: German industry was able to acquire the ultramodern machines of the postwar era.

A final disposition of the Yalta and Potsdam Conferences was the conversion of Nazi Germany to democracy. This was to be achieved through denazification, demilitarization, decentralization, decartelization, and reeducation. By assigning this responsibility to themselves, the occupation powers again deprived the Germans of the opportunity to make their own revolution. Instead of being an act of self-liberation, throwing off the nightmare of the past, denazification became a measure imposed by the former enemies, accepted reluctantly and in a spirit of sneering defensiveness. Every German in the U.S.-occupied zone had to fill out a long questionnaire about his party, police, and army affiliations, wartime activities, etc.; the British questionnaire was shorter.

One million in the west, a million and a half in the east, paid fines, were barred from employment, or were indicted as war criminals. With the Americans ignorant of the pressures of the Nazi state on the one hand, and of the web of contacts in German society on the other, it was inevitable that the crude procedure resulted in unjust convictions as well as undeserved clearances. Those who passed spoke flippantly of having gotten their "Persil certificate" (Persil being a popular soap powder). Ernst von Salomon, a self-confessed terrorist under the Weimar Republic, wrote a self-righteous and self-pitying best-seller, *The Questionnaire*, defying and ridiculing the occupiers.

No one would expect that forty million Nazi followers would instantly be converted to democracy. They were stunned by their sudden fall and sobered by the growing recognition of what had happened to them. They felt humiliated by their defeat at the hands of nations that had been characterized to them as either decadent or barbarian, and even more by the revelation of the lies they had fallen for and the crimes that had been committed in their name. Now they were torn with conflicting desires: to atone (Jaspers) by adopting worthier ideals and better models; to associate themselves with the powers that clearly had been favored by God; to forget everything and "start from point zero" (Jünger), as the existentialists, thinking of Sisyphus, were to say; or to "come to grips with the past" (*die Vergangenheit bewältigen*, which may also be rendered "to overcome the past"—an ambiguous phrase and, perhaps for that reason, very popular, encompassing both the ideas of facing it and of having done with it).

The bewilderment was not diminished but increased by the clarity of the issue. This time no "encirclement," no "stab-in-the-back" myth could explain or excuse what so patently was their moral guilt and their physical defeat.

In the west, denazification ended abruptly and disappointingly when the Allies discovered that most people who were competent in their fields had in some way contaminated their hands with Nazi contacts, while those who were innocent often either were not very helpful or would have nothing to do with the occupation authorities. Thus, after furious purges, many subordinate officials, teachers, policemen, judges, etc., were called back. Managers of the big industrial companies benefited from an informal pardon. Many who had prospered under the Nazis regained positions of influence, and the German pecking order was quickly restored—sometimes with the Allies' help. The Americans appointed Dr. Fritz Schäffer as prime minister of Bavaria, only to discover that he had voted for Hitler's Enabling Act on March 24, 1933. Later he became finance minister. In 1966 Dr. Kurt Kiesinger became chancellor, although he had been a minor official in Hitler's Foreign Office. When in 1959 Heinrich Lübke became president of the Federal Republic, the East Germans revealed that he had supplied materials for a concentration camp.

The greatest outrage was the employment of Hans Globke as state secretary under Adenauer (see Chapter 27). It may well be that he had been spying for the Catholic Church in Hitler's police—but did that entitle him to be the chancellor's man Friday? The East German authorities—in possession of secret Nazi archives which they still refuse to make public—gleefully chose their time to release documents embarrassing to West German officials.

The East German system of denazification was different. They fired every big shot, whether guilty or not, and let the small fry get away. They employed former Gestapo officers in their People's Police; Generals Arno von Lenski and Vincenz Müller had held high office under Hitler. But they also had their share of infiltrators. It was discovered too late that one Ernst Grossmann, a member of the Central Committee of the SED, had been an overseer in the Sachsenhausen concentration camp.

For those who felt that Germany's big industrialists had to answer for many of Hitler's crimes, the Allies' policies of reconstruction were a disappointment. The greatest failure of the occupation mandate was, without doubt, decartelization. The conflicting interests of the powers and their domestic industries, the changing climate of European politics, and the Germans' successful resistance foiled all attempts to "democratize" German industry. Eventually the Bundestag adopted a British-American plan for a new order in the coal and steel industry— only to see it superseded by the Schuman Plan (see Chapter 27).

No one expects an occupation regime to be popular. Its mere presence reminded the Germans of their misfortune. Often that presence was all too visible and humiliating, and its effects were painful: houses were confiscated; the gap in living standards between occupier and occupied seemed to emphasize the Germans' inferior status. When fraternization finally was permitted, the results were often embarrassing. There were 15,000 prostitutes in Cologne alone, and uncounted illegitimate children, including black children, a new experience in German schools. It is true that some fraternization ended in great careers—see *The Gift Horse* by the actress Hildegard Knef.

However, the occupation regime laid the foundations of the new Germany in more than one respect. It took responsibility for measures that German politicians themselves would not have been able to take responsibility for—and that could not pass in France, England, or the United States because of political opposition. The British Labour government introduced *Mitbestimmung* (workers' codetermination) in the Ruhr industry; it reformed state and municipal administrations and installed socialists and democrats such as Hinrich Kopf as governor of Hanover and Wilhelm Kaisen in Bremen. The French picked Theodor Heuss, Carlo Schmid, and Reinhold Maier, great liberals.

Occupation authorities in the west also assumed responsibility for the currency reform of June 1948, which launched the "economic miracle" on its fascinating career and at the same time sealed the separation of the eastern from the western zone. In January 1947 the British and American zones were merged to form Bizonia; the French joined later. Bizonia was governed by a joint economic council and state assemblies. These prepared the necessary steps for the great "capital cut."

That currency reform was the military regime's outstanding success. A hundred old marks were reduced to 6.5 new marks; but each person could exchange up to 60 old for 60 new marks. The black market with its inflated price levels was eliminated in one stroke. Wage earners were the gainers; savers were the losers. Whoever had hoarded anything that could be sold was lucky; the immediate result of the reform was that all merchandise was brought out at once.

This was all to the good. But currency reform also brought with it a contingent decision which determined Germany's fate for the coming generation. Having split the country into two economically independent parts, it reinforced the Iron Curtain that separated the zones administratively and militarily. It also delineated a capitalistic, free-enterprise economy as against a collectivist economy. Eventually, the two acts of separation were linked into the pattern of ideological, diplomatic, and economic warfare known as the Cold War.

25

The Partitioning of Germany

*We have not been able to agree on the question of
what Germany is.*
—Secretary of State George Marshall at the
London Conference, 1948

ONE ASPECT OF THE MILITARY REGIME was most often criticized: it
was slow in allowing Germany a political rebirth. Democracy was to
be learned by reeducation rather than by doing. The press was strictly
controlled. Under the American "license" system a paper had to
have editors from all parties, but they were not permitted to criticize
any occupation power. The Soviets, who had some experience with
the operation of licensed parties in eastern Europe, were the first to
allow zonewide political organizations; but they had to be "antifascist,"
and they consisted of offices rather than masses—except for the two
labor parties. In the west, parties were allowed only on the county
or state level.

This changed, however, when the Cold War broke out. Repeated
ministerial conferences had not been able to agree on an agenda,
let alone on peace treaties for Germany and Austria. On February
9, 1946, Stalin announced the imminence of a new depression in the
west, and denounced the Popular Front illusions of the war period.
On March 5 Churchill, in Truman's presence, declared that "an Iron
Curtain" had descended across the European continent. These were
the first shots of the Cold War. Now the big powers began to vie
for the friendship of their former enemies. In July Molotov promised
the Germans a united and protected country. James Byrnes, speaking
at Stuttgart on September 6, stated that the era of punitive action
was ended and that Germany should be one and independent. Both
sides appealed to German democracy.

In October 1946 state assemblies were to be elected. The parties
presenting themselves to the voters were somewhat different from
those of the Weimar Republic. On the right, a local farmers' party
had been formed. Called the German Party (DP), it probably also

got votes from unreconstructed survivors of the Hitler era. The liberals had reorganized as the Free-Democratic Party (FDP); but, as is usual with liberals, it included right-wing as well as moderate attitudes— intellectuals like Heuss and business representatives like Erich Mende. In East Germany, the party was called the Liberal Party (LDP), and its platform had to include some Soviet planks.

The political center was occupied by a large concentration of "Christians," ranging from the conservative banker Robert Pferd-menges to the trade union leader Jakob Kaiser, from the Catholic, West-leaning Konrad Adenauer to the Protestant, all-German Eugen Gerstenmaier, from the European, anti-Soviet Franz Josef Strauss to the pacifist Gustav Heinemann. In the north of the (future) Federal Republic it called itself the Christian-Democratic Union (CDU); in Bavaria, where the bishops objected to the word "democratic," the Christian-Social Union (CSU). This was the party most willing to cooperate with the Western powers to restore "normalcy."

In its beginnings, the CDU/CSU had not been as conservative and western-oriented as it became under the leadership of Adenauer and Heinrich Krone, two politicians of the former Center Party. At the founding of the party in Berlin, Jakob Kaiser of the Christian Trade Unions, who desired to live in harmony with the new communist authorities, hoped to give the new party a more leftist coloration—as his contemporary counterparts in France and Italy had done. In the Rhineland Karl Arnold strove for a progressive orientation; under his influence the party program, adopted in Ahlen in 1947, called for nationalization of monopolistic industries. The alliance of Adenauer, the former mayor of Cologne, with industrial interests turned the CDU into a conservative party; the CSU had been con-servative from its inception as successor of the Bavarian People's Party.

The Social-Democratic Party had changed the least. It was still reformist and democratic. But it had absorbed the small activist groups that had split away at some time in the past. With them came Willy Brandt, who as an exile had worn the Norwegian uniform. The new party was led by new men: the charismatic Kurt Schumacher, a Religious Socialist who had emerged from the concentration camp as a martyr and hero; the learned and eloquent Professor Carlo Schmid; the flexible, shrewd ex-communist Herbert Wehner. These men remembered that in the Weimar Republic the SPD had suffered from being too "responsible" and not socialist enough; it had been attacked by the communists for its role in coalition governments and by the Nazis for its lack of patriotism. Schumacher, a crippled, bitter man marked by death, decided that this time the SPD would speak for both: the patriots who resented the occupation regime and the partitioning of the country, and the underprivileged who resented the restoration of a capitalist Europe. Since he did not suspect that the German economy would recover as fast as it eventually did, he felt safe in choosing opposition as his stance. He proudly declared: "When these people [the Allies] were making deals with Hitler, we were dying in the concentration camps."

The SPD had been the only party that had never harbored any illusions about the Nazis and never assented to their assaults on western values. It was a party of unsung martyrs, and for all his strong-headedness, Schumacher had a better right to speak for all the victims of militarism and fascism than the communists, who were quick to appoint themselves their official spokesmen. In the eastern zone, the SPD was also soon to become the only party that resisted absorption into the communist front and refused to collaborate with its fake "People's Congress." The Soviet authorities banned the SPD and persecuted its members (even while they thoughtfully provided a successor party to the NSDAP for ex-Nazis).

Farther on the left, there was an unreconstructed KPD, led by Stalin's trusted satraps. In West Germany it remained small and ineffective. In the Soviet zone, however, heavy pressure was brought to bear on SPD militants to "unite" with the communists into a Socialist Unity Party of Germany (SED). Those who resisted often found themselves in the same concentration camps from which they had just been liberated. Only in Berlin did a few very brave leaders hold their own so that the SPD remained independent.

The result of local elections in 1946 was surprising in that it showed a distribution not dissimilar to that of a normal Weimar year: In the west, the CDU/CSU got 38 percent, the SPD 35 percent, KPD and FDP 9 percent each, and DP 2 percent. The other local parties are too small and not easily identified with any of the larger groups. In the east, the SED polled 47 percent, CDU and LDP 25 percent each. In Berlin, still an undivided city, the SPD got 49 percent, the CDU 22 percent, the SED 20 percent, and the LDP 9 percent.

In 1948 the state assemblies sent representatives to a *Länderrat* (Council of States), and then the three western powers invited the Germans to convene a constituent assembly for the three western zones. But the hopes for eventual unification of Germany were still alive. Cautiously, therefore, a parliamentary council was charged with drawing up a "basic law," something less than a constitution.

While the western part was on its way to statehood, the Russians had not been idle in their zone. Since the election had failed to produce an SED majority, an extraparliamentary movement was started, which culminated in the convening of a "German People's Congress" in December 1947. Nominally its members were deputies of the SED, the Free German Trade Union League (FDGB), the Free German Youth (FDJ), the Peasants' Mutual Aid (VdgB), etc. Actually they were all directed by the SED, and the congress adopted the proper resolutions. In February 1948 the German Economic Commission (DKW) took charge, and its secretariat exercised all functions of government except defense and foreign affairs. It was supported by a well-trained, garrisoned "People's Police." In March, coinciding with the centennial of Germany's first revolution, a "German People's Council" was appointed to draw up a constitution, and a year later a definitive "People's Congress" was elected. In the one-slate election the official list received 66 percent of the vote—a poor performance for a totalitarian government.

In February 1948, when the communists seized power in Czechoslovakia the western commanders in Europe got nervous. Communications in the Central Control Council—the last, tenuous remnant of four-power rule in Germany—had practically stopped, and in March, while the German People's Council was meeting, Marshal Sokolovsky walked out of the Control Council. The pretense that Germany was one country under tripartite occupation was dead. A foreign ministers' meeting in London (February to June 1948) failed to produce any hope of agreement; there would be no peace treaty with an all-German government. The powers could not agree on a currency reform, and so the west went ahead unilaterally (see Chapter 24).

In 1949 first the eastern and then the western parts adopted constitutions. They still contained protestations about the aim of unity, but for all practical purposes they made its achievement impossible. On both sides of the Iron Curtain, institutions were created which could never be merged. Property rights had been overridden in the east, while the west had written different laws on restitution and on the equalization of losses. Reuniting the country would have amounted to sorting out scrambled eggs. Moreover, there was now a distinct income differential between east and west.

The big powers stood behind their respective Germans, urging them on, and each side anxiously tried to prevent "its" Germans from joining up with the other's. This is what we call the Cold War. Three assumptions must be made to explain this peculiar contest. One is that Stalin was attempting to dominate, and conquer for communism, as much of Europe as he could; the second is that the United States

Federal Republic of Germany ▨ **GDR** ☐

FIGURE 2. THE TWO GERMAN STATES

meant to preserve as much as possible of the old continent for its own social-economic system; the third is that neither side wished to incur an excessive risk of war over this, but each was content to protect what it had against encroachment from the other.

This was the policy of "containment" as spelled out by George Kennan in the now-famous article, signed "Mr. X," in *Foreign Affairs* (July 1947). The entire conception, however, was attacked in a series of articles by Walter Lippmann entitled "The Cold War"—introducing an unfortunate coining into the political vocabulary—in the *Washington Post*, and by Aneurin Bevan, the British minister of health (see Chapter 26).

When spheres of influence had been distributed at Yalta and Potsdam, the ultimate disposition of Germany and Austria had been left pending. Should they remain divided into occupation zones? Or should they be unified—and in that case, would they not eventually side with either the east or the west, either voluntarily or forced by coup, pressure, or conquest? The so-called Cold War was a series of diplomatic maneuvers by which the Soviet Union on the one side and the United States and England on the other tried to lure the Germans into their respective camps, or—if that was prevented by the other side's measures—at least to bind the Germans on their side of the Iron Curtain more solidly to their respective blocs.

This anxiety resulted from the linkup of hegemony with economic system. Stalin held, with Machiavelli, that upon conquering a country one must impose one's system of government (and he added: one's economic system) on it. Hence the succession of coups in Rumania, Bulgaria, and Czechoslovakia, which Washington and London saw with increasing alarm, and the determined effort to bring the Soviet zone of Germany under a similar government. The British and Americans countered by merging their zones, though the French hesitated. This established a Western position of strength in Central Europe.

This was also the idea behind the Marshall Plan: restoring the web of multilateral trade relations which would give the non-Soviet world stability and cohesion. Even before that plan, one billion dollars in United Nations aid, mostly American, had been given to Europe; half of it went to Germany. In subsequent years, West Germany received two billion dollars in Marshall aid. East Germany, Poland, and Czechoslovakia, which had been invited to the founding session of the European Recovery Program in 1947, were ordered by Stalin to stay away, and he established his own COMECON in eastern Europe.

The currency reform in Bizonia was carried out in spite of a

Russian veto in the Control Council. Its political importance was to be revealed at once. Which currency should circulate in Berlin? Both? The Russians declared that they would not allow western money in any sector of Berlin. The mayor of Berlin, Ernst Reuter, declared that the currency amounted to sovereignty.

Berlin was a four-power enclave 100 miles inside the Russian zone. Right after the war it was still thought that Berlin would again be the capital; the western powers therefore had insisted that they have occupation rights there. To obtain these rights, Dwight Eisenhower, at the time the Allied commander, paid a heavy price: he evacuated two highly industrialized states west of the Elbe—Saxony and Thuringia—which he had conquered, and he did not insist on having a land connection from the west to the isolated city. Nor did anyone think, at the time, of having it put in writing that the right to be an occupying power implies the right to bring supplies to the occupied area. Suddenly, in June 1948, Stalin declared a blockade of all land and water communications with Berlin.

He meant to drive the western powers out of Berlin and to starve the city's population into submission. For there was this political dimension to the conflict: of all the cities in the eastern zone, Berlin alone had withstood Soviet pressure to merge SPD and KPD. The Social-Democrats ruled city hall—which unfortunately was situated in the Russian sector (for Berlin, too, was divided into four occupation zones). Now the communists occupied the assembly hall and denied Mayor Reuter access to his office. In World War I he had been a prisoner of war in Russia and had become a communist and cofounder of the Communist International; later he broke with the communists and became Social-Democratic mayor of Magdeburg. Now he had been elected in Berlin. He knew the Russians and the communists.

Resolutely he moved city hall to the American sector, declared the western mark legal tender for the three western sectors of Berlin, and made the besieged city an island of freedom in a totalitarian sea. Two million Berliners accepted the challenge of Stalin's blockade and at once became heroes of the western world. Supplies of food, coal, drugs, and machines were flown in by American planes on a minute-by-minute precision schedule—the magnificent airlift, literally, air bridge (*Luftbrücke*). For nearly a year, undaunted, the Berliners held out on their slim diet. Stalin did not dare interfere with the airlift and finally lifted the blockade.

The blockade must also be seen in the wider context of security in Europe. On April 4, 1949, the United States and Canada had joined forces with ten European nations—later augmented by Greece and

Turkey—to form the powerful North Atlantic Treaty Organization (NATO), which declared itself responsible for the defense of West Germany. At the same time, on May 23, 1949, the Federal Republic of Germany was founded, with Bonn as its capital. As its first chancellor it elected Konrad Adenauer, a staunch anticommunist and an advocate of German integration into the western system.

Obviously, Stalin had not been simply furious about Berlin. The blockade was meant to deter the West Germans from establishing a state in their zones and from integrating it into the western system. When Stalin saw that he could not prevent either, he authorized "his" Germans to declare themselves a nation, too (May 30). It was called the German Democratic Republic (DDR); but since it was neither German nor democratic, West Germans continued for a long time to refer to it as "the zone," as though it were an irredenta still to be recovered.

At the same time that NATO came into existence, the Soviet bloc founded COMECON (RGW) as an instrument for close economic cooperation (see page 307). Later, the Warsaw Military Pact came into existence. The DDR was thoroughly integrated into the East European empire, which the Soviet Union exploited ruthlessly for the reconstruction of its own economy.

Germany was split into the ramparts of two superpowers confronting each other economically, militarily, and ideologically. Like Homeric heroes, the "cold warriors" attacked each other verbally— by radio and pamphlets, by profound philosophical works, by congresses and rallies, by insults and by diplomatic moves—without, however, going to battle. The Cold War stayed cold.

Perhaps some West German leaders had hopes that the western powers would push Soviet influence back and liberate "the zone." But in September 1949 the Soviet Union exploded an atomic bomb—five years earlier than had been thought likely—and established a military balance. Europe's two blocs were trapped in the contest that forced the small powers on either side to seek protection under the umbrella of big brother's big guns. In doing so, the two Germanies accepted their division: they had to coexist as polarized parts. Thus, the Cold War became the Cold Peace, at least in Europe.

In Asia, meanwhile, it was turning into a hot war. On October 1, 1949, Mao Tse-tung founded the People's Republic of China. In Vietnam, France was fighting Ho Chi Minh, whose government the Soviet Union recognized in January 1950. On June 25, 1950, North Korean troops invaded South Korea, which the Americans had evacuated a year earlier. Would this remain a brushfire war or explode into another world conflagration? The United States Pentagon felt that its European defenses were too weak. Its apprehensions were quite understandable: Germany and Korea were similar in being divided, and Stalin was making belligerent gestures. American policy-makers therefore were casting about for supplementary recruitment. Adenauer had offered a German contribution to western defenses almost on the morrow of his election; Britain's Foreign Secretary Ernest Bevin, an impetuous Labourite who had clashed with Molotov often, supported him vigorously. U.S. Secretary of State Dean Acheson, was "converted" to German rearmament, as he says in his memoirs, by the events of 1950.

There were, however, two problems. One was German, the other European. Having been taught just recently that militarism was their national vice, how were the Germans to be re-reeducated? And having fought German militarism just five years ago, how were the Europeans to accept the idea that they were to sponsor its resurgence and to be allied with it against their recent ally of the great war? Further, how was this project to be presented without provoking a strong Russian response?

The answer to all these questions was the European Defense Community (EDC), a joint army in which Germans were to serve on a regimental level, well integrated into a watchful, purely defensive organization, incapable of striking out independently, but formidable if used for agreed-upon purposes of collective security. Solomonic as the solution appeared, it provoked indignant outcries on all sides. The French, who had suggested it to begin with, now did not want to serve in the same army with "krauts"; the British Labour Party, once again in opposition and deprived by death of Bevin's leadership, returned to its customary Germanophobia. German nationalists would not accept service as mere foot soldiers; German neopacifists would not serve anybody. A movement with the slogan *Ohne mich* ("Count me out") spread among young people who were loath to lose a year just when business opportunities seemed to be multiplying.

Stalin exploited these sentiments by launching a peace offensive. Picasso designed his symbolic dove; in Paris, a "Peace Congress" assembled delegates from fifty countries; Soviet diplomats proposed plans to "neutralize" a reunited Germany—a design that appealed to many people, inside and outside, as fair to both Germany and those who still were suspicious of it. Stalin's appeals were also tempting to those who, looking at a map of the world divided into red and blue, saw safety in a belt of white neutrality that would run from Sweden in the north through Germany, Austria, and Yugoslavia, and farther south and east to India. But coming from Stalin, such proposals could never stand the scrutiny of experts, who found in them the legal trip wires: in one way or another, the proposals always amounted to something the western powers could not accept—a merger of the two German governments on equal terms, giving the communists all the advantages of their monolithic organization.

The Allies countered with proposals to let the Germans freely elect a joint government. Thus the themes of unity, peace, and freedom were used as propaganda weapons in the Cold War. Trying to win the Germans to their side, the Soviets monopolized the words "unity" and "peace" and managed to paint their opponents with the "Cold War" brush.

26

Neutralism

We, who would not have won with Hitler, nevertheless
were beaten with him.

—Bertolt Brecht

THE ATOMIC BALANCE TRANSFORMED ALL PREVIOUS NOTIONS of diplomacy. "Tension" now meant stability. "Relaxation" meant the unleashing of unpredictable developments. Polarization meant security. A fluid situation might bring risks. This was difficult to stomach. The new code of diplomacy required the smaller nations to subordinate their power to the grand design of the bigger ones. That meant not only dependence but perpetuation of the status quo. Again and again, therefore, during the 1950s, movements both right and left of both nationalists and socialists would look for new solutions, deny the necessity of polarization, define independence in defiance of the "big brother." These movements are variously known as "neutralist" or "third force." Intellectually they were sponsored by Tito, who had broken out of the Soviet empire, and by the French existentialists. In Germany the sentiment found expression in all parties, but especially on the extreme left and extreme right.

Salomon's *Questionnaire* spoke for many Germans who felt that they were being punished for historical mistakes in which the victorious powers had participated. They reacted against "reeducation"; they had received enough education in panzer battles and air raids. Not only nationalists felt that way. A group of young socialist writers led by Hans Werner Richter and Alfred Andersch had founded a paper, *Der Ruf* (*Calling Out*), in an American prisoner-of-war camp. Returned home, they found a wide audience by boldly demanding freedom, truth, and justice, criticizing reeducation and "occupation democracy," rejecting the western power policies as colonialist, inhuman, and backward-looking. Predictably, the paper was banned in 1947; but from its ashes rose the most powerful voice German literature ever had: "Group 47." Its members included many who were soon to emerge as Germany's major writers and critics: Heinrich Böll, Günter Grass, Hans Magnus Enzensberger, Günther Eich, Carl

Amery, Fritz Raddatz, Siegfried Lenz, Wolfdietrich Schnurre. They tied free writing firmly to left-wing politics and neutralism. They intended to stay in the no-man's land that the collapse of the Third Reich had created.

Many saw the destruction, misery, and privations as a chance to turn away from the ugly past, from its materialism and false glories, to get a new start—morally, at least, to escape from the charge that all Germans shared responsibility for the horrors visited upon other countries. Andersch, a former Communist Youth leader, believed in the growing democratization of the Soviet Union and the socialization of western economies.

> We are threatened by twofold education—for planning in the East, for freedom in the West. We are in danger of being split into a totalitarian socialist state on the other side of the Elbe, and a democratic government of laws this side of it. . . . This means dividing not only Germany, but Europe, too. . . . In the second half of this century the young generation wants to develop toward a new form of government and of life where democracy overcomes the limitations of nineteenth-century liberalism, and where socialism as an economic system abandons its totalitarian claim.

There was even a Hegelian ring in this claim to overarching and overcoming all contradictory systems: "By absorbing Eastern socialism and Western democracy, [Germany] can unite the two on a higher level" and develop "a synthesis that might serve the entire world as a model." Likewise, Professor Paul Noack, who became the leader of the *Ohne mich* movement, told the Rhine-Ruhr Club: "A [peaceful] people of 60 million could fill the vacuum [between the blocs] with its spirit. A world with such a people would change its face." Was this a revival of the old German claim that Germans had a special mission among the nations?

They asked the victors' conference at Moscow to release the prisoners of war, to stop the dismantling, to abolish the zones, to restore the German territory of 1937, and to allow a national government to conclude peace. Remembering the recent record of German imperialism, these intellectuals wished to take Germany out of world politics for good. They would have liked to see a Swiss future for their country: forever neutralized and federated despite a diversity of social systems. What they abhorred most was a West German state fostered by the western powers to complement a capitalistic world economy or, even worse, to support an anti-Soviet encirclement policy. "Containment" to them, and to many other Germans at the time, meant the renewal of power politics, the promotion of neo-Nazi, revanchist sentiments, and the final breakup of German unity.

From the opposite side of the political spectrum, nationalists and capitalists also objected to the formation of two German states. Refugees feared that drawing a border would write finis to their hopes of going home; patriots and anticommunists were loath to give up the lost territories, industrialists hoped for the large eastern markets. We therefore find Thomas Dehler, leader of the FDP, and Hans-Joachim von Merkatz, leader of the DP, and Paul Sethe, the influential editorialist of the *Frankfurter Allgemeine Zeitung*, making common cause with the Social-Democrats in attacking the treaties that their coalition partner, Chancellor Adenauer, was negotiating with the Allies.

Drawing on nationalist and pacifist, anticapitalist and irredentist, arguments, the SPD under Schumacher became the most articulate opponent of the containment policy and of the "small-German" western state. Schumacher in 1946 told the first postwar congress of the SPD that 35 percent of the Germans had not suffered any losses during the war, but 25 percent had lost nearly everything, and 40 percent had nothing left at all. The industrial proletariat was now in the same boat with refugees, dispossessed middle-class people, civil-service and commercial employees, unemployable war victims, and cripples. A "party of the poor" was therefore bound to win. The party's first aim was to redistribute resources, equalize losses, and nationalize large estates and corporations. Schumacher was convinced that only the occupation powers prevented this revolution.

As a wounded veteran of World War I, Schumacher was able to tell the nationalists that a German rebirth should not be conceived by military revival; and as a veteran of the concentration camp he could talk back to those in the western capitals who wanted to punish all Germans for the sins of the Nazis. He demanded equal rights for the Germans, and he reminded the Allies of the havoc the Treaty of Versailles had wrought in the politics of the Weimar Republic. He boldly declared that only a Germany in full possession of its rights would be able to rejoin the family of nations; and he added that only Social-Democratic leadership could guarantee that such a Germany would not be a threat to peace.

However, the SPD was beaten at the polls in 1949. Undaunted, Schumacher pursued his theme that patriotism and socialism had the same enemy. This argument grew more urgent when in April 1951 the European Coal and Steel Community was founded. Could anything be more suggestive than a new international cartel of the hated "coal and smokestack barons" under the aegis of the three Catholic-conservative governments of Adenauer, Alcide De Gasperi, and Robert Schuman?

The SPD arduously and stubbornly resisted the formation of a western state at each step; and with increasing vehemence it resisted the West German state's integration into the western system. At one point Schumacher called Adenauer "the chancellor of the Allies," for which he was suspended from the Bundestag for two weeks. Sick and desperate, he could not master his rage at having miscalculated.

However, the SPD had long-term political grounds for opposing the western orientation, too. Its strongest constituencies had always been the cities now in the east; in a western state, with its Roman Catholic majority, it might be condemned to permanent minority status.

For similar reasons Protestant leaders like Niemöller, Bishop Otto Dibelius, Bishop Hanns Lilje, Congregation President Gerstenmaier, and the president of the Evangelical Synod, Gustav Heinemann (the last two founding members of the CDU), were against the formation of a Western European union in which Catholics not only would be in the majority but were anchored in strong societal structures. The left, or trade union, wing of the CDU too was reluctant to commit itself to one-half of Germany. It had powerful support in Berlin, where its leaders believed that they might be able to influence policy in the eastern zone. J. Kaiser and Ernst Lemmer—who had both been active in the Resistance—tried to "build a bridge" between east and west. Unfortunately, Soviet authorities could not and still cannot tolerate independent forces even if friendly; they voided the election of Christian trade unionists into the presidium of the eastern CDU and in their place installed Otto Nuschke, formerly editor of a liberal paper but by then a collaborationist, who led the CDU into the National Front—a mere appendix to the SED. Kaiser lost all influence and eventually had to flee to the west. He has summed up his experience of the summer of 1948:

> People have called us illusionists because we thought it possible to combine rejection of totalitarianism with the desire to build bridges between the nations. We would have been irresponsible, however, had we not tried everything to mitigate the conflict that threatened the unity of our unhappy country. We could not abandon this policy before we had convinced ourselves that Soviet power knows only enmity toward peoples or parties that do not submit to its doctrine or serve its will to dominate.

Thus ended the only serious attempt to design a political "third way" in Germany. Having failed, Kaiser could not find many who would listen to him in the western CDU; and so, by throwing away this chance of a friendly Christian-Democratic movement, Stalin tossed the CDU leadership into the lap of the conservatives: Adenauer, Pferdmenges, the *Frankfurter Allgemeine Zeitung*, and Professor Ludwig Erhard, a Bavarian Protestant and a partisan of Wilhelm Röpke's economic doctrine, which advocated the return to old-fashioned free enterprise.

Religious, national, and social issues thus were interwoven in the great debate between "Atlanticists" and "Neutralists" which was to engage public opinion for almost twenty years. Protestants, socialists, the CDU's left wing, even big industry wanted a policy of reconciliation with the east. Catholics, old monarchists, refugees from the east, and admirers of the American system allied themselves with the great number of people who feared the Russians even when they seemed to offer unity. (In fact, this was the most telling argument in the arsenal of Walter Lippmann, who had coined the term "Cold War." One day, he believed, the Russians would offer the Germans reunification, provided they surrendered to communism or Russian control; the United States therefore should try to negotiate mutual withdrawal from all parts of Germany. Lippmann also expressed the fear, wide-spread among American liberals, that the United States might get permanently involved in the defense of West Germany—a role that U.S. liberals, with many Jews among them, found repulsive. Opposition to the Cold War was intimately linked with aversion to Germany and with both American leftists' and American conservatives' aversion to military involvements abroad. Thus, surprisingly, George Kennan, the architect of containment, now came out for a policy of "dis-engagement." He was a hero of the German left until it discovered that his motives were quite different from theirs.)

The debate reached a climax in March 1952, when Stalin made a last, desperate attempt to prevent West Germany's entry into the European Defense Community (EDC). He offered free elections, reunification, and neutralization. His concessions this time went so far that Britain's Foreign Secretary Anthony Eden found it necessary to respond: would Stalin allow a United Nations commission to supervise the elections? Would he permit the elections before a peace treaty was signed? Would the peace treaty supersede the Potsdam agreements? Would a future German government have power to decide freely on its foreign alignment?

The answer to all these questions, never delivered, was an implicit "no." Stalin intended to merge the governments *before* the election and to use the electoral law of the east, where candidates for the single slate are provided by loyal organizations. Nor did he mean to have observers ("spies") snooping around in his zone. He gladly accepted the western rejection of his proposal and did not insist.

Nor did his proposal deflect the West German government from signing the EDC treaty on May 27, 1952. He did succeed in passing the "old maid" to the western diplomats: they had to take the blame for rejecting "neutralization," "unification," and "peace." To this day, neutralist and revisionist historians deplore the lost opportunity of Stalin's offer of March 10, 1952. Despite all the revelations about Stalin only three years later, they continue to ask whether the western powers should not have trusted him.

They are asking the wrong question. Perhaps the western governments did make a mistake—but not in misjudging Stalin's intentions. Had they, deadpan, pretended to respond to Stalin's initiative, had they stirred German hopes for unity in freedom and launched a movement for free organization and free speech in East Germany—who knows if the masses might not have risen, as they did only a year later, and swept away the odious regime Stalin had installed in East Germany?

That risk, obviously, the Cold War strategists were not prepared to take. They had conceded to Stalin the areas his arms had conquered in Hitler's war. They were occupying Germany not so much because they were confronting the east but because they feared that the Germans, if left alone, might start a third world war. Only a few years later, Khrushchev was to say to the British: "You watch your Germans, I'll watch mine."

Naturally, the more self-assertive industrialists hated to see Germany in that position. Their party, the small FDP, therefore was rent by internal strife over the foreign policy issue. In 1956, younger members in Rhineland-Westphalia staged a revolt to break the coalition with the CDU in their state, and aligned their party with the SPD. Among these insurgents were nationalists like Erich Mende and liberals like Walter Scheel.

Ironically, in 1972, when the Federal Republic finally recognized the status quo of the two Germanies, the relevant documents were signed by the former critics of the status quo: Willy Brandt as chancellor, Heinemann as president, Scheel as foreign minister, and Egon Bahr as state secretary.

27

The Federal Republic—I

The Adenauer Era

*It is for the German people in its entirety to accomplish
its unity and liberty in free self-determination.*
—from the Preamble to the Basic Law

ON MAY 23, 1949, THE STATE ASSEMBLIES of the three western zones
ratified a "Basic Law" which their joint parliamentary council had
worked out in heated debate and in consultation with the occupying
powers. Bavaria failed to ratify it but accepted the other states' decision
as binding. With that, the Federal Republic of Germany (BRD)
was born.*

The occupation powers, however, imposed an "Occupation
Statute," which specifically reserved to them military and foreign
affairs, control of the Ruhr, decartelization, restitution, and foreign
claims. The Federal Republic was still not sovereign.

In broad outline, its constitution is parliamentary. † The president
is strictly ceremonial. He is elected by the Bundestag and an equal
number of delegates from the state assemblies. The first president
was the amiable Professor Theodor Heuss, who in the 1920s had been
a Democratic representative, besides presiding over the *Hochschule
für Politik* in Berlin.

The Bundestag is elected by a complex system combining the
advantages of one-man constituencies with those of proportional
representation. Each voter has two votes: one he gives to a person,

---

***Bundesrepublik Deutschland* (BRD); the English rendering is "FRG"
or "Germany, F.R." The Soviet zone is named *Deutsche Demokratische
Republik* (DDR), German Democratic Republic (GDR) in English. In the
following, I use the German initials BRD and DDR; for international
organizations (like EEC) I use the English initials.

† The term "Basic Law" was used to avoid the neutralist criticism that
a constitution might prejudice unification.

the other to a party. Half of the members are elected directly, the other half from lists that have been presented by the parties. With an eye to the unhappy experience of the Weimar Republic, splinter parties are discouraged by the provision that no seats will be allotted to any list carrying less than 5 percent of the vote. This leaves to a popular man without a party a chance of direct election.

The Bundestag elects the chancellor, who then selects a cabinet. In practice, of course, cabinet seats have been distributed beforehand by deals among the parties. Since under normal conditions no party wins a majority, coalition governments are the rule. To prevent frequent changes of government—the plague of Weimar—the constitution excludes votes of no confidence which are not "constructive": while the chancellor and his cabinet need the confidence of the Bundestag to assume office, they can be overthrown only by a majority that has designated a replacement. Under this provision, Brüning could have survived the depression.

In contrast to the Weimar constitution, the Basic Law is designed to strengthen the government. But even more than the Weimar constitution, it favors government by the parties, and especially by the power brokers in the party organizations. Special laws give federal subsidies to the established parties and their youth organizations. Parties must publish their sources of income. The SPD, in a typical year, collected 19 million marks in membership dues, the CDU/CSU 8 million, the FDP 1 million; they also received "donations" of, respectively, 2.5 million, 7 million, and 2 million.

The Bundesrepublik is federal in theory; in practice its administration tends toward centralism. Only education, policy, and religious affairs are under state jurisdiction. Interestingly, when the Basic Law was being debated, the Social-Democrats insisted on a strong federal government, especially in matters of finance and economic policy. The CDU/CSU, supported by both French and American authorities, preferred a looser structure. But with the exception of Bavaria, the states had to be newly created, some without regard to historical tradition. They are: North Rhine–Westphalia, Lower Saxony (the former Hanover), Rhineland-Palatinate, Baden-Württemberg, Bavaria, Saar, Hessen, Hamburg, and Bremen. (Berlin has special status and is not represented in the Bundesrat.)

As the names Federal Republic, Federal Chamber (Bundestag), Federal President, etc., indicate, the states have retained or regained some sovereignty. They are represented in an upper chamber, the Federal Council (Bundesrat)—some states by five delegates, others by four or three, who must vote as directed by the state governor

(*Ministerpräsident*). The Bundesrat therefore cannot achieve the stature of the U.S. Senate. In crucial situations its majority may differ from that of the Bundestag; chancellors now and then have intervened in state politics to obtain like-minded coalitions in state governments. The question of Bundesrat agreement was critical in the rearmament and the Berlin Treaty debates. In recent years, the government parties lacked a majority in the Bundesrat. No agreement, therefore, was achieved on the right of extremists to employment in the civil service. Each state has its own screening procedure.

On the other hand, the Constitutional Court (*Verfassungsgericht*) is very similar to the U.S. Supreme Court. It is the arbiter between the two chambers, between parliament and administration, between federal and state governments. It rules on the constitutionality of elections and of parties—it has pronounced both the Neo-Nazi Party (DRP) and the old Communist Party (KPD) illegal; it was invoked, much to its discomfort, to decide on the constitutionality of rearming Germany. Though equipped to interpret the law, it has often been reluctant to make decisions that properly belong to the legislature.

A detailed Bill of Rights permits conscientious objection to military service and explicitly admits "restrictions of national sovereignty in the interests of a peaceful and permanent order in Europe and between the nations of the world." But, mindful of the Weimar experiment, it denies the enjoyment of civil rights to "associations whose purpose is contrary to the law, or which are directed against the constitutional order or the idea of peace," and to "persons who will use the freedom of speech, the freedom to teach, to assemble, to form coalitions, etc., to fight against a liberal democratic order" (*freiheitliche demokratische Grundordnung*). Also, "the freedom to teach does not suspend loyalty [*Treue*] to the Constitution."

Although in its last article the Basic Law emphasizes that a "constitution" will be adopted only after the German nation in its entirety has won its self-determination, the makeshift document has served the BRD well for almost thirty years now—longer than the Weimar and Hitler regimes put together. But it still bears the marks of improvisation. As the republic's capital Adenauer selected the quiet university town of Bonn—Beethoven's birthplace—whose facilities were inadequate even then. Government agencies, embassies, pressure groups, and foundations had to build their quarters all along the Rhine in neighboring communities. Frankfurt—buzzing, commercial, and liberal, with its black, red, and gold tradition—would have been the logical choice for a capital; but that would have meant admitting that the Federal Republic expected to stay. Berlin, especially

TABLE 4. THE FEDERAL REPUBLIC: BUNDESTAG ELECTIONS (PERCENTAGE OF TOTAL VOTE)

	1946[a]	1949	1953	1957	1961	1965	1969	1972	1976
CDU/CSU	38	31	45	50	45	48	46	45	49
SPD	35	29	29	32	36	40	43	46	45
FDP (liberals)	9	12	10	8	13	10	6	8	6
DP-GDP (nationalists)	2	4	3	3 ⎫		—	—	—	—
GB-BHE (refugees)	2	—	6	5 ⎬	3	—	—	—	—
BP (*Bayernpartei*), Center	2	4	2	1 ⎭	1	—	—	—	—
DRP-NDP (neo-Nazi)	—	2	1	1		2	4	less than 1	—
Communists	9	6	2	—	—	—	⎫	1	—
Ultraleftists	—	—	1	—	2	1	1 ⎬	1	1
Other	3	12[b]	1	—	—	—	—	—	—

a Local elections.
b Mostly local parties.

Note: Due to rounding, totals may deviate from 100.

after the blockade, was out of the question. And so Dr. Adenauer, the Rhinelander, got his way: he could stay where he had bred roses after the Nazis had dismissed him.

No other person has shaped the Federal Republic as tellingly as this septuagenarian whose public life had begun under the empire. During the first republic he was mayor of Cologne and Prussian delegate to the State Council (Reichsrat). He was religious but anti-clerical, conservative but republican, and so anti-Prussian that he was suspected of "separatism"—the worst charge a nationalist can prefer against a Rhinelander. His close relations with industry have been revealed in Erik Reger's novel *The Vigilant Cockerel*. His party passed him by when it preferred Brüning for the chancellor's office. The Nazis suspended and later arrested him. He was reappointed as mayor by the Americans but fired by the British—which gave him leisure to devote himself entirely to politics. He built the CDU and chaired the Parliamentary Council, and was now elected chancellor at the head of a middle-class coalition.*

Adenauer has often been attacked as being provincial, or as biased in favor of a western, even a Roman Catholic, orientation. Perhaps at that moment Germany needed a leader who was deeply rooted in a humanistic tradition older than nationalism. He did not like Berlin and all it stood for, and he suspected Protestantism of being a camouflage for Asian paganism—which seemed to begin somewhere in the sandy soil of Brandenburg. Or so his enemies have charged. His limitations were more obvious than his strengths. He was authoritarian and wily; his nickname, when it was not *Der Alte* (The Boss), was The Fox. His policies and his character wrenched German politics, but he also gave the state stability. His steady fourteen-year tenure compares favorably with the fourteen years of Weimar which had been so turbulent.

Two things helped: the unprecedented boom which soon came to be called "the German economic miracle," and Soviet pressure, which discouraged defections from the government camp. Even the opposition would not forgo the security which American protection gave all Germans—and that was to be had only on Adenauer's terms. Since he dominated his party and his coalition partners, the regime had a Gaullist structure; though it was not a presidential republic, friends

---

*139 CDU/CSU delegates, 52 FDP, 17 DP, against 131 SPD, 15 KPD, 17 Bavarians (see Table 4).

and critics called it a *Kanzlerdemokratie*. Heuss as president backed the chancellor; Schumacher, made impotent by his dogmatism and temper, had condemned the opposition to sterility.

Nevertheless, the majority did not rule arbitrarily. While Adenauer was inexorably antisocialist, he enjoyed a personal friendship with the president of the DGB (the national trade union organization), and he consented to union participation (*Mitbestimmung*) in the big Ruhr concerns. He recognized the neutralists by including in his cabinet Jakob Kaiser, after his return from Berlin, and Gustav Heinemann, president of the Evangelical church (who in 1950 left the cabinet to protest against rearmament).

The first business of the new republic obviously was to increase the area of its sovereignty. Adenauer obtained the return of the Saarland and, by joining the Ruhr Authority, asserted German rights there on equal terms. He also joined the Council of Europe. On July 9, 1951, his western orientation was rewarded by a solemn declaration of the western powers terminating the state of war.

This recognition in the west, however, was paid for by deteriorating relations with the east. While day by day the two German states were gaining reality, uneasy Germans refused to believe that this could be final. They had to deny the legitimacy of the BRD, to doubt its viability, to question its spirit. On both the right and the left, people rejected the idea of a West German nation. Even more dogmatically, the government refused to admit that another German state was being built in the east. This twofold inability to recognize facts made it nearly impossible to conduct any foreign policy—except one that promised reconquest of the "lost provinces."

Adenauer therefore made a fateful decision. In his second incumbency he allied himself with irredentists and nationalists of the extreme right. Nine million people who had been expelled from eastern countries, or who had voluntarily come from the provinces yielded to Poland, lived in West Germany. In addition, a steady stream of immigrants came from East Germany. In some areas, as in Schleswig-Holstein, they constituted 20 percent of the population. Such a mass of newcomers is not easy to absorb, and whether their grievances were just or exaggerated, the refugees had become a political factor which in some states unsettled the parliamentary balance.

From 1951 they banded together in a League of the Expelled and Dispossessed (BHE), whose politics was intensely nationalistic, pan-German, and antibolshevist. They thought only of reconquering their lost homelands and could not condone any compromise with the eastern governments that not only had expropriated their farms, shops, and houses, but had scrambled them irretrievably. As a party the BHE represented concrete, material interests, and in that capacity it joined government coalitions. In Schleswig-Holstein it grouped with the SPD; elsewhere it preferred right-wing partners. Its leaders often were demagogues and careerists who eventually discarded their party to join the CDU. Ten years later, leaderless and eroded by Adenauer's successes, the BHE collapsed; but its phraseology by then had been assimilated by the CDU. It spoke the language of the Cold War, and was spoiling for a hot war—at American expense, of course.

The German Party (DP), also nationalistic and militaristic, shared the BHE's fate. Its minister, Hans-Christoph Seebohm, who stayed in office under the CDU flag until 1966, never conceded the loss of the Sudeten area. (The problems of the refugees were overcome first by the boom conditions, which reconciled them with their new country, and eventually through intermarriage, education, and assimilation.)

Thus tilting to the right, Adenauer was able to unite the middle classes. His policies seemed to succeed: West Germany's rearmament, her admission to NATO, the return of the Saarland and the European integration of the Ruhr, finally recognition by the Soviet Union—all this seemed worth the temporary sacrifice of unification. But did the children of the economic miracle really want to be reunited with their poor eastern brothers? As the gap between incomes here and there grew wider, BRD citizens realized that reunification would mean higher taxes. On the strength of its economic success, Adenauer's party increased its vote from 31 percent in 1949 to 45 percent in 1953, and in 1957 he obtained half of the vote—more than any party had ever received in a free German election.

He then formed a cabinet of his own men: for vice-chancellor Professor Erhard, called "The Fat," the popular symbol of the economic miracle; for foreign affairs a polished yes-man, Heinrich von Brentano; for the interior a Saarlander, Gerhard Schröder; for defense the up-and-coming, pushy, and efficient Franz Josef Strauss, the bright young Bavarian. In minor posts he had three defectors from the DP and BHE of questionable political past. A trade unionist who had first helped to build the new army was given the Labor Department.

In the middle of his third term, Adenauer began to lose his touch. President Heuss wished to retire in 1959, and Adenauer, at 83, might still have succeeded him. He would have gained honor but lost power. Therefore he proposed to elevate Erhard to the presidency. When Erhard refused a scandal broke, and with some loss of prestige an undistinguished minister of agriculture was shoved into the president's palace, where he entertained the nation with malaprop episodes.

Adenauer won his fourth election, but with a less impressive margin, and again had to work in tandem with the FDP. In 1962 the boisterous Strauss got him into trouble. Strauss was the bête noire of Germany's most successful magazine, *Der Spiegel*, which combined the *Time* formula with muckraking, scandalmongering, and neutralist politics. Its self-made publisher and editor, Rudolf Augstein, may have had political ambitions of his own. He published a book-length research report on the Reichstag fire which cleared Göring of all blame. *Der Spiegel* had frequently attacked the new German army as both useless and inefficient, and in 1962 it published a critique of recent maneuvers which was clearly based on inside memoranda. Strauss, hit where it hurt, ordered a search of *Der Spiegel*'s offices— allegedly for evidence of who had leaked—and had Augstein and the author of the article arrested on charges of treason. The editor was able to show that the substance of his revelations had been in the public domain; Strauss was caught lying to the Bundestag; and Adenauer, instead of staying clear, tried to defend his minister with more lies. The FDP forced Strauss to resign, and in 1963 Adenauer's authority had become so eroded that he kept his promise to resign. Erhard formed a new cabinet.

It was a sad manner of parting for a man whose merits outshine, in retrospect, his shortcomings. His dignified demeanor, his clear recognition of Germany's debts to the victims of German aggression, his equally clear discernment of the limited options Germany had for recovery and political rehabilitation, his acceptance of the ir- revocable verdict of history, his clever exploitation of the opportunity for Germany to play a role in European and world politics—all this will be duly marked on the credit side.

It is true that with advancing age Adenauer was difficult to talk to, and that he had never conducted open policies. Even his cabinet colleagues were not informed about important decisions. He ruled them with methods bordering on blackmail. To enemies he was unfair and vengeful or high-handed. He did not hesitate to use Willy Brandt's illegitimate birth and his service in the Norwegian army as arguments in the electoral campaign. He knew how to use others for his purposes and, having used them, felt no obligation to them. When asked, once, whether he would propose a successor, he said: "Let them fight over it."

But his stubborn convictions won the confidence of foreign statesmen, and his firm leadership assured Germany a place in Europe— stronger than anyone would have suspected. True, he was favored by luck and longevity; but history has vindicated his judgment on the potential of Germany within Western Europe. Had he taken the presidency in 1961, he might not have been charged with wanting grace and humility.

Ironically, the father of the economic miracle was greeted by a recession that lasted through his tenure. People began to wonder whether the miracle of the 1950s might not have had other fathers. As a politician, too, Erhard revealed himself as less capable than his party had hoped. He allowed the reins of government to slip. Unlike his predecessor, he was not the master of his cabinet, of his party, of his coalition in the Bundestag. Although the 1965 election brought the CDU/CSU close to a majority once more, the coalition fell apart. Erhard had to make room for a new generation.

Even in his failure, Erhard had brought about another miracle: unlike the Weimar system, the Federal Republic survived. The "chancellor democracy" had transformed itself smoothly into a parliamentary republic. The halfway house of Bonn, which had enjoyed neither legitimacy nor love, which had no vision and no tradition, seemed to fulfill a mission nevertheless. Of all the misshapen bastards of history, this child of the Cold War was the least wanted; and yet, precisely when the economic miracle ran out of steam and political ineptitude provoked a crisis, the inner strength of this emergency structure withstood the test. The provisional became permanent. Stability came to be seen no longer in terms of the person or party that ruled, but in terms of the system of government.

Growing up politically meant some change in attitudes and doctrines of the parties. Those who had taken it for granted that they would rule learned now to share power with their opponents, the SPD. Those who had seen themselves as permanent underdogs, as critics not only of the government but of the state as it had emerged from the witches' brew of postwar diplomacy, had to learn constructive participation. Acceptance of the BRD as a state no less legitimate and no less permanent than any other in Europe was indispensable also for pacifying the troublesome issue of "bleeding frontiers." The so-called German question no longer held first priority; the danger of irredentism receded. Adenauer's sobriety had finally won.

Last, to everyone's credit, the extreme right had been tamed, at least temporarily. Its leaders had been absorbed into the big CDU/CSU, or even captured by government positions. The masses, aroused at election season, were held in line the rest of the time. At the end of the Erhard administration, the electorate had grown so polarized that observers began to speak of "Americanization," meaning a two-party system. This did not happen, since the small FDP survived.

But extremism, which at certain times had shown strength locally, nationally remained below the statutory threshold of 5 percent and thus never became a power factor.

The neo-Nazi movement, favored by the uncertainties of the postwar adjustment, by the refugee problem, by the frustration of reunification and the dreams of one-time grandeur, nevertheless has remained small. Its core is, quite understandably, the irreducible leftover of Hitler's veterans and of people who like the paraphernalia of Nazi ceremonies, medals, flags, parades, and the like. The "leader" is one aptly named Adolf von Thadden; though his NPD has also appealed to some younger people, its total outlook is toward the past. Even if a crisis as deep as that of the 1930s were to occur now, their type of propaganda would have little effect. A word of warning, however: history does not repeat itself. The danger of German politics does not lie in the occasional desecration of a Jewish cemetery but in the persistence of nationalism within the CDU and CSU, in the militaristic propaganda of Franz Josef Strauss and Baron Karl Guttenberg (now dead), and in the spirit cultivated by the *Deutsche Soldatenzeitung* (*German Soldiers' Times*).

28

Stalin's German Satellite

*The democratic dictatorship of the workers and peasants
is the Soviet power applied to Germany.*
—Otto Grotewohl

THE SOVIETS HAD COME TO GERMANY AND AUSTRIA with no long-range plan except to plunder whatever they could. They had several options for the future and kept them open. In Austria they experimented with a four-power regime that gave them control in one zone and a veto in the others. In Germany they rightly foresaw that their bid for admission to the Ruhr would be frustrated; so they waited for the Americans to get tired of Europe and for economic chaos in Europe to become critical before they made their next move.

Neither of these hopes was fulfilled; but in the meantime they had organized their own zone tightly enough to retain power (see Chapter 24). Three men were put in charge: veteran Spartakist Wilhelm Pieck, a benevolent but not-too-bright figurehead; Popular Front leader Paul Merker, who had survived both Hitler's and Stalin's campaigns against the Jews; and the martinet of the Stalinist apparatus, Walter Ulbricht.

As with other countries under occupation, the USSR's first step was to force the merger of the two workers' parties, giving the better-disciplined cadres of the KPD multiplied leverage in mass organizations. The most prominent Social-Democrats who thus became quislings of the SED regime were Otto Grotewohl, head of the Berlin SPD, and Friedrich Ebert, the late president's son. Secondly, mass organizations were created to transform SED power into the power to dominate and control all activities: trade unions, "fronts" of all sorts, culture leagues, women's leagues, the Victims of Fascism League, sports organizations, the Free German Youth (FDJ), etc. Liberal and Christian-Democratic politicians were also assigned honorary cabinet posts—always with an effective administrative delegate who was a communist. Only the Ministry of Justice—the terror machine—was consigned to the hands of "Bloody Hilde" Benjamin, an old communist.

The big estates were parceled out to the landless peasants and to new settlers, and with the new order came communist bosses to the farm areas, in the guise of a new "Peasants' Party." Likewise, the ex-Nazis were given a party of their own, and the call went out to all "to prove themselves in socialist reconstruction." On the other hand, whoever resisted the SED takeover found himself tarred with the "fascist" or "war-profiteer" brush. There was rarely time to investigate such charges; and anyway, nobody would dare to defend someone who was charged with Nazi connections.

But the takeover was not to lead to workers' control or co-operatives. All expropriated enterprises were declared "people's property," i.e., the state took possession of them. In the beginning, small enterprise was not touched. But—as in Russia after the October Revolution—where control was essential, big firms were expropriated, banks and insurance companies nationalized. Retail trade was concentrated in state-owned "H.O." (Handels-Organisation) stores.

Senselessly, a billion dollars worth of equipment was moved to the Soviet Union—which meant breaking up installations worth a multiple of that—and one-third of current production was levied as reparations. Labor too was recruited for Russia. It would have been more economical to receive reparations in form of merchandise; but Stalin may not have trusted that he would retain permanent control of his "zone." Companies were forced to accept 51 percent Russian partnerships and Russian directors. Either the disruption of normal exchanges or deliberate policy ruined many small businesses.

For all these reasons, production did not recover as fast as in the west; consumption and distribution lagged even more. For years people stood in long lines in front of any store that had anything to sell. No wonder a steady stream of emigrants crossed over into the western zones—three million all told between 1946 and 1961— further weakening the economy. It looked as though someone in Moscow had speculated: the worse off our East German hostages are, the larger a ransom will the West Germans and their friends be prepared to pay for their release.

The Christian-Democrats in Berlin were assigned to convey this message, and were summarily dismissed when they failed to stop the creation of the BRD. It probably was then, in 1948, simultaneously with the Prague coup, that a twofold decision was made: to organize the Soviet zone as a satellite state, and to transform it into a "People's Democracy"—i.e., to absorb the independent middle-class parties into a "National Front," to tighten and purge the SED so as to weld it into a Leninist party, to collectivize the recently divided estates, and to nationalize industrial companies.

The changeover could not be introduced, however, without floating a smoke screen of propaganda for "unity." A succession of "movements" was launched in cautious stages between May and October 1949—from the "People's Congress" and the "German People's Council" to the adoption of the constitution and eventually the proclamation of the German Democratic Republic. The constitution includes "Basic Rights of the German People"—which, however, as Grotewohl explained, were "not rights of individuals but policies of the state."

Pieck was elected president and Grotewohl prime minister. But the real power was in the hands of the party secretary, Ulbricht, a stubborn, hard-working Stalinist. In a People's Democracy, parties other than the Communist Party may exist; but the communists must be in command positions. The parliamentary representatives of these parties are admitted to a common list, the National Front. Moreover, half of the delegates to the People's Chamber are designated by the "mass organizations." In its own name the SED required only 25 percent of the seats.

The legislature has no power, anyway, in the People's Democracy. And not even the administration makes policy; it is merely an executive organ. The real power to make policy lies with the party, and within the party with the small clique that lives in a segregated district of North Berlin, Pankow. (The DDR government, therefore, is often referred to as "the Pankow regime.")

The DDR has eliminated the former states and divided its territory into fourteen districts of similar size. It has created an efficient "People's Police" (*Volkspolizei*, colloquially called Vopo) equipped with tanks, artillery, and airplanes, and a "People's Army." In addition, a Sports Association teaches parachuting, signaling, navigating, and other skills that might be needed in case of mass mobilization. The militaristic aspects of the state, the role played by the army officers of the "Free German Committee," the deliberate cultivation of the "spirit of Potsdam" and of Frederick the Great's enlightened despotism (the Prussian goose step is practiced in the East German army, not in West Germany), and the general pardon for all Nazi officers: all this has alienated old Social-Democrats from the SED. Their resistance, their old-fashioned internationalism, their solidarity with their colleagues in the west, may have suggested to the Stalinist leaders that the merger had been a tactical success but a strategic mistake. "Social-Democratism" threatened to take over the SED, and unless a wrong answer to Lenin's question "Who runs whom?" was to be tolerated, a purge was in order.

The spirit of the purged SED may best be illustrated from the titles in the songbook of the Free German Youth, which has many texts and tunes in common with the Hitler Youth songbook:

"Whatever tries to resist we push away"; "Down with the enemies of peace!"; "Take our hand, Fatherland, Deutschland . . ."; "No enemy shall prevail over us"; "The enemy of our happiness is still around"; "If will binds us we have the power"; "March, march! People in brigades, we win!" "Hit hard, young guard of the proletariat!" "We Communists have stormed / the land, the sea, and the hills. / We Red Guards will storm / the cities, the fields, and the mills."

The problems besetting the regime during its first years may be gauged from the agenda of a delegates' conference. Top priority was given to the relationship with the Soviet Union and to the "national question"—the strategy of asking for unification in propaganda while abandoning it in practice. The item "The Oder-Neisse Line" indicated that the membership was not yet sold on giving up the eastern provinces to Poland. Finally: "The performance [*Leistung*] principle as opposed to equality-mongering [*Gleichmacherei*]."

This points to the great problem of increasing productivity. Following the Russian example, the SED regime introduced the system of crash squads (*Stossbrigaden*) and "socialist competition." The ten thousand "best workers" received premiums, titles, and medals. A worker named Hennecke was cited for hauling an astonishing amount of coal, and promptly everywhere "Hennecke teams" sprouted up. Meanwhile the system has grown pervasive. From their early school days, children earn medals for "good learning," for "being ready to work for peace," and, on graduation, the Lessing Medal. On the job, workers can earn "merit medals" in each trade, from mining to dentistry; they can become "activists," "meritorious activists," and "heroes of labor." An entire team can get "meritorious," etc., and win a "national prize," a "patriotic medal of merit," a Karl Marx Medal, or a Peace Prize.

On the twentieth anniversary of the SED, special praise was lavished on the "socialist principle of performance wages," strictly linking piecework to remuneration and admonishing workers whose "social consciousness" was somewhat retarded—mired in old-fashioned trade-union, Social-Democratic thinking—that "a people-owned plant cannot be exploitative" and therefore they should accept piece wages.

The first Five-Year Plan, begun in 1951, had these goals: increasing output, collectivizing most of the farms, nationalizing most industrial companies, and redirecting foreign trade so that the DDR would become integrated into the eastern system.

In 1949 the Soviet Union had formed its own answer to the Marshall Plan: COMECON, or Council for Mutual Economic Assistance (German: RGW)—with a difference, however: the East European economies were reorganized and exploited for the benefit of the Soviet Union. Although not formally a member, the DDR was its foremost producer: 50 percent of its exports went to the Soviet Union, 30 percent to other COMECON countries, 12 percent to the Federal Republic, and 8 percent elsewhere.

At the end of the Five-Year Plan, 80 percent of industry and farming had been collectivized. The DDR was the fifth industrial country of Europe, the eighth in the world. Despite plundering, reparations, and the unequal terms of trade with COMECON, the standard of living in the DDR was rising; by 1953 workers were beginning to ask: what is socialism doing for us?

This coincided with Stalin's death and the brief "thaw"—when elsewhere Stalin statues were toppled and Stalin's handpicked satraps demoted. In the DDR, too, new leaders arose who pleaded for relaxation of censorship, for concessions to consumers and a less Spartan regime for the workers. The spokesmen for some relaxation in the DDR were not only former Social-Democrats like Paul Fechner—a concentration-camp veteran—but proven communists like Rudolf Herrnstadt, editor of the SED paper *Neues Deutschland*, and Wilhelm Zaisser, minister of the interior, who had led an international brigade in the Spanish Civil War. They were supported by Lavrenti Beria and the Russian commander in Berlin, Vladimir Semyonov. Perhaps the soft-liners in Russia felt that they could not hold on to the empire by sheer force; to consolidate their power they may have been ready for a deal on Germany. Churchill responded by calling for talks. This was probably the only time when a bolder initiative in the west might have led to a general détente, a thinning out of the occupation on both sides, and possibly a step toward unification of the two Germanies.

It was very unfortunate that at this moment McCarthyism in the United States barred any flexible U.S. policy. President Dwight Eisenhower, lacking experience in diplomacy, relied on John Foster Dulles, who substituted righteousness for policy. He found his views confirmed when Beria was murdered, the Malenkov government returned to Cold War rhetoric, and the Stalinists seemed to gain the upper hand in Pankow. They not only rejected all proposals for "thinning out" and withdrawing but also increased the pressure on their own population. Concessions to the workers that already had been made were withdrawn; efficiency standards were tightened instead of relaxed.

Instead of obeying, construction workers in Berlin struck on June 16, 1953. Their protest march, the following day, was joined by thousands who eventually occupied or surrounded government buildings in Berlin, hauled the communist insignia down, and hoisted a red flag on the Brandenburg Gate; they also set an H.O. store on fire. While the communist leaders went into hiding, Soviet tanks restored order in the streets; the crowds dispersed; the People's Police arrested some opposition leaders, while others fled to the West. When word got around, similar uprisings occurred in Magdeburg, Halle, in the Leuna area of heroic memory, and elsewhere—but again with no definite aim or result.

There followed trials and 141 executions (in addition to about 400 dead, fatally shot in the shuffle). In a poem, Bertolt Brecht sardonically advised the government, if it had lost confidence in the people, to elect itself another people.

With the fall of Beria, whose policy was a shambles, Zaisser and Herrnstadt were discredited too. Ulbricht—nicknamed The Goatee, a rigid, pedantic hard-liner and bureaucrat, an insensitive and mindless follower of Stalin—emerged as the victor. His insatiable appetite for work, unfailing memory, and ruthless use of power put a stamp of efficient desolation on the DDR. He wiped out all opposition and defended Stalinist ideas to the end of his days. Ulbricht was interested in German unification only as a means to expand communist influence, and he agreed with his master's view that it is better to have "socialism" in a small country than to have something less over an entire continent.

The first test came at the Berlin Conference (January 1954), at which the western powers submitted a plan to hold free elections in all Germany, to be followed by unification and a peace treaty with a new, all-German government. This, of course, the Russians rejected. Their plan was to write the peace treaty first, constituting a German joint government which then would impose elections (they called them "really free elections") but the outcome of the vote was not supposed to change the composition of the government—a replay of Stalin's record (see page 291).

After each of these proposals had been duly rejected by the other side, no one—except the Foreign Office in Bonn and the SPD— questioned the existence of the two German states any longer. West German policy was informed by the premise: no East German state, no Ulbricht. From this same premise, Ulbricht concluded that he had to pursue one strategic aim: getting recognition of the DDR.

As Stalin's true heir, Ulbricht exercised considerable influence on the leadership of other communist countries, notably in matters of interbloc relations. In 1956 he was to support Khrushchev's decision to intervene in Hungary; he formed a "strategic triangle" with Poland and Czechoslovakia in defense of the status quo in Eastern Europe; he resisted the disengagement policies that at the time were proposed by some statesmen in both east and west. After the Hungarian uprising in 1956, the communist empire was no longer taken for granted. Ulbricht was constantly on the lookout for "deviationists" who failed to appreciate what the Soviet Union was doing for the German workers, or who were laggard in seeing the light of dialectical materialism. Ulbricht personally called to order intellectuals who failed to comply with "democratic centralism" or hankered after the pseudo-liberties of neighboring "imperialist Germany." It became necessary to expel from the SED people who opposed an aggressive style in campaigning for the correct line, and to unmask those revisionists and agents of imperialism who used economic difficulties to demand rights.

Eventually, the continued exodus of skilled workers forced the DDR government to take drastic action against this flight from socialist duty. To run ahead of our story: in 1961 Ulbricht put up the Berlin Wall, which holds eighteen million Germans and ninety million East Europeans in a collective prison; in 1968, when Dubček threatened to weaken that wall, Ulbricht urged the Warsaw Pact nations to intervene against the deviant.

29

Toward European Integration

Between the Loire and the Weser, the heart of the Christian Occident once beat. The style of the Cologne Cathedral has its roots in French soil. Only a meeting between France and Germany can renew the Occidental idea. —Adenauer

CHANCELLOR ADENAUER HAD FELT, FROM THE BEGINNING, that Germany's future lay in cooperation with the west, and in particular its reconciliation with France. Toward this political option he was predisposed by his Catholic background and his experience as mayor of Cologne. Other Germans of the right, who had previously considered France the archenemy, now—belatedly but not too late—saw the light and, with almost suspicious eagerness, paraded their newly won Europeanism and humanism. During the last year of the war, Ernst Jünger had circulated a pamphlet, "Peace." Franz Josef Strauss was a most enthusiastic, and sincere, advocate of a Europe united against the east.

From a practical point of view, it simply made sense for Germany to insert itself into the Western European efforts toward a common reconstruction plan. Since Germany needed export markets and the east was closed, the BRD had to seek outlets in the west. The west's hunger for coal and manufactured goods helped, and the Marshall Plan gave developments a strong underpinning. The BRD joined the European Recovery Program in January 1950. Also in 1950, the European countries reorganized the Reparations Bank (BIZ) and formed a European Payments Union, pegging all values to the American dollar. In April 1951 France, Italy, the Benelux countries, and West Germany signed the first supranational authority into being: the European Coal and Steel Community (ECSC), with the aim "to eliminate the centuries-old rivalries." It had an assembly, a ministerial council, and, most important, a permanent bureaucracy: the high authority in Luxemburg. The Common Market was to grow from this seed.

In 1950 Adenauer used the Korean calamity to offer a defense contribution to NATO; as we have seen, this was not accepted until

May 1952, in the draft treaty of a European Defense Community (EDC). The neutralist opposition fought both this treaty and the formation of a German army bitterly. It went so far as to bring suit before the Constitutional Court, charging that a standing army was implicitly inconsistent with the Basic Law. But while rejecting the idea, it also contributed to its realization: it introduced democratic features in recruitment and promotion rules. The rights of conscientious objectors were safeguarded; a complex grievance procedure was introduced, culminating in the office of an independent ombudsman, called *Wehrbeauftragter*; the generals who came to command the new army were carefully screened, though of course most officers came from Hitler's *Wehrmacht*. The new Bundeswehr has 420,000 men, about half of them volunteers serving either professionally or for two years, the other half drafted for eighteen months.

The EDC treaty was unpopular in France. Frenchmen did not want German rearmament, did not want to spoil France's relationship with Russia, did not want to give up any of their sovereignty. On August 30, 1954, the National Assembly refused to ratify the treaty.

Now American diplomats went to work and obtained from Premier Pierre Mendès-France something neither he nor his voters wanted: the entry of the BRD, with fully independent armies, into the Western European Union, the nucleus of the reorganized NATO. Instead of being truly part of a European defense establishment, German troops would now have their own command. France had preserved her cherished sovereignty—but Germany became America's closest ally. The Paris Treaties sealing these developments were ready in October 1954, giving Germany and Italy full sovereignty.

The BRD voluntarily renounced nuclear, biological, and chemical weapons; but for its own safety it invited American, British, and French troops to stay on German soil. Of course, Germans, loath to see their country become a battlefield, favored a NATO strategy of "forward defense," i.e., of carrying the war into enemy territory. They referred to Allied troops in Germany, especially those in Berlin, as "hostages" or "trip wires": ensuring that a Russian attack on Germany would unleash the full force of NATO's nuclear deterrent against the aggressor. This threat may have saved the freedom of Berlin in 1960.

The German threat of joining NATO jolted the new team in the Kremlin into a new diplomacy. Finland was offered a treaty of friendship; Austria, which for ten years had languished without a peace treaty, was finally evacuated—not only by Russian but by NATO troops. Austria paid Russia a hefty sum of money to "repurchase" its expropriated oil wells and mixed enterprises, and had to promise strict neutrality.

Germany, too, was offered neutralization and unity, though no free elections; and on their own, the Soviets declared the state of war terminated on January 25, 1955. Such benevolence now came too late; even among Social-Democrats the Russian initiatives had lost all credibility. The Bundestag adopted the NATO treaties by a two-thirds majority on May 3, 1955. No constitutional objections could be raised any longer, and a week later the BRD was admitted to NATO as a full member.

After acquiring sovereignty, the BRD appointed a foreign minister (Heinrich von Brentano, Adenauer's former parliamentary aide) and a defense minister (Theodor Blank, a Christian trade union leader). Professor Walter Hallstein, who so far had been Adenauer's assistant in foreign affairs, went on in the direction he had pursued so ardently: he became West Germany's representative in the Council of Europe and helped prepare the Common Market.

As a reward for his steadfast course, Adenauer now had the satisfaction of seeing the Soviet Union reverse its course. In September 1955 he was invited to Moscow to resume diplomatic relations and to negotiate the return of the prisoners of war whom the Soviet government apparently had held for just such a purpose. It was a great personal triumph for him, although recognition by the Soviet Union of the BRD implied recognition by the BRD that there were two Germanies.

Some more perfunctory summit meetings took place; ritualistic resolutions on German reunification were adopted, and Bonn's Foreign Office continued to fight for its right to represent all of Germany. Hallstein had formulated the "doctrine" that the BRD could not have diplomatic relations with any country that recognized the "Soviet-occupied zone" as a state. The Soviet Union itself was to be the only exception. When Tito defied the doctrine, Bonn punished him by breaking off relations; other countries were effectively kept from extending recognition to the DDR for two decades.

Ten years after the war, the BRD was a respected ally in the NATO community, a strong economic power in the world, even an intellectual leader if we judge from the interest abroad in Germany philosophy and drama, and certainly a stauncher defender of nonbolshevik values than Hitler had ever been. The entire western world looked to Berlin as a heroic city, the envy of the surrounding east, a thorn in the flesh of the Soviet empire, and an outpost of western culture.

Germany paid a price: the gulf between her two parts grew wider. Each now spoke a different language, using different concepts, different

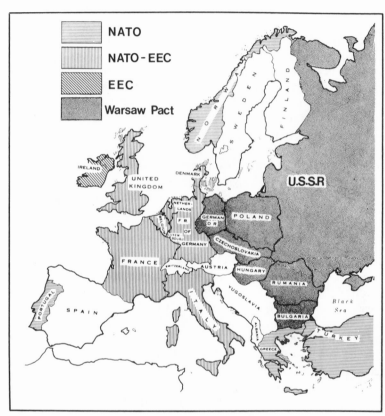

FIGURE 3. THE TWO GERMANIES IN THE EUROPEAN ALIGNMENT

acronyms in its daily dealings with authorities, different frames of reference in judging the world political situation. A cabaret skit showed a family visiting relatives on the other side and parting without having had any real communication. Uwe Johnson wrote novels about people who lost identity because of the partition.

The Russians countered NATO with the Warsaw Pact (May 1955), to which the DDR was admitted in January 1956. But meanwhile the integration of the west had made further strides. The dynamic French Minister of Development Jean Monnet had the vision of abolishing, between the members of the European Coal and Steel Community, all barriers of economic sovereignty: barriers of finance, commerce, social legislation, defense. He won the Council of Europe over, and in March 1957 the six countries signed the Treaty of Rome creating the Common Market (European Economic Community, EEC) and Euratom, a "chosen instrument" to control the development of nuclear energy in Europe.

The EEC was intended to be more than a customs union, and it has become the most important economic factor in the lives of its member countries—though not a union, yet a community. It directs the flow of funds and investments; it stabilizes exchange rates, co-ordinates social legislation, unifies the communication system, the road signs, and—eventually—the price levels. The French also demanded "harmonization of welfare costs," since their workers put in fewer hours, had longer vacations, and received comparatively higher wages and fringe benefits (which were equal for both sexes). Although this provision was not adopted, living standards have become more comparable in EEC countries. Germany became so prosperous that jobs had to be offered to Greeks, Turks, Spaniards. Trainloads of Sicilians leave the Volkswagen works at Wolfenbüttel when vacation time comes. These "guest workers" have created problems in certain neighborhoods and have met with problems of their own, but the effect of their coming and going has been nothing less than revolutionary. They have learned the ways of highly industrialized countries and are transplanting them into backward areas. They make demands on their employers and political bosses which no one thought of before. They are changing the social structures of their native villages. They are making Europe a more homogeneous continent, and this makes it ready for a more intimate union.

The Common Market has a commission headquartered in Brussels. It was given broad powers to initiate legislation, and it has often behaved like a sovereign power, though it is not a superpower. Its nine members, appointed for four years, are independent of the federated governments. Its first president was Walter Hallstein; he was followed by Jean Monnet. It is true that de Gaulle later reduced the commission's powers, but other organs took over its vitality.

The enthusiasm for Europe was great in Germany. Obviously it was as Europeans that the Germans hoped to get all those attributes of power they had renounced as Germans. As members of a European community, all sister countries would accept the diminished sovereignty that had been forced on Germany. France might struggle to preserve its identity within Europe; but Germans expected to live better, individually and collectively, under the European flag. It was reaction to the horrid experience of extreme nationalism that had first made Germans receptive to the idea of Europe; now they were able to see it as a cooperative venture. Hence the paradox of a nation that had first been Pan-German and was now the most Pan-European.

One area where Europeanism pays is the use of superweapons. In 1957 the Western European Union (WEU) decided that to complete its capabilities it needed nuclear arms. German soldiers were therefore trained in the United States to use the weapons systems America had stationed in Germany; but nominally the BRD stood by its renunciation of nuclear arms under its own jurisdiction.

Meanwhile some changes were occurring in the East. Khrushchev, at the Twentieth Congress of the Communist Party of the Soviet Union, made the famous speech exposing Stalin's crimes. He proclaimed the doctrine of coexistence, meaning the perpetuation of the status quo in Europe. Indeed, when the Poles and Hungarians rose to challenge the Soviet empire, Soviet tanks crushed the rebellion, and President Eisenhower honored the tacit agreement that neither side would take advantage of the other's difficulties. These were anxious moments for the BRD: standing idly by while almost next door freedom was being murdered. But this time the East German workers did not stir, and Austria, the only channel of access to the beleaguered Hungarians, did not care to become a battlefield; it became only a corridor of flight from the bloody repression.

Once again, the western powers might have helped a Soviet dictator off the hook and simultaneously helped several countries to liberate themselves from Soviet domination—if at the time an imaginative secretary of state had suggested to Khrushchev that both the United States and the Soviet Union should withdraw from Central Europe. No such deal was offered, and we shall never know whether genuine neutralization would have worked. Somewhat belatedly, Polish Foreign Minister Adam Rapacki made a proposal pointing in that direction. Anxious to get the Russians off his back, he offered "denuclearization" of Poland, Czechoslovakia, and all of Germany. Anthony Eden, who had succeeded Churchill as prime minister, countered this rather unilateral proposal with a plan to "thin out" conventional as well as nuclear arms in Europe.

But the propitious moment had passed. In both camps the advocates of "immobilism" carried the day. Adenauer, strongly backed by Dulles, rejected all blandishments and stuck by the strategy of European integration. The defeat of the Hungarians, while the western powers wrung their hands, ought to have taught the Germans that the world had been divided for good and the Iron Curtain was there to stay—unless some unforeseen event were to drastically change the power balance.

Change it did, all too soon—but in the opposite direction. In October 1957, the Russians sent their first sputnik into space, and demonstrated their ability to send ballistic missiles across the globe. Suddenly, America was no longer protected by two oceans. On the strength of his new weapon, Khrushchev lost no time demanding de jure recognition of all World War II conquests, and again, Berlin was selected as the point where the west could be squeezed. In November 1958 he gave the western powers six months to "get out," or else control of the access to Berlin would be yielded to the DDR. Was he really prepared to break the Potsdam agreements and surrender to Ulbricht the trigger of World War III?

Eisenhower invited him to Washington, where Khrushchev tactfully used every opportunity to remind his hosts of the sputnik. Eisenhower—bereft by death of the steadfast Dulles' advice—allowed that Berlin's situation was indeed "anomalous," and agreed to a summit meeting where the Germans would get the Munich treatment. Elated, Khrushchev tried to cash his check before it had been signed. Issuing new transit regulations for the autobahn, he required the use of forms that implied recognition of the Pankow regime. Alerted by Adenauer, both Washington and Paris had second thoughts. When Khrushchev arrived in Paris for the summit in May 1960, de Gaulle informed him that recognition of the DDR was out of the question— unless he settled all east-west matters. Angered by what he considered a breach of faith, Khrushchev used a nasty incident—the flight over Sverdlovsk of a U.S. reconnaissance plane—for a very statesmanlike "out." He blew the summit conference to smithereens and flew to Berlin, where he told Ulbricht that this was not the time to transfer control.

De Gaulle considered this his great opportunity. He had returned to power in 1958 and gained great prestige by settling the Algerian war and liberating France's colonies. With Dulles dead, Eisenhower fumbling, and England in the hands of weak leaders, he saw himself as the outstanding statesman of the western world, and at the same time he perceived his chance to challenge the Anglo-Saxon hegemony under which he had suffered. He had just rendered Adenauer an invaluable service; the moment was opportune for a bold attempt to win him for a diplomatic pirouette.

The approach was made easier a year later, when a change of power in Washington led to a weakening of German-American ties. John F. Kennedy did not like Adenauer and was bored by the legalistic arguments of his ambassador in Washington. Some of his advisers were critical of the Cold War stance and sought ways of making U.S. military commitments in Europe more flexible. The U.S. generals found the doctrine of instant retaliation dangerous and recommended a strategy of "staggered defense"—which, of course, meant the possibility of war on German soil and therefore met with strong resistance in Germany. Americans did not like to expose their own cities to destruction should the next Berlin crisis prove unmanageable; Germans preferred to see ICBMs fly over their heads between Washington and Moscow while they would be able to duck underneath the fracas. The new American doctrine no longer offered the Germans the protection of an atomic umbrella.

De Gaulle offered Adenauer a way out of his predicament: a Bonn-Paris axis. A European, Gaullist defense might replace the "Atlantic conception" that had so far prevailed in NATO. As de Gaulle saw it, the rigid NATO structure would be loosened, permitting the powers to regain the command over their several troops. (Indeed, de Gaulle was to withdraw his forces from the NATO command in 1966.) But for Germany to have to choose between Washington and Paris was, to say the least, embarrassing.

The issue was raised, however, the next year by a new Berlin crisis—brought on, this time, not by deliberate diplomatic intrigue but by the mass exodus from Ulbricht's socialist fatherland. Apparently people, after the aborted summit, sensed that a new crisis was impending and were suddenly seized by a panicky desire to leave before it might be too late. Year after year since 1950 between 200,000 and 300,000 persons had gone west—among them thousands of workers and technical intelligentsia who saw greater opportunities in a free economy, but also hundreds of writers, artists, ideologists, and even high party officials: Ernst Bloch the philosopher; Alfred Kantorowicz, editor of the DDR's highbrow magazine *Sinn und Form*; Rudi Dutschke, rebel leader and Marxist thinker; Hans Mayer, Marxist critic; Uwe Johnson, novelist; Erich Gniffke, member of the Central

Committee. It was most embarrassing.

The DDR government had laid waste a five-kilometer-wide strip of land along its border, and mined it, to prevent illegal exit; but there was still the Berlin hole: once in Berlin, a DDR citizen had only to take the subway from the Russian to the American sector, register there in a reception center, and be taken by air to freedom in the BRD. Physicians, engineers, agronomists, electricians, economists, and other experts disappeared by the thousands—a drain of needed skills and a loss of educational investment. The harder the authorities fought against this flight, the more urgent they seemed to make it for people to flee. By 1961 more than 2.5 million had gone; late in July the migration swelled to 10,000 a week, in the first week of August to 20,000.

On August 13, the DDR began to build a fence, which by the end of the month became a wall and is now a two-block-deep fortification that makes flight impossible for all but the most daring or desperate. The sudden interruption of all traffic on August 13, 1961, caught many people unawares. Thousands of East Berliners who were in the West on legitimate business could not get back to their families. Those who lived in one sector and worked in the other lost their jobs. Streets that used to be arteries of traffic were cut into two dead ends.

But Ulbricht had made his point: the two Germanies were now definitively and effectively divided. Whether or not the west recognized the status quo de jure, there would be no doubt for citizens of the DDR where their de facto government was.

The West Germans were stunned, and their allies could not help them. Vice-President Lyndon Johnson went to Berlin to reassure the Berliners. President Kennedy himself went to the Wall with Adenauer and Willy Brandt and said to the people, in German: *"Ich bin ein Berliner"*—"I am a Berliner." Despite their enthusiasm, the Germans could not help noticing that mighty America did not dare take down a fence which Ulbricht had erected.

The partitioning of Europe was almost complete by now, and Germans began to listen to de Gaulle; Defense Minister Strauss proclaimed himself a Gaullist. Adenauer went to Paris in 1962; de Gaulle returned the visit in September, to great acclaim. He, too, spoke German. "For de Gaulle to be here," he told the steelworkers in Duisburg, "and for you to give him this warm welcome, there must be trust between our nations." A treaty of friendship was signed in January 1963.

Although the Germans were aware that de Gaulle had his ulterior plans, they hailed the treaty as a necessary act of reconciliation, the final burial of a centuries-old antagonism. Some even talked, more or less ironically, of the restoration of Charlemagne's empire (and de Gaulle was at least a tall Charles), with France, Germany, Italy, and Burgundy (the Benelux countries) in harness under Christian-Democratic leaders. However, when de Gaulle vetoed England's entry into the Common Market, it became clear that he did not think European but merely meant to use Adenauer's friendship to pursue his maniac defiance of "les Anglo-Saxons."

The Bundestag attached to its ratification of the treaty of friendship a preamble safeguarding the framework of NATO and the EEC as well as German interest in unification. Although for the first time the BRD saw options and perhaps necessary moves that pointed to a more independent policy, it remained "Atlantic."

These events coincided with the retirement and subsequent death of "der Alte." In his fourteen years of leadership he had raised Germany from helplessness to power, from contempt to respect, from hostility to reconciliation, from isolation to integration, from Pan-Germanism to Europeanism. Without being distracted by what others might deem desirable, he recognized what was possible at all times. The building of the Berlin Wall—which Berliners call *die Schandmauer*, the Wall of Shame—indicated the limit of his policy. The Cold War thinking, the fortification of the two camps, now had to give way to more flexible policies.

Even so, the era of *Ostpolitik*—détente or rapprochement with the east—that followed did not reverse the basic Western orientation imprinted on the Bonn Republic from its birth. In 1960 half of German imports came from Western Europe; in 1970, two-thirds. Exports to Western Europe rose from thirty billion marks to eighty-seven billion.

The new chancellor, Ludwig Erhard, and his foreign minister, Gerhard Schröder, were strongly committed to the Atlantic alliance, but they cautiously opened a dialogue with some Eastern European countries. The aim was still to isolate the DDR—a policy that certainly did not serve unification, still the professed objective of all German policy—and many Germans began to wonder whether the BRD had a policy at all. The French alliance was dormant; the American alliance did not pay any dividends. On the contrary, it brought new humiliations. One of Kennedy's harebrained schemes to revive NATO had been a multinational navy; and the Germans saw this as an opportunity to get their hands on another lever of command. When Lyndon Johnson dropped the project, they felt cheated. They suffered another humiliation when Johnson somewhat brutally told Erhard that German industry must not supply China with a steel mill that had been contracted for.

In other areas, too, the Erhard administration lacked brilliance, and in dealing with party politicians the chancellor's performance was disappointing. Worst of all, he was beaten in his own field, economics. It was under his chancellorship that Germany suffered her first postwar recession. The man who had claimed credit for the economic miracle now had to take the blame for the lack of an economic policy. In typically German manner he had built a theory on his good luck in starting the postwar boom; he did not know that it takes more than a formula to sustain prosperity.

30

The Miracle of the Western World

Wir Wunderkinder
—Movie title, 1958

FROM COMPLETE RUIN IN 1946, THE WEST GERMAN ECONOMY has soared to third place in the world in an almost uninterrupted sequence of successes. Supported by consistent good luck and skillful government guidance, its managers have turned obstacles into opportunities. The influx of twelve million refugees who had to be housed, clothed, fed, and provided with schools and community facilities; the bombed-out cities that had to be rebuilt; the occupation armies that required maintenance and logistic foundations—all this constituted a head of steam for postwar demand. The injections of United Nations Relief and Rehabilitation Aid and Marshall aid could be used to better advantage than in countries that had no reserves of skilled labor or production capacity. Even the dismantling of equipment and the low exchange rate of the mark turned out to be blessings in disguise. With brand-new machinery Germany quickly became Europe's biggest exporter of manufactured goods, which a war-starved world market gobbled up voraciously.

German industriousness and ingenuity used the propitious conditions well. The Zeiss optical works were transplanted to the west; the Volkswagen started out to conquer the world's roads. Although Germany is not an atomic power, its atomic reactors are now sold in the Third World against American competition, and even against American attempts to interpose moral-political pressures. BRD production now is 50 percent greater than the production of all of Germany was before the war. Even farm production, on the reduced area of less-rural West Germany, exceeds in value the production of the former Reich. Decartelization, ordered by the Allies, was a joke. Each of the four companies into which I. G. Farben was divided produces more chemicals, dyes, and medicines than the entire firm had done under Hitler. West Germany is second in automobile production, third in steel. (Statistical figures on the economic miracle must cover, of course, a longer period, and therefore will be found in Tables 7, 8, and 9 at the end of Chapter 33.)

Although recently some stresses have appeared in the German economy, it is stronger than any other on the continent and has frequently been called upon to help other members of the Common Market. Three times the mark has been revalued—in 1961, 1969, and 1976—for a total of 16 percent. Its exchange rate against the dollar has improved from 4.25 to 2.0.

The performance has generally been hailed as an economic miracle; the Germans themselves at first were not so sure that it would last. When the traditional carnival was revived, they sang a ditty: Who has ordered all that? Who's going to pay? A cabaret sketch, later expanded into a film, inquired what had made them into such *Wunderkinder* ("children of the miracle," but also "prodigies"). What indeed?

The fathers of the 1949 currency reform took credit for making Germany a neoliberal showcase—the model of a free-enterprise economy unhampered by government relations, rationing, price and wage controls. It was also an economy unburdened by debts, and of course Professor Erhard was able to use the indirect monetary controls and tax incentives that belong in the arsenal of a modern, managed economy. The system was by no means "free" but, by Erhard's own definition, "structured." It encouraged investment and directed a large percentage of the product to foreign markets, while keeping the expansion of domestic consumption within limits and avoiding inflationary pressures.

Despite these strategic restraints, the system earned the name "social market economy" by redirecting a large proportion of income into welfare projects. The government pays restitution to victims of the Nazi regime and pensions to war victims, the disabled, widows, orphans; it contributes to insurance plans against sickness, old age, and unemployment. A 1952 law "equalizes the burden" of war losses by taxing away up to 50 percent of everybody's pre-1945 assets over a period of thirty years. Moreover, the government owns the railways, the airlines, telephone and telegraph lines, television and radio, postal savings banks, and many utilities; it controls coal, steel, and aluminum production. In short, it influences almost one-half of all capital expenditure in one way or another.

Neoliberal theory is happily mitigated by the goals and techniques of the welfare state, and social policies are further expanded by a

TABLE 5. INCOME DISTRIBUTION IN EAST AND WEST GERMANY
(Percentage of total income)

	Percent in the BRD	Percent in the DDR
Lowest quintile	10.5	10.4
Second quintile	16.0	15.8
Third quintile	16.8	19.8
Fourth quintile	23.3	23.3
Highest quintile	33.4	30.7

strong trade union movement. It was fortunate that, in the first phase of the economic miracle, the 6.5-million-member DGB was led by Hans Böckler, who enjoyed the chancellor's confidence. In return for voluntary wage restraints, Adenauer granted the union leader concessions which in the long run strengthened the trade unions' position. The number of strike days was held to a minimum; the fruits of technological progress were shared among capital, labor, and the public. While the productivity of labor increased 100 percent during the first fifteen years, real wages increased 50 percent.

The Codetermination Law of 1951 (*Mitbestimmungsgesetz*) gave labor a share of responsibility. At first it applied only to the coal and steel industry; later, in 1956, it was expanded to holding companies, and in 1976 to the rest of big industry. All companies employing more than a thousand workers must give one-third (in coal and steel, one-half) of the seats on their boards to representatives of labor; the executive committee must include a labor director appointed by the union to handle grievances and personnel policies. The unions' avowed aim is to acquire commanding positions in the economy so that they, too, can influence national economic policies. At their insistence, the government must now submit an annual "State of the Nation" report. The unions own the fourth-largest bank in Germany. They control an insurance company, 6,000 cooperative stores, a fishing fleet, and a building corporation renting 300,000 apartments.

The work week has been shortened from forty-eight to forty hours. Weekly earnings are twice as high as ten years ago. Unemployment is low. Workers may own houses with many middle-class comforts; they can travel through Europe and beyond in their own cars. Consumption per capita has tripled in fifteen years. The 1966 average family income was 1,000 marks a month—after Sweden the highest in Europe.

A vast consumer market has been created, and expectations are still rising. So far, one-half of the nation's product has been distributed in the form of wages and salaries; obviously, such a policy can be sustained for a certain time only. It seems that the moment is coming closer when a larger proportion of the national product must be consumed.

Great inequalities still exist. Dividing the nation's families into five classes of equal size, according to their income, in 1970 we find the distribution noted in Table 5.

The median monthly income in the BRD is now between 1,200 and 1,300—a deceptive figure which tempts us to disregard 16,000 families who earn a million, and 500,000 who have no income. One-fifth of all families in the BRD earned one-third of all income; surprisingly, the proportion is not much lower in the DDR. (The calculation has been made by the BRD Statistical Office. We have no way of determining whether the original data are comparable; fringe benefits are one-third of wages in the west, but probably more in the east.)

One phenomenon characteristic of advanced industrial societies has appeared in the BRD, too. The "income pyramid" no longer resembles a triangle but an onion. At its base, it no longer spreads out but tapers in, because the "pauper class" decreases as workers achieve middle-class incomes. Moreover, a large proportion of the paupers no longer consists of potentially employable people but of those who have either dropped out of the labor force or will never be employable. This includes the youth gangs (*Halbstarke* and *Gammler*), who for awhile were the terror of the cities and are still a problem for social agencies. It also includes students who extend their stay at the university to five years or longer.

One million (formerly two million) foreign workers—Yugoslavs, Turks, Greeks, Iberians, Italians, even Arabs—live in the Federal Republic of Germany. Some came from places so remote that they had never encountered indoor plumbing. They work both in the interstices of the economy and in big industry. Their living conditions have been the subject of sensationalist reporting, much of it apparently inspired by propaganda hostile to the BRD. They are hired for exacting work which more affluent Germans will no longer take upon themselves, on a temporary basis but at union rates. They are not expected to blend into the population; but many intend to stay or have married in Germany. Communal frictions have marred relations, and legal problems of a new kind may arise when EEC passports become available and guest workers demand voting rights, schools in their languages, etc. For the moment the problem has been just barely manageable. Since the workers send part of their income home, their living standard is low and neighborhoods where they live deteriorate.

The waning peasantry is another stratum that feels less than integrated. Farming as a way of life is no longer attractive, farming as a source of income even less. The industrial revolution has definitely come to the farm, and the government, putting sentimentality aside, has agreed to accelerate it. The farm law of 1955 has given incentives for all kinds of modernization: merging of small farms, mechanization, consolidation of scattered property, switching to high-priced dairy and meat production (*Veredlungswirtschaft*). Eight hundred thousand farms under fifteen hectares (thirty-six acres) have disappeared since 1949; of the million that are left, perhaps another 40 percent will disappear, either to be merged with larger units or to be given over to more remunerative land uses. The farm population has declined from 10 to 5 percent of the total.

Efficiency, by contrast, has risen phenomenally. Acre yields have been doubled; dairy farms have increased productivity by 50 percent. The 1957 Treaties of Rome ought to have benefited all European peasants; actually German peasants felt that their interests were being sacrificed to Adenauer's policy of Franco-German friendship. In 1969 the Peasants' League told the CDU that it would vote NPD unless the government obtained more concessions for them in the Common Market. Fortunately, the farm revolution has not created the kind of social hardship that occurred in last century's industrial revolution; but it is changing the social balance.

Another twentieth-century revolution has seized white-collar work, which is becoming technical. Although the skills it requires have grown more commonplace and the work is often less well paid than blue-collar work, it still commands more social respect. Professor Ralf Dahrendorf (once a high OEEC official, now director of the London School of Economics) calls such salaried employees "a false middle class." Their number is increasing because of the expansion of professional, commercial, financial, and government services, the bureaucracies' rise in industry, and the greater need for "service occupations." White-collar occupations offer more opportunities for upward mobility and are considered part of management, although in fact most of these positions are subordinate.

In the last seventy years the proportion of salaried employees to wage earners has risen from 1:13 to 1:3. But again, such overall figures conceal conflicting trends: on the one hand the increase of clerical and sales personnel, whose individual contribution is more and more replaceable; on the other hand the rise of individuals whose special skills and services have gained in appreciation and remuneration. Such persons are now the heads of institutes, service firms, or associations, even industrial concerns, government agencies, and the like. Institutionalization in the service industries (and in academia) is the equivalent of concentration in manufacturing industries. One need only compare the old-fashioned family doctor with the head of a modern hospital or health agency, the family counselor with the corporation lawyer, the old-fashioned scholar with the research tycoon, and it will be apparent that a new class of people is gaining access to the ruling class at the head of new industries.

To be counted among the mighty, it is no longer sufficient to be rich, or even to have a high income. One must have a function; one must command influence or have power over people and things. A survey of the men (and very few women) who "run" the country will reveal that few of them have inherited their positions, and that quite a few who might have inherited one are now forgotten. The Krupps, the Stumms, the Thyssens are remembered only because industrial plants still bear their names. Some of the men who made their way under Hitler are still, or were until recently, among the movers and shakers: Berthold Beitz, the manager of the Krupp works, or Hermann Abs, the remarkable banker who was ostracized by the Allies but reappeared as negotiator for the Adenauer government at international conferences and has meanwhile collected several dozen directorships.

Very different types of leaders are exemplified by three presidents of the Association of German Industrialists. The first, Fritz Berg, had owned a small metal firm, and he fought hard against the trade unions. The second, Hans-Günther Sohl, was a manager who followed modern ideas about cooperation between employers and unions. The third, Hanns-Martin Schleyer, whom terrorists kidnapped and killed in 1977, had been a personnel manager and unpopular with the unions.

The trade union leaders, who now sit with industrialists on the boards of directors, or who negotiate with them on matters far surpassing wage levels, are no longer faceless sellers of labor; their personalities are commented upon in newspapers and they have indeed played an important role in the unions' political alignments. Böckler was accommodating; leaders who followed, such as Viktor Agartz and Ludwig Rosenberg, had strong reservations against western orientation and rearmament policy and maneuvered the trade unions into a more radical stance. Young union leaders are often found on the left of the SPD.

Another group from which new political leaders were recruited is academia. Professors Erhard, Hallstein, and Wilhelm Grewe served under Adenauer; Karl Schiller was economics minister in the Broad Coalition; Werner Maihofer and Horst Ehmke were members of the Schmidt government. Professor Kurt Biedenkopf is secretary of the CDU; Professor Richard von Weizsäcker rewrote its program in 1973. This new interest of academic persons in power reflects the changing sociological climate: experts need power, and power needs experts.

This does not exhaust the scope of elite recruitment; the Bonn Republic has not yet developed an establishment. It is "open" to an extent unknown to any other system. It has tolerated the rise of the great opinion makers, Axel Springer on the right and Augstein left of center. It has had one chancellor who was a minor official in Ribbentrop's Foreign Office, and another who does not know his father. Its nouveaux riches are not rooted in German culture but belong to the international jet set. It is a republic whose elites are both "revolving" and adding to each other; belonging to the leading strata does not imply any commonly agreed set of beliefs or assumptions. Although in Germany class is still determined by education, there is nothing comparable to the old fraternities or to the club atmosphere that was characteristic of the Weimar days. Attempts have been made to revive the fraternities; but while they may cater to some people's craving for snobbery, they cannot satisfy their desire for social distinction.

To be sure, German education is not egalitarian. Although tuition fees are negligible throughout the system, workers hesitate to send their sons to university, or even to high school. Only 30 percent of university students are women; tradition more than necessity keeps it that way. Of all eighteen-year-olds only 10 percent graduate from high school (up from 5 percent previously), and only 400,000 places are open at all universities, engineering schools, and art academies. Admission depends on highly competitive examinations. All students, from the upper classes of high school through university, complain about *"Leistungsdruck"*—the pressure to perform.

Mobility there is—at a price, and only individually. In practice, selection of the fittest by examinations has not broken down the class barriers. The vast differentiation between strata continues; civil servants and professionals often have parents of the same class, and the diplomatic service still abounds with aristocratic names. The Brandt administration promoted journalists, labor organizers, and other outsiders; but interestingly, among these too there were aristocrats. A new civil-service consciousness seems to be evolving in the industrial and political bureaucracies of the Common Market, the agencies of foreign aid and development, and other promoters of the international welfare economy—the "Eurocrats." Dedicated to their assignments rather than to personal power, party or nation, these men and women share with their peers a new experience of management. They have outgrown the profit motive and think in terms of their responsibility to the future.

As in other countries, the meritocracy is on the rise. In 1964 Ewald Zepf found that of 250 prominent people, 14 percent had only grade-school and 23 percent only high-school diplomas. Dahrendorf estimated in 1964 that only 1 percent of the population belonged to the "upper class": wealthy capitalists, landowners, high officials and top professionals, managers, and political elite—the same proportion as under the Weimar Republic and as today. He counted 12 percent as "service class"—middle management, professionals and officials; 12 percent "false middle class"—salaried employees and salespeople; 20 percent "old middle class"—shop owners, peasants, the self-employed. He divided the working class into an "elite" constituting 5 percent of the total population, lower-class workers (another 5 percent), and the rest of the workers (45 percent). As there is no agreement on method between scholars, these percentages are difficult to compare with others. But his classification system allows him to better show opportunities for social mobility, both individually and as a category.

Clearly class differentiation is now functional rather than in life-styles. The advanced industrial economy has produced, as elsewhere, a consumer ideology which tends to equalize values, tastes, and habits. Prepackaged experience is on sale for everyone, and cultural differentiation defines the old classes, but not the new ones.

In 1965 Helmut Schelsky maintained that "economic classes" may have been a useful concept for studying society in the nineteenth century; but "in highly industrialized countries the structure of leisure-time behavior and consumption patterns determines the nature of a society, and consumer position becomes the determinant of cultural and political behavior." Schelsky certainly does not deny that there are more paupers than millionaires in the BRD; his claim is that 90 percent of the population adhere to (or are caught up in) a middle-class system of values which integrates their life-styles into a graded, unstratified scale of basically identical consumer satisfactions and therefore has overcome the compartmentalized structure of antagonistic classes. Paradoxically, this conservative theory of a "consumer society" is echoed on the far left by the Frankfurt School's attack on "one-dimensional man" and "consumerism." In the consumer society, everybody seems to be equal at least in aspirations and opportunities, though not in achievement; if some fail, it is not because of insurmountable class barriers but because they are less competitive.

As we shall see presently, only a small percentage hold the "system" responsible for their malaise; problems have to be resolved within the framework of society and with the means of conflict resolution it provides. "Critique" is the specialty of a small academic sect, not of a politically or socially active force.

Helmut Schelsky and the neo-Marxists offer new versions of the managerial-revolution theory. The technical intelligentsia bids for a share in the spoils of the domination which it helps to maintain; it is challenged by others coming from the same stratum and sharing the same education, who have allied themselves with the "marginal people": dropouts, unemployables, lumpen proletarians, and proletarian nations. This theory and its totalitarian implications have been challenged by Richard Lowenthal of the Free University of Berlin, and by Minister for Research and Technology, Horst Ehmke. They see German society as composed of economic classes and social-status groups whose relationships are in rapid development. The frictions that necessarily occur in the continuing process of adjustment may engender extreme attitudes of elitism or of a counterculture. More recently, disturbing interviews with high school students have revealed anomic attitudes, lack of any sense of purpose and meaning, indifference to the national culture and the state.

The outbreak of this social malaise was not altogether unforeseen. Back in 1957, Schelsky predicted "a secessionist generation, producing senseless outbreaks from a modern world which has been wrapped in the cotton of manipulated humanity and welfare." As in other countries, radicalism is mostly an upper-class phenomenon. Willy Brandt's sons were active in the New Left; almost all members of the terrorist groups come from highly educated families. The young people detest their parents' materialism, their conformism, their standards of success; they identify with Third-World heroes: Castro, Che Guevara, the PLO, Ho Chi Minh, even Idi Amin. They question the social structure of the Western world and abhor the dictatorship of the East.

Partly, the problem is generational. Those born after the war have enjoyed peace under the threat of atomic warfare and prosperity without responsibility. They have been offered all the opportunities without having to earn them or to fight for them. They have benefited from the achievements of the restoration without experiencing its difficulties, and they are impatient of its shortcomings without knowing yet how to overcome them. Anxious to realize their own values or to apply new methods, they frequently see the system, which invites them to compete for cooptation, as "a cartel of anxiety-ridden incumbents" (Ralf Dahrendorf). The ticket for admission to this establishment is performance (*Leistung*). The rules of the game are those of material achievement; the value system underlying this society's life is as materialistic as are the rewards it promises for compliance.

The anti-Nazi ideology of the early years of the republic and the anticommunism of the Cold War years, were no longer sufficient to legitimatize a regime that seemed to have no idea—it was neither "building socialism" like its eastern neighbor nor guaranteeing the "pursuit of happiness" like its western ally; it had neither a king nor a mystique. Half in despair and half in hope of some act of creative imagination, the socialist minister Erhard Eppler exclaimed: "Without a future there is no living."

Ironically accepting this sentiment, young people decided to live for the present. Worrying about a future or about "meaning" in life was middle-class mentality. The "now" generation sought instant gratification in a culture of its own. Its distinctive tastes in music and life-style, its sexual and sartorial habits, first looked like gestures of defiance; but business was quick to exploit the new "youth" fashions. The profitable industries that were built on the counterculture demonstrated the infinite versatility and adaptability of "the system."

More successful than its predecessor, the "second youth movement" has seen its life-styles adopted and absorbed by society. A relaxed, sensualistic culture coexists with the "performance" culture of the German tradition. The establishment has coopted the leaders of the youth revolt; the elites are constantly recruiting new talent. Contrary to the notion of students vainly knocking on closed doors, the society is rather open; its elites are, though not "revolving," yet renewing its cadres.

They do experience a serious problem of selection, however: the wider the doors of competition are opened, the tougher the competition will be. This is a new phenomenon in Germany, where choosing a university used to be in the student's hands and accession to the upper classes largely a matter of education and connections. It is not surprising that the new conditions of competition should arouse resentment and disgust among those whose notions of culture were formed on the basis of tradition. What they call vulgar mass culture is democracy—precisely in not a formal but a material sense.

31

Winds of Change

For the first time we can say Vaterland *once more.*
—Election speech, 1969

GERMANY IN THE LATE 1960s WAS NOT JUST TWENTY YEARS OLDER than at the end of the war. It was a different country. The terrible memories were neither forgotten nor overcome, but one no longer thought about them. For indeed—why should those under twenty-five, that third of the population that had not been born when Hitler started the war, feel any guilt about it? Or indeed the two-thirds who had been under twenty or unborn in 1933 and therefore could not have voted for Hitler in a free election? Many of the younger people felt a revulsion against a generation that had given Germany a bad name; but they wished to be judged by their own deeds, not by those of their fathers. The postwar period, with its depressing sense of being second rate, of being ostracized, of being watched and scrutinized, was over.

By now, the Adenauer era was seen as the time of contempt rather than as the time of meritorious efforts toward rehabilitation; and the Erhard regime as merely its extension. The chancellor had, upon request, endorsed the American effort in Vietnam, and although most Germans felt the same way, they saw no need to follow every American lead publicly. When Egypt gave Ulbricht a rousing welcome, public opinion in the BRD reacted in an unexpected manner. Erhard had recognized Israel and withdrawn development aid from Nasser— who promptly hit the BRD with a Hallstein-in-reverse, suspending relations. That unleashed a storm of criticism in the BRD against Erhard. Writers who just a few years before would have felt obliged to favor Israel now charged that Erhard—of all people—had sacrificed German trade interests to ideology. The change in German self-confidence could not have been expressed more drastically.

The postwar era was over also in the relations between the two Germanies. Ever since the Berlin Wall had gone up, people had come to realize that the partition was here to stay for at least a generation.

333

They began to see that in order to live with the situation, one had first of all to recognize the existence of the DDR—still called "the so-called DDR" in the west, even though the two states were important trading partners for each other, and Berlin depended on the DDR for its water and electric current. But West German industry now became impatient to export into the East European market, which also was coveted by the French and British; putting anticommunism and politics on one side, its representatives urged the government to defy or circumvent the American objections to an "opening to the East." Foreign minister Schröder had begun to exchange trade missions with Bulgaria, Rumania, and Poland. He had even relaxed the Hallstein Doctrine in its application to satellite countries; but he tried to make the shift seem as insignificant as possible.

By contrast, the FDP and SPD wanted a spectacular gesture symbolizing a basic change in attitudes, and their governing position in Berlin gave them an opportunity for such a demonstration. The Wall had caused hardships to thousands. Families had been separated. The Social-Democrats felt that they could do two or three things at a time: recognize a de facto situation; help alleviate the hardship for people; administer a moral rebuke to Ulbricht; and, with all this, outflank the CDU on the reunification issue and create a popular movement for German brotherhood.

Mayor Willy Brandt's aide, Egon Bahr, a fervent patriot, negotiated with DDR authorities an agreement permitting West Berliners to visit their relatives in East Berlin between Christmas 1963 and New Year. It was a shameful agreement: the greedy Ulbricht government levied a fee on each visitor (as it levied fees on arrested "spies" or "traitors" whom it released to the west, and as it levied a fee on each ton of supplies that came into West Berlin). But 1,300,000 West Berliners suddenly remembered their distant aunts and cousins and, in bitterly cold weather, lined up at the few checkpoints with their gift parcels and good Western money. Bahr claimed that the humanitarian action was a great political success. During 1964, 1965, and 1966, eight more visiting periods were allowed, and the SPD drove its message home: the partition of Germany must not end contacts between the German people; it could be overcome only by patient methods of rapprochement; the west must pay the eastern governments to educate them to human decency.

As opposition, the SPD was close to conducting its own foreign policy. SPD leaders blithely went to Moscow to confer with Khrushchev. Although they never brought home any concessions, they contended that indulgence on prestige matters was more than compensated for by the gain in political initiative. This is what Germans mean by *Ostpolitik*. They wanted to see a change of pace, since the Cold War stance had obviously brought no visible results.

Dissatisfaction with the status quo was not confined to the opposition. Erhard's coalition partner was restive; in his own party, criticism was rife. He did win another election, but after that his government fell apart. In 1964 the CDU obtained 47 percent of the vote; but the SPD finally broke out of its traditional one-third confinement, winning 40 percent of the vote at the expense of smaller parties.

After Erhard's resignation in 1965, the SPD and CDU formed a "Broad Coalition." The new chancellor was a suave Swabian, Kurt Kiesinger of the CDU. Willy Brandt, the personable, dynamic mayor of Berlin, became vice-chancellor and foreign minister. As finance minister, the power-hungry Franz Josef Strauss had his comeback. Professor Karl Schiller of the SPD was economics minister; Schröder had to trade the Foreign Office for the Defense Office; and Herbert Wehner, the Social-Democratic boss of bosses, was given responsibility for "joint-German issues." To Germans who wanted to overcome the postwar era, this was an interesting combination: Kiesinger and Schiller had both joined the Nazi party in 1933, when Brandt, the young revolutionary, had gone into exile. Wehner had been a communist and was now a religious socialist. Although the Adenauer cabinet, too, had included ex-Nazis, it was now said that the composition of the cabinet symbolized a new general forgiveness and an attempt to bring all Germans together. Even Strauss, the villain of the Spiegel affair, was included in this overcoming of the past.

For the SPD this was the first opportunity in a generation to prove that it could govern. Although it had shared responsibility in state governments, its one-sided, negativistic reaction to the creation of a western republic and to rearmament had branded it as a party of the discontented—doomed to be in eternal opposition. Since its Godesberg congress in 1959, it had striven hard to rid itself of that image. It also needed to do away with the notion that it was a mere class representation. Its new program, therefore, declared that "the SPD has turned from a working-class party into a party of the people"; it proclaimed that its aims were based on the western inspiration of Christianity, humanism, and classical philosophy. Contrary to its previous tenets, it condemned monopolies "even in the hands of the state," and although it demanded "a far-seeing policy of full employment," it designated "free competition and free enterprise" as its instruments: "competition wherever possible, planning where necessary."

The architect of the new strategy was Herbert Wehner, an opportunist who had learned from the communists to respect power. He also recognized the importance of selling a personality. After Schumacher's death the SPD had slipped back into its organizational routine and elected as leader Erich Ollenhauer, a colorless party boss who was no match for Adenauer. Now he graciously stepped aside so that the charismatic Willy Brandt could lead the ticket—a politician with a heart, also a man who had been doubtful about Schumacher's negativism and who had rapport with John Kennedy. He led the SPD out of the tower, and in the coalition cabinet he outshone the chancellor.

As foreign minister, Brandt initiated *Ostpolitik* and thereby gave the Germans pride. Although it was supported by the Johnson administration, it seemed to be independent, the opposite of Cold War policies, an echo of Bismarck's Reinsurance Treaty and Rathenau's Rapallo policy. Relations with Yugoslavia and Rumania were restored, and when Dubček came to power in Czechoslovakia, an informally cordial relationship was developed. Border guards were withdrawn, making it once more possible for East Germans to escape from their prison.

But when added up soberly, the change was in name and philosophy rather than in substance. The BRD's foreign policy remained solidly anchored in the Western alliance—with the difference, however, that the Germans had so decided of their own will and reflection. If *Ostpolitik* did not bring many successes, it was at least an independent way of dealing with the realities of Germany's postwar geography; and gradually it educated the Germans to admit that they had lost World War II, that the Oder and Neisse rivers were the Polish boundary, and that between the BRD and Poland there was a country called the DDR. The generation that had grown up with this condition no longer needed to shun, as a humiliating admission of defeat, recognition of the status created by war.

Brandt's *Ostpolitik* in this first phase was based on the mistaken premise that to "soften" the solidness of the Soviet bloc, one must begin by drawing the satellites into a conversation. Cautiously he also started to explore the avenues to Moscow. All this came to an abrupt halt when five Warsaw Pact powers—including the DDR, but not Rumania—invaded Czechoslovakia in August 1968, snuffing out Dubček's "socialism with a heart"—a venture that had evoked enormous hopes and sympathies among Germans of all parties.

In the domestic field, the Broad Coalition succeeded in overcoming the 1964-65 recession and led the German economy into another boom.

It worked out a new law on the operations of political parties, liberalized the penal code, and recognized the rights of illegitimate children.

The new code was the work of that extraordinary man Gustav Heinemann, a statesman respected beyond his party. He had been a conservative representative in the Brüning Reichstag; under Hitler he had joined the Church Bearing Witness, and after the war he became president of the Evangelical Synod. He was a cofounder of the CDU and minister of the interior under Adenauer, but broke with him and founded the neutralist, pacifist, and patriotic All-German People's Party, which failed at the polls and then fell into the hands of cranks. Heinemann joined the SPD, became minister of justice, and in that capacity pleaded for an understanding of the student protest movement. In 1969 the FDP offered to vote for him if the SPD would make him its presidential candidate. He won against Defense Minister Schröder by 512 to 506 votes and filled the office with a new sense of dignity and humanity.

Heinemann's election was the first intimation that all was not well within the Broad Coalition. The two parties were so incompatible that the leaders circumvented the danger of parliamentary disagreements by meeting privately in Kiesinger's country house. Both parties were under pressure from their more principled, or extremist, wings to resume their liberty. At the extreme right, neo-Nazi agitation threatened to make inroads into the CDU; on the extreme left, an antiparliamentary movement, mostly of university students, invaded local units of the SPD in many places, and in some cities actually conquered the leadership.

We must give this ultraleft movement a glance, since it received extraordinary publicity. In 1967, an almost ephemeral incident resulted in a major tragedy. The shah of Iran was invited to Berlin; dissident Iranians, university students there, needed little effort to incite German students to a demonstration. When the police shot and killed a student, protest rallies raged in German universities, giving Marxist and anarchist terrorists a chance to dominate the student movement. The next year, a fanatic shot their most gifted leader, Rudi Dutschke, inflicting heavy brain damage. Once again savage demonstrations swept the cities, this time mostly directed against newspapers of the Springer chain, which had asked for stern measures against the students. Simultaneously with the momentous uprisings in Paris and Prague, students in many universities threw fear into middle-class hearts. Passing from demonstrations to "direct action," they seized faculty offices and occupied campuses, or interfered with town governments and freedom of the press.

These events led to the 1968 Emergency Law (*Notstandsgesetz-gebung*), which amended the Basic Law to give the government special powers in case of danger to the state: in such emergencies the Bundestag may suspend civil liberties which otherwise are vouchsafed by the constitution. Despite heavy opposition from its youth organizations and the trade unions, the SPD leadership went along with this legislation, whose main purpose was to reassure CDU/CSU voters.

In the September 1969 election the neo-Nazi party failed to receive the 5 percent minimum, and the ultraleft and communist parties together received less than 1 percent of the vote. Hence the seats were so distributed that the FDP could form a majority by joining with either the CDU or the SPD. The conservatives had long since left the FDP; the liberal-industrial wing, with Scheel and Hans-Dietrich Genscher at its head and favored by Heinemann, decided to throw in its lot with the SPD. Since 1969, therefore, West Germany has had Social-Democratic chancellors and liberal foreign ministers.

These two parties do not see eye to eye on social policy; but they are congenial on cultural affairs and foreign policy. The new tone was set by Brandt's government declaration of October 28, 1969, from which we cite the beginning and the end:

> Mr. President, ladies and gentlemen. We are determined to protect the security of the Federal Republic of Germany and the cohesion of the German nation, to keep the peace, and to work together for a European peace settlement. . . . The Germans are bound together by their language and history—with all its splendor and misery; we are all at home in Germany. We still have common tasks and common responsibility: for peace among ourselves and Europe. Twenty years after the founding of the Federal Republic of Germany and the DDR, we must prevent a further estrangement of the German nation. We must go from a regulated next-to-each-other to a with-each-other. This is not only a German interest; it has significance for peace in Europe, too, and for the relationship between the East and West. . . . The Federal Government . . . once again offers the Ministerial Council of the DDR negotiations without discrimination on either side, at government level, which should lead to cooperation agreed on by treaty. International de jure recognition of the DDR by the Federal Government cannot be considered. Even though two states exist in Germany, they are not foreign to each other; their relations to each other can only be of a special nature. . . .

> In a democracy, a government can work successfully only if it is supported by a democratic commitment of its citizens. We need blind approval no more than we need pomp and high-and-mighty aloofness. We do not

seek admirers. We need critical people to think with us, to decide with us, to take responsibility with us. The self-awareness of this government will show itself in tolerance, so it will know how to treasure a solidarity that expresses itself in criticism. We are not the chosen, we are the elected. That is why we seek a dialogue with all who exert themselves for this democracy. In recent years, some in this country feared the second German democracy would go the way of the first. I never believed it. Today I believe it less than ever. No. We are not at the end of our democracy. We are just beginning. We want to be a nation of good neighbors—inside Germany and outside.

Parallel movements in literature and philosophy on both sides of the Iron Curtain will be explored in Chapter 34.

*   *   *

THE PASSING OF THE ADENAUER ERA, twenty years after the end of World War II, brought to an end the climate of restoration and of intellectual timidity (see Chapter 34). It brought university reform, the new life-styles of the affluent society, and an end of the siege mentality that had been a heritage of the war. The "postwar period" was gone, indeed.

The late 1960s will be remembered as the watershed in public attitudes, the period of student rebellions the world over, the May 1968 movement that led to the demise of de Gaulle the next year, the tragically ended "Spring of Prague," the rapid liberalization of the Catholic Church, and the social activism of priests. Unfortunately, a similar "softening" did not occur in the Marxist camp. The unspeakable Ulbricht sent East German troops once more into Czechoslovakia to help Brezhnev crush the Dubček experiment. The so-called "European communism" needed another decade to develop. We shall turn now to the developments in the DDR.

32

The Other German Miracle

*It is in the worker's interest to fulfill with all his power
the task set by the SED.*

—Ulbricht

THE CHANGE THAT CAME TO EAST GERMANY was of a different kind. The building of the Wall in 1961 not only stopped people's actual escape; it stopped those eighteen million who remained in captivity from even thinking of escape. From then on the DDR was their country, in which they had to realize whatever happiness they hoped to find in life. They had to give up the dream that one day they would be liberated by the west. If they wished to achieve something for themselves, they had to work for the SED, for the DDR, for Ulbricht.

Neither Nazism nor communism had changed that extraordinary quality of the German worker: wanting to be proud of his work, whether on the job or in his home. So people simply got busy, with amazing results. Despite its unfavorable terms of trade with the Soviet Union, the DDR has the highest standard of living in the COMECON area— 30 percent better than that of the Soviet Union. Its citizens have refrigerators, television sets, washing machines (if they are lucky enough to have a place to put them, for housing construction still lags badly), and even cars (if they wait long enough; most cars are still exported). Moreover, DDR citizens can now eat tropical fruit (on days the store has had a delivery) or buy western records and fashions. They can also take their vacations at the Black Sea (though of course not on the Riviera).

This miracle has been achieved in the new climate of political hopelessness and by an economic reform that seemed to make concessions to capitalism. In 1963, wage scales were revised to give higher pay to those with higher skills. Plant managers were told that it was not enough to fulfill the quotas set by the Five-Year Plan; the merchandise also had to be produced "at a profit." This ominous word was used in the new directives defining "socialist principles." The official *Handbook of the DDR* chided managers who failed to use the most efficient technology, or who earned high premiums by exceeding fictitious "targets." Instead of this corrupt system, the SED introduced "economic levers . . . the most important of which is profit." From now on, production costs had to be covered by income from sales, and research had to be financed out of profits. Write-off was to be regulated by the cost of replacement or credit and similar capitalistic devices. And finally, prices were allowed to float, though within limits, and consumption is still channeled by subsidies and levies.

Needless to say, the new system meant closer control of productivity. The increase in the rate of surplus value had to be explained to the workers as another step toward socialism. A conference of 950 political, economic, and trade union leaders was called to launch a "new economic system of planning and directing" based on wage and profit, competitive production, and rational organization. Shock brigades were sent to the factories to teach workers how to use the new incentives and produce more goods more cheaply. The Sixth Trade Union Congress (FDGB) affirmed the workers' "great responsibility for increasing production. The workers' interest lies in putting all their strength to work for the fulfillment of the task set by the SED in the field of economics." A competitive program was designed to stimulate productivity; special care was taken to increase the scientific input. "The race between the two systems will be decided in favor of that system which uses science and technology to best advantage," said Ulbricht.

The results have been spectacular. National income has doubled in fifteen years. Exports, which had been eight billion eastern marks in 1958, rose to sixteen billion in 1968 and twenty-five billion in 1974. Of that, 40 percent went to the Soviet Union, 22 percent to other COMECON countries, 10 percent to the BRD, and 10 percent to underdeveloped countries. The DDR spends 390 marks per person yearly on defense—5.9 percent of national income compared to only 3.2 percent for the BRD. Monthly incomes have risen from 665 eastern marks in 1967 to 784 in 1971, compared to 1,282 western marks in the BRD. Since the two marks are hard to compare (though the official exchange rate remains one for one), Table 6 shows hours and minutes of labor required to buy specific items of merchandise.

Produced national income rose from 72 billion eastern marks (in stable prices of 1969) to 120 billion in 1972, electricity consumption from 1,059 kilowatts per capita in 1950 to 4,072 in 1971, car ownership from 230,000 in 1960 to 1,160,000 in 1970 (compared to 13,940,000 in the BRD). The number of milk cows has increased from twenty-five to thirty-five per 100 hectares, the number of houses built from 31,000

TABLE 6. PRICES IN TERMS OF LABOR TIME (HOURS AND MINUTES)

	BRD	DDR
1 kilogram rye bread	0:12	0:07
1 kilogram sugar	0:10	0:23
1 kilogram margarine	0:29	0:29
1 kilogram steak	1:29	2:21
1 kilogram coffee	2:19	16:40
10 cigarettes	0:09	0:23
Suit, 50 percent wool	25:58	44:46
Men's shoes, leather	5:18	11:29
Portable manual typewriter	31:40	100:43
17-jewel watch, stainless steel	11:32	37:16
45-horsepower car	878:00	4,226:00
100 square meters apartment space (monthly rent)	40:00	20:00

to 76,000 (compared to 544,000 in the BRD, where the size of dwelling space is also 50 percent larger).

These successes were due to the total mobilization of the population and the intensity of the work. As just one way of appraising the drive, in the BRD only half of all women between fifteen and sixty years of age work; in the DDR—80 percent of women work.

In the first fifteen years, collectivization of farms had been a slow process. By 1959 only 40 percent of the cultivated land was in the hands of 10,000 Agricultural Production Cooperatives. Then a new statute urged "voluntary collectivization"; activists swarmed over the countryside to persuade the reticent. By the end of 1961 the number of cooperatives had doubled, covering 85 percent of all usable land; but mergers later reduced the number to 7,500, some of them are as large as 12,000 hectares. Peasants may bring into the collective either their arable land; or the land plus their meadows and cattle; or all they have except one-half hectare of vegetable garden, two cows, and two pigs. Their wages are figured in terms of "labor units," which are staggered according to skill; at the end of the year, when the cooperative draws up its balance sheet, it can tell how many marks to pay for each labor unit.

These arrangements describe the perfect "agro-city" as Khrushchev had first envisaged it in the Soviet Union. Everything is calculated to produce the highest yield; the prime incentive, again, is monetary. Although the plan sets targets, managers have freedom as to how to seek the best results for their units. Prices are allowed to fluctuate in response to demand—which, of course, is controlled by the planning agency.

It is remarkable that a regime as rigid and Stalinist as Ulbricht's was able to abandon features of socialist planning which to this day are stubbornly enforced in the Soviet Union. Overall planning has been retained, but its implementation has been decentralized and liberalized. By contrast, the political regime was never liberalized; if anything, it was tightened.

A division of labor and mutual toleration prevails between political and economic managers. Even after so many years, the two elites have not merged. The party, which has two million members, produces its own leaders on the local, provincial, and national levels in factories, collectives, and mass organizations. Despite great efforts to make the party bosses experts in production, the political elite tends to separate itself out at the higher echelons. Simple members still have to have jobs. A party worker may be, for instance, a fully employed miner who gets leave ten days a year to participate in a *Volkskammer* (People's Chamber) vote and engages in party business in the evenings. Only persons with real power work full time for the party. One out of four citizens of voting age has some "function," whether economic or political, and hundreds of thousands have been promoted from the workbench to the office.

Economic, technical, and scientific managers may have subordinate positions in the party. They rarely need, or care, to hold high party rank. Even the higher civil servants, except those in sensitive positions, are not necessarily high-ranking party members, and in some cases special care has been taken to appoint a noncommunist, for instance as foreign minister.

The regime allows both elites to enjoy privileges: special housing, travel abroad, preferential school admission for their children, and even something their West German peers no longer have, the services of a maid; but above all, powers of decision. This sets them apart as "the new class." The new class includes the older generation of communists who survived war and persecution—a generation that is now dying out—and the "new men," grown up under the SED educational system and trained in its cadre schools.

Though capable of mouthing Marxist jargon, socialist managers are not committed to socialism as an ideology. They see it as a technique of management; they consider their administration system the matrix of their jobs, and they know no better system. Among the intelligentsia there may be more descendants of the managerial classes, former and present, than among the politicians; but they are strictly technocrats and have no quarrel with the system as such—only with any malfunctions. They convinced the political leaders that a more flexible price system would make the plan work better. Their suggestion was not meant to undermine the idea of planning; they are system adjusters, not "revisionists."

Liberalizing the price system, therefore, has not implied liberalizing the system of thought control. In fact, repression seems to be more effective in the DDR than in other satellite countries. Despite the closeness of West German radio and TV transmitters, the DDR does not have a civil rights movement or an underground literature. The few overt dissenters were easily isolated. Professor Robert Havemann, a respected physicist, does not believe in historical materialism, therefore he cannot teach. (His published works do not indicate that he is a major thinker.) Wolf Biermann, whose naughty songs attack the squares of the new class, lived under house arrest for years and was, of course, forbidden to perform; but his audience was considerably larger in West Germany than in East Germany. He was finally allowed a concert tour abroad and was then prevented from returning. Other free-thinking writers had to follow him into exile—none voluntarily, for they are not "dissenters" but critical communists.

A few non-Marxist authors were published in the DDR, including Christa Wolf, a sensitive chronicler of the inner life, and Stephan Hermlin, a stylish poet. Stefan Heym, an older communist, was allowed to write critically of the bureaucracy provided the story glorified communism as a whole. Many of the deviants are Jews.

After each period of relaxation, censorship was tightened again, and the official Writers' Association came down with a sledgehammer of socialist criticism on any writer who would not be a literary Hennecke. Not even for their own enjoyment will the ruling technocrats tolerate literature that is concerned with the human side of life. They will do anything to stifle the development and the appreciation of such literature; they discourage reading and writing poetry, except that addressed to tractors and lathes. The high school is called "polytechnical school" because it teaches what is useful for the state. The old humanist curriculum, which even the Nazis dared only reform and distort, has been abolished.

The school is responsible for producing obedient and enthusiastic servants of the system. Nevertheless, it is the one feature of the DDR that is generally admired by western visitors. In theory, it is totally egalitarian. Kindergartens and day-care centers are available to all children whose mothers work. All children pass through a unified ten-grade school, topped by the "polytechnical" high school. Instruction is integrated with industrial training, and an efficient tracking system guides the talented to the most rewarding careers. Workers are graded as "unskilled," "skilled," and "masters" in "cadres with professional training" or "cadres with academic training." The sudden boost in the number of universities and the influx of party men into academic teaching have tended to lower scholastic standards; humanist research not related to class war is considered a pastime of bygone leisure classes. The new DDR universities and technical institutes produce usable knowledge and a technical intelligentsia that is happy to fulfill its function in the socialist community.

Neither liberalization in the economy nor the democratization of education has brought any audible call for relaxing the party regime. The new constitution of 1968 emphasized SED "leadership" even more boldly than the previous one. It also gave the secretary of the party the ex-officio position of head of state who appoints the council of ministers. This was Ulbricht and, after his resignation, his hand-picked successor, Erich Honecker.

Although the constitution was debated in the party and in the mass organizations before it was adopted, it means very little. The cabinet is a technical apparatus that carries out the party's orders and keeps the daily administration routine lubricated. The party secretary is also chairman of the *Staatsrat* (State Council), the highest organ of the state, which is composed of mayors of big cities, scientists, and other notables. It meets only intermittently and has only a small staff of its own.

The *Volkskammer* (People's Chamber) is the highest legislative organ. It is "elected" on a single slate without opposition and meets once every few weeks to approve the laws that the government has published in the meantime. The list of the National Front candidates has been drawn up by the SED and the "mass organizations."

The *Grundrechte* (Bill of Rights) includes no rights of the individual vis-à-vis administration, police, or courts, but a number of collective rights, such as the right to work, the right to education, the right to leisure time and recreation, the right to "encouragement of youth"—notions defying any definition that might stand up in court.

The constitution was Ulbricht's last great work. After 1968, his stubborn immobility began to get in the way of Brezhnev's ideas on détente. He opposed the BRD's no-force treaties (see Chapter 33) with Poland and the Soviet Union (1970), on which Brezhnev set high hopes for talks on disarmament and mutual withdrawal of forces, and he raised difficulties against an agreement on Berlin without which the BRD would not ratify the two no-force treaties. So in 1971, finally, he was retired "for reasons of health."

If the idea of replacing The Goatee was to rid the DDR of his image, his successors deflated all such hopes. Erich Honecker, the new party secretary, and Willi Stoph, the prime minister, are of the old school and no less opposed to détente than Ulbricht was. Only under heavy pressure from Moscow did they consent to an agreement with the BRD, signed late in 1972, which led to a considerable improvement in the DDR's international status but fell short of the SED's ideological aim—recognition by the BRD. Nevertheless, after its admission to the United Nations, the Honecker regime felt secure enough to release 20,000 political prisoners. Life became "normal." The siege mentality was played down at Brezhnev's prompting—at least momentarily.

Recognition was completed in the Helsinki Agreements of 1975, in which the western powers subscribed to the status created in Eastern Europe after the war. In return, they exacted from the communist nations promises concerning the right to emigrate and the right to free thought. At the time, these promises were believed to be too vaguely worded to be of any legal consequence. With no "teeth" or material sanctions to guarantee fulfillment, the communist powers felt that they could sign them and get something for nothing. Ever since, though, they have been plagued by demands for greater freedom.

The DDR government has reacted quite nervously to the slightest sign of dissident stirrings. It feels insecure again. Its legitimacy problems cannot be solved by international treaties, because they derive from its origin, from the way it operates, and from its continuing subservience to Moscow. For the majority of its citizens the regime is still "they"; it is an odious police state which, to this day, in spite of all its social and economic achievements, has not achieved legitimacy in its own eyes.

Seizing power in the heartland of Marxism, the German communists have made great efforts to create a Marxist science and literature. After thirty years, it must be said that they have succeeded in stifling Marxist thought. Orthodoxy rather than creativity rules the East German schools. Poetry and philosophy must conform to the party's directives. A physicist cannot without endangering his institute and himself express doubt about "dialectics in nature," because Engels believed in it. Literary production is as closely controlled as coal output.

A directive on literature issued by the Central Committee of the SED asked writers to be "true to life" but defined life as "the new social reality in the DDR," and truth as the fight for a "unified, democratic, peace-loving, and independent Germany, fulfilling the Five-Year Plan." Ulbricht assigned to literature the task of "educating people to be true patriots." As a result, novels like *Menschen an unserer Seite* are little more than clever reportage with editorials. Even if a writer succeeds in putting real people into his book and letting them speak real language, the Writers' Collective, sitting in judgment on the proofs, usually makes him correct his ideological mistakes. Willi Bredel had tried to write a three-part historical novel of his generation—*The Fathers, The Sons,* and *The Grandsons.* The Soviet Writers' Association demanded and obtained extensive "corrections" that took all interest out of the characters. The author was not even allowed to develop psychological explanation for the behavior of noncommunist workers.

The culture czar of East Germany was Johannes R. Becher, who began as expressionist and nihilist, a rebel against all previous form, against hypocrisy and moralizing. After his conversion to communism, he wrote an epic on the Five-Year Plan:

Of tremendous things sang before us
the poets of all ages.
But the most tremendous thing remained for us to sing:
We sing the Five-Year Plan.

The poem praises Stalin's unique contribution, condemns the imperialists, whom the Red Army holds at bay, and concludes:

The boundaries of time we strode over,
and we set out into the age of communism.

In his exile poems, Becher gave moving expression to his love of Germany, its landscape, its cultural heritage. He was happy to come home and then fulfilled the wish of his Russian sponsors: to express Germany's guilt and expiation. He wrote, and Hanns Eisler set to music, the national anthem for the DDR:

Risen from death and from ruins,
Turning toward the future . . .

Writers in the DDR might have carried on the humanist tradition of the Popular Front, or they might have continued the proletarian, anti-fascist literature of the 1930s. Instead, they allowed the Soviet Writers' Association to dictate to them the norms of "socialist realism." The task was, in the words of one of their official spokesmen (Alexander Abusch, *Literatur und Wirklichkeit* [*Literature and Reality*], 1952) to "represent the struggle of the new against the old and obsolete in production and in society, the new men and the new perspectives of the future." This led to schematic, arid writing. Even eastern critics wondered why in their greatest writers' novels the bourgeois are interesting characters and the "positive heroes" remain pale.

After an initial period of threats and *Kulturkampf,* the SED regime has tried to use the Christian churches for its purposes, and the churches have been responsive. (One-half of the DDR citizens are Lutheran, one-tenth are Roman Catholic, tithe-paying members; the rest are scattered and unaffiliated.) Churches are well attended, but non-religious ceremonies (marriage, "youth initiation") are encouraged. In 1971 the state officially recognized the existing churches (and even sought a concordat with the Vatican) and allowed a loyal pastors' league to lapse. In return, the Lutherans defined their position as "the church not outside and not against, but within the socialist state," supported the international policy of the government, and even persuaded the church press in West Germany to soft-pedal its coverage of conditions in the East.

33

The Federal Republic—II
Liberals in Power

This, dear friends, is our *republic.*
—Willy Brandt

THE 1970s OPENED FOR THE BRD under the leadership of an unusual team: Gustav Heinemann, the unconventional, nonconformist president; Willy Brandt, the left-leaning chancellor; and Walter Scheel, the insurgent liberal, as foreign minister. The parliamentary leader of the SPD was Herbert Wehner, the ex-communist who had worked with Honecker in the 1934-35 Saarland fight. They were all people oriented to issues rather than to party organizations; they all represented the new attitude of détente abroad and liberalism at home. They all believed in *Ostpolitik*.

It is necessary to repeat here the earlier note on the two meanings of liberalism: the FDP advocates an old-fashioned European liberalism of Adam Smithian laissez-faire; the SPD advocates active state intervention for full employment, redistribution of incomes, and workers' participation in management—policies that are called liberal in the United States. The FDP is closely allied with big industry, the SPD with labor.

The two therefore were at odds over the most important planks in the SPD's electoral campaign: *Mitbestimmung* (union participation) and full-employment policies. On the social-economic front, class war was conducted inside the cabinet, even while Social-Democratic chancellors were getting the trade unions to tone down class struggle.

The coalition partners have more similar views on civil liberties, cultural matters, penal reform, police powers, etc., and they go a long way together in defense and foreign policies. The hallmark of their early work was acceptance of the two historical revolutions that had happened in the postwar era: the generation leap (expressed in university reform and the student movement's new life-style), and the partitioning of Germany as a result of Hitler's war.

Coming to terms with history, the new German government renounced all aspirations of becoming a big power by setting its signature to the status quo. First it signed the Nonproliferation Treaty (prohibiting the acquisition of nuclear arms by countries that did not have them at the date of signing—November 28, 1969; ratified only after a "Verification Agreement" with Euratom, April 5, 1973), which had been delayed for a year.

Brandt then proceeded to negotiate good-neighbor treaties with Poland and the Soviet Union. Twenty-five years after the war, West Germany was ready to recognize Poland's borders. Both countries renounced force in settling their disputes. A similar treaty could be negotiated with the Soviet Union (Moscow Treaty, December 7, 1970), but not yet with Czechoslovakia and the DDR—in both cases for the most ridiculous reasons of past history. Although the Munich Pact of 1938 was as dead as its authors, the West German government was reluctant to renounce it formally because of the private lawsuits that had resulted from property transfers. With the DDR, on its part, no treaty could be concluded because in West German eyes it lacked the attributes of a sovereign state.

Rapprochement with the east (*Ostpolitik*) had many critics. The CDU/CSU (now in opposition) objected to the conclusion of any treaty with the Soviet Union as long as the DDR government prevented Germans from meeting with Germans. The critics felt that the west should not make unilateral concessions but should bargain for a material quid pro quo. Because Moscow was at odds with China at the time and most anxious to obtain a détente with NATO, such suggestions were not without merit. Indeed, in the three years of negotiations that followed, Moscow was found responsive to firmness. As a first token of Brezhnev's earnestness, Ulbricht was sacrificed to détente: he had to abandon his office in May 1971. His successor Honecker was no more amenable; but at least another symbol of the Cold War had gone.

Soon after Willy Brandt became chancellor, he met the DDR's prime minister, Willi Stoph, in the East German town of Erfurt for the kind of "dialogue" which at one time had been demanded by the East, and which now was one of Egon Bahr's "small steps" to lowering the barriers between Germans. When the two leaders appeared at the hotel window, the crowd that had gathered on the plaza outside broke into unending shouts for "Willy"—and there could not be the slightest doubt about which of the two was meant. Another such meeting, which took place in Kassel, West Germany, was less successful as Nazi crowds tried to break it up, giving Stoph an excuse to complain about the so-called democrats' hostility to peace. He returned home without giving any satisfaction to those who had hoped that a show of good will would soften the eastern regime. Egon Bahr's slogan, "unification by rapprochement," so far has remained a rather one-sided wish; as a policy it has failed.

Yet it signifies an attitude and a faith—a conviction that peace is possible in our generation and that neither the unity of Europe nor indeed that of Germany is lost forever. Perhaps this is a nostalgic view—like the "Great-German" dream that lingered among the liberals of 1848 long after Prussia and Austria had gone their separate ways. It is a view, also, which occasionally separates Germans from their American and NATO allies.

The negotiations with Moscow and Warsaw went at a quick pace despite reservations and protests. Brandt himself went to the communist capitals. Before signing the treaty with Poland, he visited the Warsaw Ghetto Memorial and fell on his knees, making amends on behalf of all Germans. The gesture stayed in the minds of his hosts: there was a German—there were Germans—different from those they had known and different also from those they knew in COMECON.

But with all the good will he was bearing and suing for, Brandt made one thing clear to the Russians and Poles: the no-force treaties they wanted so badly would not be ratified unless similar guarantees were given for the safety of Berlin. Brandt ostentatiously visited the city where he had been mayor, disregarding Ulbricht's protest that no German chancellor had rights in that "free city." But Berlin is within the DDR's territory, not part of it.

On the basis of the West German declarations, the three western powers—which still were and are responsible for West Berlin—were able in 1971 to negotiate with the Russians a new statute that gives Berliners as much security as any treaty can, assuring them of undisturbed access and supplies. They were also given new visiting rights, which they had been denied since 1967. For this treaty, full credit should go to U.S. ambassador Kenneth Rush: he withstood the impatient eagerness of Germans who might have signed a less favorable treaty with less ironclad guarantees. The West Germans have often blamed the United States for "Cold War" attitudes that were mere bargaining positions; the aim was a treaty that would hold.

Meanwhile in the west, Brandt persuaded the new French President Pompidou to withdraw de Gaulle's veto against England's admission to the Common Market. *Ostpolitik* required a strong European balance. At that moment, Brandt's international stature was so eminent that he was awarded the Nobel Peace Prize for 1971.

Stresemann and Carl von Ossietzky, the anti-Hitler pacifist and martyr, had been the last Germans to obtain it.

The prestige that went with this award did not much help the chancellor in overcoming nationalist opposition at home. His margin in the Bundestag was slim to begin with; Pan-Germans and refugees from the East were defecting from both the Free-Democratic and the Social-Democratic parties. In a venomous and obstructionist debate— in which Brandt had to pay for Schumacher's one-time truculence in fighting Adenauer's foreign policy—the opposition tried to prevent ratification of the treaties, which both Russians and German liberals considered the foundation of future relations. (The U.S. government, which had first encouraged *Ostpolitik*, then warned against going too far too fast, eventually supported Brandt. It was aware, though, that German patriots like Bahr and Scheel were prepared to proceed from *Ostpolitik* to Rapallo policy.) Brandt had to assure his opponents that "we are not giving away anything [*de jure*] which we have not lost long ago [*de facto*]." The Poles helped create a favorable climate by allowing 40,000 ethnic Germans to leave. Eventually, a few votes had to be bought to assure adoption of the treaties by the slimmest majority, on May 17, 1972. (The disclosure, three years later, caused the government considerable embarrassment.)

Having forced open the way for *Ostpolitik*, the Bonn government concluded a coexistence treaty with the DDR (whose government had to be coaxed by Moscow) late in 1972. This "Treaty on Basic Relations" (*Grundlagenvertrag*) styles both DDR and BRD as "states" which must fulfill the obligations of sovereign United Nations members and, indeed, opened the door of the world organization to the two Germanies, in 1973. But it could not have been ratified by the Bundestag had not the chancellor and the foreign minister denied, in the same breath, that thereby the DDR had been recognized as a sovereign state. Brandt again used his formula, "two states within the German nation," and opined that the DDR "lacks certain attributes of a state."

DDR and BRD agreed to establish "representations" in each other's capitals, but to this day they have no embassies. In its fanaticism, the CDU/CSU voted against entry into the United Nations. The incubus of reunification still distorts the foreign policy of any German opposition into a psychotic syndrome.

With these treaties, the way was cleared for the Conference on European security, which after long preparation took place at Helsinki in 1975. By this time the United States, which had been a reluctant participant in the earlier stages of the project, was actively interested in détente as an opener to the ongoing negotiations on strategic arms limitation (SALT) and on mutual withdrawal of troops. It has not given up its Atlantic conception or its basic view of a polarized world; it still sees détente as basically an instrument in bilateral relations with the Soviet Union. The Germans, like many other Europeans, tend to see détente as a means to liberate them from that polarity.

Nevertheless, no responsible German politician wants international chaos or American disengagement from European security. In the Helsinki agreements, therefore, it was at German insistence that the United States became a guarantor, together with the Soviet Union, of the status quo in Europe.

The Helsinki agreements, which indeed seal the status quo in Europe, have met with the strongest criticism on the German right: the west gave away legal claims and in return got vague promises, and at that not for its own interests but on behalf of dissenters and minorities in the Soviet empire. As was pointed out in Chapter 32, however, the agreements did not remain a dead letter but are frequently flourished before the oppressors of freedom as a new Magna Carta.

On the other hand, détente so far has not advanced SALT or the negotiations on reduction of troop levels in Europe. Rather, both Warsaw Pact and NATO forces in Germany have been increased. Although one does not speak anymore of the Cold War in polite society, the cold peace does not look so very different. Those who had anticipated wonders from *Ostpolitik* were deeply disappointed; some suspected that the break with the past had not been radical enough.

So when Brandt came home from his search for international peace, he received less than a hero's welcome. In fact, he had to face a rebellion of the young in his own party. The *Jusos* (Young Socialists— not a teenage group but a recruitment organization for future leaders) reopened the old criticism of coalition politics. Socialist students came up with blueprints for a new society; impatient members asked for extraparliamentary action. Whole series of radical literature were published by old, established publishing houses. And this movement was by no means confined to leftist sects. Even the "Young Democrats" and the "Young Union," under-thirty organizations affiliated with the FDP and CDU, respectively, appeared to be left of the government. "The Constitution should not be interpreted mainly as an instrument of defense against its enemies, but as a mandate to build a better society, to fill all the lacunae that still exist between the reality and the vision of the Constitution," said Wissmann, chairman of the *Junge Union*. Apart from the virtual takeover by Marxists of some universities or departments (*Fachbereiche*), riots had occurred in 1969 at the Frankfurt book fair; books by hated authors and publishers had been burned. The Socialist Students' League (SDS), which had been expelled from the SPD in 1960, conquered the National Students' League in 1970 and tried to convert it into a "Militant League for Socialism." The less radical Socialist University League (SHB), which the SPD now sponsored, also kept itself far to the left of the party and occasionally collaborated with Spartakus, the communist students' association. In Munich, Heidelberg, and other cities, *Jusos* and SHB succeeded in dominating the SPD locals' regular meetings and in denying reelection to socialist mayors who had become popular with middle-class voters (see page 337).

This wave of radicalism ran its course. The SPD leadership remained flexible enough to prevent the activists from leaving the party, and firm enough to retain the image of a "people's party." The radicals were left with the choice between "marching through the institutions" and disappearing in the ultraleft nirvana. At election time, all the left sects taken together, including the communists under a new name, again polled less than 1 percent of the vote. More significantly, the students have nowhere been able to influence the trade unions or to radicalize any substantial number of blue-collar workers: the workers kept faith with their old party.

In 1972, the voters gave the SPD-FDP coalition a margin of twenty-three seats—54.3 percent of the popular vote. In the north the victory was even greater, since Strauss's CSU carried Bavaria with 55 percent. The CDU was in a shambles and leaderless. An attempt by Rainer Barzel, the CDU candidate for the chancellorship, to unseat Brandt through a parliamentary intrigue was repulsed and discredited him with his own followers—regrettably, since Barzel might have reduced the far right within the party. In 1976 the impetuous Strauss renounced the thirty-year-old alliance of the Bavarian CSU with the CDU to found a party that would appeal to the more right-wing voters outside Bavaria in traditional CDU territory. The CDU then was led by a triumvirate consisting of the prime minister of Rhineland-Palatinate, Helmut Kohl, the able Professor Kurt Biedenkopf, who shrewdly came out for *Mitbestimmung* and social legislation, and a highly articulate diplomat, Karl Carstens.

In 1974 the CDU was to obtain a sad sort of satisfaction. Its constant warnings that the advocates of *Ostpolitik* were naive and, in particular, that Brandt was too trusting, were vindicated in a spectacular though frightening way. A certain Günter Guillaume—who was in charge of Brandt's personnel appointments and of his party liaisons—was unmasked as a DDR spy. The discovery was doubly embarrassing as there had been warnings; but in their anti-anti mood, those reponsible for the chancellor's security had made a point of not panicking. Brandt resigned—the more readily as his leadership, or lack of it, had lately been attacked by Wehner and other party dignitaries.

His successor was the sharp-witted and sharp-tongued Helmut Schmidt, who had gained experience in the Ministries of Defense and Finance. At the same time Heinemann, at 75, yielded the presidency to Scheel, who yielded the Foreign Office to the chairman of the FDP, Hans-Dietrich Genscher, a man without knowledge of foreign languages or foreign countries.

The Schmidt administration is one of technocrats; the chancellor is in the right wing of his party and more popular with industrialists than with trade unions. This is not altogether his fault. Expansion was over and unpleasant choices had to be faced. Schmidt was not responsible for the disasters that befell the west one after the other during his tenure: the Nixon administration's carelessness in dealing with allied governments, followed by the total paralysis of Washington in the throes of the Watergate crisis; the oil embargo in the Middle East war, and the subsequent tribute exacted by the OPEC monopoly; the lack of decisiveness in Paris during these crises; the coincidence of recession and inflation, with financial and monetary calamities in EEC countries.

All of this led to a crisis of confidence. Once again, state and nation were not at one. People with long memories saw ominous parallels with the fate of the Weimar Republic. While the Schmidt administration was acting as a financial fire brigade in the Common Market and exerting itself to help restore democracy in Greece, Portugal, and Spain, German intellectuals questioned its legitimation or proclaimed their estrangement through new theories: it was not the *Gammler* who disturbed law and order, but the prevailing order that was disturbing to adolescents, claimed sociologists and psychologists. In the theater and in the arts, too, these misgivings found poignant expression (see Chapter 34).

Students concluded from the theories of their sociology professors that they were living in a society of material constraints (*Sachzwänge*) whose established bureaucracy manipulated the lives of all citizens and forced them to "wear character masks" (*Rollenträger*). The neo-liberal, democratic form of "domination" was said to conceal a totalitarian structure of state monopoly capitalism (*Stamokap*). Reform action within this system would merely fortify its deception; therefore, "direct action" would have to force it to take off the mask of liberalism and democracy.

Jürgen Habermas and Horst Ehmke, both men of the left, have called the ideology of these desperadoes "left fascism" and have condemned their automatic anti-Americanism, blind Arabism, and anti-intellectualism. Horst Ehmke, who has pleaded for forbearance with some of the youthful excesses, nevertheless accused the New Left ideologists of taking "spite" attitudes just opposite the Social-Democratic position even though they may lead into absurd anti-democratic alliances. Unfortunately, their political isolation has also led them to acts of despair and terrorism and to unwitting service of outside powers—perhaps of international mobsters.

A series of terrorist attacks had been launched against the Federal Republic and especially against the Brandt government, which an insane gang had singled out as its pet villain. At the Munich Olympic Games they seized and killed the Israeli team; abroad they killed German diplomats and hijacked Lufthansa planes. The German branch of this international band (with Japanese, Palestinian, and Libyan connections) was the infamous Baader-Meinhof group, which committed kidnappings, bank robberies, and murders. Surprisingly, it elicited perverse sympathies among the intellectuals. Heinrich Böll used Ulrike Meinhof's life as a model in his novel *Katharina Blum*. Public demonstrations and lawyers' antics turned the monster trial of the gang into a circus which made the court look ridiculous and the government despotic. After the collective suicide of some of the terrorists, thousands came to their funeral, and for weeks the papers were carrying a debate on the tragic misunderstandings that led so many intelligent, nice middle-class kids astray. Society stood accused of having driven these criminals to their destruction. The discussion revealed that thousands who did not join the disciples of Nechaev nevertheless felt deep hostility against society and against the republic.

The alienation of students produced an executive order that may have helped to reduce radical activities at the universities, but at the same time has deepened that alienation. The order allowed authorities to investigate whether an applicant for a civil-service job was loyal to the constitution. Since every teacher and every judge, as well as every railway motorman, is a civil servant, opponents of the order charge that it amounts to a denial of employment (*Berufsverbot*) to radicals. At least among intellectuals, conservatives find themselves in a united front with radicals and liberals in opposing this abridgement of civil rights. The federal government therefore has abandoned the order, saying that the existing civil-service law is sufficient to screen applicants (see page 295).

As the result of all these developments, the government was losing its popular base. In the 1976 elections it squeezed through with a slim majority, largely on the strength of Schmidt's credit with the middle classes and thanks to the CDU's disorientation. But the SPD must once again worry about its relations with the trade unions. The workers were proud as long as they felt that it was their own chancellor who had opened the dialogue with the east; but the socialist peace resembles the capitalist war too closely. They are also proud of *Mitbestimmung*; but it has not increased the weekly paycheck. On the contrary, it may have saddled the unions with responsibility for an income policy that is obviously not liked by the workers. Moreover, miscalculation or mismanagement has put a strain on the civil-service pension fund, and while inflation eats away the value of the wages, workers are asked to give up fringe benefits or at least to postpone wage demands. Again, Schmidt may boast that "his" inflation is the mildest in the world; but to the consumer it is still inflation, and the trade unions are voicing their dismay.

The government has had to face criticism by the unions, and the union leaders have had to face wildcat strikes. It would be an exaggeration to speak of "radicalization" among union members. Even during the honeymoon of the Brandt government, union members judged the republic by the share of the product that came to them. Despite *Mitbestimmung* and fringe benefits, they still felt that their class was at the bottom of the pyramid. They appreciate improvements and expect a steady increase in the benefits of growth and technological progress. When these expectations are disappointed, they might not throw away what they have, as many did in the 1920s and 1930s, but instead defend it. The old issue of reform versus revolution will not reappear in this form. It has been said that "Bonn is not Weimar." Nor it the worker of 1977 the worker of 1927. The system is capable of absorbing conflicts; it may even need them.

Thus, communists may not again make great inroads into the SPD's working-class constituency, though they may win a shop-steward election here and there. But if the SPD finds itself in opposition it may pass into a more radical leadership. For its left wing, represented not only by the *Jusos*, is painfully aware that the SPD is once again acting as the physician of capitalism and defender of democracy instead of pursuing its own great reform aims. The Bonn republic, child of reeducation, anti-Nazism, and anticommunism, has developed the impulses of individual liberty and of free enterprise in relation to the state, but it has not yet developed the positive freedoms of social and economic association which would complete democracy.

TABLE 7. THE ECONOMIC MIRACLE IN FIGURES:
REAL SOCIAL PRODUCT PER CAPITA (BRD)

Year	In comparison with base year 1913 = 100	In comparison with England (as percentage of British income)
1900	80	68
1913	100	73
1925	100	72
1938	137	82
1950	118	65
1969	276	124
1977	549	117

Source: Statistisches Jahrbuch, BRD, recalculated.

TABLE 8. THE ECONOMIC MIRACLE IN FIGURES: NATIONAL
PRODUCT AND LABOR INCOME (BRD)

Year	Net national product (in billion marks)	Average yearly salary (in marks)
1950	75	3,200
1955	139	4,850
1960	230	6,900
1968	403	12,500
1977	877	24,000

Source: Statistisches Jahrbuch, BRD, recalculated.

TABLE 9. THE FIFTY LARGEST COMPANIES (BRD)

Year	Sales volume (in billion marks)	Percentage of total industrial sales
1954	37	25
1963	118	36
1967	360	42

Parliamentary government is a necessary condition of democracy, but not its goal. It originated in an era when the individual needed to assert his rights vis-à-vis the crown; today the problem is whether a sovereign nation can assert its overriding rights and interests vis-à-vis particular powers (pressure groups, corporations). Then, state and society were each acting upon the other from outside; today they are intimately interwoven, and neither can move without requiring support from the other as well as influencing it. In the process both lose their sovereignty, and especially democracy may no longer assume that its decisions can be imposed on the technological, bureaucratic, and corporate processes of economic development. The attempt to make the institutions human, modern, and democratic cannot be based on the assumption that all social factors are allied with each other and can ride on inherent trends of industrial growth.

The public expects the state to provide services—employment, security, health, housing, roads, etc.—which it cannot provide without planning. That means a certain degree of independence from the pushing and pulling of interest groups. Pluralism and respect of individual freedom cannot be totally reconciled with public welfare; the general will is not the will of all. Only extremists of the right or left have a pat answer to this dilemma. Social-Democrats and advocates of social liberalism must negotiate an obstacle course between the demands of freedom and the demands of public welfare. Not only may they fail to strike a happy balance; the attempt itself may be criticized as contradictory or, worse, as an evasion of decisive action. In a programmatic "perspective" the SPD therefore envisages both greater independence of the executive organs and intensified citizen participation in their decisions; less administration, and greater efficiency of the administration.

Participation must be seen in two ways: as satisfaction of a democratic need to control the decision makers, and as giving all citizens a sense of belonging to the republic. The West German state has always been considered a halfway house—part of neither a united Europe nor a united Germany—and its citizens still have not developed a nationalism of the BRD. Their identity, their first loyalty, is not with that country. Would participation give them a feeling of "we"?

This problem very often is presented in social terms: the West German state is seen as the servant either of international capitalism or of native corporations. The citizens do not see it as "their" state that they could influence by appropriate participation.

34

The Uncertain Trumpet

Geist in Postwar Germany

The writer acts by uncovering something: a common tone, a common passion, a hope, a joy, a threat that concerns all.

—Siegfried Lenz

WHAT DO GERMAN WRITERS OF THE PAST THIRTY YEARS tell us about common joys, threats, and hopes? The consciousness of a nation—its understanding of its history and destiny—is reflected and created by its mythmakers: historians, philosophers, poets, playwrights, and novelists. But the German writers who came home from the war, from exile, or from prisoner-of-war camps wanted anything but myths; they knew neither hope nor joy. The future looked dismal; and all values of the past had fallen to pieces.

All of them! The postwar generation would not even hear of Goethe and of other traditions that might have given it pride, something to hold on to. No—that, too, had been part of the web of lies. If the past was to be "overcome," no ideology would help. Culture, too, had to start from "point zero." The first business was "derubblization" (*Entrümpelung*) of the language, "clear-cutting" (*Kahlschlag*) of phraseology.

When Thomas Mann returned to celebrate the Friedrich Schiller bicentennial, he invoked the classics' purpose to "build new forms, purer principles, nobler morals—for the betterment of the human condition." But the younger writers no longer understood this message. "The flags that have been hoisted [after the Nazi rule] will not be our old banners but colored rags that have been sanctioned once again. We shall live in a world where all flags have died," said Alfred Andersch (an ex-communist). Wolfdietrich Schnurre put it more poignantly, and also more typically of the younger writers: "After long suffering, which he bore with heavenly patience, died, neither loved nor hated by anybody—God." The obvious allusion to Nietzsche makes the difference painfully clear: what once had been tragic is now sad. As though they had never heard of Nietzsche's other famous epigram, the new generation of Germans wanted to be free *from* all ideas but not free *for* any in particular.

Cool sobriety was the watchword. Günter Eich, who had not been known previously, won instant fame with a poem entitled "Inventory," which began:

> This is my cap,
> this is my coat,
> here is my razor
> in the bag of canvas. . . .

Wittgenstein's arid philosophy took the place of the flowery obscurantism that had been taught under the Nazis. Historians like Meinecke and Dehio revised the earlier perspectives of German history and criticized its heroes: there was no way back to a better past. Younger revisionists (Golo Mann, Fritz Fischer, Karl Bracher, Wolfang and Wilhelm Mommsen—great-grandsons of Theodor Mommsen) reduced the pretensions of the German *Geist* to the pursuit of power and material gain; to the coming generations of Germans they held out the more modest prospect of a nation that turns down world and political ambitions and does not seek its identity in delusions of past greatness. Formerly, such an attitude had been scorned as *Geschichtslosigkeit* (historylessness) or "Swissification." Under Allied supervision, school textbooks were rewritten to suggest a critical view of German history. Thomas Mann gave his own interpretation of Germany's frightening hubris and fall in his grandiose novel *Doktor Faustus*.

Reactions to this shattering comedown were different in the east and in the west. The Marxist perspective allowed DDR citizens to repudiate the capitalist-fascist heritage by accepting the Soviet regime, and at the same time to claim the worthy heritage of the German—and especially the Prussian—past, which conformed so well to the Spartan ideas of eastern socialism. The communist government adopted— rather unabashedly—usable pieces of history such as Frederick the Great and the War of Liberation (1813); its ideologists even tried to find the revolutionary spirit in the German classics.

The West Germans, by contrast, found little of the German past suitable for building an identity on; they had to seek roots or affinities in the "modern" developments of the western countries. Inevitably, therefore, the DDR and BRD found their respective cultural orientations, not to say role models, in the Soviet and western literature that

Germany had missed during the previous two decades.

West Germans eagerly absorbed the avant-garde works that poured in to fill the cultural vacuum, along with behaviorist research, communications science, supermarkets, discotheques, blue jeans, cool jazz, beat, and rock. European youth snapped up American fads and fashions. German writers and critics had to catch up on Genet, Sartre, and Faulkner or to renew their acquaintance with Kafka, Pirandello, Joyce, Proust, Hemingway, Dos Passos; with Döblin's *Berlin Alexanderplatz*, Brecht's "epic theater" and the *Three-Penny Opera*. Soon they were also to absorb abstractionism, the "theater of the absurd," reflected points of view, and other innovations of western "decadent" literature. German writers used their conceits as monitors to purge literature of clichés. Even in their rage, the postwar authors had to write soberly, analytically, taking nothing for granted, giving the reader no chance to identify with any hero or heroine (Brecht's *Verfremdungseffekt*), rejecting the temptation to impose their own feelings on the readers, or on the characters.

Indeed, the true objectives of postwar literature were not the obvious themes of recent experience, but suggestions of a new approach: distrust any Pied Piper, even the author. Beware of his eloquence. Do not assume that he is omniscient or that his story may be true. Distrust even the language—the very words that carry such a load of history. The novel acquired a new function: *umfunktionieren* (to change function) would soon become one of the most popular new words; for everything now could (or had to) be seen in new contexts and be made to serve new purposes. Thus, plain narrative was no longer acceptable; the story had to be told from different perspectives, or filtered through different consciences; the author had to let the reader decide what was true about the characters. Anyway, "literature," meaning entertainment, was taboo—and besides, how does one write about the Nazis without either demonizing or minimizing them? Straight narrative was left to lowbrows like Hans Kirst, whose *08/15* (with two spin-off volumes) was a best-seller but does not appear in histories of literature. As the *All Quiet on the Western Front* of World War II, it was not adequate to the enormity of the recent experience.

Besides, there was a personal reason for the new, cool style. Writers who were young when Hitler came to power—Richter, Andersch, Eich, Arno Schmidt, Schnurre—had enjoyed no youthful period of experimentation. They emerged after the war as activists and writers; many of them had been politically militant before 1933. They had no time, or they were not allowed, to be poets at an age when writers usually grow to maturity. They had no manuscripts hidden in their desks, and they viewed writing first of all as a political mission: overcoming the past, preaching new attitudes, reorienting the mind of Germany.

Perhaps it was natural that among those who published the first antiwar, anti-Nazi novels, many had been abroad—as Jews, as communists and socialists, as writers unable to collaborate. A few like Richarda Huch and Bergengruen had been "exiles at home." Some of them had been well known before Hitler—Brecht, Thomas and Heinrich Mann, Theodor Plievier, Anna Seghers, Zuckmayer—but many others had not been published in the Weimar period: Elias Canetti, Nelly Sachs, Stefan Andres, Wolfgang Koeppen, Stephan Hermlin, Hans Erich Nossack, Wolfgang Hildesheimer, Hilde Domin. A group of minor lights came from Moscow, led by Johannes R. Becher and Friedrich Wolf (whose *Professor Mamlock* had been a stirring anti-Nazi film). There were two children of exiles, Peter Weiss and Ilse Aichinger (who married Günter Eich). The founders of *Der Ruf*, Andersch and Richter, had been prisoners of war in the United States (see page 287), and Arno Schmidt a prisoner of war in England. A number of exiles chose not to return—Oskar Maria Graf, Erich Fried, Jakov Lind, Paul Celan (a Rumanian Jew living in Paris who was said to have written the finest German verses before he committed suicide), and Hermann Broch—but nevertheless rejoined the new German anti-Parnassus.

The impact of repatriated writers was reinforced by that of critics and philosophers like Hannah Arendt, the thinkers of the Frankfurt School, Hans Mayer, Ernst Bloch, and historians Carl Friedrich and Hans Rothfels. They mediated the process of catching up and strongly influenced the choice of literary subjects and the critique of the German past. Thus Celan became famous because of his "Death Fugue," Stefan Andres wrote the *Deluge* trilogy, Hermann Kasack *The City Beyond the River*, Arno Schmidt *Leviathan*, Richter *The Defeated*, Andersch *The Cherries of Freedom* and *Zanzibar*, Thomas Mann *Doktor Faustus* and *The Holy Sinner*—all concerned with the legacy of the Nazi episode and the problems of responsibility. Karl Jaspers—who, as an "exile at home," rejected the notion of collective guilt—nevertheless acknowledged "collective shame"; Hannah Arendt discovered "the banality of evil." Ralf Dahrendorf, the sociologist, whose father had been a Social-Democratic representative and was jailed by the Nazis, searched for the structures in German society and history that had favored the dictatorship. Younger writers who had grown up in Nazi schools were not content with easy condemnation of the guilty, but spoke of those who had suffered without resisting and those who had failed to look and see, of all those who had not cared enough to try to prevent the catastrophe. The first serious postwar movie was entitled *The Murderers Are Among Us*.

If we group the writers by generation, the procession will be led, obviously, by authors who had done their best work before the Nazis and saw no reason to change their style. Carl Zuckmayer in the west and Anna Seghers in the east, Ernst Jünger on the right and Döblin on the left, are typical of this generation. Zuckmayer, in *The Devil's General*, addressed himself realistically to the Nazi period, and he wrote a beautiful volume of memoirs. Anna Seghers wrote her moving *The Seventh Cross* in exile, returned to East Germany, and now follows the precepts of "socialist realism."

Another group of older writers learned from Joyce, Kafka, Döblin, or the expressionists. Canetti, Kasack, Koeppen, and Hans Henny Jahnn may be typical of this "Weimar avant garde," although they came to be recognized only after World War II. Spanning the generations are writers, either modern or traditional in manner, whose themes or inspirations are religious. Foremost among them are two women, the Catholic Elisabeth Langgässer and the protestant Ina Seidel. Stefan Andres, who spent the war in Positano, Italy, also belongs in this company of Christian mystics, while the younger Heinrich Böll developed his own militant and existentialist Catholicism. Both turned the critical shafts of their Christian conscience against the consumer culture of the Bonn republic.

The next generation is those who were between twenty-four and thirty-three years old in 1945—writers in search of new bearings. To this generation belong Arno Schmidt, Ilse Aichinger, Andersch, Schnurre, Peter Weiss, Böll; the poets Celan, Helmut Heissenbüttel, Hermlin, Karl Krolow, and Rudolf Hagelstange; and two Swiss authors, Max Frisch and Friedrich Dürrenmatt. These formed the core of Group 47; despite differences among themselves, they provided an audience for each other and created the postwar audience for their new attitude. Günter Grass, Enzensberger, Peter Rühmkorf, and Peter Handke were under twenty in 1945.

Some younger novelists engaged in a strenuous search for the roots of evil. Disdaining the easy ways of overcoming the past, they suggested that people were no better now than at the time of the Nazis. They also used modern techniques—Brecht's *Verfremdungseffekt*, Döblin's open novel, Hesse's reflective poetry, Benn's expressionism— to prevent their works from becoming a ritual through which a reader might vicariously purge himself of sin. Thus, Heinrich Böll used *The Opinions of a Clown* to confront his contemporaries with unpleasant truths, and Günter Grass created what must be the most obstreperous, obscene, and vile brat in world literature (*The Tin Drum*) to "tell it like it is." Martin Walser X-rayed postwar society in *Marriages in Philippsburg*; Siegfried Lenz earnestly taught his people a *German Lesson*, and returned to the theme in *The Model*. In his play *Time of the Guiltless*, he went beyond Zuckmayer's *The Devil's General*: the guiltless are manipulated by the guilty. Similar questions were asked by Max Frisch in *Andorra* and in the dead-serious farce *The Firebugs*, and by Walser in *Black Swan*. Koeppen showed the persistence of the fascist death wish in *Death in Rome*. Finally, the Vienna comic Helmut Qualtinger created *Herr Karl,* the adjustable man who can serve any regime and adopt any ideology. Their characters were all descendants of Brecht's Galy Gay (in *A Man's a Man*), who was transformed from peaceful husband to bloodthirsty soldier.

All this led to the criticism of postwar society, as in the works of Koeppen and Walser, Böll and Grass. Advocating commitment, Group 47 gave German literature and criticism a radical and satirical coloration. Some writers engaged in politics, too: Grass campaigned for Willy Brandt; Walser was converted to communism; Böll took part in the progressing radicalization of independent Roman Catholics. He has been called Germany's middle-aged angry man. He and Hans Magnus Enzensberger have defended the civil rights of terrorists.

"Commitment," of course, is not confined to leftists. Heissenbüttel and Hagelstange would be found on the right; Frisch, Richter, and Lenz in the center. But there can be little doubt that politics (in a larger sense, of course) is in the writers' field of vision, perhaps even more than in the 1920s—and all writers, whether right or left, are deeply concerned with preserving the unity of German literature and German language across the artificial border. This gives their politics a special "antipolitical," neutralist flavor.

Having grouped authors first by subject matter, then by age and politics, we must now mention their choice of country. (Inevitably, some names must appear on every list.) Many of the exiled intellectuals, whether from a desire to turn a totally new leaf or under the misconception that Nazism was just a tool of capitalism, first went to East Germany; but they soon found themselves harassed. Later on, many DDR writers fled to the west: philosopher Ernst Bloch, critics Hans Mayer and Alfred Kantorowicz, novelists Theodor Plievier, Hermann Kasack, and Uwe Johnson, and militant atheist Gerhard Zwerenz. Peter Huchel—poet and editor of the highbrow magazine *Sinn und Form*—wrote in 1972: "I left a country where people like me have only one freedom: to be alone—no mail, no travel, eight years of total isolation. A sad balance sheet, not just for myself." Wolf

WRITERS (WITH YEAR OF BIRTH)

1871 Heinrich Mann	1903 Peter Huchel	1920 Wolfdietrich Schnurre
1875 Thomas Mann	1905 Elias Canetti	1921 Ilse Aichinger
1877 Hermann Hesse	1906 Stefan Andres	1921 Wolfgang Borchert
1878 Alfred Döblin	1906 Wolfgang Koeppen	1921 Friedrich Dürrenmatt
1885 Ina Seidel	1907 Günter Eich	1921 Helmut Heissenbüttel
1886 Gottfried Benn	1908 Hans Werner Richter	1926 Ingeborg Bachmann
1888 Friedrich Wolf	1911 Max Frisch	1926 Siegfried Lenz
1891 Johannes R. Becher	1912 Hilde Domin	1927 Günter Grass
1891 Nelly Sachs	1912 Hans Hagelstange	1927 Martin Walser
1892 Theodor Plievier	1914 Alfred Andersch	1929 Hans Magnus Enzensberger
1894 Hanns Henny Jahnn	1914 Arno Schmidt	1929 Günter Kunert
1895 Ernst Jünger	1915 Stephan Hermlin	1929 Peter Rühmkorf
1896 Hermann Kasack	1915 Karl Krolow	1929 Christa Wolf
1896 Carl Zuckmayer	1916 Wolfgang Hildesheimer	1931 Rolf Hochhuth
1898 Bertolt Brecht	1916 Peter Weiss	1933 Reiner Kunze
1899 Elisabeth Langgässer	1917 Johannes Bobrowski	1934 Uwe Johnson
1900 Anna Seghers	1917 Heinrich Böll	1936 Wolf Biermann
1901 Hans Erich Nossack	1920 Paul Celan	1942 Peter Handke

Biermann, the world-famous songwriter, a brother to François Villon and Bob Dylan, was given a one-way exit visa. Stefan Heym and Stephan Hermlin were disciplined for failure to conform with socialist realism; instead, workers were called upon to take pen in hand and form "writing brigades" to celebrate the joys of building socialism. Anna Seghers, Arnold Zweig, and Friedrich Wolf—and even Brecht, who died in the DDR in 1956—did not produce any significant work under that regime. Peter Weiss "chose" the DDR after his *Marat/Sade* world success; but when he also celebrated Trotsky, his permit to stay was revoked. The literary commissars of the DDR, men like Becher, Bredel, and Erwin Strittmatter, fall under Hermlin's criticism: "In striving for a new aesthetics, they overstep their poetical talent and . . . destroy the substance and law of poetry." But even Strittmatter is now in trouble, after pleading for more sensitivity in poetry.

Only in most recent years has independent creativity received some encouragement in the DDR. Honecker has declared it desirable to discuss the limits of criticism and private expression that are permissible in a socialist country, and a few authors who otherwise are good communists have dared to write about commissars who are not heroes and about plans that fail, to show an individual fate as a function of social pressures. Thus Martin Stade, in *The King and His Fool*, describes how Gundling, a favorite of the art-loving Frederick I, became a toady and butt of crude jokes under his boorish successor, Friedrich Wilhelm I—a parable on the situation of writers in the DDR which nevertheless could be published. Still more surprising was *Half Time*, the diary of Franz Fühmann, an ex-Nazi who had become a pillar of the literary GPU and then suddenly began to ask whether socialist art can do without private myths. A former exile, Carl-Heinz Danziger, delivered a systematic attack on the entire literary establishment in his autobiographical novel *The Party Is Always Right*. Christa Wolf, in her very personal novel *Reflecting on Christa T.*, was sharply critical of regimented life, and she poured satire on mechanical recipes for happiness in *Practical Wisdom of a Tomcat*. Other writers emphasizing creativity are Volker Braun (his novel *Note: Simple Truth Is Not Enough!*), Reiner Kunze (*The Wonderful Years*—a best-seller in the BRD), Günter de Bruyn (*Buridan's Ass*). Honecker, while agreeing to debate with them, nevertheless warned them "not to impose your personal sorrows on society"—a reference to Ulrich Plenzdorf's satirical novel *The New Sorrows of Young Werther*. Hermann Kant showed in *Impressum* how difficult it is for a party worker to preserve common sense and a feeling for the workers. Kunze and the abrasive

Günter Kunert were exiled in 1977.

These authors discuss questions that must nag the most sincere among the leaders: how can we reconcile all this hypocrisy with our faith in the socialist future? How do we justify the sacrifice we are imposing on the people? It is true that many of these works reduce human problems to editorials about the proper conduct of an activist; but through clever devices the proclamations of faith are exposed as lies. A satirical poem by Kunert describes a man's adjustment to the conditions of a great flood: he managed to become a fish, "the water even shut off his speech," and now he fears that drought might force him to become a man again. The lesson is obvious, and western politicians should take note: dissident DDR writers are concerned with defending the integrity of their persons, not with overthrowing the regime. Christa Wolf, Biermann, Hermlin, and Huchel have made it clear that they are communists and consider their system superior to the best western model. They are pressing for reform within it, above all for personal freedom and for freedom of speech.

Whether orthodox or dissident, eastern intellectuals endow German history with a meaning. Through a Hegelian dialectic, capitalism, imperialism, and Nazism produced their antithesis, socialism, in the most developed country with the most humanist heritage in arts and sciences. The next generation will realize the synthesis of collectivism and the individual, of socialism and freedom, of equality and distinction, of efficiency and art. Marxism has always viewed Germany—its home—as its strategic key to world domination.

Nothing comparable appears in West German literature. But it, too, is concerned with personal freedom. Throughout the works of all German writers, no theme is as pervasive as the individual's autonomy vis-à-vis the demands of "mass society." In contrast to DDR literature, no western writer praises efficiency and collectivism. Former communists, like Andersch and Koeppen, are the most outspoken critics of organization men and their ideologies. As against earlier self-interpretations, and against Group 47's original, socialist ideology, opposition to the establishment is no longer conceived in narrowly political terms but as the human protest against big organization, against alienation and reification—the old romantic rejection of technology—often in a newly found Marxist or neo-Marxist terminology. After the shame of Nazism came the shame of the economic miracle, of affluence, of expediency and calculability, of "Americanism," rearmament, and NATO. In opposition, West German writers tend to equate Germany's unity with the integrity of the human person, and withdrawal from world politics with development of the self.

In other words, this opposition is existentialist more than political. The world it sees and criticizes is Kafkaesque. The character speaking for the author is constantly fleeing, or crushed by conditions beyond his control. He cannot change the world; but he cannot escape it or even understand it. "Man asks his questions," Hildesheimer says, "but the world remains silent." Hilde Domin asks whether poetry still has a function in a manipulated (*gesteuert*) society.

This same estrangement is evident in Nossack and Andersch; but the experience is by no means confined to writers who lived through the Nazi ordeal. It is obvious in Dürrenmatt and Frisch—both Swiss, and not Jewish either. Frisch's *Stiller* and *Homo Faber*, just like Nossack's d'Arthez (in *The d'Arthez Case*), seek to hide their selves behind new identities.

They all suffer from *Lebensangst, Weltangst, Existenzangst* (fear of the world, of existence). Earlier, the theme of anxiety had played a great role in Heidegger's philosophy and in the literature of the 1920s. In a 1930 lecture, Heinrich Mann called it the predominant problem of capitalist decadence: "Man wants certainty, but we see nothing certain before us." Neither the Nazis nor World War II nor the atomic threat were needed to suggest an "end-of-the-world" panic as it appears in many postwar novels and plays. Andersch and Nossack promise to make the reader doubt the reality of the world. Lenz assures us that "it is only doubt that makes life tolerable." Peter Weiss confesses that "Auschwitz is the place where I belong." Dürrenmatt finds that "freedom today is possible only as sacrifice."

In such a world interaction is hard to conceive; most modern writers have difficulty constructing a plot and maintaining or developing a character. They escape into picaresque episodes (Grass) that take place in basically static environments. Dürrenmatt is not interested in the old man or in his jilted old love (*The Visit*) but only in the structure of the village that permits the one to buy the murder of the other. Walser's heroes (if they deserve that name at all) are so small in stature that the slightest involvement with the world either overwhelms or corrupts them. Where a generation ago Fallada's "Little Man" still was fighting back and asking "What now?" (see page 161ff.), the little man in Koeppen's novels is altogether passive and content to state that this society is sick all over. Where Brecht confronted his characters with problems whose solution was suggested to the audience, Dürrenmatt and Frisch doubt that the theater can teach anybody anything—except, perhaps, that "one cannot save the world but must endure it." While even expressionism had not despaired of the poet's mission to give sense and meaning to a world that might be temporarily out of joint, Dürrenmatt, Böll, Grass, Manfred Bieler, Peter Handke, Weiss, and other German authors seem to agree with Samuel Beckett that only fools are sane.

A similar attitude pervaded the *Lebensgefühl* (feeling for life) of postwar adolescents—especially their fringes, the *Gammler* and the beatniks. When Helmut Schelsky and Gerhard Sanden studied the youth of the first postwar decade, they found a "skeptical generation," deeply aware of the insecurities of modern life and profoundly distrustful of ideologies, conformist and averse to strong commitments, cool to romanticism and prematurely sophisticated, dedicated to the sober business of personal advancement and therefore interested in techniques rather than ideals, a generation that had learned that "everything is either illusion or hoax" and therefore tried to camouflage its true feelings. Though they did not agree with the values of society, family, and government, they considered it impractical to wax passionate about suffering and oppression. Instead of fighting for freedom, they developed private strategies for beating the system. Germany's angry young men were at the same time cagey—but that was unlikely to last.

It is remarkable that on the basis of this analysis in the 1950s, Schelsky predicted the student outbreaks of the 1960s. Private unconcern erupted in public demonstrations, rebels without a cause struggled to get the system off their backs. The students embraced philosophies that confirmed the anthropologists' and psychologists' observation that "it is order that bothers the adolescents." They adhered to existentialism or picked up misunderstood phrases from the neo-Marxist anarchism of the Frankfurt School: alienation, emancipation of the whole man, "oppressive tolerance," manipulated freedom, raising of consciousness. But actually they were motivated by "a heightened sense of their bodies, a motoric excitability" (Schelsky) that led to rowdyism and secessionism, motorcycle rampages, and academic rioting. These attempts to break out of the system mistook themselves for political revolution; but in retrospect we can say that they were merely another way of protesting against the "lack of meaning." Like the writers, the protesters were asking the technocentric society to protect their privacy against arrogant intrusion. Their most significant rationalization has been Herbert Marcuse's "great refusal"—negation as a value and purpose in itself without any relation to a cause. (The *Ohne mich* attitude is international: every Italian movie seems to say *No me frego*, I don't care.)

Almost all literature of the postwar era either deals directly with this problem or is based on the premise that it cannot be solved. This is not the familiar German father-son drama, or is only partly so. Novel and theater no longer deal with the Oedipal situation, for the father's authority is breaking down anyway. Both philosophy and belles lettres suggest the absence of strong father images and of authoritarian ideas. The West German state has not produced what German political philosophy calls state consciousness, or identification with authorities. In the absence of a superego the social commands have not been internalized, and as a result the egos have not developed strong individualities. They are conscious of their vulnerability, unsure of themselves and of the world, hence capable of great conformity or of undisciplined drifting. The state is not held together by ideas and values held sacred by all its citizens. The new German film also suggests that youth suffers from the absence of fathers rather than from their overweening authority. Ideals, this generation has learned, are mere symbols manipulated by clever pipers in quest of power. They do not stem from, or rest upon, inherited and assured standards. The writer's task is to debunk them, not to exalt them.

Beauty and meaning, too, have gone. "Is it not barbarous to write poems after Auschwitz?" asked Theodor Adorno. Younger German poets answered "no"—by writing barbarous poems drenched in contempt, fear, and suspicion of the world and of man. It is true that writers like Böll and Andersch or poets like Ingeborg Bachmann spoke of a new "aesthetics of humanism"—only to characterize its aim as "showing the disfigured face of man."

The stress is here on "disfigured." Man's real face cannot be seen. In contrast to the writers of the pre-Hitler generation, the modern writer no longer pretends to know what perhaps his characters don't know—some higher truth, some inner beauty. On the contrary, he reveals that those who pretend to know more are either self-deceived or imposters. It is true that people always try to make sure of something; but Nossack hunts that illusion down, makes the reader unsure, the world "uninsurable" (*unversicherbar*).

Such doubts have consequences. If outside reality is a dream, then the dreamer cannot be sure of himself either. Max Frisch's narrator in *A Wilderness of Mirrors* tries out various roles and names, like costumes, while he is settling on the story. Uwe Johnson has only assumptions about his hero (in *Assumptions about Jacob*), and never discerns the truth; he changes the speaker or the place in the middle of a sentence. Grass telescopes various stories into each other and lets the reader guess when he changes from reality to fantasy, from the actual to the imagined character. Although realistic detail is abundant, the reader's willingness to suspend disbelief is frequently exposed to severe strain.

Every novel therefore has more than one dimension or layer. Straight narrative is considered old-fashioned and unsophisticated. If a serious author like Lenz seems to use traditional techniques, the critics will be quick to find hidden understructures, or the author himself will point out that reality must be built up from imagination. The resulting style has been called "magic realism." It assumes that while the world must be construed, the building materials are not the so-called "facts"—which themselves are mere interpretations—but the state of our consciousness, language, the games people play.

Heissenbüttel ridicules "the human heart," whose description he calls "the lowest rung of entertainment literature." He "relegates [all] eternal values and criteria to the attic of superstition." Literature can no more be a "reflection" of something real than our senses reflect the real world. The world must be created out of the materials of language. This literature flees from humanism. The writer seems to be playing with the creations of his imagination, which must not necessarily have referents in reality.

The process has been pushed to extremes by some younger authors, like Hildesheimer, Walser, and the Austrian Peter Handke. For some of them, like Ingeborg Bachmann or Paul Celan, "pushing one step beyond the limit" of traditional literature, language itself has become the subject matter of writing (or rather, the inability to use it has become an additional dimension); finally, language no longer signifies but is made to form patterns and figures. Some of these experiments, as the author and critic Walter Jens charged, result in Byzantine games. Others help control and criticize the whole reified and cliché-ridden world of communications that besieges the mind of modern man—not just "the masses," who are all too often blamed for accepting what the elite has prepared for them.

All this literature has a strong streak of parody which seeks to disestablish and demythologize. The younger practitioners of the art—Hans Magnus Enzensberger and Peter Rühmkorf, for instance, both immensely gifted and playful—but also Grass, Böll, and Lenz, use these linguistic techniques to expose the mental habits of the affluent society. Ingeborg Bachmann and Peter Handke combat romantic notions of love or of personality. Böll demystifies power, public relations, professional jargon, patriotism. Uwe Johnson, whose eternal subject is divided Germany, in *Two Views* shows how language and mores separate two lovers from each other.

But while it is easy to shoot at national monuments, the most grandiose myth is the ego, the supposed "I" of a hero or narrator. Not by accident did the 1960s produce such interesting books by paranoiacs and on paranoia; not by accident is all this contemporaneous with the structuralists' and existentialists' linguistic explorations. The romantic myth of the omnipotent, world-destroying, and world-creating artist is dying; the artist seems to be a mere spokesman for the medium. The language is no longer seen as an instrument ready to be used by a sovereign intelligence residing in an individual; that intelligence is shown to derive its purposes from the language.

Above, we suggested that the political impotence of both the West German writers and the student rebels is related to the lack of healthy ego development in their protagonists. No tragedy is possible where instead of hubris the author posits accidents, instead of human error the blind working of a machine. Arno Schmidt is so fascinated by the materialism of the world that his characters are incapable of changing it; they can only rage against its invincible power. His outbreaks are pseudorevolutionary because he no longer believes in revolution. Nor do all the enfants terribles of postwar letters: Peter Weiss rhymes revolution with copulation; Dürrenmatt's Anabaptist leader wonders why people follow him; Nossack is "a lone-wolf guerrilla"; Andersch has progressed "from revolution to inversion."

Even the avowed radicals are not serious. Enzensberger periodically goes "into exile," whence he sends well-paid reportages to the magazines he despises. His own magazine *Kursbuch* (*Timetable*) was as much a part of the establishment as is the entire counterculture—so he left it. His own poetry is very learned, and he translates from eight languages. Aside from deeply despairing poems full of disgust and lament, he has also written some tender verse offering some small hope that poetry is possible in our age. In an essay on Pablo Neruda he deplored the error of making poetry a tool of politics; on the contrary, "We are waiting, perhaps in vain, for the poet who will neither betray poetry for the sake of his audience nor his audience for the sake of poetry, and for whom poetry is not the handmaiden of politics but politics the handmaiden of poetry, that is to say of man."

Most German writers would subscribe to this opinion. Few would claim that art has no relationship to politics or to some notion of the truth. All consider themselves moralists. But they are not, nor do they wish to be, mythmakers. They do not sing of heroes or ideas. They proclaim their dissatisfaction with the status quo blindly, not knowing what lies behind the door at which they are hammering.

Yet the source of their dissatisfaction is precisely the lack of ideals in the BRD—"a land without mysteries," says Andersch; no place for poets, complained Eich and Huchel. The classical formula of antagonistic coexistence between *Geist* and *Macht* cannot be revived to force coexistence between imagination and the economic miracle. Either the writers criticize a reality that does not respond to their spiritual aspirations, or they talk of the various strategies they are using to isolate their better from their everyday selves. They also deplore and attack collaboration with the established order—and the better a writer is "established," the more he fears the establishment. He does not express the fears and hopes of the society that sustains him, but he does not represent its future either.

In the long run, a society cannot be at war with a substantial section of its intellectuals. Herbert Marcuse's definition of art as the negative will not hold—if only because the present society of affluence and tolerance is capable of absorbing the nonrevolutionary opposition. The artists no longer find new frontiers to break open. They recognize that they are playing a game—just the thing they were accusing society of. The cycle of ever-renewed secessions somehow comes to a stop after eighty years of trying to catch up with itself. There are signs pointing to a new style of objectivity. Perhaps they indicate a reconciliation of the artists with reality, perhaps a stabilization of the republic.

If we were to look for one leitmotiv in serious writing and serious art of the postfascist era, it would be the fight against clichés, assigned roles, and predigested reality. Again and again audiences are confronted with the charge that they have betrayed their true self—or lost it in the confusion of living. But what is this self? Previous generations may have called it "humanity" with some deliberate ambiguity, and imagined they found it in some antique model or in the alleged "essence" of man, in the law of nature, in the all-pervasive majesty of reason. This century discovered that "man makes himself" or, better, that man has to invent himself—a dangerous, perhaps an illusory rope act in which that which is sought and supposed to be found must in the same act be created. The artists are showing us the building materials but not telling us what to do with them. Hence, in contrast to earlier times, the work of art no longer presents to us a view of the whole; it remains fragmentary, aphoristic.

What one writer, Schnurre, has said of one of his novels may be true of all German literature today: it is not a wide river of creative imagination but a landscape of ponds. It would be difficult to attribute to it a basic tendency or style. It does not form a school. Even Group 47 disbanded in 1977 after having agonized for a decade. Yet it seems to have a few recurrent themes or problems, all interrelated: the difficulty of knowing oneself and knowing what one's world is made of; alienation and involvement; the problematic nature of action; the dialectics of communication; the meaning of freedom.

*   *   *

LACK OF MEANING, OR OF THE FEELING THAT LIFE IS MEANINGFUL, determines the direction of religion, philosophy, and the natural and social sciences. While significant progress is being made in our knowledge of the world, our environment, and our social and political reality, in the second half of the century the western mind has not produced a grand theory in any field. Systems, or attempts at system-building (such as existentialism, structuralism, crisis theology, neo-Thomism, and neo-Marxism), have rather exposed the need for an all-encompassing theory, or perhaps the yearning for metaphysical grounding.

Even in the field of physics—the model of all science in the great tradition of Galileo—Einstein was the last even to try for a unified field theory. Those who came after him were satisfied with step-by-step enlargements of our insight; their ingenious hypotheses certainly increased our understanding of nature, but at the same time each of them brought up more questions than they answered. So far, there has been no great Copernican breakthrough which would dare to explain all phenomena. On the contrary, the prevailing philosophy and methodology of science is "positivistic": i.e., it deliberately refrains from grand theory.

Nevertheless, both the pure and popular science always strive to explain "last things," to open vistas toward ontology and ethics, to break out of the confining rigidity of positivist science. This is even more true of the social sciences, where knowledge is supposed to lead to action. There positivism and systems analysis have come under sharp attack, especially from the Frankfurt School of neo-Marxists: Max Horkheimer and Theodor W. Adorno wrote *The Eclipse of Reason* and *The Dialectics* (i.e., the self-liquidation) *of the Enlightenment*; Jürgen Habermas, a younger member of the school, exposed *Science and Technology as Ideology*. But it is in the nature of Marxism to be "critique" rather than a closed philosophy, and Herbert Marcuse, the philosopher of the student rebellion, stressed "The Negation"— the exact opposite of the discredited "system" of positive sciences that Marxism had become in the hands of Lenin and his disciples. Ernst Bloch, too, the one-time expressionist and Marxist philosopher who had come to West Germany from Leipzig, East Germany, offered no concrete solution but only his *Principle of Hope*. Neither of these thinkers was able to give the new generation that metaphysical certitude which a great movement needs to justify its actions, and no wonder that in their old age these thinkers themselves returned to religion.

Neither positivism nor orthodox Marxism or revisionism seemed to provide guidance. For a brief moment after World War II, it had seemed that existentialism might fill the vacuum. But where it seemed to support activism, it turned out to be a fad, and where it was serious philosophy, it, too, offered a method rather than a system of thought. It did leave a deep imprint, however, on German literature in the postwar era. Though no one will be able to show that the themes and problems were suggested to the writers by existentialist philosophy, the latter did provide the novelists with a vocabulary that helped them to express certain problems, as we found in our survey of postwar novels. Martin Walser's latest novella, *The Fleeing Horse*, is a good example of a theme which Hemingway treated without any knowledge of existentialism but which now could be stated anew in terms of that philosophy. However, existentialism works rather like a dowsing rod, in contrast to older philosophies which pretended to be maps of the terrain one was going to explore. It is not designed to solve the metaphysical and ethical problems which it poses. It may lead some to a religion that brings salvation but it is not, as some had thought, a substitute for such a religion.

We are then led back to the churches or at least to informal religion. Germany, too, had its "God is dead" movement, and the churches are trying to find their place in the "secular city." The movement for adaptation to the conditions of life in the twentieth century is irresistible. When we study the religious press, we find regular features devoted to the topic "God and the World," discussions on the admission to the priesthood of women and homosexuals, debates on abortion, indications of a positive involvement of the church in social affairs and, above all, concern for the poor of the overseas world. All very good—but precisely the more that churches are losing themselves in mundane affairs, the less they seem to offer that which had been their original and principal mission—salvation. That the masses are seeking a counterpoint against the demands of the world is certain—for church attendance has increased, especially in the east. Yet we see no theological movement in either part of Europe.

The great religion of the twentieth century, to be sure, is social science. Germany is no exception: social research and social theory are flourishing at the universities and in the popular magazines. Publishers find it profitable to print millions of paperbacks on social philosophy. At conventions the scholars quarrel about techniques of social engineering and guidance. Yet no school of thought so far has projected a model so convincing that it could imbue the republic with a public philosophy. (This is true even in East Germany, where no one takes Marxism very seriously any more.) Nor has either part of the country produced a grand view of history that might lead the nation together again or light up the arduous path toward Europe.

Other concerns, however, enliven postwar historiography. Beginning with *The German Catastrophe* by Friedrich Meinecke, dean of German historians, the German self-image has been revised, the main lines of nationalist history have been criticized, a larger outlook on world history has been achieved. Specific controversies have raged over the foundations of Bismarck's Reich, the German war aims in World War I, the Treaty of Versailles, the prospects of the Weimar Republic and the significance of its culture, the responsibilities for bringing the Nazis to power, the nature of National Socialism and the character of its leader, the meaning of the July 20, 1944, uprising, and *Ostpolitik* (see bibliography). All of these topics involve a new conception of Germany's place in European history. There also has been more research on heretics and rebels in German history, and the Marxist school has thrown new light on some interesting relationships between history and literature. Yet again, these revisions and retouchings have not resulted in a new grand view of history.

Hegel defined history as "progress in the consciousness of freedom." Has this principle been realized in Germany? If by freedom we mean the permission to "sing like the bird," the answer is yes. If freedom means the mastery of the human condition, we are reminded of the other Hegelian principle—that freedom can be realized only in the continued struggle for it. As long as this struggle goes on, there is hope. As Paul Celan says:

> Therefore
> temples still stand. One
> star
> may send light
> Nothing
> nothing is lost.

Postscript

Woe to the age that needs heroes.
—Brecht

FROM TIME TO TIME historians must take stock of their knowledge and present a new view of "what really happened" (to use Leopold von Ranke's famous formula). In writing a new German history, therefore, my first task was to summarize the present state of scholarship. Beyond that, however, a new age has a different conception of what was important. Events that once dominated the headlines did not make a lasting impact; others, less noticed by contemporaries, wrought important changes in the structure of society. Thus our attention must shift from political and military to the social and cultural events, and a new "mix" of significant trends in the various fields of national endeavor will necessarily require a reevaluation of the whole.

The attempt to make sense of a national history, to find some coherence or inner logic in it, will result in a different view and a different style for each generation of historians; this, in turn, may shed new light on individual phenomena. For a national history should be more than a collection of monographs. Whether I have succeeded in integrating all aspects of German history I must leave to the reader's judgment.

Here I shall discuss only a few problems that arose in the course of work. As in my European history of the same period, *The Fall and Rise of Europe*, I have found it useful to refer to popular culture and lowbrow art as often as to the highest products of the human mind; for however great the latter may be, they often are not representative of the contemporary state of consciousness. Some writers and artists who in my youth were hailed as leaders are all but forgotten; but as a rule I have included their works rather than those that posthumously emerged as immortal. The latter I chronicled at the time of their recognition rather than their creation.

Similar considerations have guided my treatment of artists, writers, and philosophers, even of scientists. In a survey of cultural history that aims to integrate itself into the general stream of national history, it is obviously impossible to discuss the true meaning—or even to describe comprehensively—the whole work and final significance of each writer or thinker, nor is this book the place to trace the history of each important idea. In contrast to the history of ideas, a cultural and sociological history must be concerned with the reception and popular effect of those ideas and their impact on or relation to the general development of the national culture and of the public mind. Even misunderstandings or gross vulgarizations are of greater consequence in some cases than an author's "true meaning," which might have been recognized only by the few or unearthed only by the diligent research of more recent scholarship. Thus, for instance, Nietzsche's impact had to be presented by the lights of people whom he certainly would have despised, and the Marx who launched a worldwide movement was not the sentimental utopian whom students of his unpublished manuscripts have reconstructed.

This leads me to a second observation on intellectual history. It is often assumed that artists, writers, and philosophers have a presentiment of their age or, at the least, "reflect" its image more truly than, say, advertisements or editorials. I do not make such an assumption. Artists may create the mood of a culture, or they may lag behind it, or they may even be "alienated" from it and resist it. In the last case, they are apt to suggest that the age as a whole is "alienated" or (as a recent school suggests) that only the fools are sane.

To believe that the artist expresses anything but his own reaction to his age, however, is to miss the real problem. There are indeed ages in which *Geist* (philosophy and art) is at one with the aspirations of the people, is perhaps their spokesman or indeed their prophet; at other periods the two are at war, and this may be both symptom and cause of a deep crisis. No doubt such a divorce between the intellectuals and the nation has occurred in our century, and most certainly this falling-out has characterized the crisis of our time. A nation's relationship with its professional mythmakers—writers, poets, philosophers, theologians, and historians, among others, more recently joined by certain scientists, psychologists, sociologists and popularizers, journalists, agitators, etc.—is unlike that with other classes which leave less visible monuments to posterity, and therefore must be studied with especially critical care.

In judging the Weimar period, for instance, one must not be blinded by the brilliance of its intellectual lights, which have induced later historians to paint that period in colors never seen by the vast majority of its contemporaries. Conversely, the caviling, querulous tone of much contemporary writing in Germany and on Germany has given the Federal Republic a bad reputation—even its achievements are held up against it in some quarters. The present study has tried to place both the Weimar and Bonn republics into historical perspective. The Bonn republic has mastered some problems that ruined the Weimar republic. But its intellectuals seem to look back to Weimar with longing.

Germany has come a long way through these last hundred years— from imperial hubris to partnership in a European association, from a class society to a welfare state, from military heroes to the pursuit of happiness, from the fantasy of the master race to the acceptance of defeat and partition. It was not a straight path, but one lined with temptations that led the nation astray, causing it to turn its back on the heritage of European civilization. Friedrich Meinecke asked whether it was an aberration or a misfortune—*Irrweg* or *Unglücks-weg*—whether national socialism has a place in German history or can be forgotten. Those who came after him spent the labors of a generation to overcome their past, and in the process learned to accept their present—the loss of territory that had once been settled by the Teutonic knights and ruled by German kings; the division of the nation that had once fought for its unity under the black, red, and gold republican banner; dependence of the two parts on larger international blocs, the passing of the helm of history into other hands, the diminution of sovereignty.

Germans are living now in six countries: apart from the Federal Republic and the German Democratic Republic, they live in Austria, Luxemburg, Switzerland, even in France. They belong to the NATO bloc, to the Warsaw Pact, and to the neutrals; they are the strongest, most active and most enthusiastic partner of the European Economic Community; they have taken a hand in saving Mediterranean countries for democracy—is their partition perhaps to be interpreted as a device of Providence? Has it been their lot to be divided so that they can play a role in unifying the rest of Europe?

German postwar historians have taken comfort in the thought that German history may after all have a meaning—that the arrogant reach for world domination which ended in a tragic fall nevertheless bequeathed to this nation a mission. Others have taken a more apocalyptic view of this same sense of "chosenness": have not Germans, again and again, in the excesses of their wars of religion and in the excesses of world politics, in the radicalism of their philosophies and in the boldness of their views of history, tasted the depths of every aberration? If Germany was not the cradle of every heresy, it was the antichrist of all other nations. Thus, in a perverse way, some providential meaning can be read into the German catastrophe and give support to the critique of the middle-class mentality which prevails on both sides of the wall. The young activists protest against the utilitarian spirit, the lack of commitment; and indeed most citizens of the Federal Republic look at the political structures in present-day Europe as mere practical arrangements with little ideological content.

International agencies do not seem to take the place in people's hearts that was once held by the national state. They do not inspire the same kind of loyalty and they do not embody ideals of similar intensity. I have quoted the distich in which Friedrich Schiller admonished his countrymen never to build a nation; instead, he counseled, they should "strive to be freer as men." His cosmopolitan, humanist, and humanitarian ideal happens to coincide today with the national aim of the Germans as people—they will be able to communicate once more across the wall only if freedom of movement, expression, and exchange is restored in the east. If the rivalry between the two states can be defused, the cold war overcome by détente, and a new generation grows up without the ideologies of hate and mission, then the movement of people, goods, and ideas may eventually remove the barriers between nations and systems. "Silent history" may then do its work: just as German culture once forged a national unity across dynastic, regional, and religious differences, so the European spirit may overarch the ideological, economic, and national differences that still obstruct the movement toward unity.

In recent years the movement toward West European unity has lost momentum; a common currency will not be introduced as early as had been envisaged, and a genuine European parliament is still far away in time. Nothing in the preceding history points to an automatic, predetermined goal of history; just as German unity had to be willed and won, European unity will not come by itself but must be planned and fought for against both inside and outside resistance. The arguments in its favor are reason and necessity; but these alone, even with the help of silent history, are not enough to make actual what can be discerned only as a potential now.

One argument for European unity is the community of its interests vis-à-vis the Third World. The BRD has inherited the guilt of white western colonialists, and it is bound to respond in solidarity with the industrialized nations to the demands of raw-materials producers for a New International Economic Order. It has contributed generously, with capital and know-how, to development aid; it has its own version of the Peace Corps; and it has agreed to the stabilization of import payments from developing countries (the Lomé Convention of 1973 between the Common Market and certain African, Pacific, and Caribbean countries). Its yearly budget of bilateral and multilateral grants-in-aid amounts to three to four billion marks, compared to less than one billion by the DDR. The latter supports the New International Economic Order and votes in the United Nations for resolutions favoring the Third World at the expense of the capitalist countries. But in the long run, these political gestures will not liberate COMECON from the demands of the world's surplus population.

Two world wars have ended European predominance in the world, but they have not liquidated the heritage of distrust and of racial strife. Europe is no longer the model of development for other continents, and some of the developing nations may well decide to go their own ways. While commercial and technological interdependence is increasing, the continents may actually move apart, and Europeans may have to remember what they have in common and what unites them—not necessarily in contestation with other continents, but in differentiation from them.

The German school of historicism, which goes back to J. G. Herder, has always celebrated the variety of peoples within the unity of their cultural advance. The ideologies that claimed a providential role for the German nation are now recognized as aberrations from the chosen path of European culture. German historians no longer look back to Barbarossa and Frederick the Great; if they look back to Bismarck, it is only to compare his rationality with Hitler's immoderation. For the first time those whose calling it is to review the nation's past and its myths are critical of their history; they help the Germans to redefine their place in Europe and in the world.

At the end of our survey, we cannot draw the likeness of a German self-image for the end of this century, as we did for its beginning. The divided nation has no identity and neither half can define itself now without referring to the framework of a larger culture. Our survey of four generations has shown that national habits and ideas can change, that opinion can be molded, that social and political goals are flexible. A nation that once took pride in being apolitical and individualist was seized by a paroxysm of political enthusiasm, and then fell back into the pursuit of private happiness. A nation reputed to be obedient to authority became critical and self-doubting. A nation that only a generation ago seemed to be dedicated to the life ot the state is now devoting all its energies and thoughts to the diverging interests of groups and individuals.

Inevitably, the problems of such a society also are likely to multiply—be it because of the variety of interests or because their conflicts are allowed in the open. The Weimar republic failed to meet this challenge; the Bonn republic is better equipped to master the difficulties.

Bibliography

THE HISTORICAL LITERATURE IN THE GERMAN LANGUAGE is immense and should be looked up in special monographs. In the interest of saving space, I shall confine this survey to books available in English, although, of course, my own research has been based on German sources. In some cases a translation of a German book is available only in a British edition; these are indicated by the place of publication. I have not included memoirs, general biographies, or most government and international agency reports, which can easily be located in public libraries.

Translations from current newspapers and magazines are published in the weekly *German Tribune* and *Aussenpolitik—Foreign Affairs Quarterly* (Übersee Verlag, Hamburg). The government of the Federal Republic issues a yearly booklet, *Germany Today*, with excerpts from its statistical yearbook. The German Information Center in New York is equipped to provide background material. Diplomatic documents have been collected by the U.K. Foreign Office for the 1898-1914 period in *British Documents on the Origins of the [First World] War* (ed. Gooch-Temperley, 1926-1930) and by the U.S. Department of State for 1918-1945 in *Documents on German Foreign Policy* (Washington, D.C.: Government Printing Office, 1949 ff.). Also useful are Louis Snyder's *Documents of German History* and *Chronicle of German History*, both published by Rutgers University Press (New Brunswick, N.J.: 1958 and 1968).

Since the present history can refer only briefly to the context of European and world events, it is advisable to read for background a work whose horizon is wider—e.g., my own *The Fall and Rise of Europe* (1975) or George Lichtheim's *Europe in the Twentieth Century* (1972), both from Praeger Publishers, New York.

To place recent German history into the context of the preceding century, I recommend K. S. Pinson, *Modern Germany* (New York: Macmillan, 1959), and Hans Kohn, *The Mind of Germany* (New York: Charles Scribner's Sons, 1960). An abstract of comprehensive German works is found in Sigmund Neumann, ed., *Modern Political Parties* (Chicago: University of Chicago Press, 1960). Also useful are

Gwendolyn Carter and John Herz, *Government and Politics in the Twentieth Century* (New York: Praeger Publishers, 3rd ed., 1973) and William Andrews, ed., *European Politics* (New York: Van Nostrand Reinhold Co., 1969). Slightly different from my own approach are two good but less comprehensive accounts: A. J. Ryder, *Twentieth Century Germany* (New York: Columbia University Press, 1973), and Gordon Craig, *From Bismarck to Adenauer* (Baltimore, Md.: Johns Hopkins University Press, 1958).

The following books reflect the postwar effort to "overcome the past": Ludwig Dehio, *Germany and World Politics* (New York: W. W. Norton & Co., 1967); Hans Kohn, ed., *German History—Some New German Views* (New York: Foreign Policy Association, 1954); and Friedrich Meinecke, *The German Catastrophe* (Boston: Beacon Press, 1950).

A similar effort governs Golo Mann's *German History in the Nineteenth and Twentieth Centuries* (New York: Praeger Publishers, 1968) and the works of the late Hajo Holborn, a German-born Harvard historian.

*   *   *

CHAPTER 1: The best overall view is Ralf Dahrendorf, *Society and Democracy in Germany* (Garden City, N.Y.: Doubleday & Co., 1968). Three good but somewhat dated economic histories are W. F. Bruck, *Economic and Social History of Germany 1888-1938* (New York: Russell and Russell, 1962); John Clapham, *The Economic Development of France and Germany 1814-1914* (New York: Cambridge University Press, 1935); and Gustav Stolper, *The German Economy 1870-1914* (New York: Reynald & Hitchcock, 1940).

Two grandiose views are offered by Josef Schumpeter in *Capitalism, Socialism, and Democracy* (New York: Harper & Row, 1950) and by the neo-Marxist Fritz Sternberg in *Capitalism and Socialism on Trial* (New York: Alfred A. Knopf, 1957).

See also Jürgen Kuczynski, *A Short History of Labor Conditions*, vol. 3, *Germany since 1888* (London: Gollancz, 1945).

*   *   *

CHAPTER 2: *Weimar Culture* by Peter Gay (New York: Harper & Row, 1968) covers much of the pre-Weimar period. Barbara Tuchman's *Proud Tower* (New York: Macmillan, 1962) questions the notion that the pre–World War I period was a golden age. Introductions to literature: Ronald Gray, *The German Tradition in Literature* (New

York: Cambridge University Press, 1965) and Felix Berteaux, *A Panorama of German Literature 1871-1931* (New York: Whittlesay, 1935). For a nostalgic view: Stefan Zweig, *World of Yesterday* (New York: Viking Press, 1943). Useful but somewhat marred by a Jewish bias are the cultural and intellectual histories by George Mosse. An excellent monograph is *Young Germans* by Walter Laqueur (New York: Basic Books, 1962).

See also L.J.C. Cecil, *Albert Ballin* (Princeton, N.J.: Princeton University Press, 1967); Peter Gay, *The Dilemma of Evolutionary Socialism* (New York: Columbia University Press, 1963); G. Masur, *Imperial Berlin* (New York: Basic Books, 1971); and J. P. Mayer, *Max Weber and German Politics* (London: Faber and Faber, 1956).

As sources, it pays to reread the works of Max Weber (selection by Gerth and Mills, New York: Grosset & Dunlap, 1946) and Georg Simmel (selection by Kurt Wolf, New York: Free Press, 1946), and of course the literature of the age, especially Rainer Maria Rilke; the early works of Thomas Mann and Heinrich Mann; the naturalistic drama of Sudermann, Hauptmann, Max Halbe and Georg Kaiser; and the novels of Kellermann, Wassermann, Ricarda Huch, and Gustav Frenssen. See also Raymond Aron, *German Sociology* (Glencoe, Ill.: Free Press, 1957) and Robert Michels' classic *Political Parties* (Gloucester, Mass.: Peter Smith, 1960).

On the extreme left: C. E. Schorske, *German Social Democracy 1905-17* (Cambridge, Mass.: Harvard University Press, 1955); J. P. Nettl, *Rosa Luxemburg* (New York: Oxford University Press, 1967); James Joll, *The Second International* (London, Routledge, 1955); Carl Landauer, *European Socialism* (Berkeley: University of California Press, 1959).

On the extreme right: Fritz Stern, *The Politics of Cultural Despair* (New York: Anchor, 1965); Peter Viereck, *Metapolitics* (New York: Capricorn, 1941); G. J. Pulzer, *The Rise of Political Anti-Semitism in Germany and Austria* (New York: John Wiley & Sons, 1964, with a good bibliography).

* * *

CHAPTER 3: See Walter Kaufmann, *From Shakespeare to Existentialism* (Boston: Beacon Press, 1959); also his *Nietzsche* (Princeton, N.J.: Princeton University Press, 1968). Obviously, science and philosophy cannot be treated in the framework of any single nation; but since Germans were intimately connected with relativity and quantum theory, with neopositivism, neo-Kantianism, phenomenology, existentialism, psychoanalysis and its derivations, Gestalt, and non-Euclidian mathematics, German authors will here be cited: Hans Reichenbach, *The Rise of Scientific Philosophy* (Berkeley: University of California Press, 1951); Edmund Husserl, *Philosophy and the Crisis of European Man* (New York: Harper & Row, 1965); Karl Jaspers, *Man in the Modern Age* (New York: Humanities Press, 1966); Ernst Cassirer, *The Problem of Knowledge* (New Haven, Conn.: Yale University Press, 1950), *Substance and Function* (New York: Dover Publications, 1952), and *An Essay on Man* (New Haven, Conn.: Yale University Press, 1962); Max Planck, *The Universe in the Light of Modern Physics* (New York: W. W. Norton & Co., 1931); Werner Heisenberg, *The Physicist's Conception of Nature* (Westport, Conn.: Greenwood, 1958) and *Physics and Beyond* (New York: Harper & Row, 1971), a beautiful autobiography as history of ideas; Albert Einstein, *Relativity: A Popular Exposition* (New York: Crown Publishers, 1961); Ronald Clark, *The Life and Times of Einstein* (New York: World Publishers, 1971); Wolfgang Köhler, *The Task of Gestalt Psychology* (Princeton, N.J.: Princeton University Press, 1969); and Ernest Jones, *The Life and Work of Sigmund Freud* (New York: Basic Books, 1953-1957).

For general orientation I recommend three admirable intellectual histories: Crane Brinton, *The Shaping of the Modern Mind* (New York: New American Library, 1950); John H. Randall, Jr., *The Making of the Modern Mind* (Boston: Houghton Mifflin Co., 1940); and H. Stuart Hughes, *Consciousness and Society 1890-1930* (New York: Alfred A. Knopf, 1958).

Also interesting are Thomas Molnar, *The Decline of the Intellectual* (New York: World Publishers, 1965) and Hayden V. White, *The Ordeal of Liberal Humanism* (New York: McGraw-Hill Book Co., 1970).

*   *   *

CHAPTER 4: See A.J.P. Taylor, *The Struggle for Mastery of Europe* (London: Oxford University Press, 1954). Luigi A. Albertini, *The Origins of the War of 1914* (London: Oxford University Press, 1952-1957) supersedes the representative German text by Erich Brandenburg, *From Bismarck to the World War* (London: Oxford University Press, 1927). The nature of imperialism has been discussed by Lenin, Schumpeter, William Langer, Hannah Arendt, and others; opposing views are collected in Harrison Wright, ed., *The New Imperialism* (Lexington, Mass.: D. C. Heath & Co., 1961).

On militarism see Alfred Vagts, *A History of Militarism* (Cleveland, Ohio: Meridian, 1959); Karl Demeter, *The German Officer Corps* (New York: Praeger Publishers, 1965); Walter Görlitz, *The German General Staff* (New York: Praeger Publishers, 1953); Marlene Wertheimer, *The Pan-German League* (New York: Columbia University Ph.D. dissertation, 1924).

* * *

CHAPTER 5: The controversy about war guilt and war aims has recently been revived by Fritz Fischer's massive *Germany's Aims in World War I* (New York: W. W. Norton & Co., 1967). For criticism of his views, see *Historische Zeitschrift*, passim.

See also Gerhard Ritter, *The Schlieffen Plan* (London: O. Wolff, 1958) and *The Rise of German Militarism* (Coral Gables, Fla.: University of Miami Press, 1966, 2 vols.); Barbara Tuchman, *The Guns of August* (New York: Dell Publishing Co., 1962); Z.A.B. Zeman, *From Vienna to Versailles* (New York: Coward, McCann & Geoghegan, 1956); G. Feldman, *Army, Industry and Labor in Germany, 1914-1918* (Princeton, N.J.: Princeton University Press, 1967); Harry Kessler, *Walther Rathenau* (New York: Harcourt Brace, 1929); Winston Churchill, *The World Crisis 1911-18* (New York: Macmillan, 1937); J. Wheeler-Bennett, *Brest-Litovsk* (London: Macmillan, 1938), *Hindenburg* (London: Macmillan, 1967), and *The Nemesis of Power* (New York: St. Martin's Press, 1954); and A. Mendelssohn-Bartholdy, *The War and German Society* (New Haven, Conn.: Yale University Press, 1937).

* * *

CHAPTERS 6 AND 7: Arthur Rosenberg, *The Birth of the German Republic* (New York: Oxford University Press, 1931) and *History of the German Republic* (New York: Russell and Russell, 1965) are still the best around. All major participants on both sides, including generals have written memoirs. See Klaus Epstein, *Matthias Erzberger and the Dilemma of German Democracy* (Princeton, N.J.: Princeton University Press, 1959); Günter Roth, *The Social Democrats in Imperial Germany* (Totowa, N.J.: Bedminster Press, 1913); R. Coper, *Failure of a Revolution* (New York: Cambridge University Press, 1955); Kenneth Calkins, *Hugo Haase* (Kent, Ohio: Kent State University Ph.D. dissertation, 1976); A. Joseph Berlau, *The German Social Democratic Party 1914-21* (New York: Columbia University Press, 1949); Ralph A. Lutz, ed., *The Fall of the German Empire* (Stanford, Calif.: Hoover Institution Press, 1932).

On Bethmann-Hollweg: Konrad Jarausch, *The Enigmatic Chancellor* (New Haven, Conn.: Yale University Press, 1973); Allan Mitchell, *Revolution in Bavaria* (Princeton, N.J.: Princeton University Press, 1965); David Morgan, *The Socialist Left and the German Revolution* (Ithaca, N.Y.: Cornell University Press, 1975); and A. J. Ryder, *The German Revolution* (New York: Cambridge University Press, 1967).

* * *

CHAPTER 8: See Arno J. Mayer, *The Politics and Diplomacy of Peacemaking* (New York: Alfred A. Knopf, 1967); Gordon A. Craig and Felix Gilbert, eds., *The Diplomats* (Princeton, N.J.: Princeton University Press, 1953); J. M. Keynes, *The Economic Consequences of the Peace* (New York: Charles Scribner's Sons, 1952); I. J. Lederer, ed., *The Versailles Settlement* (Lexington, Mass.: D. C. Heath & Co., 1960); Harold Nicolson, *Peacemaking* (New York: Grossett & Dunlap, 1943); Erich Eyck, *A History of the Weimar Republic* (Cambridge, Mass.: Harvard University Press, 1962); H. E. Carr, *The Twenty Years' Crisis* (New York: St. Martin's Press, 1958) and *International Relations Between the Wars* (New York: Macmillan, 1959); and Charles S. Maier, *Recasting Bourgeois Europe* (Princeton, N.J.: Princeton University Press, 1975)—a very original, basic contribution.

* * *

CHAPTERS 9 THROUGH 11: See J. W. Angell, *The Recovery of Germany* (New Haven, Conn.: Yale University Press, 1929); F. L. Carsten, *Reichswehr and Politics* (New York: Oxford University Press, 1966); A. Dorpalen, *Hindenburg and the Weimar Republic* (Princeton, N.J.: Princeton University Press, 1966); Hans Gatzke, *Stresemann and the Rearmament of Germany* (Baltimore, Md.: Johns Hopkins University Press, 1954) and *European Diplomacy 1919-39* (New York: Basic Books, 1972); R. N. Hunt, *Social Democracy 1918-33* (New Haven, Conn.: Yale University Press, 1953); F. K. Ringer, ed., *German Inflation 1923* (New York: Oxford University Press, 1969); H. A. Turner, *Stresemann and the Politics of the Weimar Republic* (Princeton, N.J.: Princeton University Press, 1963); and John A. Leopold, *Hugenberg* (New Haven, Conn.: Yale University Press, 1978).

* * *

CHAPTERS 12 AND 13: For a bibliography of Weimar culture, the reader is referred to the Wiener Library in London and the Leo Baeck

Institute in New York. See also Walter Laqueur, *Weimar* (New York: G. P. Putnam's Sons, 1974); Otto Friedrich, *Before the Deluge* (New York: Harper & Row, 1972), with an excellent bibliography of English books (originals and translations) on popular and high culture in Germany; and Harry Kessler, *In the Twenties* (New York: Holt, Rinehart and Winston, 1971).

Only a few books on German culture have been translated. Martin Esslin has written on Brecht, the theater of the absurd, and expressionism; Erich Heller has written on Thomas Mann and on *The Disinherited Mind* (New York: Harcourt Brace Jovanovich, 1975); H. F. Garten has dealt with Gerhart Hauptmann and with *Modern German Drama* (London: Methuen, 1958). Adorno's learned pamphlet *The Philosophy of Modern Music* (New York: Seabury, 1972) is now available. Siegfried Kracauer's film book *From Caligari to Hitler* appeared in 1974 (Princeton, N.J.: Princeton University Press). Walter Sokel's *The Writer in Extremis* (Stanford, Calif.: Stanford University Press, 1959) gives an interpretation of expressionism. Gropius himself published a book on the Bauhaus (New York: Museum of Modern Art, 1938); see also his *Apollo in the Democracy* (New York: Macmillan, 1968). See also Werner Haftmann, *History of Modern Painting* (New York: Praeger Publishers, 1965); Franz Roh, *German Painting in the Twentieth Century* (Greenwich, Conn.: New Graphic Society, 1968); Charles Kuhn, *Expressionism* (Cambridge, Mass.: Harvard University Press, 1967); Victor Miesel, ed., *Voices of German Expressionism* (Englewood Cliffs, N.J.: Prentice-Hall, 1968); Peter Selz, *German Expressionist Painting* (Berkeley: University of California Press, 1957); and Bernhard S. Myers, *The German Expressionists* (New York: Praeger Publishers, 1963). Christopher Isherwood's *The Berlin Stories* was used for the American film *Cabaret*. German films of the period occasionally may be viewed at the Museum of Modern Art in New York.

*   *   *

CHAPTER 14: See Arthur Koestler, *Arrow in the Blue* (New York: Macmillan, 1952); Walter Mehring, *The Lost Library* (Indianapolis, Ind.: Bobbs-Merrill Co., 1961).

On the left: Werner T. Angress, *Stillborn Revolution* (Princeton, N.J.: Princeton University Press, 1963); Istvan Deak, *Weimar Germany's Left-Wing Intellectuals* (Berkeley: University of California Press, 1968); Ruth Fischer, *Stalin and German Communism* (Cambridge, Mass.: Harvard University Press, 1948; to be used with caution); Martin Jay, *The Dialectical Imagination* (Boston: Little, Brown and

Co., 1973); Kurt Tucholsky, *What If . . . —Satirical Writings* (New York: Funk & Wagnalls Co., 1967); Harold Poor, *Tucholsky and the Ordeal of Germany* (New York: Charles Scribner's Sons, 1968).

* * *

CHAPTER 15: On the right: Klemens von Klemperer, *Germany's New Conservatism* (Princeton, N.J.: Princeton University Press, 1957); Aurel Kolnai, *The War Against the West* (London: Gollancz, 1938); Herman Lebovics, *Social Conservatism and the Middle Class* (Princeton, N.J.: Princeton University Press, 1965); George Mosse, *The Crisis of German Ideology* (New York: Grosset & Dunlap, 1966).

. Of particular interest are the writings of Ernst Jünger and Carl Schmitt.

* * *

CHAPTERS 16, 17, 18, AND 19: Two early biographies of Hitler—A. Bullock, *Hitler* (New York: Harper & Row, 1964) and Konrad Heiden, *Hitler* (London: Gollancz, 1949)—are still among the best. Little worth knowing has been added by most of the recent spate of Hitler biographies. From this judgment I exempt two profound works: Ernst Nolte, *Three Faces of Fascism* (London: Weidenfeld, 1966) and Joachim C. Fest, *Hitler* (New York: Harcourt Brace Jovanovich, 1975).

German historians have analyzed the agony of the republic in detail—best perhaps Bracher and Wolfgang Sauer. But the general hostility against the Weimar establishment has so far prevented any adequate treatment of the period 1930-1933. Nor have Brüning and Schacht yet been thought worthy of biographies. See Theodor Eschenburg, ed., *The Path to Dictatorship* (New York: Praeger Publishers, 1966), and D. Orlow, *History of the Nazi Party* (Pittsburgh, Pa.: University of Pittsburgh Press, 1969).

The most up-to-date accounts are Karl Bracher, *The German Dictatorship* (New York: Praeger Publishers, 1970) and Joachim C. Fest, *Faces of the Third Reich* (New York: Pantheon Books, 1970). The best analysis of "totalitarianism" still is Franz Neumann, *Behemoth* (New York: Oxford University Press, 1941). A vast controversy exists on the notion of totalitarianism. See Hannah Arendt, *Origins of Totalitarianism* (Boston: Beacon Press, 1951); Z. Brzezinski and Karl Friedrich, *Totalitarian Dictatorship* (Cambridge, Mass.: Harvard University Press, 1956); and David Spitz, *Patterns of Anti-Democratic Thought* (New York: Macmillan, 1949).

On the Nazis' way to power: K. Sontheimer, ed., *The Road to*

Dictatorship (London: Cambridge University Press, 1964); William S. Allen, *The Nazi Seizure of Power* (New York: Quadrangle/The New York Times Book Co., 1965).

An important question is whether the Nazi regime introduced a social revolution. On this see David Schoenbaum, *Hitler's Social Revolution* (Garden City, N.Y.: Doubleday & Co., 1966); Alexander Gerschenkron, *Bread and Democracy in Germany* (Berkeley: University of California Press, 1943); and Richard Grünberger, *The Twelve-Year Reich* (New York: Holt Rinehart & Winston, 1971). See also A.R.L. Gurland, *The Fate of Small Business in Nazi Germany* (Washington, D.C.: Government Printing Office, 1943); Arthur Schweitzer, *Big Business in the Third Reich* (Bloomington: Indiana University Press, 1964); and Jürgen Kuczynski, *Germany, Labor under Fascism* (New York: Greenwood Press, 1968).

Among other special subjects, that of the relations between army and Nazis has received attention: R. J. O'Neill, *The German Army and the Nazi Party* (London: Corgi Books, 1966); Francis L. Carsten, *The German Army in Politics* (Berkeley: University of California Press, 1964); and Felix Gilbert, *Hitler Directs His War* (New York: Oxford University Press, 1954).

Some Nazi leaders (Göring, Goebbels, Himmler, Quisling) have been the subjects of biographies—none worth reading. Some of the survivors, like Schacht and Speer, have had the nerve to publish sensationalist memoirs. Even fellow travelers of Hitler's, like Unity Mitford and Putzi Hanfstängl, have attracted interest either as memorialists or as objects of study. These have recently opened the way to a "revisionist" literature which denies some or all of the well-established facts: that Hitler was anti-Semitic, that he caused World War II, that he deliberately destroyed six million Jews; that he planned to subject other nations, especially those of the Slavic family, and to keep them in subjection.

Fritz Tobias tries to exculpate Göring and the S.A. from the charge of arson in *The Reichstag Fire* (New York: G. P. Putnam's Sons, 1964).

*   *   *

CHAPTER 20: The main revisionist work is A.J.P. Taylor's *The Origins of the Second World War* (New York: Atheneum Publishers, 1962). It has been answered by H. R. Trevor-Roper in *Hitler's War Directions* (London: Sidgwick, 1966) and Allen Bullock in *Hitler and the Origins of World War II* (London: British Academy Proceedings, 1967). A summary appears in E. M. Robertson, ed., *The Origins of the*

Second World War (London: Macmillan, 1971). See also Klaus Hilde-
brand, *The Foreign Policy of the Third Reich* (Berkeley: University of
California Press, 1973); and Norman Rich, *Hitler's War Aims* (New
York: Macmillan, 1973).

On special phases of the road to war: B. H. Liddel Hart, *The
Second World War* (London: Cassell, 1970); Elizabeth Wiskemann,
Europe of the Dictators and *The Rome-Berlin Axis* (both New York:
Oxford University Press, 1966); Keith Eubank, *Munich* (Norman:
University of Oklahoma Press, 1963); Gordon Brook-Shepherd, *The
Rape of Austria* (New York: Macmillan, 1963); Francis Loewenheim,
ed., *Peace or Appeasement* (Boston: Houghton Mifflin Co., 1963);
Gustav Hilger, *We and the Kremlin* (New York: Macmillan, 1959).
The U.S. State Department also has published documents on the
Soviet-German rapprochement in 1939.

*   *   *

CHAPTERS 21 AND 22: Churchill's breathtaking history of the war is
still a good introduction for the general reader. But obviously it must
be read critically, and it has been superseded by scholarly research.

*   *   *

CHAPTER 23: On the resistance: *Germans Against Hitler* (Bonn: Press
and Information Office of the BRD, 1964); Hans Rothfels, *The German
Resistance* (Chicago: Regnery, 1948); Gerhard Ritter, *Goerdeler* (New
York: Praeger Publishers, 1951); H. Graml, H. Mommsen, H. J.
Reichardt, and E. Wolf, *The German Resistance to Hitler* (Berkeley:
University of California Press, 1970); Peter Hoffmann, *The History
of the German Resistance 1933-1945* (Cambridge, Mass.: M.I.T. Press,
1977). Unfortunately, these books are almost exclusively concerned
with the generals' conspiracy of July 20, 1944, rather than with the
numerous underground organizations of the left. For this see Annedore
Leber, *Conscience in Revolt* (London: Vallentine, 1957).

*   *   *

SPECIAL SUBJECTS: On the situation of the churches: E. Bethke,
Dietrich Bonhoeffer (London: Collins, 1975); G. Lewy, *The Catholic
Church and Nazi Germany* (New York: McGraw-Hill Book Co., 1964);
S. Friedlander, *Pius XII and the Third Reich* (New York: Alfred A.
Knopf, 1966); Rolf Hochhut, *The Deputy* (New York: Grove Press,
1963); J. S. Conway, *The Nazi Persecution of the Churches* (New York:
Basic Books, 1968).

On concentration camps: Eugen Kogon, *The Theory and Practice of Hell* (London: Octagon, 1959); H. Höhne, *The Order of the Death's Head* (New York: Coward, McCann & Geoghegan, 1970).

On the "final solution": Lucy Dawidowicz, *The War Against the Jews* (New York: Holt Rinehart and Winston, 1975); Raoul Hilberg, *The Destruction of the European Jews* (New York: Quadrangle/The New York Times Book Co., 1961); Gerald Reitlinger, *The Final Solution* (New York: Beachhurst Press, 1961).

On propaganda: Henry Pachter, *Nazi Deutsch* (New York: Ungar, 1946); E. K. Bramsted, *Goebbels* (Lansing: Michigan State University Press, 1965); E. Hartshorne, *The German Universities and National Socialism* (London: Allen & Unwin, 1937); Z.A.B. Zeman, *Nazi Propaganda* (New York: Oxford University Press, 1964).

*   *   *

PART FOUR: It is obvious that the literature on the last thirty years of German history is less complete and less definitive than on earlier periods, and that less of it has been translated into English. A rather comprehensive survey of the scene in both parts of Germany is Professor Alfred Grosser's excellent *Germany in Our Time* (New York: Praeger Publishers, 1974), which also has a comprehensive bibliography of German titles. Indispensable for the analysis of West Germany is Ralf Dahrendorf, *Society and Democracy in Germany* (Garden City, N.Y.: Doubleday & Co., 1967). Equally indispensable for understanding the DDR are the publications of Peter Christian Ludz, most of which are available in English.

Most of the politicians who participated in the formation of the two states have left memoirs or collections of speeches, and the BRD government has published extensive memoranda on every aspect of development in both states. Documents of foreign affairs and a yearly Bonn *Almanach* are available in English.

The best guide through the maze of claims and counterclaims of the Cold War controversy is still Louis Halle, *The Cold War as History* (New York: Harper & Row, 1967). See also Robert McGeehan, *The German Rearmament Question* (Urbana: University of Illinois Press, 1971).

See also Lewis J. Edinger, *Kurt Schumacher* (Stanford, Calif.: Stanford University Press, 1965); Edgar Alexander, *Adenauer* (New York: Farrar Straus & Cudahy, 1957); Terence Prittie, *Adenauer* (London: Tom Stacey, 1971); Carola Stern, *Ulbricht* (New York: Praeger Publishers, 1970); Lyman H. Legters, ed., *The German Democratic Republic* (Boulder, Colo.: Westview Press, 1977); David R.

Binder, *The Other German* (Willy Brandt) (Washington, D.C.: New Republic Co., 1975); Joachim Braun, *Gustav Heinemann* (London: Oswald Wolff, 1972); Guido Goldman, *The German Political System* (New York: Random House, 1974); D. Childs, *East Germany* (New York: Praeger Publishers, 1969) (see also his writings on German labor); W. F. Hanrieder, *West German Foreign Policy* (Stanford, Calif.: Stanford University Press, 1967); Hans Speier, *The Soviet Threat to Berlin* (Santa Monica, Calif.: Rand Corporation, 1961). Ruhm von Oppen, *Germany under Occupation* (London: Oxford University Press, 1955); Kurt B. Tauber, *Beyond Eagle and Swastika,* 2 vol. (Middletown: Wesleyan University Press, 1967); Institut für Demoskopie, *The Germans in Public Opinion 1947–68* (Allenbach: Verlag für Demoskopie, 1968).

On the intellectual situation since World War II: Theodor W. Adorno et al., *The Positivist Dispute in German Sociology* (New York: Harper & Row, 1976); Paul Connerton, ed., *Critical Sociology* (Baltimore, Md.: Penguin Books, 1976); Jürgen Habermas, *Toward a Rational Society* (Boston: Beacon Press, 1970); Edmund Husserl, *Phenomenology and the Crisis of Philosophy* (New York: Harper & Row, 1965) Max Horkheimer, *Eclipse of Reason* (New York: Seabury Press, 1974); George Lichtheim, *Collected Essays* (New York: Viking Press, 1973); and Herbert Marcuse, *One-Dimensional Man* (Boston: Beacon Press, 1964). (Although Marcuse is a permanent resident in the United States, his thinking is determined by German philosophy, especially Hegel, Marx, and Heidegger.) See also Harold Morick, ed., *Wittgenstein and the Problem of Other Minds* (New York: McGraw-Hill Book Co., 1967); Albrecht Wellmer, *Critical Theory of Society* (New York: Seabury Press, 1974); David Pears, *Ludwig Wittgenstein* (New York: Viking Press, 1970); and Ernest Gellner, *Thought and Change* (London: Weidenfeld & Nicolson, 1964).

Documents: D. Siegel, *The German Question* (Bonn: Press and Information Office of the BDR, 1960); Walther Hubatsch et al., eds., *The German Question* (New York: Herder Book Center, 1967); *A Decade of U.S. Foreign Policy 1941-49* (Washington, D.C.: Government Printing Office, 1950); Wolf Hadelmeyer, ed., *Documents on Berlin 1943-63* (Bonn and Munich, 1964); *Documents on Germany, 1944-61* (U.S. Senate, Washington, D.C.: Government Printing Office); and *Documents on Germany under Occupation 1945-54* (London: Royal Institute of International Affairs, 1955).

Name Index

Subject Index

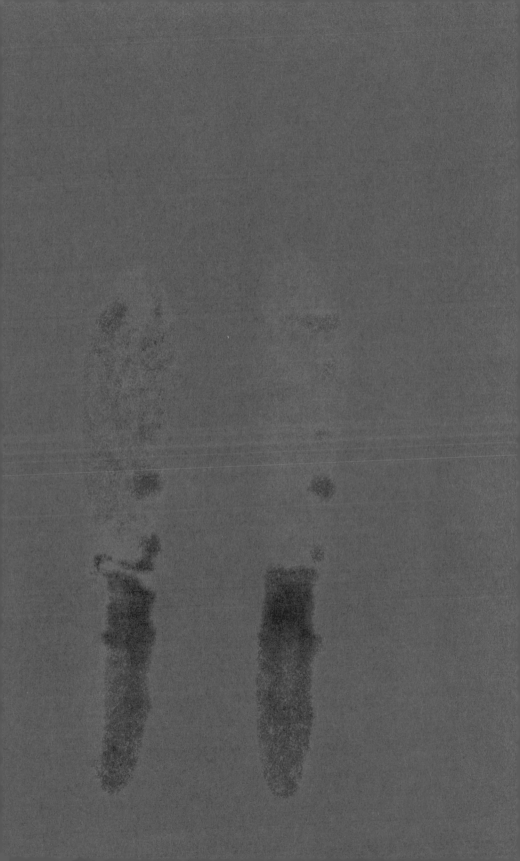

DATE DUE	